AMOS

Baylor Handbook on the Hebrew Bible

General Editor

W. Dennis Tucker Jr.

AMOS
A Handbook on the Hebrew Text

Duane A. Garrett

BAYLOR UNIVERSITY PRESS

Cover Design by Pamela Poll
Cover photograph by Bruce and Kenneth Zuckerman, West Semitic Research, in collaboration with the ancient Biblical Manuscript Center. Courtesy Russina National Library (Saltykov-Shchedrin).

Library of Congress Cataloging-in-Publication Data

Garrett, Duane A.
Amos : a handbook on the Hebrew text / Duane A. Garrett.
p. cm. -- (Baylor handbook on the Hebrew Bible series)
Includes bibliographical references and index.
ISBN 978-1-932792-69-0 (pbk.)
1. Bible. O.T. Amos--Criticism, Textual. 2. Bible. O.T. Amos--Language, style. 3. Hebrew language--Grammar. I. Title.

BS1585.52.G37 2008
224'.8044--dc22

2008010617

Printed in the United States of America on acid-free paper with a minimum of 30% pcw recycled content.

TABLE OF CONTENTS

INTRODUCTION

The book of Amos, the superscript tells us, was composed by Amos of Tekoa in the mid-eighth century B.C. Although from Judah, Amos directed his message against the aristocratic and priestly upper-classes of Samaria and Bethel. Israel at this time, during the reign of Jeroboam II, was in the midst of a misleading period of prosperity and military power. Deceived by their affluence and territorial expansion, the Israelites supposed that God was on their side and that the good times would never end. Cruelty to the poor, religious arrogance, and an unbounded sense of confidence in the might of their fortifications characterized the upper echelons of society. They could not imagine that their cities were only decades away from total destruction, and they counted Amos a charlatan and blasphemer for his predictions of their imminent demise. The book of Amos is a carefully crafted indictment against Israel, an apologia for Amos' claims to the prophetic office, and a prediction of calamity for Israel followed by a final, eschatological salvation.

The focus of this commentary is the Hebrew text of Amos. Discussions of the book's social and historical background, of insights gained from archaeology, and of its theology are secondary and purposefully kept to a minimum. In addition, this commentary works from the received Masoretic Text of Amos and makes no effort to include an exhaustive record of textual variants, of versional readings, and of conjectural emendations proposed by biblical scholars. Discussions of text-critical issues therefore will appear only when either the obscurity of the received text or some other considerations require it. This commentary is intended primarily for the student of Hebrew and the Bible translator, but it should be helpful also for any teachers of the Bible who believe that wrestling with the original language of the text to be valuable.

Redaction and Structure of the Book of Amos

In current OT studies, the question of the structure of Amos is closely linked to the question of its redaction history, as scholars seek to show both what was the original form of the book and how it evolved. A famous example of this method is the commentary by H. W. Wolff which, on the basis of a form-critical analysis, argues that Amos went through six redactional stages (Wolff 1977, 106–13). But Dirk Rottzoll argues that it went through no less than twelve stages of redaction (Rottzoll 1996, 285–90)! A more recent example is Wood (2002), which argues that the book was originally seven poems written and performed by the prophet as a poetic tragedy. Wood asserts that a second edition of the prophet's book was produced by an exilic author who inserted a running commentary on the original work, thereby not only greatly expanding and reordering the original but also transforming it into a comedy (by giving it a redemptive, happy ending). This revised version, the present book of Amos, is in ten parts. Wood's theory, like others of its kind, is at times forced and is not persuasive. Nevertheless, some may find the ten divisions that Wood proposes as the structure of Amos helpful. Similarly, but with very different results, one sees structural analysis mixed in with a proposed redaction history in Park (2001). The results of redaction-critical studies are in fact exceedingly diverse. There is no consensus (see Möller 2003, "Reconstructing and Interpreting Amos's Literary Prehistory" for a survey of recent redaction-critical analyses; see also Möller 2003, *A Prophet in Debate*, which argues on the basis of a rhetorical-critical analysis that the text of Amos did not have an extensive redaction history). In my view, redaction-critical approaches are neither compelling nor heuristically valuable.

Although certain divisions of Amos are obvious in even a casual reading of the text (e.g., that the eight oracles against the nations in

1:3–2:16 constitute a single division), many aspects of the structure are obscure and debated, and readers will find an abundance of proposals in the scholarly literature. For example, O'Connell (1996) argues that, following the pattern of seven nations plus Israel in 1:3–2:16, Amos uses an "N +1" pattern throughout (where "N" is some stereotypical number such as 3 or 7, and the additional item is some element of surprise, such as adding Israel to the list of condemned nations). O'Connell does not, however, convincingly demonstrate that this pattern governs the whole book. Boyle (1971) says that 3:1–4:13 is a covenant lawsuit, but this, too, is unpersuasive. Koch (1974) argues that the hymn fragments in Amos 4:13; 5:8; 9:5-6 are redactional but that they demarcate divisions of the book. Noble (1995) says that Amos is in three parts (1:2–3:8; 3:9–6:14; 7:1–9:15). He claims that the middle section is a chiasmus, but he must relocate or delete several verses to make it work. Every major commentary on Amos, moreover, has its own presentation of the structure of the book. While there are some areas of agreement (again, that 1:3–2:16 belongs together), it would be a mistake to speak of anything like a standard view. The reader should consult the commentaries for various alternatives to the structure suggested here.

The starting point for the outline of Amos proposed in this commentary is Limburg (1987), where he states that there are fifty divine speech formulas (such as אמר יהוה, "says YHWH," and נאם יהוה, "the oracle of YHWH") in Amos. These are, he says, distributed as follows: one at 1:1–2, fourteen in 1:3–2:16, and seven each in 3:1–15; 4:1–13; 5:1–6:14; 7:1–8:3; and 8:4–9:15. Thus there are seven divisions in the book. Limburg points out that the number seven (or seven plus one) is very important in Amos. There are seven accused nations plus Israel in 1:3–2:16, for example, and the call for justice in 5:21-24 lists seven thing that YHWH hates: feasts, solemn assemblies, burnt offerings, cereal offerings, peace offerings, noise of songs and melodies of harps.

As remarkable as Limburg's analysis is, there are aspects of it that are not satisfying. For example, 1:2 has no divine speech formula (וַיֹּאמַר has no explicit subject and is not a divine speech formula), and therefore there are forty-nine, not fifty, such formulas. This is not really a problem, however. The whole of 1:2 is about divine speech and serves to introduce this as the motif that governs the book. Limburg counts 3:1 twice, apparently on the strength of its having דִּבֶּר יְהוָה and לֵאמֹר, but he does not count 3:8, which has אֲדֹנָי יְהוִה דִּבֶּר. But לֵאמֹר should not be counted separately (it is joined to דִּבֶּר יְהוָה; see Miller 1995 on quotative frames), but certainly אֲדֹנָי יְהוִה דִּבֶּר should be counted. Also, Limburg gives little attention to showing that the structure of Amos actually does fall into the seven groups he mentions. If, for example, one cannot show that 8:4–9:15 belongs together as a single division, there is no reason to count this as one passage that has seven speech formulas.

Slightly modifying Limburg's presentation, one can see how the various formulas are used. After 1:2 sets forth divine speech as the governing motif of the book, the divine speech formulas all occur in groups of fourteen or seven in the six large divisions indicated by Limburg. With two exceptions, every major division in Amos is introduced with a plural imperative of שׁמע. These exceptions are 1:3–2:16, which is a series of oracles, each begun with כֹּה אָמַר יְהוָה, and the vision report section at 7:1–8:3, which is introduced by a hiphil of ראה. Thus, the seven divisions of Amos after the superscript (1:1) and the poetic proclamation of YHWH making his voice heard (1:2), are as follows (the opening words of each division are in parentheses):

I. 1:3–2:16 (כֹּה אָמַר יְהוָה)
II. 3:1–15 (שִׁמְעוּ אֶת־הַדָּבָר הַזֶּה)
III. 4:1–13 (שִׁמְעוּ הַדָּבָר הַזֶּה)
IV. 5:1–6:14 (שִׁמְעוּ אֶת־הַדָּבָר הַזֶּה)
V. 7:1–8:3 (כֹּה הִרְאַנִי אֲדֹנָי יְהוִה)
VI. 8:4–9:15 (שִׁמְעוּ־זֹאת)

I.	II.	III.	IV.	V.	VI.
1:3^ 1:5	**3:1**	_4:3_	5:3^*	7:3	_8:9*_
1:6^ 1:8*	**3:8***	_4:5*_	5:4^	7:6*	_8:11*_
1:9^ 1:11^	_3:10_	_4:6_	5:16^+	7:8&	_9:7_
1:13^ 1:15	3:11^*	_4:8_	5:17	7:15&	_9:8_
2:1^ 2:3	3:12^	_4:9_	5:27+	7:17^	_9:12_
2:4^ 2:6^	_3:13*_	_4:10_	_6:8+_	8:2&	_9:13_
_2:11_ _2:16_	_3:15_	_4:11_	_6:14+_	_8:3*_	9:15++

Key to Divine Speech Formulas in Amos		
אמר	אמר יהוה	plain text
	כה אמר יהוה	plain with caret
	אמר אדני יהוה	plain with asterisk
	אמר יהוה אלהי צבאות	plain with plus sign
	אמר יהוה אלהיך	plain with two plus signs
	ויאמר יהוה	plain with ampersand
דבר	דבר יהוה	bold
	אדני יהוה דבר	bold with asterisk
נאם	נאם יהוה	italics
	נאם אדני יהוה	italics with asterisk
	נאם־יהוה אלהי צבאות	italics with plus sign

The table above and its accompanying key shows what formulas are used in what verses. The table is in six columns corresponding to the six major divisions of Amos.

From this alone one can see certain revealing patterns. As mentioned above, 1:3–2:16 has fourteen divine speech formulas. Amos five times begins and ends each of these eight oracles with a divine speech formula. If he had consistently done this for all these oracles, there would of course be sixteen. But he skips the second formula at Tyre (1:9-10), Edom (1:11-12) and Judah (2:4-5), and he adds a third formula for Israel at 2:11. Thus, the text seems to deliberately aim at having fourteen formulas. More interestingly, every major division except for the last ends with at least one **נאם** formula (see the bottom row of the table). The formula at 9:15, which uniquely is **אמר יהוה אלהיך**, "says YHWH your God," seems deliberately set at the end of the restoration prophecy (9:11-15) to reassure Israel that YHWH will again be their God. Note, however, that every other formula of 8:4–9:15, the last division of the book, is a **נאם** formula, which corresponds to the fact that every other division ends with a **נאם** formula. It is also noteworthy that just as the **נאם** formulas dominate the last division of the book, 8:4–9:15, so also in 4:1-13 every formula is of the **נאם** kind. This suggests that the book is in two parts, 1:3–4:13 and 5:1–9:15, and this is supported by the overall structure of the book, as described below. By contrast, **אמר** type formulas are more common in all other divisions of the book. The division 7:1–8:3 is more narrative in nature, and the formula **ויאמר יהוה**, with the *wayyiqtol* verb, occurs twice there. The most exalted, pleonastic formulas (**אמר יהוה אלהי צבאות** and **נאם־יהוה אלהי צבאות**) all occur in 5:1–6:14, and the two formulas with **דבר** both are in 3:1-15. There does not appear to be any pattern to the usage of **אדני** in the formulas except that it appears in every major division.

This commentary will attempt to demonstrate that each division described above has internal coherence and structure (for discussions of each division's structure, see the introductions to the major divisions). In addition, there is an internal logic to the arrangement of the six major divisions, with a chiastic structure, as follows:

A. 1:3–2:16 Judgment on the nations, with the unexpected inclusion of Israel.
  B. 3:1-15 First defense of Amos' prophetic office against those who assert that he has no right to prophesy against Israel
    C. 4:1-13 First major accusation against the materialistic and religious arrogance of the Israelites.
    C'. 5:1–6:14 Second major accusation against the materialistic and religious arrogance of the Israelites.
  B'. 7:1–8:3 Second defense of Amos' prophetic office against those who assert that he has no right to prophesy against Israel
A'. 8:4–9:15 Final accusation and verdict against Israel, with the unexpected revival of Israel and inclusion of the nations in Israel's glory.

Conventions of this Commentary

Throughout the commentary, the Hebrew text of Amos appears with full cantillation marks (accents, or טְעָמִים). When a Hebrew word is discussed, it is written without the cantillation marks, and citations of passages outside of Amos generally lack cantillation marks. When verbs are parsed, the traditional stem names are used (qal, piel, etc.). Conjugations, however, are named with the terminology that has become increasingly more the standard in Hebrew studies, as follows:

qatal = perfect (קָטַל)
yiqtol = imperfect (יִקְטֹל)
wayyiqtol = imperfect with "vav consecutive" (וַיִּקְטֹל)
weqatal = perfect with simple conjunction (וְקָטַל)
weyiqtol = imperfect with simple conjunction (וְיִקְטֹל)

Although one might debate whether *qatal* and *weqatal* should be considered to be separate conjugations, in the syntax of the language, each of the five forms listed above has a distinctive set of functions. Therefore, one cannot treat the *qatal* and the *weqatal* simply as the same verbal form; the former is generally perfective in aspect and indicative in mood, and it typically deals with past, present, or gnomic actions. The latter is generally imperfective and may be subjunctive or volitive, and it often is used for a future indicative or an apodosis. Similarly, one should never regard the *weqatal* as the same as a *wayyiqtol*, or fail to take note of the relatively rare presence of a *weyiqtol* in Amos (it is used seven times).

A major issue in Amos is distinguishing prose from poetry. In this commentary, Hebrew that is reckoned to be prose is printed as whole verses in paragraph form. After this, the prose text is analyzed on a clause-by-clause basis, and each clause is individually printed in a smaller typeface. This is done because, in my estimation, the clause is the ideal level at which to approach the analysis of Hebrew prose. Within the clause, one can see how each constituent and morpheme functions at the clause level, and at a higher level, one can describe how each clause functions in the discourse.

Colometry (or "stichometry") is the division of a poem into its individual lines. The colometry of a poem being fundamental to its analysis, every poetic section of Amos is set forth on a line-by-line basis. The basis for the line divisions used here are two-fold. First, the major disjunctive marks of the cantillation system are taken into account (see Hoop 2000). In the majority of cases, line breaks occur at the *silluq*, the *athnach*, and the *zaqeph qaton*, with some breaks occurring at the *pashta*, *revia*, or *tifha*. As a general rule, when a disjunctive accent serves to mark a line break, it will have a weaker disjunctive accent within its domain. As is done here, names of accents are given in italics in a simplified transliteration. In situations where the line divisions do not, in my view, coincide with the major disjunctive accents, some comments are made in the discussion of that text.

Second, in determining the colometry of a poem, the "line constraints" as described in O'Connor (1980) and refined in Holladay (1999) are taken into account. These constraints state that in any Hebrew line of poetry, there must be:

- *From 0 to 3 clause predicators.* A line may have no predicator, but it should have no more than three. A clause predicator may be a finite verb, an infinitive absolute that functions as a finite verb, an infinitive construct phrase functioning as a finite verb (e.g., an infinitive construct that has a suffix functioning as the subject of the action), a participle functioning as a periphrastic finite verb, and the particles אֵין and יֵשׁ. O'Connor also counts the vocative as a predicator, and I have followed that rule.
- *From 1 to 4 constituents.* A constituent is a word or phrase that fills one grammatical slot. Examples would be a subject, a predicate, or a prepositional phrase. Although it has more than one word, a construct chain functioning as a subject or vocative, for example, is a single constituent.
- *From 2 to 5 units.* A unit is basically a word, but small particles such as כִּי or אִם or prepositions such as אֶל do not count as units. One may debate what does or does not count as a unit. I treat לֹא as a non-unit, and only count כֹּל as a unit if it is absolute.

As an example, we have the following line in Amos 1:9:

עַֽל־הַסְגִּירָ֞ם גָּל֥וּת שְׁלֵמָ֖ה לֶאֱד֑וֹם

Because they handed over a full-scale exile to Edom.

Here, we see that the line ends with the disjunctive *zaqeph qaton.* There is 1 predicator, עַֽל־הַסְגִּירָם. This infinitive construct is reckoned to be a predicator because it works like a finite verb, taking the suffix as its subject. There are also 3 constituents and 4 units. The constituents are the infinitive construct phrase עַל־הַסְגִּירָם, the direct object גָּלוּת שְׁלֵמָה, and the prepositional phrase לֶאֱדוֹם. The units are הַסְגִּירָם, גָּלוּת, שְׁלֵמָה, and לֶאֱדוֹם. The preposition עַל does not count as a unit (and no suffix or prefix counts as a unit). The presence or absence of maqqeph is irrelevant.

Neither the cantillation marks nor the line constraints should be regarded as inviolable; occasionally this commentary will point out lines that, in my opinion, violate one or both of these (e.g., a line ending with a conjunctive accent, or a line with only one unit). Nevertheless, in the overwhelming number of instances, lines both end with a "normal" final accent and also conform to the line constraints. In my view, other approaches to Hebrew colometry (such as counting stresses, words, or syllables) produce no meaningful results and are not valid.

In the discussion of the content of a poem, each line is analyzed separately. First, every line is described in terms of what accent marks the end of the line and in terms of the aforementioned poetic constraints. Then, each "constituent" of the line is analyzed separately.

Sometimes this commentary will speak of devices that occur in the poems. These include:

- *Gapping* (also called "double-duty"), in which a word in one line also governs or modifies an adjacent line. For example, the verb וְהִכְרַתִּי in line Bd of 1:5 also governs line Be.
- *Dependence*, in which a line is grammatically incomplete and depends upon either the previous or following line. For example, in 1:3, lines Aa and Ac both depend on line Ab.
- *Semantic matching*, in which a word or phrase in one line is synonymous or nearly synonymous with a word in an adjacent line. See line b of 1:2.
- *Semantic parallelism*, in which one line more-or-less has the same meaning as an adjacent line. See lines a and b in 1:2. It

is widely understood today, after Kugel (1981), that the lines rarely simply repeat the same idea; usually the second line in some way advances or in some way modifies the thought of the first.

- *Syntactic parallelism*, in which two adjacent lines have the same grammatical structure, as in lines c and d in 1:2.

Having broken down a poem into its lines, the lines need to be grouped into meaningful collections. Unfortunately, there is little consistency in the use of terms such as stanza and verse. This commentary adopts the following conventions. At the highest level is the poem. A poem is made up of one or more stanzas, and each stanza is made up of one or more strophes, and each strophe is made of one or more lines. The term "verse" is used in this commentary exclusively for the numbered verses of the MT. In other words, "verse" is not used to describe poetic structure but to locate a text in the book. A single major division of Amos may have several poems of varying length as well as passages in prose.

To aid in the discussions, poetic lines are tagged according to stanza (uppercase Roman letters), strophe (Arabic numerals), and line (lowercase Roman letters). For example, "line A3b" would be the first stanza ("A"), the third strophe ("3"), and the second line ("b") of that strophe.

- If a poem has only one stanza, or if a stanza has only one strophe, that single stanza or strophe will not be designated by letter or number. For example, line 2c would refer to the third line ("c") in the second strophe ("2") in a poem with only one stanza.
- If a poem has only one stanza and only one strophe, each line of the poem is designated only with a lowercase Roman letter (e.g., "line c").

A HANDBOOK ON THE HEBREW TEXT OF AMOS

1:1-2: Profile of Introduction

The opening of the book, this contains a prose superscript (1:1) and a poem of one strophe (1:2). The superscript gives the name of the book's author as well as the name of the author's city. It also states the time of composition by means of three synchronisms: with the names of the reigning kings of Judah and of Israel and with a significant event, a major earthquake). The poem declares the major theme of the book, that YHWH has spoken in anger and therefore that his prophet must proclaim God's message of doom.

[1]The words of Amos, who was from the shepherds of Tekoa, which he received by vision concerning Israel in the days of Uzziah, the king of Judah, and in the days of Jeroboam the son of Joash, the king of Israel, two years before the earthquake. [2]And he said,

YHWH will roar from Zion,
And he will give his voice from Jerusalem;
And the pastures of the shepherds will dry up
And the top of Carmel will wither.

1:1: Superscript

The book opens with a standard prophetic superscript naming the author with the date of his prophecy correlated to contemporary Israelite and Judean kings.

1:1 דִּבְרֵ֣י עָמ֔וֹס אֲשֶׁר־הָיָ֥ה מִתְּק֑וֹעַ אֲשֶׁ֨ר חָזָ֜ה עַל־
יִשְׂרָאֵ֗ל בִּימֵ֣י ׀ עֻזִּיָּ֣ה מֶֽלֶךְ־יְהוּדָ֗ה וּבִימֵ֞י יָרָבְעָ֤ם
בֶּן־יוֹאָשׁ֙ מֶ֣לֶךְ יִשְׂרָאֵ֔ל שְׁנָתַ֖יִם לִפְנֵ֥י הָרָֽעַשׁ׃

Prose Clause: דִּבְרֵ֣י עָמ֔וֹס

Title of book; a construct chain.

Prose Clause: אֲשֶׁר־הָיָ֥ה בַנֹּקְדִ֖ים מִתְּק֑וֹעַ

Relative clause in apposition to עָמוֹס. After the relative pronoun אֲשֶׁר, the verb הָיָה is a qal *qatal* 3 m s of היה. בַנֹּקְדִים is a prepositional phrase with בְּ ("with" or "among"), but נֹקֵד ("shepherd") is found only here and in 2 Kings 3:4, where we read, וּמֵישַׁע מֶלֶךְ־מוֹאָב הָיָה נֹקֵד ("And Mesha, the king of Moab, was a sheep-breeder"). It is related to נָקֹד ("speckled"), a term used for sheep in Genesis 30:32-33, 35, 39; 31:8, 10, 12, and its meaning is not in any real doubt. Also, from Ugarit, UT 6 (I Ab) VI, 55 has the title *rb nqdm*, "chief of the shepherds." A number of scholars, on the basis of its being used to describe a king, believe that Amos was a well-to-do sheep breeder and not an impoverished shepherd (see Hasel 1991, 35–40, for further discussion). מִתְּקוֹעַ is a prepositional phrase (מִן) with a proper noun. The Tekoa mentioned here is almost universally assumed to be the small village of Judah located about twelve miles south of Jerusalem, although Rosenbaum (1990, 29–40) argues (not convincingly) that Amos was from the north and, following the medieval rabbi David Kimchi, suggests that Tekoa may have been in the tribe of Asher.

Prose Clause: אֲשֶׁ֨ר חָזָ֜ה עַל־יִשְׂרָאֵ֗ל בִּימֵ֣י ׀ עֻזִּיָּ֣ה מֶֽלֶךְ־יְהוּדָ֗ה וּבִימֵ֞י יָרָבְעָ֤ם בֶּן־יוֹאָשׁ֙ מֶ֣לֶךְ יִשְׂרָאֵ֔ל שְׁנָתַ֖יִם לִפְנֵ֥י הָרָֽעַשׁ

Relative clause (headed by אֲשֶׁר) in apposition to דִּבְרֵי. The verb of the clause is חָזָה, a qal *qatal* 3 m s חזה. It is odd to speak of "words that he saw," but in this case חזה means to receive a message via a revelatory vision. In עַל־יִשְׂרָאֵל the preposition עַל may be either "concerning" (Ruth 2:4) or "against" (Judg 9:18). Three temporal phrases that locate Amos' ministry historically follow:

בִּימֵ֣י׀ עֻזִּיָּ֣ה מֶֽלֶךְ־יְהוּדָ֗ה. A prepositional phrase with בְּ attached to the construct plural of יוֹם, with the proper noun עֻזִּיָּה serving as the absolute. מֶלֶךְ־יְהוּדָה is in apposition to עֻזִּיָּה. Although Amos' message is primarily against Israel, the king of Judah as a chronological indicator precedes mention of the king of Israel. This suggests that Amos considered the Davidic king to have a superior claim to legitimacy.

וּבִימֵ֞י יָרָבְעָ֤ם בֶּן־יוֹאָשׁ֙ מֶ֣לֶךְ יִשְׂרָאֵ֔ל. The conjunction coordinates this construct chain with בִּימֵי עֻזִּיָּה. Again, we have a construct chain with a proper noun. The two construct chains בֶּן־יוֹאָשׁ and מֶלֶךְ יִשְׂרָאֵל are in apposition to יָרָבְעָם.

שְׁנָתַ֖יִם לִפְנֵ֥י הָרָֽעַשׁ. The dual of שָׁנָה ("year") with the prepositional phrase לִפְנֵי הָרָעַשׁ is used adverbially for a temporal phrase. The earthquake (רַעַשׁ) was evidently of such severity that it was remembered for years thereafter simply as "the earthquake." It is here mentioned not only for chronological purposes but also as an allusion to theophany and the day of the Lord, as in Isaiah 29:6, "From YHWH of hosts you will be punished with thunder and earthquake. . . ." See also Ezekiel 3:12. Stating that Amos gave his message two years before the earthquake, it is as though the text were claiming that the earthquake were a vindication of Amos' claim that the day of YHWH was about to break out against Israel. The chronological precision, that it was "two years" before the earthquake, suggests that Amos gave all of his prophecies in the space of a fairly short time.

וַיֹּאמַ֓ר׀ 1:2

A prose quotation formula for the poetic stanza in lines a–d. It lacks explicit reference to the deity, and therefore is not a divine speech formula even though God is obviously the speaker. וַיֹּאמַר is a qal *wayyiqtol* 3 m s of אמר.

1:2: Introductory Proclamation

Four lines (a-d) in one strophe. Line a is syntactically and semantically parallel to b (line a = X + *yiqtol*, and line b = ו + X + *yiqtol*), with gapping of יהוה in line b. Line c is syntactically and semantically parallel to d (both are *weqatal* clauses). The *weqatal* clauses indicate that the action of c-d is consecutive to that of a-b.

a יְהוָה֙ מִצִּיּ֣וֹן יִשְׁאָ֔ג
b וּמִירוּשָׁלִַ֖ם יִתֵּ֣ן קוֹל֑וֹ
c וְאָֽבְלוּ֙ נְא֣וֹת הָרֹעִ֔ים
d וְיָבֵ֖שׁ רֹ֥אשׁ הַכַּרְמֶֽל׃ פ

Line a: The colon-marker is *zaqeph qaton* and the constraints are: 1 predicator, 3 constituents, and 3 units.

יְהוָה֙. The subject; the first word of the prophecy is YHWH.

מִצִּיּ֣וֹן. The word order in יְהוָה מִצִּיּוֹן might suggest that מִצִּיּוֹן could be taken with יְהוָה as an appellation, "YHWH of Zion," and as a single constituent. Against this, however, is the disjunctive *pashta* in יְהוָה and the conjunctive *munah* in מִצִּיּוֹן. As such, the prepositional phrase מִצִּיּוֹן adverbially modifies the verb יִשְׁאָג and is not bound to the noun יְהוָה.

יִשְׁאָ֔ג. Qal *yiqtol* 3 m s of שׁאג. The X + *yiqtol* pattern (the fact that the *yiqtol* is non-initial) suggests that the verb is indicative and not modal. It may be future or present iterative.

Line b: The colon-marker is *athnach* and the constraints are: 1 predicator, 3 constituents, and 3 units.

וּמִירוּשָׁלִַ֖ם. The conjunction indicates clause-level coordination with line a. The absence of an explicit subject is gapping of the subject, and it confirms that the prepositional phrase is bound to the verb, and so affirms the implication of the accents in יְהוָה מִצִּיּוֹן.

יִתֵּ֣ן. Qal *yiqtol* 3 m s of נתן.

קוֹלוֹ. Noun with 3ms suffix. The phrase יִתֵּן קוֹלוֹ semantically matches יִשְׁאָג.

Line c: The colon-marker is *zaqeph qaton* and the constraints are: 1 predicator, 2 constituents, and 3 units. This line is sequential to lines a–b.

וְאָבְלוּ. Qal *weqatal* 3 c p of אבל. This is אבל II, to "dry up" and not אבל I, "to mourn." See *HALOT*.

נְאוֹת הָרֹעִים. Feminine plural noun from נָוֶה, "a green meadow," in a construct chain with הָרֹעִים.

Line d: The colon-marker is *silluq* and the constraints are: 1 predicator, 2 constituents, and 3 units. This line has syntactic parallelism with and amplifies line c.

וְיָבֵשׁ. Qal *weqatal* 3 m s of יבשׁ. Because of the parallel structure of lines c–d, the action of this *weqatal* is not sequential to that of the previous line.

רֹאשׁ הַכַּרְמֶל. A construct chain. The gentle, and usually green, slopes of Mt. Carmel provide a specific example, after line c, of a pastureland that is parched.

1:3–2:16: Oracles against the Nations

This, the first major division of Amos, is a series of eight poems, each one an oracle of judgment against a nation (1:3-5, Damascus [Syria]; 1:6-8, Gaza [Philistia]; 1:9-10, Tyre [Phoenicia]; 1:11-12, Edom; 1:13-15, Ammon; 2:1-3, Moab; 2:4-5, Judah; 2:6-16, Israel). Some suggest that Amos is geographically encircling Israel, moving from northeast (Damascus), to southwest (Philistia), to northwest (Tyre), to southeast (Edom), to the transjordan states (Ammon and Moab), to Judah, and finally to Israel. Others suggest that he bases his rhetoric on ethnicity, beginning ethnically distant or unrelated peoples (Arameans, Philistines, and Phoenicians), moving to closely related nations (Edom, Ammon, and Moab) and finally to Judah, who were of the same people as the northern Israelites, before addressing Israel itself.

It is clear, however, that Amos is rhetorically entrapping the Israelites by beginning with Gentile states and progressively moving closer until he reaches the main object of his denunciations, Israel and its capital city, Samaria. Steinmann (1992) argues that other patterns are evident in the order of the poems. For example, the first three are directed against city-states, the next three are directed against peoples, and the last two are directed against the covenant nations.

One may assume that the inclusion of Israel among the condemned nations is intended to be unexpected and therefore rhetorically effective. There are several indicators of this. First of all, Israel is placed last, after a condemnation of seven states, and the audience might have assumed that the oracles were finished at seven. Second, in condemning Gentile nations, Amos was probably playing the role of the "optimistic prophet" who predicts only salvation for Israel but disaster for its enemies; the people may well have expected a prophet to condemn foreign nations (Barton 1980, 5). Third, by beginning with a condemnation of Samaria's ancient rival Damascus, Amos lulled his audience into thinking that this would be a jingoistic message.

Formally, the following characteristics are evident in the first seven poems (i.e., in all but the Israel poem). Each is in two stanzas, an accusation (one or two strophes) and a prediction of judgment (always one strophe). The accusation stanza always begins with a standard three-line formula in which each line begins with עַל (or וְעַל). The judgment stanza always begins with the formula וְשִׁלַּחְתִּי אֵשׁ . . . וְאָכְלָה ("and I will send fire . . . and it will consume . . ."), although the judgment on Ammon at 1:14 distinctively begins with וְהִצַּתִּי אֵשׁ ("and I will kindle fire") instead of וְשִׁלַּחְתִּי אֵשׁ. The judgment stanza can be expanded to seven lines, or it may consist of only the two-line formula headed by וְשִׁלַּחְתִּי.

Three patterns are found among the first seven poems. In the oracles on Damascus (1:3-5), Gaza (1:6-8), Ammon (1:13-15), and Moab (2:1-3), the accusation is a single strophe of three or four lines, and the judgment is a single strophe of seven lines dominated by the *weqatal* verb. In the oracles on Edom (1:11-12) and Judah (2:4-5), the accusation is in two strophes, the first strophe being four lines (the first three headed by the standard עַל) and the second strophe being a bicolon headed by a *wayyiqtol* verb. The judgment stanza in these two poems is minimal, consisting of only the bicolon headed by the וְשִׁלַּחְתִּי אֵשׁ formula. The third pattern and the shortest poem is the judgment on Tyre (1:9-10). It has a four-line accusation stanza and the minimal two-line judgment formula. Except for the fourth line of the first stanza, the Tyre oracle has only the minimal features for these oracles.

Another feature of the first seven oracles is concatenation, in which one or more elements in one oracle are repeated in the next. For example, the structure and much of the content of Damascus oracle (1:3-5) are repeated in the Gaza (Philistine) oracle (1:6-8). Both, for example, speak of God removing the one who sits (on the throne) and who holds the scepter (יוֹשֵׁב and וְתוֹמֵךְ שֵׁבֶט; 1:5 and 1:8). In the Philistine oracle, God sends fire on the wall of Gaza (1:7); in the next oracle, God sends fire on the wall of Tyre (1:10). Tyre in 1:9 is criticized for not remembering the covenant of brothers, whereas Edom in 1:11 pursued his brother with a sword. Edom in 1:11 slaughtered רַחֲמָיו (which here means "his childbearers"; see discussion below), whereas Ammon in 1:13 cut open the pregnant women of Gilead. Ammon will go into exile בִּתְרוּעָה, "amid the battle-cry" (1:14), and Moab will be defeated בִּתְרוּעָה בְּקוֹל שׁוֹפָר, "amid the battle-cry, with the sound of the shofar." In 2:2, God says that he will send fire on Moab (the region), and it will consume Kerioth (the principal city). In 2:5, God will send fire on Judah (the region), and it will consume Jerusalem (the principal city). For further discussion and elaboration, see Paul (1971).

[3]*Thus says YHWH:*
Because of three rebellions of Damascus,
And because of four, I will not revoke it;
Because they threshed Gilead with the iron sledges.

[4]*And I will send fire on the house of Hazael,*
And it will consume the citadels of Ben-hadad;

[5]And I will shatter the gate-bar of Damascus,
And I will cut off the seated (ruler) from the Valley of Aven
And the one who holds a scepter from Beth-eden,
And the people of Syria will go into exile to Kir.
Says YHWH.

[6]Thus says YHWH:
Because of three rebellions of Gaza,
And because of four, I will not revoke it;
Because they carried off a full-scale exile to hand them over to Edom.

[7]And I will send fire on the wall of Gaza,
And it will consume its citadels;
[8]And I will cut off the seated (ruler) from Ashdod
And the one who holds a scepter from Ashkelon,
And I will send back my hand against Ekron,
And what remains of the Philistines will perish.
Says the Lord YHWH.

[9]Thus says YHWH:
Because of three rebellions of Tyre,
And because of four, I will not revoke it;
Because they handed over a full-scale exile to Edom
And did not remember a fraternal covenant.

[10]And I will send fire on the wall of Tyre,
And it will consume its citadels.

[11]Thus says YHWH:
Because of three rebellions of Edom,
And because of four, I will not revoke it;
Because he pursued his brother with the sword
And was exterminating their child-bearers.
And his rage tore on and on
While his wrath remained ever vigilant.

[12]And I will send fire on Teman,
And it will consume the citadels of Bozrah.

[13]*Thus says YHWH:*
Because of three rebellions of the Ammonites,
And because of four, I will not revoke it;
Because they split open the pregnant women of Gilead
In order to enlarge their territory.

[14]*And I will kindle a fire on the wall of Rabbah,*
And it will consume its citadels
With a war-signal, on a day of battle,
With a wind-storm, on a day of tempest.
[15]*And their king will go into exile—*
He and his princes together.
Says YHWH.

[2:1]*Thus says YHWH:*
Because of three rebellions of the Moab,
And because of four, I will not revoke it;
Because they burned the bones of the king of Edom to lime.

[2]*And I will send a fire upon Moab,*
And it will consume the citadels of Kerioth
And Moab shall perish with clamor,
With a war-signal—with a blast of a shofar.
[3]*And I will cut off a judge from the midst of it,*
And I will kill its princes with him.
Says YHWH.

[4]*Thus says YHWH:*
Because of three rebellions of the Judah,
And because of four, I will not revoke it;
Because they rejected the Torah of YHWH,
And they did not keep his statutes,

[5]*And their lies led them astray—*
(Lies) which their fathers followed.

And I will send a fire upon Judah,
And it will consume the citadels of Jerusalem.

[6]*Thus says YHWH:*
Because of three rebellions of the Israel,
And because of four, I will not revoke it;
Because they sell a righteous man because of silver
And an impoverished man because of a pair of sandals;
[7]*They are people who sniff at the dust of the earth after the heads of the poor*
And stretch out the way of the weak.

And a man and his father go to the same girl
In order to profane my holy name,
[8]*And on garments taken in pledge they stretch out*
Alongside every altar,
And they drink wine taken from people by fines
At the house of their God.

[9]*But I destroyed the Amorite before you*
Whose height was like the height of cedars,
And he was as strong as oaks;
And I destroyed his fruit above
And his roots below.

[10]*And I brought you up from the land of Egypt,*
And I took you through the wilderness for forty years
To possess the land of the Amorite.

[11]*And I raised up some of your sons as prophets*
And some of your young men as Nazirites.
Is not this in fact the case, Sons of Israel?
The oracle of YHWH.

[12]*And you made the Nazirites drink wine,*
And you prohibited the prophets, saying:
"Never prophesy!"

[13]*Look! I am weighed down under you,*
Just as a cart is weighed down—
One that is full of sheaves.

[14]And retreat shall escape the swift:
A strong man will not rally his strength,
And a warrior will not save his life,
[15]And one who bends a bow will not stand,
And one swift on his feet will not save (his life),
And one riding a horse will not save his life,
[16]And one mighty of heart among warriors
Will flee naked on that day.
The oracle of YHWH.

1:3-5: First Oracle (Damascus)

After the prose heading (כֹּה אָמַר יְהוָה), the poem has two stanzas. The first stanza (1:3) gives the reasons God will judge Damascus (three lines) in which each line is headed by the preposition עַל. The second stanza (1:4-5) gives the punishment (seven lines), in which each line is headed by a *weqatal* verb, except for line Be, where there is gapping with the verb וְהִכְרַתִּי in line Bd doing double-duty, and line Bg, which is the concluding אָמַר יְהוָה.

1:3a כֹּ֚ה אָמַ֣ר יְהוָ֔ה

Prose Clause: A prose divine speech formula for the following oracle. אָמַר is a qal *qatal* 3 m s אמר with the particle כֹּה, and יְהוָה is the subject of the verb.

1:3b: First Stanza. Three lines. Each is headed by עַל or וְעַל.

1:3b Aa עַל־שְׁלֹשָׁה֙ פִּשְׁעֵ֣י דַמֶּ֔שֶׂק
Ab וְעַל־אַרְבָּעָ֖ה לֹ֣א אֲשִׁיבֶ֑נּוּ
Ac עַל־דּוּשָׁ֛ם בַּחֲרֻצ֥וֹת הַבַּרְזֶ֖ל אֶת־הַגִּלְעָֽד׃

Line Aa: The colon-marker is *zaqeph qaton* and the constraints are: 0 predicators, 1 constituent, and 3 units. This line is grammatically dependent on לֹא אֲשִׁיבֶנּוּ in the following line.

עַל־שְׁלֹשָׁה֙ פִּשְׁעֵ֣י דַמֶּ֔שֶׂק. A prepositional phrase. עַל is regularly used in these oracles to indicate the reason God is bringing down judgment, and it should be translated "because." פִּשְׁעֵי דַמֶּשֶׂק is a construct chain bound to the number שְׁלֹשָׁה. Damascus was the dominant city of Syria, north of Israel. פֶּשַׁע, "crime" or "act of rebellion," indicates that YHWH is the legitimate sovereign over even this Gentile state.

Line Ab: The colon-marker is *athnach* and the constraints are: 1 predicator, 2 constituents, and 2 units.

וְעַל־אַרְבָּעָ֖ה. There is gapping with the previous line, the phrase פִּשְׁעֵי דַמֶּשֶׂק being understood here. The significance of the formula "for three . . . for four" in Amos is debated. In Proverbs, the N . . . N+1 formula generally indicates that the latter number is the specific number of examples that the teacher will enumerate. For example, Proverbs 6:16 says, "There are six things that the Lord hates, seven that are an abomination to him," and verses 17-19 go on to list seven sins. This is not the case in Amos, where for Damascus he cites only one specific sin. The "for three . . . for four" therefore could simply mean, "for several." It is noteworthy, however, that 3 + 4 = 7, and this is an important number for Amos. The oracles against the nations specify 6 Gentile states plus Judah, the covenant people, for seven oracles of judgment (the fact that Israel is the eighth nation is significant, as discussed below). As is well known, the number seven generally signifies completion. Thus, the point of "for three . . . for four" is probably that Damascus has reached the maximum allowed number of transgressions. That is, the cup of their iniquities is full. Amos therefore asserts that the number of Damascus' sins has reached the critical point, demanding divine judgment, but he only specifies one particular sin.

לֹ֣א אֲשִׁיבֶ֑נּוּ. Negated hiphil *yiqtol* 1 c s of שׁוב with 3 m s suffix. It marks the apodosis of a "because . . . therefore" construction, in which the protasis lines are marked by עַל. The verb signifies "to cause to turn back" but here, in a judicial context, means to "revoke."

The thing not revoked (indicated by the suffix) is the implied punishment. For a summary of alternative interpretations of לֹא אֲשִׁיבֶנּוּ, see Barton (1980, 18).

Line Ac: The colon-marker is *silluq* and the constraints are: 1 predicator, 3 constituents, and 4 units. This line is grammatically dependent on the previous line.

עַל־דּוּשָׁם. Qal infinite construct of דּוּשׁ with 3 m p suffix and preposition עַל. The verb means to "trample" or "thresh." The preposition resumes the explanatory or causal sequence of the protasis.

בַּחֲרֻצוֹת הַבַּרְזֶל. A prepositional phrase (בַּחֲרֻצוֹת) in construct with the noun הַבַּרְזֶל. The preposition בְּ is instrumental. Sledges were heavy wooden platforms studded with nails or spikes on the bottom. Drawn by oxen, farmers used such tools to thresh grain. The image is a metaphor of harsh military conquest, ripping apart people and communities just as a sledge rips apart wheat. This metaphor for military subjugation also appears in Akkadian texts from Tiglath-pileser I and Esarhaddon (Barton 1980, 19).

אֶת־הַגִּלְעָד. The direct object. Gilead, east of the Jordan, was disputed territory that was at times held by Israel and at times by Damascus. The Omride kings of Israel fought a series of battles against Damascus in an attempt to maintain control of Gilead. The conquest alluded to here may be that carried out by Hazael (2 Kgs 10:32-33). See Barton (1980, 26–31) for a survey of the history of the conflict between Damascus and Israel.

1:4-5: Second Stanza. Seven lines. Each line is headed by a *weqatal* except where there is gapping (line Be) and in the final line. The seven lines of divine judgment correspond to the seven (3 + 4) sins of Damascus in 1:3.

וְשִׁלַּחְתִּי אֵשׁ בְּבֵית חֲזָאֵל Ba 1:4
וְאָכְלָה אַרְמְנוֹת בֶּן־הֲדָד׃ Bb
וְשָׁבַרְתִּי בְּרִיחַ דַּמֶּשֶׂק Bc 1:5

וְהִכְרַתִּ֤י יוֹשֵׁב֙ מִבִּקְעַת־אָ֔וֶן Bd
וְתוֹמֵ֥ךְ שֵׁ֖בֶט מִבֵּ֣ית עֶ֑דֶן Be
וְגָל֧וּ עַם־אֲרָ֛ם קִ֖ירָה Bf
אָמַ֥ר יְהוָֽה׃ פ Bg

Line Ba: The colon-marker is *athnach* and the constraints are: 1 predicator, 3 constituents, and 4 units.

וְשִׁלַּ֥חְתִּי. Piel *weqatal* 1 c s of שׁלח. The *weqatal* is significant for two reasons. First, it continues the apodosis begun by לֹא אֲשִׁיבֶנּוּ. Second, this and all subsequent *weqatal* forms constitute the main-line framework of an anticipatory (future tense) narration. Five specific calamities are predicted for Damascus, as represented by the five *weqatal* verbs in lines Ba, Bb, Bc, Bd-e, and Bf.

אֵ֖שׁ. The direct object. Fire here connotes the destruction of the city.

בְּבֵ֣ית חֲזָאֵ֑ל. A prepositional phrase (בְּבֵית) in construct with the proper noun חֲזָאֵל. The preposition בְּ is locative, but it also indicates the secondary object. Hazael, like Ben-hadad, was apparently a throne-name; the history of Damascus is difficult to reconstruct because many kings are identified by the same name (it appears that at least three different kings of Damascus are called Ben-hadad in the Bible). The famous Hazael of the Bible (2 Kgs 8–12; latter part of the ninth century) was a scourge to Israel, inflicting severe defeats upon them, although Israel recovered after his death. The "house of Hazael" refers to the dynastic succession of rulers over Damascus. Not all members of the ruling line were related; Hazael himself was a usurper. But the entire line of Damascus kings, the text says, will come to an end.

Line Bb: The colon-marker is *silluq* and the constraints are: 1 predicator, 2 constituents, and 3 units.

וְאָכְלָ֖ה. Qal *weqatal* 3 f s of אכל. The subject is the fire of line a.

אַרְמְנוֹת בֶּן־הֲדָד. The direct object, a construct chain. The destruction of the "citadels" of a city in Amos is formulaic for the destruction of that city and for the end of that state. The word אַרְמוֹן may mean "palace," but it is also construed as fortified, suggesting that an English term such as "citadel" is appropriate. It could refer to the acropolis around which most ancient cities were built, as that position was most easily defended and would also often be the location for a palace or temple. בֶּן־הֲדָד is the other throne name used in Damascus; it is a Hebrew version of the Aramaic Bir-Hadad, "son of (the god) Hadad." Hazael and Ben-hadad form a merism indicating that there will be no more Aramean kings of Damascus.

Line Bc: The colon-marker is *zaqeph qaton* and the constraints are: 1 predicator, 2 constituents, and 3 units. Despite the verse numbering, this continues the strophe begun in v. 4.

וְשָׁבַרְתִּי. Qal *weqatal* 1 c s of שׁבר. This continues the mainline prediction begun in the previous lines.

בְּרִיחַ דַּמֶּשֶׂק. The direct object. The bar of Damascus, by synecdoche, represents the gate of the city, which in turn represents its defenses. The point is that all of the city's defenses will fail.

Line Bd: The colon-marker is *zaqeph qaton* and the constraints are: 1 predicator, 3 constituents, and 3 units (בִּקְעַת־אָוֶן is regarded as a proper name and therefore as 1 unit).

וְהִכְרַתִּי. Hiphil *weqatal* 1 c s of כרת.

יוֹשֵׁב. Qal participle m s of ישׁב, this could mean, "inhabitant" and refer to all the citizens. However, it is paired with "the one who holds a scepter" in line e (semantic matching) and therefore it refers to a person who "sits (upon a throne)"; that is, to the king.

מִבִּקְעַת־אָוֶן. A prepositional phrase with מִן. The location of the "Valley of Aven" is unknown, but the title is probably a cacophemism (a term of disparagement) rather than the actual name of a place, as it means "valley of iniquity." It probably refers to the valley area north of Galilee between the Lebanon and Anti-Lebanon mountains.

Line Be: The colon-marker is *athnach* and the constraints are: 0 predicators, 3 constituents, and 3 units. There is gapping, in that this line is governed by וְהִכְרַתִּי from line d. Taking into account the gapping, lines d and e syntactically parallel one another, each having a participle or participial phrase (יוֹשֵׁב and וְתוֹמֵךְ שֵׁבֶט) followed by a prepositional phrase in which a two-word proper name is governed by מִן. The gapping here indicates that the ruler from the Valley of Aven and of the scepter-holder from Beth-eden are conceptually a single person. Probably the ruler of each place is one and the same man, the king of Damascus.

וְתוֹמֵךְ. Qal active participle m s of תמך with conjunction. The participle is substantival.

שֵׁבֶט. The direct object of וְתוֹמֵךְ.

מִבֵּית עֶדֶן. A prepositional phrase with מִן. Beth-eden is known as *Bit Adini* in Assyrian texts and was located on the Euphrates River about 200 miles northeast of Damascus. With the Valley of Aven, apparently in the southwest, this indicates that the kings of Damascus will lose power over all of their territory, from the southwest to the northeast.

Line Bf: The colon-marker is *tifha*. The constraints are: 1 predicator, 3 constituents, and 4 units. If אָמַר יְהוָה were treated as part of this line, there would be too many constituents and units. Several times in Amos a *tifha* will mark a line break before a divine speech formula.

וְגָלוּ. Qal *weqatal* 3 c p of גלה. This is the last in a series of five mainline predictions marked by the *weqatal*.

עַם־אֲרָם. A construct chain serving as the subject. Amos foresees a mass deportation of the Aramean people.

קִירָה. A proper name, Kir, with a directive ה. Kir's location is not certain, but Isaiah 22:6 suggests that it was in the area of Elam, east of southern Mesopotamia. Amos 9:7 indicates that this is the original homeland of the Arameans, and that text asserts that God brought up the Arameans in an "exodus" from Kir. Now, he says, their exodus will be reversed. See Amos 2:10, where the implication is that Israel's exodus from Egypt will also be reversed.

Line Bg: The colon-marker is *silluq* and the constraints are: 1 predicator, 2 constituents, and 2 units.

אָמַ֖ר. Qal *qatal* 3 m s of אמר. The divine speech formula terminates the poem.

יְהוָֽה. The subject.

1:6-8: Second Oracle (Gaza)

After the prose heading (כֹּ֖ה אָמַ֣ר יְהוָ֑ה), the poem has two stanzas, each a single strophe. This poem is structurally identical to 1:3-5. The first stanza (1:6) gives the reasons God will judge Gaza and the Philistines in three lines, with each headed by the preposition עַל. The second (1:7-8) gives the punishment in seven lines, with each line headed by a *weqatal* verb, except for line Bd, where there is gapping with the verb וְהִכְרַתִּי in line Bc doing double-duty, and line Bg, which is the concluding אָמַר אֲדֹנָי יְהוִה. Scholars have noted that this oracle includes every city of the Philistine pentapolis except Gath (Gaza, Ashdod, Ashkelon, and Ekron are all mentioned). It appears that Gath was relatively insignificant by the time of Amos. The last known king of Gath was Achish (mentioned in 1 Kgs 2:39-40, from the early part of Solomon's reign), and Gath is absent in cuneiform sources from this time (for further information, see discussion at 6:2).

כֹּ֚ה אָמַ֣ר יְהוָ֔ה 1:6a

See 1:3.

1:6b: First Stanza. Three lines. Each is headed by matching עַל or וְעַל.

עַל־שְׁלֹשָׁה֙ פִּשְׁעֵ֣י עַזָּ֔ה Aa 1:6b
וְעַל־אַרְבָּעָ֖ה לֹ֣א אֲשִׁיבֶ֑נּוּ Ab
עַל־הַגְלוֹתָ֞ם גָּל֥וּת שְׁלֵמָ֖ה לְהַסְגִּ֥יר לֶאֱדֽוֹם׃ Ac

Line Aa: The colon-marker is *zaqeph qaton* and the constraints are: 0 predicators, 1 constituent, and 3 units. This line is dependent on the following line.

עַל־שְׁלֹשָׁה֙ פִּשְׁעֵ֣י עַזָּ֔ה. Gaza is mentioned here as the representative city of the Philistines either because it is the southernmost Philistine city (and thus is at the extreme southeast corner of Amos' map of condemned nations, opposite Damascus), or because it was the most powerful of the city-states, or because its place along the coastal trade-route made it an important junction in the slave trade (Paul 1991, 56). By the late eighth century Gaza was under the domination of Assyria. Gaza gave tribute to Tiglath-pileser III of Assyria (ruled 745–727) according to an Assyrian building inscription (*ANET* 282). Thereafter rulers of Gaza were tributary vassals of Assyria and are mentioned as such in texts connected with Sennacherib (704–681), Esar-haddon (680–669) and Ashurbanipal (668–633); see *ANET* 288, 291, 294.

Line Ab: The colon-marker is *athnach* and the constraints are: 1 predicator, 2 constituents, and 2 units.

וְעַל־אַרְבָּעָ֖ה. Prepositional phrase with עַל used causally.

לֹ֣א אֲשִׁיבֶ֑נּוּ. Negated hiphil *yiqtol* 1 c s of שׁוּב with 3 m s suffix.

Line Ac: The colon-marker is *silluq* and the constraints are: 1 predicator (הַגְלוֹתָם), 4 constituents, and 5 units.

עַל־הַגְלוֹתָ֛ם. Hiphil infinitive construct with 3 m p suffix with עַל used causally.

גָּל֥וּת שְׁלֵמָ֖ה. The direct object. The word גָּלוּת is a cognate accusative with הַגְלוֹתָם. The word שְׁלֵמָה is adjectival, giving the meaning "a complete exile." It may refer to raiding villages and taking their entire populations as captives to sell into slavery.

לְהַסְגִּ֥יר. Hiphil infinitive construct of סגר with לְ. It is here a complement to הַגְלוֹתָם. On סגר, see 1:9.

לֶאֱדוֹם. Prepositional phrase with לְ, which may be regarded as both directional and as a dative of advantage. Edom is mentioned here and in 1:9 as the recipient of a large number of persons kidnapped for slavery. Edom apparently either served as a middleman for transporting slaves to Arabia or itself used the slaves in its copper mines.

1:7-8: Second Stanza. Seven lines. The initial *weqatal* verbs constitute a mainline series of future events. Four lines end with references to names of Philistine cities (Gaza, Ashdod, Ashkelon, and Ekron), one line (Bb) ends with אַרְמְנֹתֶיהָ ("her [Gaza's] citadels"), and one line (Bf) ends with שְׁאֵרִית פְּלִשְׁתִּים ("the remainder of the Philistines"). In short, the first five lines each describe the destruction of a Philistine location, and the sixth broadly states that all Philistia will be destroyed.

וְשִׁלַּ֥חְתִּי אֵ֖שׁ בְּחוֹמַ֣ת עַזָּ֑ה Ba 1:7
וְאָכְלָ֖ה אַרְמְנֹתֶֽיהָ׃ Bb
וְהִכְרַתִּ֤י יוֹשֵׁב֙ מֵֽאַשְׁדּ֔וֹד Bc 1:8
וְתוֹמֵ֥ךְ שֵׁ֖בֶט מֵֽאַשְׁקְל֑וֹן Bd
וַהֲשִׁיב֨וֹתִי יָדִ֜י עַל־עֶקְר֗וֹן Be
וְאָֽבְדוּ֙ שְׁאֵרִ֣ית פְּלִשְׁתִּ֔ים Bf
אָמַ֖ר אֲדֹנָ֥י יְהוִֽה׃ פ Bg

Line Ba: The colon-marker is *athnach* and the constraints are: 1 predicator, 3 constituents, and 4 units.

וְשִׁלַּחְתִּי. Piel *weqatal* 1 c s from שׁלח. As in 1:4, the *weqatal* forms here continue the apodosis and give a mainline sequence of future events.

אֵשׁ. The direct object.

בְּחוֹמַת עַזָּה. Prepositional phrase with בְּ. Three times YHWH sends fire on the חוֹמָה ("wall") of a city (1:7, 10, 14). חוֹמָה is a defensive wall around a city, building, or vineyard. The more general term for a wall is גָּדֵר (Hammershaimb 1970, 31), and קִיר is an internal, structural wall (see Amos 5:19).

Line Bb: The colon-marker is *silluq* and the constraints are: 1 predicator, 2 constituents, and 2 units.

וְאָכְלָה. Qal *weqatal* 3 f s from אכל.

אַרְמְנֹתֶיהָ. Direct object with 3 f s suffix (antecedent is עַזָּה).

Line Bc: The colon-marker is *zaqeph qaton* and the constraints are: 1 predicator, 3 constituents, and 3 units.

וְהִכְרַתִּי. Hiphil *weqatal* 1 c s of כרת.

יוֹשֵׁב. Qal participle m s of ישׁב. As in 1:5 this word represents the ruler, one who sits on a throne, and not an ordinary "inhabitant." It is matched by וְתוֹמֵךְ שֵׁבֶט in Bd.

מֵאַשְׁדּוֹד. Prepositional phrase with מִן. The eighth-century city of Ashdod suffered two conflagrations. It was subdued in around 760 by Uzziah (2 Chr 26:6) and then in 712 by the Assyrian Sargon II (721–705 B.C.). It is thereafter mentioned as a tributary state of Assyria (see *ANET* 288, 291, 294).

Line Bd: The colon-marker is *athnach* and the constraints are: 0 predicators, 2 constituents, and 3 units. There is gapping of the verb וְהִכְרַתִּי in line Bc.

וְתוֹמֵךְ שֵׁבֶט. A qal active participle m s of תמך with conjunction and in construct with שֵׁבֶט, an objective genitive. The participle is substantival.

מֵאַשְׁקְלוֹן. Prepositional phrase with מִן. Ashkelon was located on the Mediterranean coast between Gaza to the south and Ashdod to the north. Tiglath-pileser III twice confronted Ashkelon, a member of an anti-Assyrian coalition led by Damascus, while campaigning in the Levant. See *ABD*, "Ashkelon."

Line Be: The colon-marker is *revia* and the constraints are: 1 predicator, 3 constituents, and 3 units.

וַהֲשִׁיבוֹתִי. Hiphil *weqatal* 1 c s of שׁוּב. The verb, with the direct object יָדִי and the preposition עַל, means, "I will send back my hand against" (see Isa 1:25). Elsewhere in Amos 1–2, the hiphil of שׁוּב means to "revoke" a judgment.

יָדִי. The direct object.

עַל־עֶקְרוֹן. Prepositional phrase with עַל. Ekron was located more toward the interior and further from the coast, making it a border city between Judah and Philistia. Currently identified at Tel Miqne, it, too, came under Assyrian domination in the late eighth century. In his campaign of 701, Sennacherib assaulted Ekron and killed its leading citizens, impaling them about the city wall; see *ANET* 287–88).

Line Bf: The colon-marker is *zaqeph qaton* and the constraints are: 1 predicator, 2 constituents, and 3 units.

וְאָבְדוּ. Qal *weqatal* 3 c p of אבד. This final *weqatal* completes the mainline series and indicates the complete end of Philistine civilization.

שְׁאֵרִית פְּלִשְׁתִּים. This construct chain, "the remainder of the Philistines," acknowledges that there were other Philistine cities and villages, including what remained of Gath. The point is that all of Philistia will be swept away.

Line Bg: The colon-marker is *silluq* and the constraints are: 1 predicator, 2 constituents, and 3 units.

אָמַר. Qal *qatal* 3 m s of אמר.

אֲדֹנָי יְהוִה. Subject. The addition of אֲדֹנָי (literally "my lords" but used frequently as an honorific for YHWH and simply translated as "lord"), over against the shorter אָמַר יְהוָה in 1:5, illustrates the kind of minor variation Amos frequently employs.

1:9-10: Third Oracle (Tyre)

After the prose heading (כֹּה אָמַר יְהוָה), the poem has two stanzas. The first stanza (1:9) gives the reasons God will judge Tyre and the

Phoenicians. The second (1:10), in a truncated fashion, describes the calamities that will befall Tyre. The abbreviated judgment clause does not indicate that Tyre will experience a less severe trauma. Although Amos employs repetition throughout his first two chapters, he avoids the tedium of structuring every poem in exactly the same manner. As described above, only two elements are repeated verbatim in every poem. First, every poem employs the same opening in three lines. Second, in the pronouncement of judgment, every oracle except that on Israel has the two lines . . . וְשִׁלַּחְתִּי אֵשׁ and . . . וְאָכְלָה. The oracle on Tyre is unique in that it has only these requisite five lines plus one additional line, Ad.

1:9a כֹּה אָמַר יְהוָה

Prose Clause: See 1:3.

1:9b: First Stanza. Four lines. Each is headed by עַל or וְעַל, except that the fourth line (Ad) is headed by וְלֹא זָכְרוּ. This line is exposition on Ac, indicating the especially heinous nature of this act of kidnapping people for slavery.

1:9b Aa עַל־שְׁלֹשָׁה פִּשְׁעֵי־צֹר
Ab וְעַל־אַרְבָּעָה לֹא אֲשִׁיבֶנּוּ
Ac עַל־הַסְגִּירָם גָּלוּת שְׁלֵמָה לֶאֱדוֹם
Ad וְלֹא זָכְרוּ בְּרִית אַחִים׃

Line Aa: The colon-marker is *zaqeph qaton* and the constraints are: 0 predicators, 1 constituent, and 3 units. This line is dependent on the following line.

עַל־שְׁלֹשָׁה פִּשְׁעֵי־צֹר. Tyre was the dominant Phoenician city in the eighth century, Sidon at this time being in vassal status to Tyre (Paul 1991, 59).

Line Ab: The colon-marker is *athnach* and the constraints are: 1 predicator, 2 constituents, and 2 units.

וְעַל־אַרְבָּעָה. Prepositional phrase with עַל used causally.

לֹא אֲשִׁיבֶנּוּ. Negated hiphil *yiqtol* 1 c s of שׁוּב with 3 m s suffix.

Line Ac: The colon-marker is *zaqeph qaton* and the constraints are 1 predicator, 3 constituents, and 4 units. This line is the concatenous link to a similar accusation leveled against Gaza in 1:6, but as is common in Amos, there is minor variation in the wording (see line Ac in 1:6).

עַל־הַסְגִּירָם. Hiphil infinitive construct of סגר with 3 m p suffix and a causal preposition עַל. The infinitive here serves as a predicator; by contrast, in 1:6, הַגְלוֹתָם is the predicator and לְהַסְגִּיר is its complement. But the meaning of both lines is essentially the same. סגר in the qal means to "shut" but in the hiphil it means to "hand (a refugee) over" to a pursuer or enemy. The usage in Deuteronomy 23:16 (E 15) is particularly apropos.

גָּלוּת שְׁלֵמָה. The direct object. The adjective שָׁלֵם ("whole, complete") suggests that an entire community was seized and carried off into slavery.

לֶאֱדוֹם. Prepositional phrase with לְ. As in 1:6, Edom is the recipient of the captured slaves. It is perhaps noteworthy that places from which these slaves were taken is not indicated in the text. One might assume that they are snatched from Israel or Judah, but the text does not say this. The important point is that these nations engaged in the crime of seizing peoples to sell as slaves. Whether or not the people they seized were Israelite is secondary.

Line Ad: The colon-marker is *silluq* and the constraints are: 1 predicator, 2 constituents, and 3 units. Within the accusation stanzas of the oracles of this poem, the lines headed by עַל may be regarded as mainline elements of the protasis, listing the principal reasons that God's judgment is coming. This וְלֹא + *qatal* clause, as is normally the case, is offline, and it here comments on the accusation. In this case, the act of attacking villages and taking people to sell into slavery is made all the more heinous by the fact that the peoples they attacked were treaty-allies and thus should have been under their protection.

וְלֹ֥א זָכְר֖וּ. Negated qal *qatal* 3 c p of זכר. The term זכר is used for remembering (i.e., for abiding by the terms of) a covenant, as in Genesis 9:15 and Exodus 2:24.

בְּרִ֥ית אַחִֽים. A construct chain serving as the direct object. The covenant alluded to here may be the treaty relations between Israel and Tyre. Such a treaty was made between David and Hiram of Tyre (2 Sam 5:11), and it was maintained under Solomon and Hiram (1 Kgs 5:1-12). There was also a marriage alliance involving Ahab of Israel and Jezebel daughter of Ethbaal of Sidon (1 Kgs 16:31). Again, however, the lack of specificity is important. The crime of Tyre is not that they acted against Israel, but that they kidnapped people for slavery and violated treaties in order to do so. "Brothers" (אַחִים) is in the ancient Near East a technical term for treaty partners (see 1 Kgs 9:13). See Priest (1965).

1:10: Second Stanza. Two lines. Both are headed by *weqatal* verbs, indicating that this strophe is the apodosis. As described above, these two lines constitute the minimal configuration for a judgment stanza in the first seven poems.

1:10 Ba וְשִׁלַּ֥חְתִּי אֵ֖שׁ בְּח֣וֹמַת צֹ֑ר

Bb וְאָכְלָ֖ה אַרְמְנֹתֶֽיהָ׃ פ

Line Ba: The colon-marker is *athnach* and the constraints are: 1 predicator, 3 constituents, and 4 units.

וְשִׁלַּ֥חְתִּי. Piel *weqatal* 1 c s from שׁלח.

אֵ֖שׁ. The direct object.

בְּח֣וֹמַת צֹ֑ר. Prepositional phrase with בְּ on a construct chain.

The destruction of Tyre represents the end of Phoenician independence and of its hegemony over the northern Levant.

Line Bb: The colon-marker is *silluq* and the constraints are: 1 predicator, 2 constituents, and 2 units.

וְאָכְלָה. Qal *weqatal* 3 f s from אכל (the subject is אֵשׁ).

אַרְמְנֹתֶיהָ. The direct object. The 3 f s suffix has Tyre as its antecedent; cities are construed as feminine.

1:11-12: Fourth Oracle (Edom)

After the prose כֹּה אָמַר יְהוָה, the poem has two stanzas, the first having two strophes and the second having one.

1:11a כֹּה אָמַר יְהוָה

See 1:3.

1:11b-c: First Stanza. Two strophes. The first is a standard accusation strophe, but the second is conjoined to it with a *wayyiqtol* and gives a secondary accusation.

1:11b: First Strophe. 4 lines. Each is headed by עַל or וְעַל, except that the last line (1d) is headed by the *weqatal* וְשִׁחֵת.

1:11b A1a עַל־שְׁלֹשָׁה פִּשְׁעֵי אֱדוֹם
A1b וְעַל־אַרְבָּעָה לֹא אֲשִׁיבֶנּוּ
A1c עַל־רָדְפוֹ בַחֶרֶב אָחִיו
A1d וְשִׁחֵת רַחֲמָיו

Line A1a: The colon-marker is *zaqeph qaton* and the constraints are: 0 predicators, 1 constituent, and 3 units. This line is dependent on the following line.

עַל־שְׁלֹשָׁה פִּשְׁעֵי אֱדוֹם. Edom, located south of the Dead Sea, was a nation whose people were most closely related to the Israelites but who often were their most bitter enemies. Edom is mentioned four times in these poems, twice as the recipient of slaves (1:6,9), once as the victim of a crime (2:1), and here, where Edom is the object of divine judgment.

Line A1b: The colon-marker is *athnach* and the constraints are: 1 predicator, 2 constituents, and 2 units.

וְעַל־אַרְבָּעָה. Prepositional phrase with עַל used causally.

לֹא אֲשִׁיבֶנּוּ. Negated hiphil *yiqtol* 1 c s of שׁוּב with 3 m s suffix. As usual, it marks the apodosis.

Line A1c: The colon-marker is *pashta* and the constraints are: 1 predicator, 3 constituents, and 3 units. The use of *pashta* at the end of a line is unusual, but for two reasons this line should terminate here. First, if וְשִׁחֵת רַחֲמָיו were added to this the line would be too long (five constituents). Second, the parallelism, with רדף corresponding to שׁחת and with אָחִיו corresponding to רַחֲמָיו, suggests that וְשִׁחֵת רַחֲמָיו is a separate line.

עַל־רָדְפוֹ. Qal infinitive construct of רדף with 3 m s suffix and preposition עַל used causally. This serves as the predicator of this line.

בַחֶרֶב. Prepositional phrase with instrumental בְּ. The sword is metonymy for military action.

אָחִיו. The direct object. As in 1:9, "brother" could here represent a treaty partner, but in this case it probably represents the racial kinship between Edom and Judah, their neighbors to the north. Again, the fact that Judah is not explicitly named indicates that it is the nature of the crime, not the fact that Judah was the victim, that is the focus. Because of the condemnation of Edom in the book of Obadiah, set apparently at the time of the exile, some suggest that this oracle is a later insertion condemning Edom for the role it played during the fall of Jerusalem to Nebuchadnezzar II (in 586). This conclusion is unnecessary. There were no doubt many incursions and battles along the border of Edom and Judah throughout their long history, and Amos probably had an incident in mind that we have no specific knowledge of. This appears to have been an especially vicious attack, however; it was an attempt to carry out a policy of genocide against Judah.

Line A1d: The colon-marker is *zaqeph qaton* and the constraints are: 1 predicator, 2 constituents, and 2 units.

וְשִׁחֵת. Piel *weqatal* 3 m s of שׁחת. The verb means to destroy, ruin, or exterminate. The use of the *weqatal* for the past tense is unusual and demands attention. Amos 1–2 has a large number of *weqatal* verbs, but almost all represent a mainline future tense exposition, as is common. Normally a conjoined past tense action is expressed with the *wayyiqtol*, but the use of the *wayyiqtol* here would suggest a separate, sequential action. The *weqatal* suggests two things. First, as mentioned above, the action of this line (A1d) is simultaneous with that of the previous line, A1c. Second, the action is imperfective ("and he was exterminating") and not perfective ("and he exterminated"). The latter would be represented by the *wayyiqtol*.

רַחֲמָיו. The word רַחֲמִים is used abstractly for "compassion" or "pity," and thus most versions take this line as "he destroyed his pity," understanding that to mean that he showed no compassion. However, as Shalom Paul states, such an interpretation "is a makeshift one and is totally unattested" (Paul 1991, 64). Various interpretations for רַחֲמִים here have been proposed, including the unconvincing notion that it refers to treaty partners (see Fishbane 1970 and 1972; Coote 1971; Barré 1985). It is more likely here that רֶחֶם ("womb") is used by metonymy for "women" especially in their capacity as child-bearers. Similar usage appears in Judges 5:30:

הֲלֹא יִמְצְאוּ יְחַלְּקוּ שָׁלָל
רַחַם רַחֲמָתַיִם לְרֹאשׁ גֶּבֶר

"Won't they find [and] divide plunder?
A womb, two wombs, for the head of each warrior?"

Here, the sexual language is quite graphic. Women taken in plunder are described as "wombs" for the "head" (i.e., for the sexual organ) of each soldier. In Amos, the women are similarly the victims of enemy soldiers, and again they are by metonymy referred to as רחם because it is their sexual capacity that is in view. In Amos, however, the women are represented as childbearers and are not objects of rape but of slaughter, because Edom's objective is genocide. The term רחם in Ugaritic also can mean "woman," as it is used in parallel with *btlt*, "virgin" (*CTA* 6:ii:26–27; cited in Paul 1991, 65). In addition, the concatenation pattern described for this poem indicates that the slaughter of women is in view, since the principal crime of the Ammonites in 1:13 is that they cut open pregnant women. On the other hand, the fact that רַחֲמִים means "compassion" is not lost on Amos. Making a wordplay on the two senses of the word as "child-bearers" and "compassion," he speaks of how the Edomites gave full expression to their rage in the next strophe (2a-2b). The antecedent of the 3 m s suffix on רַחֲמָיו is "brother" in the previous line. As "brother" a collective reference to the people of Judah, the suffix can be translated as "their."

1:11c: Second Strophe. Two lines. The lines are plainly parallel (אַפּוֹ with וְעֶבְרָתוֹ, and לָעַד with נֶצַח), and constitute a bicolon. The initial *wayyiqtol* is used here and in 2:4 to introduce a secondary accusation.

וַיִּטְרֹף לָעַד אַפּוֹ A2a 1:11c
וְעֶבְרָתוֹ שְׁמָרָה נֶצַח׃ A2b

Line A2a: The colon-marker is *zaqeph qaton* and the constraints are: 1 predicator, 3 constituents, and 3 units.

וַיִּטְרֹף. Qal *wayyiqtol* 3 m s of טרף. In prose narrative the *wayyiqtol* typically gives the mainline structure for a historical sequence of events. This text, however, although past tense, is not strictly a narrative but an accusation. The *wayyiqtol* is not temporally sequential but it is secondary, being an additional accusation. The verb טרף ("to tear") is often emended to נטר ("to guard") on the grounds that it is a better parallel to שמר in line 2b, and also because of the usage in Jeremiah 3:5, הֲיִנְטֹר לְעוֹלָם אִם־יִשְׁמֹר לָנֶצַח ("Will he guard [his anger] forever? Will he keep [it] continually?"). This emendation is appealing and may be correct, but one can maintain the MT as it stands.

לָעַד. The noun עַד means "lasting time" or "future," and the idiom לָעַד means "permanently."

אַפּוֹ. It is not certain whether this is to be construed as the subject or object of the verb, but since "he tore his wrath" is unclear and actually suggests that he destroyed his wrath (i.e., brought it to an end), it is more like that that אַפּוֹ is the subject, "his wrath tore."

Line A2b: The colon-marker is *silluq* and the constraints are: 1 predicator, 3 constituents, and 3 units.

וְעֶבְרָתוֹ. As with אַפּוֹ, it is unclear whether this word is the subject or object of the verb. The parallel with the previous line, however, suggests that it is the subject.

שְׁמָרָה. As it stands, this appears to be a Qal *qatal* 3 m s with 3 f s suffix, but without the normal *mappiq* (such forms are rare but attested; see *GKC* §58g). If this is correct, the suffix must be a resumptive pronoun referring back to the direct object וְעֶבְרָתוֹ. This construction ("his rage, he kept her") is quite peculiar, and some simply emend the verb to שָׁמַר, dropping the suffix. An alternative is to repoint the verb as a simple Qal *qatal* 3 f s, שָׁמְרָה, a minor emendation that leaves the consonantal text intact. So understood, וְעֶבְרָתוֹ is the subject rather than the object of the verb. A difficulty here is that this requires taking שמר in an intransitive sense, as "to continue" or "remain vigilant," although it almost always is transitive, to guard or keep something. It is possible that we have an intransitive usage in 2 Samuel 11:16, where the infinitive construct of שמר seems to mean to "keep watch" or "maintain vigilance" (even there, however, there is an indirect object). Nevertheless, it appears that reading שמרה as a *qatal* 3 f s used intransitively with וְעֶבְרָתוֹ as the subject is the best option. The use of the וְ + [X] + *qatal* pattern after the *wayyiqtol* here indicates that the two lines describe a single action. Two lines headed by *wayyiqtol* verbs would suggest two separate, sequential actions.

נֶצַח. This means "duration" and, as an adverb, "endlessly."

1:12: Second Stanza. Two lines. This is the standard judgment stanza in its shortest form.

וְשִׁלַּחְתִּי אֵשׁ בְּתֵימָן Ba 1:12
וְאָכְלָה אַרְמְנוֹת בָּצְרָה׃ פ Bb

Line Ba: The colon-marker is *athnach* and the constraints are: 1 predicator, 3 constituents, and 3 units.

וְשִׁלַּחְתִּי. Piel *weqatal* 1 c s from שלח.

אֵשׁ. The direct object.

בְּתֵימָן. Prepositional phrase with בְּ. Teman was the name of the region of north Edom.

Line Bb: The colon-marker is *silluq* and the constraints are: 1 predicator, 2 constituents, and 3 units.

וְאָכְלָה. Qal *weqatal* 3 f s from אכל.

אַרְמְנוֹת בָּצְרָה. A construct chain and the direct object. Bozrah was the chief city of Edom; it was about thirty miles southeast of the Dead Sea.

1:13-15: Fifth Oracle (Ammon)

After the heading (כֹּה אָמַר יְהוָה), the poem has two stanzas. The structure of this poem is thus similar to the oracles on Damascus (1:3-5) and Philistia (1:6-8).

כֹּה אָמַר יְהוָה 1:13a

See 1:3.

1:13b: First Stanza. It gives the reasons God will judge Ammon in four lines, in which each line is headed by the preposition עַל except for line Ad, which is a purpose clause dependent on line Ac.

עַל־שְׁלֹשָׁה֙ פִּשְׁעֵ֣י בְנֵֽי־עַמּ֔וֹן	Aa	1:13b
וְעַל־אַרְבָּעָ֖ה לֹ֣א אֲשִׁיבֶ֑נּוּ	Ab	
עַל־בִּקְעָם֙ הָר֣וֹת הַגִּלְעָ֔ד	Ac	
לְמַ֖עַן הַרְחִ֥יב אֶת־גְּבוּלָֽם׃	Ad	

Line Aa: The colon-marker is *zaqeph qaton* and the constraints are: 0 predicators, 1 constituent, and 3 units. This line is dependent on the following line.

עַל־שְׁלֹשָׁה֙ פִּשְׁעֵ֣י בְנֵֽי־עַמּ֔וֹן. This indictment uniquely has "sons of Ammon," the name of the people, rather than the name of a territory (such as "Moab") or leading city (such as "Tyre"), as the designation for the accused state.

Line Ab: The colon-marker is *athnach* and the constraints are: 1 predicator, 2 constituents, and 2 units.

וְעַל־אַרְבָּעָ֖ה. Prepositional phrase with עַל used causally.

לֹ֣א אֲשִׁיבֶ֑נּוּ. Negated hiphil *yiqtol* 1 c s of שׁוּב with 3 m s suffix.

Line Ac: The colon-marker is *zaqeph qaton* and the constraints are: 1 predicator, 2 constituents, and 3 units.

עַל־בִּקְעָם֙. The preposition עַל is causal; בִּקְעָם is a Qal infinitive construct of בקע, with a 3 m p suffix serving as the subject of the action.

הָר֣וֹת הַגִּלְעָ֔ד. A construct chain as direct object; the adjective הָרָה ("pregnant") is here f p and used substantively. This is the second time Gilead is mentioned as the object of aggression (see 1:3). This atrocity, ripping open pregnant women, is sequential to the slaughter of childbearers (1:11) in the concatenous structure of the poem.

Line Ad: The colon-marker is *silluq* and the constraints are: 1 predicator, 2 constituents, and 3 units (taking לְמַעַן as a unit).

לְמַ֫עַן הַרְחִ֫יב. A purpose clause with הַרְחִיב, a hiphil infinitive construct of רחב ("enlarge").

אֶת־גְּבוּלָֽם. The direct object. The Ammonites desired more *Lebensraum*; to gain this they were willing, as were the Edomites, to slaughter pregnant or childbearing women.

1:14-15: Second Stanza. This is another seven-line description of punishment. Lines Ba, Bb, and Be are each headed by the standard *weqatal* verb. Lines Bc and Bd are prepositional phrases dependent on Bb. Line Bf has gapping, with וְהָלַךְ in line Be governing both lines. Line Bg is the standard concluding אָמַר יְהוָה.

וְהִצַּ֤תִּי אֵשׁ֙ בְּחוֹמַ֣ת רַבָּ֔ה Ba 1:14
וְאָכְלָ֖ה אַרְמְנוֹתֶ֑יהָ Bb
בִּתְרוּעָה֙ בְּי֣וֹם מִלְחָמָ֔ה Bc
בְּסַ֖עַר בְּי֥וֹם סוּפָֽה׃ Bd
וְהָלַ֥ךְ מַלְכָּ֖ם בַּגּוֹלָ֑ה Be 1:15
ה֥וּא וְשָׂרָ֛יו יַחְדָּ֖ו Bf
אָמַ֥ר יְהוָֽה׃ פ Bg

Line Ba: The colon-marker is *zaqeph qaton* and the constraints are: 1 predicator, 3 constituents, and 4 units.

וְהִצַּ֤תִּי. Hiphil *weqatal* 1 c s from יצת. This root is unusual in that in all of its inflected forms (Qal, Niphal, and Hiphil), it follows the morphology of the I-נ root (such as נפל), in which the first radical assimilates to and doubles the second. This is the only place in the first seven oracles where the judgment stanza begins with וְהִצַּתִּי אֵשׁ

instead of וְשִׁלַּחְתִּי אֵשׁ. We probably should not make too much of this variation; throughout the oracles, Amos uses formulas and repetition without rigidly adhering to fixed patterns.

אֵשׁ. The direct object.

בְּחוֹמַת רַבָּה. A construct chain with preposition בְּ. Rabbah was located at the site of the modern capital of Jordan, Amman. In Hellenistic times it was called Philadelphia. In the Iron Age, it was the capital city of the Ammonites.

Line Bb: The colon-marker is *athnach* and the constraints are: 1 predicator, 2 constituents, and 2 units.

וְאָכְלָה. Qal *weqatal* 3 f s from אכל.

אַרְמְנוֹתֶיהָ. Direct object with 3 f s suffix whose antecedent is רַבָּה.

Line Bc: The colon-marker is *zaqeph qaton* and the constraints are: 0 predicators, 2 constituents, and 3 units. This line relates to the previous line adverbially, describing circumstances.

בִּתְרוּעָה. Prepositional phrase with בְּ for attendant circumstances.

בְּיוֹם מִלְחָמָה. Prepositional phrase on a construct chain with בְּ. Asyndeton (lack of conjunction) here indicates that this phrase and בִּתְרוּעָה are understood to be in apposition, simultaneous, and descriptive of a single event.

Line Bd: The colon-marker is *silluq* and the constraints are: 0 predicators, 2 constituents, and 3 units. This line grammatically matches the previous but is not semantically equivalent, although it metaphorically treats the same circumstances.

בְּסַעַר. Prepositional phrase with בְּ, here used for attendant circumstances.

בְּיוֹם סוּפָה. Prepositional phrase on a construct chain with בְּ, used temporally. Asyndeton again indicates that this phrase and בְּסַעַר are understood to be in apposition, simultaneous, and descriptive of a single event. The storm or whirlwind is metaphorical for the chaos and destructiveness of battle, thus suggesting a metaphorical rather than literal semantic unity with the previous line.

Line Be: The colon-marker is *athnach* and the constraints are: 1 predicator, 3 constituents, and 3 units.

וְהָלַךְ. Qal *weqatal* 3 m s of הלך.

מַלְכָּם. The subject, מֶלֶךְ with a 3 m p suffix. Several Greek recensions read Μελχομ here, and thus some believe that this word should be read as "Milcom," god of the Ammonites. However, the subsequent line and also the tendency of Amos to speak of sending rulers into exile (1:5, 8) indicate that this refers to the king and not to the god. There may be, however, a wordplay on Milcom in Amos' use of the term מַלְכָּם instead of the term for monarchs that he uses above, יֹשֵׁב.

בַּגּוֹלָה. Prepositional phrase with בְּ, used here to describe attendant circumstances as a complement to הלך.

Line Bf: The colon-marker is *tifha* and the constraints are: 0 predicators, 1 constituent, and 3 units. The use of *tifha* for a colon-marker is unusual, but several times in these oracles a weak disjunctive precedes a formula of divine speech, which should be regarded as a separate line. The line has gapping, with וְהָלַךְ in the previous line governing this line also.

הוּא וְשָׂרָיו יַחְדָּו. The subject of the verb וְהָלַךְ is secondarily expanded to include the king's high officials. This is thus a compound subject and therefore a single constituent. Rhetorically, this suggests that no one in leadership will escape.

Line Bg: The colon-marker is *silluq* and the constraints are: 1 predicator, 2 constituents, and 2 units. Another divine speech formula.

אָמַר. Qal *qatal* 3 m s of אמר.

יְהוָה. The subject.

2:1-3: Sixth Oracle (Moab)

After the heading (כֹּה אָמַר יְהוָה), this poem has two stanzas. The first stanza (2:1) gives the reasons God will judge Moab (three lines) in which each line is headed by the preposition עַל. The second (2:2-3) gives the punishment (seven lines), in which each line is headed by a *weqatal* verb, except for line Bd, where there is gapping with the verb וּמֵת in line Bc doing double-duty, line Bf, which is tied to line Be by a chiastic structure, and line Bg, which is the concluding אָמַר יְהוָה. The structure of this poem is a variation on the pattern found with Damascus (1:3-5), Philistia (1:6-8) and Ammon (1:13-15). Barton (1980, 33–35) has a good survey of possible historical backgrounds for the warfare alluded to in this oracle, but he concludes that it is not possible to know with certainty what incident Amos here alludes to.

2:1a כֹּה אָמַר יְהוָה

See 1:3.

2:1b: First Stanza. Three lines. Each is headed by causal עַל or וְעַל.

2:1b Aa עַל־שְׁלֹשָׁה פִּשְׁעֵי מוֹאָב
Ab וְעַל־אַרְבָּעָה לֹא אֲשִׁיבֶנּוּ
Ac עַל־שָׂרְפוֹ עַצְמוֹת מֶלֶךְ־אֱדוֹם לַשִּׂיד׃

Line Aa: The colon-marker is *zaqeph qaton* and the constraints are: 0 predicators, 1 constituent, and 3 units. This line is dependent on line Ab.

עַל־שְׁלֹשָׁה פִּשְׁעֵי מוֹאָב. Moab, located east of the Jordan and north of Edom, is accused of violence toward its southern neighbor.

Line Ab: The colon-marker is *athnach* and the constraints are: 1 predicator, 2 constituents, and 2 units.

וְעַל־אַרְבָּעָה. Prepositional phrase with עַל used causally.

לֹא אֲשִׁיבֶנּוּ. Negated hiphil *yiqtol* 1 c s of שׁוב with 3 m s suffix.

Line Ac: The colon-marker is *silluq* and the constraints are: 1 predicator, 3 constituents, and 5 units.

עַל־שָׂרְפוֹ. The preposition עַל is causal; שָׂרְפוֹ is a Qal infinitive construct of שׂרף with 3 m p suffix serving as the subject of the action.

עַצְמוֹת מֶלֶךְ־אֱדוֹם. A construct chain serving as direct object. It is noteworthy that Edom is the victim of Moab's atrocity, indicating that it is the nature of the crime itself and not the identity of the victim that is Amos' concern. In other words, nations are not condemned simply for being opposed to Israel.

לַשִּׂיד. Prepositional phrase with לְ and definite article serving as a complement to the verb. The significance of burning bones to lime (שִׂיד) is disputed. There is no evidence supporting an alternative translation for שִׂיד or an emendation. Some suggest that burning bones to lime is simply disregard for human dignity, but of itself this offense seems rather paltry compared to the crimes attributed to the other nations. Others suggest that this is a religious act and that burning the bones was meant to prevent the deceased from attaining resurrection (Stuart 1987, 314). There is, however, no evidence from Iron Age Levantine states of a widespread belief that the bones had to be preserved in order to insure a resurrection (indeed, we have no reason to believe that people in either Moab or Edom believed in a resurrection at all). Reverence for the bones of the dead is not a feature of Iron Age burial sites in the Levant. It is best to follow the *Targum Jonathan* on Amos in its assertion that the body was burned to lime in order to make plaster for the walls of a room. That, after all, is what lime is was used for. We may suggest specifically that the lime was used to whitewash the throne room of the king of Moab. Such a practice would be analogous to the Assyrian practice of decorating the walls of their palace rooms with scenes depicting their victories over their enemies and even of displaying proudly Assyrian atrocities against their enemies. The north palace at Nineveh, for example, has a relief showing Ashurbanipal and his troops sacking an Elamite city. More significant for biblical scholars are the Lachish reliefs from Sennacherib's palace at Nineveh, showing not only his taking of the city but the Assyrians' impaling of their prisoners. Moab's burning of bones to lime could be regarded as similar—gruesome celebration of their own violence on the walls of their palace. It thus implied that they had become inhuman in their viciousness.

2:2-3: Second Stanza. Seven lines in one strophe, following with minor variation the structure of the judgment stanzas against Damascus, Gaza, and the Ammonites.

2:2	Ba	וְשִׁלַּחְתִּי־אֵ֥שׁ בְּמוֹאָ֔ב
	Bb	וְאָכְלָ֖ה אַרְמְנ֣וֹת הַקְּרִיּ֑וֹת
	Bc	וּמֵ֤ת בְּשָׁאוֹן֙ מוֹאָ֔ב
	Bd	בִּתְרוּעָ֖ה בְּק֥וֹל שׁוֹפָֽר׃
2:3	Be	וְהִכְרַתִּ֥י שׁוֹפֵ֖ט מִקִּרְבָּ֑הּ
	Bf	וְכָל־שָׂרֶ֛יהָ אֶהֱר֥וֹג עִמּ֖וֹ
	Bg	אָמַ֥ר יְהוָֽה׃ פ

Line Ba: The colon-marker is *zaqeph qaton* and the constraints are: 1 predicator, 3 constituents, and 3 units.

וְשִׁלַּחְתִּי. Piel *weqatal* 1 c s from שׁלח.

אֵשׁ. The direct object.

בְּמוֹאָב. Here, fire is said to be sent against the region or nation, Moab, instead of against the capital city. But the next line mentions the city Kerioth.

Line Bb: The colon-marker is *athnach* and the constraints are: 1 predicator, 2 constituents, and 3 units.

וְאָכְלָה. Qal *weqatal* 3 f s from אכל.

אַרְמְנוֹת הַקְּרִיּוֹת. A construct chain used as a direct object. Kerioth was one of the principal cities of Moab, and it is mentioned in Jeremiah 48:24 as well as in line 13 of the Mesha Stele (also known as the "Moabite Stone"), where it is said to have been the site of a temple to Chemosh, the principal deity of Moab.

Line Bc: The colon-marker is *zaqeph qaton* and the constraints are: 1 predicator, 3 constituents, and 3 units.

וּמֵת. Qal *weqatal* 3 m s of מות.

בְּשָׁאוֹן. Prepositional phrase with בְּ used adverbially for attendant circumstances. שָׁאוֹן (from שאה II; Isa 17:12). The word describes a loud noise, often one made by a crowd of people (Isa 5:14; 13:4; 24:8; Hos 10:14; Ps 74:23), but also the noise of the ocean (Isa 17:13; Ps 65:8 [E 7]). Here the source of the noise is not disclosed, but it probably includes the burning of the city, the lamentation of the inhabitants, and the war-cries and battle signals of the attackers.

מוֹאָב. The subject. Remarkably, an entire nation will "die."

Line Bd: The colon-marker is *silluq* and the constraints are: 0 predicators, 2 constituents, and 3 units. This line is structurally identical to line Bc in the previous poem (1:14), with which it is a concatenous link.

בִּתְרוּעָה. Prepositional phrase with בְּ for attendant circumstances (adverbial of וּמֵת in the previous line).

בְּקוֹל שׁוֹפָר. Prepositional phrase with בְּ on a construct chain. This phrase could be strictly appositional with בִּתְרוּעָה, identifying the noise of battle as a shofar, but it is probably cited as an example of one of the noises of battle.

Line Be: The colon-marker is *athnach* and the constraints are: 1 predicator, 3 constituents, and 3 units.

וְהִכְרַתִּי. Hiphil *weqatal* 1 c s of כרת.

שׁוֹפֵט. The direct object. For the sake of assonance with שׁוֹפָר,

Amos employs שׁוֹפֵט rather than terms he has used previously, such as יֹשֵׁב. As is common, שׁוֹפֵט connotes a ruler rather than simply someone who judges in legal proceedings.

מִקִּרְבָּהּ. Prepositional phrase with מִן and the 3 f s suffix. The antecedent to the feminine suffix is the implied ארץ מואב, the land of Moab.

Line Bf: The colon-marker is *tifha* and the constraints are: 1 predicator, 3 constituents, and 3 units.

וְכָל־שָׂרֶיהָ. A direct object construct chain with 3 f s suffix. שַׂר refers to a high official; the older translation "prince" is misleading since a שַׂר is not necessarily royalty.

אֶהֱרוֹג. Qal *yiqtol* 1 c s of הרג. The sequence *weqatal* with a direct object in line Be followed by a direct object with *yiqtol* in Bf implies that the slaying of the "judge" (שׁוֹפֵט) and all the officials (וְכָל־שָׂרֶיהָ) are not sequential but are conceptually part of a single event. There is an inversion here, with line Be having a verb, object, and prepositional phrase while line Bf has the object, then the verb, and then a prepositional phrase.

עִמּוֹ. Prepositional phrase with עִם and a 3 m s suffix; the antecedent is שׁוֹפֵט.

Line Bg: The colon-marker is *silluq* and the constraints are: 1 predicator, 2 constituents, and 2 units. This is another divine speech formula.

אָמַר. Qal *qatal* 3 m s of אמר.

יְהוָה. The subject.

2:4-5: Seventh Oracle (Judah)

This poem, with minor variation, follows the pattern of the Edom oracle (1:11-12).

כֹּה אָמַר יְהוָה 2:4a

See 1:3.

2:4b: First Stanza. Two strophes. The first is a standard accusation strophe with lines headed by עַל, but the second is conjoined to it with a *wayyiqtol* and gives a secondary accusation.

2:4b: First Strophe. Four lines. Each line is headed by עַל or וְעַל except for the fourth, line 1d, which is bound to line 1c by a chiastic structure.

עַל־שְׁלֹשָׁה֙ פִּשְׁעֵ֣י יְהוּדָ֔ה	A1a	2:4b
וְעַל־אַרְבָּעָ֖ה לֹ֣א אֲשִׁיבֶ֑נּוּ	A1b	
עַֽל־מָאֳסָ֞ם אֶת־תּוֹרַ֣ת יְהוָ֗ה	A1c	
וְחֻקָּיו֙ לֹ֣א שָׁמָ֔רוּ	A1d	

Line A1a: The colon-marker is *zaqeph qaton* and the constraints are: 0 predicators, 1 constituent, and 3 units. This line is dependent on the following line.

עַל־שְׁלֹשָׁה֙ פִּשְׁעֵ֣י יְהוּדָ֔ה. The accusations against Judah are not general crimes against humanity, as was the case in the accusations against the Gentiles, but concern covenant violations.

Line A1b: The colon-marker is *athnach* and the constraints are: 1 predicator, 2 constituents, and 2 units.

וְעַל־אַרְבָּעָ֖ה. Prepositional phrase with עַל used causally.

לֹ֣א אֲשִׁיבֶ֑נּוּ. Negated hiphil *yiqtol* 1 c s of שׁוּב with 3 m s suffix.

Line A1c: The colon-marker is *revia* and the constraints are: 1 predicator, 2 constituents, and 3 units.

עַֽל־מָאֳסָ֞ם. Qal infinitive construct of מאס with 3 m p suffix (the implied antecedent is the people of Judah) and the preposition עַל used causally. This infinitive functions as a predicator.

אֶת־תּוֹרַ֣ת יְהוָ֗ה. The direct object.

Line A1d: The colon-marker is *zaqeph qaton* and the constraints are: 1 predicator, 2 constituents, and 2 units. This line forms a chiasmus with the previous line.

וְחֻקָּיו. Direct object with 3 m s suffix and conjunction; it parallels **אֶת־תּוֹרַת יְהוָה**, and the antecedent to the suffix is **יְהוָה**.

לֹא שָׁמָרוּ. Negated qal *qatal* 3 c p of **שׁמר**.

2:4c: Second Strophe. 2 lines. As in the Edom oracle, this strophe, headed by a *wayyiqtol*, constitutes a secondary accusation.

2:4c A2a וַיַּתְעוּם כִּזְבֵיהֶם

A2b אֲשֶׁר־הָלְכוּ אֲבוֹתָם אַחֲרֵיהֶם׃

Line A2a: The colon-marker is *zaqeph qaton* and the constraints are: 1 predicator, 2 constituents, and 2 units.

וַיַּתְעוּם. Hiphil *wayyiqtol* 3 m p of **תעה** with a 3 m p suffix referring to the people of Judah. The *wayyiqtol* is here logically secondary to the previous accusation but it is not temporally sequential. It is both a secondary accusation and an example of how Judah went about abandoning the law of YHWH.

כִּזְבֵיהֶם. The subject; it has a 3 m p suffix. The noun **כָּזָב** ("lie") here probably refers to idols.

Line A2b: The colon-marker is *silluq* and the constraints are: 1 predicator, 3 constituents, and 4 units.

אֲשֶׁר . . . אַחֲרֵיהֶם. A relative clause whose antecedent is **כִּזְבֵיהֶם**. The relative **אֲשֶׁר** is bound to the resumptive 3 m p pronoun suffix in **אַחֲרֵיהֶם**. Literally, "which their fathers went after them," it means, "after which their fathers went." Relative clauses constitute a special problem in delineating the constituents of a line according to the constraints, since elements of the relative, as here, may come at the beginning and end of the clause, with other constituents inserted between the two parts.

הָלְכוּ. Qal *qatal* 3 c p of הלך ("walk"). The verb here connotes believing in something and engaging in the practices associated with it.

אֲבוֹתָם. The subject; it has a 3 m p suffix whose antecedent is the implied people of Judah.

2:5: Second Stanza. Two lines. This is the standard judgment stanza in its shortest form.

2:5 Ba וְשִׁלַּחְתִּי אֵשׁ בִּיהוּדָה
Bb וְאָכְלָה אַרְמְנוֹת יְרוּשָׁלִָם׃ פ

Line Ba: The colon-marker is *athnach* and the constraints are: 1 predicator, 3 constituents, and 3 units.

וְשִׁלַּחְתִּי. Piel *weqatal* 1 c s from שׁלח.

אֵשׁ. The direct object.

בִּיהוּדָה. As in the oracle against Moab, fire is here sent against the nation, Judah, instead of against the capital city; but as in 2:2, the next line mentions the principal city of the nation, Jerusalem.

Line Bb: The colon-marker is *silluq* and the constraints are: 1 predicator, 2 constituents, and 3 units.

וְאָכְלָה. Qal *weqatal* 3 f s from אכל.

אַרְמְנוֹת יְרוּשָׁלִָם. Apart from 1:2, this is the only mention of Jerusalem in Amos (although 6:1 refers to Zion). Strikingly, 1:2 represents Jerusalem as the abode of YHWH, the place from which he roars, whereas this verse describes fire from YHWH consuming the citadels of Jerusalem.

2:6-16: Eighth Oracle (Jerusalem)

The eighth stanza dramatically breaks from the pattern set in the first seven. After the normal prose heading (כֹּה אָמַר יְהוָה), it has four stanzas and a total of eight strophes. Only the first three lines of the first strophe have the standard pattern of accusations headed by the preposition עַל. Also, the standard judgment bicolon used in the seven prior oracles (with וְשִׁלַּחְתִּי אֵשׁ, etc.) is not employed in the eighth. There is a large accusation stanza in two strophes, followed by a stanza describing in four strophes God's historical acts of grace to Israel and their response. This is followed by a metaphorical description of YHWH's grief (the third stanza [a single strophe]), and concluded by a lengthy portrayal of the Israelite army routed in battle (the fourth stanza [a single strophe]).

כֹּה אָמַר יְהוָה 2:6a

See 1:3.

2:6-8: First Stanza. This is formed from two strophes of six lines each.

2:6b-7a: First Strophe. Six lines (A1a-f). Each of the first three lines is headed by the normal עַל or וְעַל. One might treat the opening two lines of 2:7 as a separate strophe, but two factors speak against this. First, the participle הַשֹּׁאֲפִים (the first word of 2:7) functions as a relative clause having as its antecedent the pronoun suffix on מִכְרָם from 2:6, suggesting that, despite appearances, it is part of the same strophe. As the head of a new strophe הַשֹּׁאֲפִים hangs in the air quite awkwardly. See also the use of הָאוֹצְרִים in 3:10, which begins a line but clearly belongs with the preceding strophe. Similar examples of a plural participle used in this way are at Amos 3:10; 4:1 and 5:6-7. Also, after the formulaic two lines that introduce the stanza (A1a-b) the following four lines (A1c-f) are bound by four nouns describing the victims of abuse: צַדִּיק (A1c), וְאֶבְיוֹן (A1d), דַּלִּים (A1e), and עֲנָוִים (A1f). This strophe, therefore, is marked by having the abuse of the poor as its central accusation.

עַל־שְׁלֹשָׁה פִּשְׁעֵי יִשְׂרָאֵל A1a 2:6b
וְעַל־אַרְבָּעָה לֹא אֲשִׁיבֶנּוּ A1b

עַל־מִכְרָ֤ם בַּכֶּ֙סֶף֙ צַדִּ֔יק A1c
וְאֶבְי֖וֹן בַּעֲב֥וּר נַעֲלָֽיִם׃ A1d
הַשֹּׁאֲפִ֤ים עַל־עֲפַר־אֶ֙רֶץ֙ בְּרֹ֣אשׁ דַּלִּ֔ים A1e 2:7a
וְדֶ֥רֶךְ עֲנָוִ֖ים יַטּ֑וּ A1f

Line A1a: The colon-marker is *zaqeph qaton* and the constraints are: 0 predicators, 1 constituent, and 3 units. This line is dependent on the following line.

עַל־שְׁלֹשָׁה֙ פִּשְׁעֵ֣י יִשְׂרָאֵ֔ל. Prepositional phrase with עַל used causally on a construct chain. Amos at last comes to the principal object of his prophecy, Israel.

Line A1b: The colon-marker is *athnach* and the constraints are: 1 predicator, 2 constituents, and 2 units.

וְעַל־אַרְבָּעָ֖ה. Prepositional phrase with עַל used causally.

לֹ֣א אֲשִׁיבֶ֑נּוּ. Negated hiphil *yiqtol* 1 c s of שׁוּב with 3 m s suffix. This serves as the apodosis to the phrases with עַל.

Line A1c: The colon-marker is *zaqeph qaton* and the constraints are: 1 predicator, 3 constituents, and 3 units.

עַל־מִכְרָ֤ם. Qal infinitive construct of מכר with 3 m p suffix and preposition עַל used causally.

בַּכֶּ֙סֶף֙. The preposition בְּ often marks the price of something; see *HALOT* בְּ definition 17. It could also express the cause or reason for something (*HALOT* בְּ definition 19).

צַדִּ֔יק. The direct object. But in what sense is the person "righteous," and how is he sold "for silver" (בַּכֶּ֙סֶף֙)? There are at least three possibilities. (1) He is sold into to slavery for a set price of silver, and צַדִּיק indicates that he does not deserve this. (2) He is sold into slavery because he owes some money, and צַדִּיק again indicates that he does not deserve this and that the penalty is too harsh. (3) He is metaphorically sold out in the law courts when someone bribes the judges for an amount of silver, and צַדִּיק indicates that he is innocent or in the right in the case at law.

Line A1d: The colon-marker is *silluq* and the constraints are: 0 predicators, 2 constituents, and 3 units. There is gapping here, with מִכְרָם in the previous line governing both lines.

וְאֶבְיוֹן. Direct object with conjunction. This is parallel to צַדִּיק in the previous line. The three possible interpretations described above for צַדִּיק apply here as well, except that וְאֶבְיוֹן stresses the victim's poverty instead of his innocence.

בַּעֲבוּר נַעֲלָיִם. As in the above line, this prepositional phrase could mean "for the price of a pair of sandals" or "on account of a pair of sandals." Should sandals be regarded as something of high value or as something that is very cheap? Clothing could be of high value because of the intensive labor required in weaving cloth, and it could be used as currency (e.g., Judg 14:13). But sandals are never spoken of in this way, and Sirach 46:19 explicitly treats sandals as something of very little value. This should rule out the idea that this person was sold for the price of a pair of sandals; whatever his oppressor thought of him, he would want to get as much money for selling him as possible. It also seems odd that the judges in a court would accept so small a bribe as a pair of sandals, although Amos could be making the point that the judges are so lacking in integrity that they will pervert justice for even the cheapest of bribes. Still, the idea of bribing someone with sandals seems very odd, and if bribery in court is the point here, it may be better to emend the text to נעלם, a "hidden (bribe)," as suggested by several scholars (Paul 1991, 78). Such an emendation is purely conjectural, however. Therefore, the best solution is to assert that the poor are sold into slavery for a very small debt that they cannot pay, such as for the price of a pair of sandals.

Line A1e: The colon-marker is *zaqeph qaton* and the constraints are: 1 predicator, 3 constituents, and 5 units. The participle הַשֹּׁאֲפִים is not substantival but serves as a predicator within a participial relative clause. It could be taken to be periphrastic and translated with a finite verb.

הַשֹּׁאֲפִים. Qal participle m p with definite article. This word is a famous conundrum; it means to "pant" or "sniff" and so seems to make no sense in context. Some interpreters say that the oppressors are so keen to get what they can from the poor that they even sniff at the dust on their scalps, but this makes for such a bizarre metaphor that it cannot possibly be right. A number of interpreters emend the text to the root שׁוּף or suggest that שׁאף here is a by-form of שׁוּף. They take שׁוּף to mean "trample," and translate the line, "those who trample the heads of the poor into the dust of the earth" (Paul 1991, 79–80). There are three reasons that this is impossible. First, if the verb means "trample," the line literally reads, "who trample on the dust of the earth at the heads of the poor." This is a very awkward and unnatural sentence, and it cannot mean that they trample the heads of the poor *into* the earth. Second, שׁוּף does not mean "trample." The verb appears in Genesis 3:15 (twice), Psalm 139:11, and Job 9:17. While the first occurrence of the verb in Genesis 3:15 might be taken to mean "trample," the second cannot mean that, and it is best to take both instances to mean "to strike." So also in Job 9:17, where is שׁוּף used in parallel to וְהִרְבָּה פְּצָעַי, "and he multiplies my wounds," it is best taken to mean "to strike." The שׁוּף in Psalm 139:11 appears to be a homonym meaning "cover" or "hide," but it clearly does not mean "trample." Third, the proposal that הַשֹּׁאֲפִים is a by-form of שׁוּף is not persuasive. Shalom Paul offers three analogies for this (Hos 10:14; 2 Sam 19:5; Zech 14:10), but these are all *qatal* or *weqatal* forms that have the א as an orthographic feature (e.g., in Hos 10:14 writing וְקָאם for וְקָם) and not as a true by-form, as the m p participle הַשֹּׁאֲפִים would be. Therefore, שׁאף as "to sniff" remains our best translation option, as that meaning is well attested (see *HALOT* שׁאף).

עַל־עֲפַר־אֶ֫רֶץ. Prepositional phrase with עַל. What sniffs at the dust of the earth? The answer is a dog when it is hunting. The oppressors are metaphorically represented as a pack of hunting dogs seeking their prey. If Samarian aristocrats enjoyed hunting with dogs in the manner of their 18th century English counterparts, this could be a deliberate recasting of their sport. They hunted for people with the same relish that they hunted for animals.

בְּרֹאשׁ דַּלִּים. Prepositional phrase with בְּ on a construct chain. The preposition marks the object and could be translated as "after." The term "head" can be metonymy for the whole person (see *HALOT* ראשׁ definition 5). It is possible that this continues the hunting metaphor. Did ancient hunters display the heads of animals they had killed as trophies, as modern hunters do? We do not know, but we do know that human heads could be displayed as trophies (1 Sam 17:54). The point here is not that they literally hunted the poor and mounted their heads as trophies, but that their treatment of the poor was equally as ruthless.

Line A1f: The colon-marker is *athnach* and the constraints are: 1 predicator, 2 constituents, and 3 units. An inclusion structure, with the predicating participle as the first word of the line A1e and the verb יַטּוּ as the last word of line A1f, suggests that these two lines are two aspects of a single action rather than being sequential or logically distinct.

וְדֶרֶךְ עֲנָוִים. A construct chain and direct object of the following verb.

יַטּוּ. Hiphil *yiqtol* 3 m p of נטה. The translation of this verb is notoriously difficult, as its meanings include "to stretch out, twist, bend, extend, spread out, steer away from, guide away, deceive, or divert." Job 24:4, יַטּוּ אֶבְיוֹנִים מִדָּרֶךְ, "they turn the poor from the way," means that the poor are shoved out of the road as a sign of no respect for their persons. But this is a false parallel to Amos 2:7; here, it is not the poor but the דֶּרֶךְ itself that is the object of the verb. Probably נטה here combines the ideas of "extend" and "divert" or "twist," and the meaning is that the path that the poor take is made long and twisted. This may continue the hunting metaphor; the poor, as the quarry of the rich, must follow an extended, evasive route to escape capture. The metaphor suggests that the lives of the poor are filled with continual harassment and danger from the upper class.

2:7b-8: Second Strophe. Six lines. This unity of this strophe is that it primarily focuses upon religious offenses, although it secondarily continues the theme of the oppression of the poor. Lines A2b, A2d, and A2f each end with reference to religious matters (שֵׁם קָדְשִׁי [A2b], מִזְבֵּחַ [A2d], and בֵּית אֱלֹהֵיהֶם [A2f]. Furthermore, the subject of יַטּוּ in A2c (2:8) is not an undefined "they" but is the father and son from line A2a. This further indicates that these lines are a single strophe and should not be further divided.

2:7b	A2a	וְאִישׁ וְאָבִיו יֵלְכוּ אֶל־הַנַּעֲרָה
	A2b	לְמַעַן חַלֵּל אֶת־שֵׁם קָדְשִׁי׃
2:8	A2c	וְעַל־בְּגָדִים חֲבֻלִים יַטּוּ
	A2d	אֵצֶל כָּל־מִזְבֵּחַ
	A2e	וְיֵין עֲנוּשִׁים יִשְׁתּוּ
	A2f	בֵּית אֱלֹהֵיהֶם׃

Line A2a: The colon-marker is *zaqeph qaton* and the constraints are: 1 predicator, 3 constituents, and 4 units.

וְאִישׁ וְאָבִיו. A compound subject; its initial position in the line makes prominent the fact that this is an entirely new subject, one the reader has not seen in this text, and that it introduces a new topic. Thus, this line begins a new strophe. The conjunction on וְאִישׁ indicates that it is continuing the previous series of accusations.

יֵלְכוּ. Qal *yiqtol* 3 m p of הלך. The use of הלך אֶל to refer to sexual union is odd, but that is no doubt the meaning here. See Paul (1982) and Bronznick (1985). The phrase בּוֹא אֶל is often used idiomatically for sexual union with a woman (e.g., Gen 16:2; 30:3-4; 38:8; Deut 22:13), but it refers to sexual relations with a woman who is part of the household (a wife, concubine, domestic slave [as in Gen

16:2], or a sister-in-law in fulfillment of levirate duties). The fact that הלך is used here probably indicates that the men are going outside of their household—to a shrine—to have sexual relations with a woman. For a man and his son to have sexual relations with the same woman violates the spirit if not the letter of Lev 18:8. The *yiqtol* here implies that the action is customary or repeated.

אֶל־הַנַּעֲרָה. The use of נַעֲרָה raises questions about the setting of this offense. נַעֲרָה simply means "girl" or "young woman" and perhaps "servant girl," and thus some argue that both the head of a household and his adult son are using one of their domestic slave girls for sexual purposes. This is against the view that the woman here is a shrine prostitute. The argument is that if Amos had meant shrine prostitute, he would have used the word קְדֵשָׁה. But קְדֵשָׁה/קָדֵשׁ is actually quite rare in the Hebrew Bible (it occurs eleven times in nine verses; three of these occurrences are masculine). It is usually found in narrative; it appears only once in the Latter Prophets (Hos 4:14, where the specified offense is that men make sacrifices with הַקְּדֵשׁוֹת). In light of the prominence of religious language in this strophe (as described in the strophe profile above), it seems that this is a cultic act and not simply men taking advantage of a household slave. As stated above, הלך אֶל strongly suggests that this woman is not part of the household of the father and son. At the same time, the use of הַנַּעֲרָה is significant. The shrine prostitute is here not portrayed as a powerful priestess with control over her own destiny; she is a lowly woman, no doubt a slave who was purchased to perform the duties of a prostitute for a shrine. The sin is manifold in nature: (1) it is participation in a fertility cult; (2) it involves father and son having sex with the same woman; (3) it involves the brutal use of an unfortunate young woman.

Line A2b: The colon-marker is *silluq* and the constraints are: 0 predicators, 2 constituents, and 4 units.

לְמַעַן חַלֵּל. The verb (חַלֵּל) is a piel infinitive construct. While לְמַעַן with an infinitive is perhaps rarely used for a final clause ("with the result that"; Deuteronomy 29:19 could be an example), its use for a purpose clause ("in order to") is overwhelmingly more common and certain. There is no basis for translating this as "*with the result that* they profane my holy name." Rather, it should be rendered, "in order to profane my holy name," but the usage is ironic. They intend this as a religious act and persuade themselves that it sanctifies God's name, but in fact it does the opposite. This further indicates that the sexual act is in the context of a religious rite.

אֶת־שֵׁם קָדְשִׁי. This construct chain, as is common, functions adjectivally ("the name of my holiness" representing "my holy name"). In this ironic setting, this expression is probably used precisely because the prostitution takes place at a shrine.

Line A2c: The colon-marker is *zaqeph qaton* and the constraints are: 1 predicator, 2 constituents, and 3 units. This could be joined with the following phrase אֵצֶל כָּל־מִזְבֵּחַ as a single line, but the *zaqeph qaton* with its subordinate *pashta* suggests it is a full line.

וְעַל־בְּגָדִים חֲבֻלִים. Prepositional phrase with locative עַל. The word חֲבֻלִים is a qal passive participle m p of חבל; the verb implies that the clothes have been seized from poor people for failure to pay a debt. In context, where there is sexual activity at a shrine, the idea may be that the men do not want to foul their own clothes by using them as sheets on which to have sex, and thus they use the poor man's cloak. The accusation is again multi-faceted: it is cultic, sexual, and involves profound disrespect for people of a lower class.

יַטּוּ. Hiphil *yiqtol* 3 m p of נטה. The verb is used reflexively here, "to stretch (oneself) out," that is, to lay oneself down. This usage may have been a vulgar idiom for having sex (cf. English "get laid"). Whether that is the case or not, we are not to assume that they simply lay down and went to sleep beside an altar. The *yiqtol* again implies that the action is frequent.

Line A2d: The colon-marker is *athnach* and the constraints are: 0 predicators, 1 constituent, and 2 units.

אֵ֣צֶל כָּל־מִזְבֵּ֑חַ. The noun אֵצֶל, "side," here serves in the construct as a preposition, and it counts as a unit. While it is true that "incubation," sleeping at a shrine in hopes of receiving a dream from a god, is attested in the ancient world, context (sexual activity in the previous lines and drunkenness in the following lines) strongly indicates that this is bacchanalian revelry at a shrine.

Line A2e: The colon-marker is *zaqeph qaton* and the constraints are: 1 predicator, 2 constituents, and 3 units. This could be joined with the following phrase בֵּית אֱלֹהֵיהֶם as a single line, but the *zaqeph qaton* with its subordinate *pashta* suggests it is a full line.

וְיֵ֤ין עֲנוּשִׁים֙. A construct chain, in which עֲנוּשִׁים, a qal passive participle of ענשׁ, refers to people upon whom a financial penalty has been imposed, which they have had to pay in kind, with wine. The use of such wine indicates that the revelers are able to carry on at no expense to themselves, because the wine was taken from others.

יִשְׁתּ֔וּ. Qal *yiqtol* 3 m p. The *yiqtol* again implies customary action.

Line A2f: The colon-marker is silluq and the constraints are: 0 predicators, 1 constituent, and 2 units.

בֵּ֖ית אֱלֹהֵיהֶֽם. A construct chain; the preposition בְּ is often implied but not present in poetry. The ambiguity of אֱלֹהֵיהֶם ("their God" or "their gods") suggests that the men consider this behavior to be in keeping with covenant fidelity to YHWH but that Amos sees it otherwise.

2:9-12: Second Stanza. This is formed from four strophes, the first three describing God's acts of mercy to Israel and the fourth describing their subversion of God's work.

2:9: First Strophe. Five lines. The conquest of Canaan is described under the metaphor of a forest. YHWH first declares that he destroyed (hiphil of שׁמד) the Amorite (B1a), and then a relative clause describes the Amorites as tree-like (B1b-c). YHWH then declares that he destroyed (hiphil of שׁמד) them from fruit to root

(B1d-e). In short, two pairs of lines (B1b-c and B1d-e) metaphorically elaborate on B1a.

2:9 B1a וְאָנֹכִ֞י הִשְׁמַ֤דְתִּי אֶת־הָֽאֱמֹרִי֙ מִפְּנֵיהֶ֔ם
B1b אֲשֶׁ֨ר כְּגֹ֤בַהּ אֲרָזִים֙ גָּבְה֔וֹ
B1c וְחָסֹ֥ן ה֖וּא כָּֽאַלּוֹנִ֑ים
B1d וָאַשְׁמִ֤יד פִּרְיוֹ֙ מִמַּ֔עַל
B1e וְשָׁרָשָׁ֖יו מִתָּֽחַת׃

Line B1a: The colon-marker is *zaqeph qaton* and the constraints are: 1 predicator, 4 constituents, and 4 units.

וְאָנֹכִ֞י. The subject, with a conjunction.

הִשְׁמַ֤דְתִּי. Hiphil *qatal* 1 c s of שׁמד. The pattern [ו + X + *qatal*] is often contrastive; here, previous acts by the subject ("and I") contrast with the previous behavior of the Israelites described above in strophes one and two.

אֶת־הָֽאֱמֹרִי֙. The direct object. The term "Amorite" is often used broadly for the pre-Israelite inhabitants of the land. The choice of the term "Amorite" instead of "Canaanite" here and in 2:10 may be driven by Genesis 15:16, "the iniquity of the Amorite is not yet complete." The implication is that the iniquity of Israel, like that of the Amorites before them, was moving toward a critical point.

מִפְּנֵיהֶ֔ם. Literally "from your face," this depicts the inhabitants of the land being driven back from before the invading Israelites under Joshua.

Line B1b: The colon-marker is *zaqeph qaton* and the constraints are: 0 predicators, 2 constituents, and 4 units.

אֲשֶׁ֨ר . . . גָּבְה֔וֹ. A relative clause. The 3 m s suffix on גָּבְה֔וֹ is resumptive of the relative pronoun; thus, "whose height."

כְּגֹ֤בַהּ אֲרָזִים֙. Prepositional phrase with comparative כְּ on a construct chain.

Line B1c: The colon-marker is *athnach* and the constraints are: 0 predicators, 3 constituents, and 3 units. This is a copular clause; it is offline and adds a second description of the Amorite after line B1b.

וְחָסֹ֥ן. A predicate adjective. חָסֹן is attested only twice in the OT (here and Isa 1:31). Its meaning ("strong"), however, is not in doubt as cognate words are well attested in other Semitic languages (see *NIDOTTE* חָסֹן). It is striking that in both OT instances the word is used to describe the strength of men metaphorically described as trees. It may be that in ordinary conversation חָסֹן was used as a clichéd adjective for strong trees, such as oaks.

הֽוּא. The subject.

כָּאַלּוֹנִ֑ים. Prepositional phrase with comparative כְּ. The אַלּוֹן is an oak.

Line B1d: The colon-marker is *zaqeph qaton* and the constraints are: 1 predicator, 3 constituents, and 3 units.

וָאַשְׁמִ֤יד. Hiphil *wayyiqtol* 1 c s of שׁמד. This continues the small historical narrative begun in line B1a of this strophe with וְאָנֹכִי הִשְׁמַדְתִּי. The *wayyiqtol* is genuinely sequential. The idea is that YHWH first cut down the trees and then ensured that they would never grow again, destroying both their seed and their roots.

פִּרְיוֹ֙. Direct object with 3 m s suffix.

מִמַּ֔עַל. Adverbial usage; literally, "from above."

Line B1e: The colon-marker is *silluq* and the constraints are: 0 predicators, 2 constituents, and 2 units. There is gapping, with וָאַשְׁמִיד from line B1d governing both lines.

וְשָׁרָשָׁ֖יו. Direct object with 3 m s suffix. The merism of fruit and root describes the two parts of the tree than might germinate or put forth new growth. Contrast Isaiah 6:13, where after the "tree" of Judah is destroyed, a stump remains to sprout again.

מִתָּֽחַת. Adverbial usage; literally, "from below" and a merism with מִמַּעַל.

2:10: Second Strophe. Three lines. Two factors suggest that this should be regarded as a second strophe and not as a continuation of the first strophe begun in 2:9. First, the fact that both 2:9 and 2:10 begin with וְאָנֹכִי followed by a hiphil *qatal* verb indicates that they are to be thought of as parallel but separate strophes. Second, there is chronological inversion, describing the conquest in 2:9 but the exodus in 2:10, which one would not expect if it were a single strophe. But why is the chronological sequence inverted? Probably it is because Amos wants to focus on the conquest rather than the exodus and wilderness sojourn, although these, too, are briefly mentioned as part of the standard recitation of Israel's formative events. Notice that the reversal of sequence allows Amos to begin line B1a with "the Amorite from before you" and to end line B2c with "the land of the Amorite," creating in inclusion structure framed by reference to the expulsion of the Amorites. The implication is that Israel, too, could be expelled.

2:10 B2a וְאָנֹכִ֛י הֶעֱלֵ֥יתִי אֶתְכֶ֖ם מֵאֶ֣רֶץ מִצְרָ֑יִם
B2b וָאוֹלֵ֨ךְ אֶתְכֶ֤ם בַּמִּדְבָּר֙ אַרְבָּעִ֣ים שָׁנָ֔ה
B2c לָרֶ֖שֶׁת אֶת־אֶ֥רֶץ הָאֱמֹרִֽי׃

Line B2a: The colon-marker is *athnach* and the constraints are: 1 predicator, 4 constituents, and 5 units.

וְאָנֹכִ֛י. Parallel to the use of וְאָנֹכִי in 2:9, this introduces a second mini-historical narrative.

הֶעֱלֵ֥יתִי. Hiphil *qatal* 1 c s of עלה.

אֶתְכֶ֖ם. The direct object.

מֵאֶ֣רֶץ מִצְרָ֑יִם. Prepositional phrase with מִן on a construct chain.

Line B2b: The colon-marker is *zaqeph qaton* and the constraints are: 1 predicator, 4 constituents, and 5 units.

וָאוֹלֵ֨ךְ. Hiphil *wayyiqtol* 1 c s of הלך. The *wayyiqtol* is sequential to the previous clause in line B2a.

אֶתְכֶם. The direct object.

בַּמִּדְבָּר. Prepositional phrase with locative בְּ.

אַרְבָּעִים שָׁנָה. An expression of duration. Numbers over 10 typically govern singular nouns; the numbers two through ten typically govern plural nouns.

Line B2c: The colon-marker is *silluq* and the constraints are: 0 predicators, 2 constituents, and 3 units.

לָרֶשֶׁת. Qal infinitive construct of ירשׁ with לְ, here expressing purpose.

אֶת־אֶרֶץ הָאֱמֹרִי. The direct object. The construct chain אֶרֶץ הָאֱמֹרִי here is in juxtaposition to מֵאֶרֶץ מִצְרָיִם in line B2a. Reference to the Amorites also provides also an inclusion with a mention of the Amorites in line B1a.

2:11: Third Strophe. Four lines. Like 2:9-10, this strophe describes YHWH's acts of grace toward Israel. Its subject-matter, however, is quite different from that of the prior two strophes. Also, it begins with a hiphil *wayyiqtol* instead of the וְאָנֹכִי + hiphil *qatal* pattern seen in 2:9-10. It also includes a rhetorical question demanding that Israel confess the validity of YHWH's claim (line B3c), and it concludes with an oracle formula (line B3d).

2:11	B3a	וָאָקִים מִבְּנֵיכֶם לִנְבִיאִים
	B3b	וּמִבַּחוּרֵיכֶם לִנְזִרִים
	B3c	הַאַף אֵין־זֹאת בְּנֵי יִשְׂרָאֵל
	B3d	נְאֻם־יְהוָה׃

Line B3a: The colon-marker is *zaqeph qaton* and the constraints are: 1 predicator, 3 constituents, and 3 units.

וָאָקִים. Hiphil *wayyiqtol* 1 c s of קוּם. The hiphil of קוּם here means to choose someone for a task, as in Judges 2:16.

מִבְּנֵיכֶם. Prepositional phrase with מִן, which is partitive here.

לִנְבִיאִים. Prepositional phrase with לְ, which here indicates the purpose for which they were chosen.

Line B3b: The colon-marker is *athnach* and the constraints are: 1 predicator, 2 constituents, and 2 units. This line has gapping with the previous line, the verb וָאָקִים governing both lines.

וּמִבַּחוּרֵיכֶם. Prepositional phrase with מִן, which is partitive here.

לִנְזִרִים. Prepositional phrase with לְ, which again indicates the purpose for which they were chosen. Nazirites are not commonly mentioned in the Old Testament; the Nazirite vow is described in Numbers 6, and Judges 13–16 describes the Nazirite career of Samson. Why are they mentioned here? Probably the Nazirites represent Israelites of exceptional devotion to YHWH. The implication is that YHWH sent such people to them as reminders of the need for a life of true piety. The Nazirite was the closest thing ancient Israel had to a man under a monastic vow, although the one Nazirite we know well, Samson, was far from fulfilling the ideal of consecration to YHWH.

Line B3c: The colon-marker is *tifha* and the constraints are: 2 predicators, 3 constituents, and 3 units. בְּנֵי יִשְׂרָאֵל is here a proper name and thus a single unit. If הַאַף were counted as a unit, the line would still be within the constraints, but it probably should not be counted. Why does Amos introduce a rhetorical question here? The probable reason is that the Israelites had not subverted the conquest or the exodus narratives and that Amos' audience would need no prompting to confess that these events had been gracious works of God. They had, however, undermined the work of the Nazirites and prophets, as the subsequent accusation indicates. Before moving into the accusation, therefore, Amos first demands that Israel acknowledge that the appearance of Nazirites and prophets among them was also a merciful act of God.

הַאַף אֵין. The negative existential אֵין serves as a predicator.

זֹאת. The subject; a feminine demonstrative, this is a neutrum that stands for preceding content. Here, its antecedent is the assertion in lines B3a-b.

בְּנֵי יִשְׂרָאֵל. A construct chain used as a vocative.

Line B3d: The colon-marker is *silluq* and the constraints are: 0 predicators, 1 constituents, and 2 units.

נְאֻם־יְהוָה. A construct chain, this is a standard oracle formula. Links tying strophe B1 to strophe B2 have already been noted, and the discussion below describes how strophes B3 and B4 are bound together. But the oracle formula נְאֻם־יְהוָה also has the function of separating the three benefits described in strophes B1, B2 and B3 from the response of Israel in strophe B4.

2:12: Fourth Strophe. Three lines. Like 2:11, this strophe begins with a hiphil *wayyiqtol*. It contends that the Israelites have sought to subvert God's work by corrupting or hindering his agents, the prophets and Nazirites. Several elements bind this strophe to strophe B3. Together, they have an inversion structure in that lines B3a-b have the order prophets–Nazirites, whereas lines B4a-b have the order Nazirites–prophets. Line B3a begins with the hiphil *wayyiqtol* וָאָקִים ("and I raised up"; God is the subject) and B4a begins with the hiphil *wayyiqtol* וַתַּשְׁקוּ ("and you made [them] drink"; Israel is the subject). Also, the oracular נְאֻם־יְהוָה of B3d is answered by the people's rejection of the prophetic word in B4c, לֹא תִּנָּבְאוּ ("never prophesy").

2:12 B4a וַתַּשְׁקוּ אֶת־הַנְּזִרִים יָיִן
B4b וְעַל־הַנְּבִיאִים צִוִּיתֶם לֵאמֹר
B4c לֹא תִּנָּבְאוּ׃

Line B4a: The colon-marker is *athnach* and the constraints are: 1 predicator, 3 constituents, and 3 units.

וַתַּשְׁקוּ. Hiphil *wayyiqtol* 2 m p of שׁקה.

אֶת־הַנְּזִרִים. The direct object.

יָיִן. A secondary direct object, indicating the substance that was drunk.

Line B4b: The colon-marker is *zaqeph qaton* and the constraints are: 1 predicator, 3 constituents, and 3 units.

וְעַל־הַנְּבִיאִים. Prepositional phrase with עַל.

צִוִּיתֶם. Piel *qatal* 2 m p of צוה. The pattern צוה + עַל may occur with a prohibition, as in Genesis 2:16-17; 28:6; Jeremiah 35:6; Nahum 1:14; Esther 2:10. Another example is Isaiah 5:6, וְעַל הֶעָבִים אֲצַוֶּה מֵהַמְטִיר עָלָיו מָטָר, "and I will forbid the clouds from sending rain upon it." There are other patterns with צוה and עַל that do not involve prohibitions, as in 2 Samuel 14:8, וַאֲנִי אֲצַוֶּה עָלָיִךְ, "and I will give orders concerning you."

לֵאמֹר. Qal infinitive construct of אמר with לְ.

Line B4c: The colon-marker is *silluq* and the constraints are: 1 predicator, 1 constituent, and 1 unit. This violates the constraints unless לֹא is here regarded as a unit. As described in the introduction, however, the constraints are not inviolable. This line is reported speech.

לֹא תִּנָּבְאוּ. Niphal *yiqtol* 2 m p with negative. The use of לֹא instead of אַל for the negation suggests that this is a standing order, "never prophesy." Cp. Exod 20:13-15.

2:13: Third Stanza. A single strophe of three lines, this has no counterpart in the first seven oracles against the nation. A description of divine exasperation, it is transitional, moving the reader toward the judgment stanza (2:14-16).

2:13 Ca הִנֵּה אָנֹכִי מֵעִיק תַּחְתֵּיכֶם
Cb כַּאֲשֶׁר תָּעִיק הָעֲגָלָה
Cc הַמְלֵאָה לָהּ עָמִיר׃

Line Ca: The colon-marker is *athnach* and the constraints are: 1 predicator, 4 constituents, and 4 units.

הִנֵּה. This familiar word often introduces dramatic pronouncements, and sometimes these are statements of despair or complaint. For example, Genesis 15:3 (וְהִנֵּה בֶן־בֵּיתִי יוֹרֵשׁ אֹתִי) could be loosely translated as, "And do you know what? My household slave will be my heir!"

אָנֹכִי. The participle that follows needs an explicit subject which is here provided by אָנֹכִי.

מֵעִיק. Hiphil participle m s of עוּק in a periphrastic construction. Contrary to a number of interpreters (e.g., Hayes 1988, 118–19), it does not mean to "press down." It appears to be used of a wagon with the meaning, "to make a rut" (see *HALOT*) and from that means, "to be weighted down." It is intransitive/passive, a middle voice, and does not take a direct object, as the usage in the next line clearly shows.

תַּחְתֵּיכֶם. Prepositional phrase with תַּחַת. This is sometimes taken to mean "in your place" (as in Exod 16:29; 2 Sam 2:23; Job 40:12), with the verb מֵעִיק interpreted as "hold down" or "restrain," and thus, "I will restrain you in your place." But this passage is not truly analogous to texts where תַּחַת means "in (your) place." For example, Job 40:12 has וַהֲדֹךְ רְשָׁעִים תַּחְתָּם ("and tread down the wicked in their place"), but note that the direct object, רְשָׁעִים, is explicit. In אָנֹכִי מֵעִיק תַּחְתֵּיכֶם, there is no indication that "you" is the direct object of מֵעִיק. Thus, תַּחְתֵּיכֶם has its normal and far more common meaning, "under you."

Line Cb: The colon-marker is *zaqeph qaton* and the constraints are: 1 predicator, 3 constituents, and 3 units.

כַּאֲשֶׁר. Meaning "just as," this word subordinates this line to the preceding line to make a comparison.

תָּעִיק. Hiphil *yiqtol* 3 f s of עוּק; the usage here is clearly middle voice and intransitive. Not every hiphil is transitive, and the verb cannot have the transitive meaning "restrain" since the cart is obviously not restraining anything. Taking this occurrence of the verb as intransitive but the occurrence in line Ca as transitive (as does Paul 1991, 94–95) is most implausible.

הָעֲגָלָה. The subject. The definite article represents a class of objects and not a specific object.

Line C*c*: The colon-marker is *silluq* and the constraints are: 0 predicators, 3 constituents, and 3 units. This line is adjectival, standing in apposition to הָעֲגָלָה.

הַמְלֵאָה. Adjective f s with definite article, in agreement with its antecedent הָעֲגָלָה.

לָהּ. Reflexive use of the preposition לְ with a 3 f s suffix. Literally "filled to herself," it means, "filled to the brim."

עָמִיר. English requires a preposition such as "with" to indicate with what the cart is filled, but Hebrew does not. עָמִיר refers to the sheaves, the cut stalks of grain that have not yet been threshed. See Jer 9:21(E 22); Mic 4:12.

2:14-16: Fourth Stanza. Nine lines. In the first seven oracles, every stanza concludes with a single judgment strophe. In some cases this strophe has only the requisite two-line formula begun with וְשִׁלַּחְתִּי, but in others there is a lengthy strophe dominated by *weqatal* verbs. Here, the two-line וְשִׁלַּחְתִּי אֵשׁ formula is missing but the judgment does begin with a *weqatal* verb (line Da). Of course, one could divide this stanza into several strophes, as in the numbered verses, but there are three reasons for taking this as a single strophe.

The first reason is the analogy to the lengthy judgment strophes against Damascus, Gaza, Ammon, and Moab. One would expect Israel, the climax of the poem, to also have a large judgment strophe.

The second reason is that lines Db-h are grammatically bound to Da. A prophetic text can bind two lines together, indicating that the two describe aspects of a single future event, by using the pattern *weqatal* + X in the first line and the pattern וְ + [X] + *yiqtol* in the second line. For example, Isaiah 3:4 reads וְנָתַתִּי נְעָרִים שָׂרֵיהֶם וְתַעֲלוּלִים יִמְשְׁלוּ־בָם, "And I will make (*weqatal*) boys their officials, and babies will govern (*yiqtol*) them." Governance by boys and toddlers are not two separate, sequential events, but is a single event in which incompetent rulers are metaphorically described in two terms. Here, a single *weqatal* + X line is followed by seven lines in the וְ + [X] + *yiqtol* pattern (there are six *yiqtol* verbs, but the sixth *yiqtol* governs both lines Dg and Dh). This suggests that the whole of Da-Dh is portrayed as a single military action in which different types of soldiers are mentioned. By contrast, an initial *yiqtol* followed by a series of *weqatal* verbs would suggest a sequential series of discrete events. Note also that we have a series of five לֹא + *yiqtol* verbs in lines Db-f; the sixth *yiqtol* in Dg-h breaks the pattern, in that it lacks the negative, thereby concluding this strophe.

The third reason for reading this as a single strophe is the content of 2:14-16; every line describes the panicked soldiers of a defeated army. These soldiers are differentiated either by their military specialization (heavy infantry, bowmen, light infantry, and cavalry in lines Dc-Df) or by their qualities as soldiers (physically tough [Db] or exceptionally brave [Dg]). But the whole strophe describes a single action—a routed army in flight. The argument of lines Da-Dh is as follows:

Da: No one in the army, however swift, will find escape. This includes:

Db: the physically tough (a desirable military quality)
Dc: the heavy infantry (a military specialization)
Dd: the bowmen (a military specialization)
De: the light infantry (a military specialization)
Df: the cavalry (a military specialization)
Dg-Dh: the courageous (a desirable military quality).

The inclusion structure of lines Db and Dg-Dh suggests that no matter how tough or courageous any members of the four specialized units are, they will all flee in terror.

2:14 Da וְאָבַ֤ד מָנוֹס֙ מִקָּ֔ל
Db וְחָזָ֖ק לֹא־יְאַמֵּ֣ץ כֹּח֑וֹ
Dc וְגִבּ֖וֹר לֹא־יְמַלֵּ֥ט נַפְשֽׁוֹ׃
2:15 Dd וְתֹפֵ֤שׂ הַקֶּ֙שֶׁת֙ לֹ֣א יַעֲמֹ֔ד
De וְקַ֥ל בְּרַגְלָ֖יו לֹ֣א יְמַלֵּ֑ט
Df וְרֹכֵ֣ב הַסּ֔וּס לֹ֥א יְמַלֵּ֖ט נַפְשֽׁוֹ׃
2:16 Dg וְאַמִּ֥יץ לִבּ֖וֹ בַּגִּבּוֹרִ֑ים
Dh עָר֛וֹם יָנ֥וּס בַּיּוֹם־הַה֖וּא
Di נְאֻם־יְהוָֽה׃ פ

Line Da: The colon-marker is *zaqeph qaton* and the constraints are: 1 predicator, 3 constituents, and 3 units.

וְאָבַ֤ד. Qal *weqatal* 3 m s of אבד. The initial *weqatal* formally follows the pattern of the previous seven judgment strophes in the previous oracles.

מָנוֹס֙. The subject of the verb. Defined as either "flight" or "place of refuge," it probably simply means "retreat" or "escape," and the usage here portrays a defeated army that will not be able to retreat in good order, resulting in a total rout and the ensuing annihilation of that army.

מִקָּ֔ל. Prepositional phrase with מִן. Why is קַל (here in pausal form), the "swift," specified in the first line, only to be repeated in line De? The expression in De probably refers specifically to light infantry as a unit of the army. Here in Da, "swift" indicates not a specific military specialization but the trait most necessary for the implied situation, running away from a defeat in battle. The point is that the whole army will flee and that even the most swift among them will not get away. Following this initial summary, lines Db-Dh describes six types of soldiers who will find no escape.

Line Db: The colon-marker is *athnach* and the constraints are: 1 predicator, 3 constituents, and 3 units.

וְחָזָק. The subject. The adjective חָזָק is used substantively, and it means "hard, strong, or severe." It here refers to the military quality of toughness, including the ability to fight, endure pain, and function under severe duress.

לֹא־יְאַמֵּץ. Piel *yiqtol* 3 m s with negative.

כֹּחוֹ. The direct object; the noun כֹּחַ with 3 m s suffix. Used with אמץ, it can refer to rallying one's strength in the midst of a military crisis (Nah 2:1).

Line Dc: The colon-marker is *silluq* and the constraints are: 1 predicator, 3 constituents, and 3 units.

וְגִבּוֹר. The subject. The word גִּבּוֹר essentially means "hero" or "warrior," and it can refer to any kind of soldier (2 Chr 14:8). The term can describe an exceptionally powerful soldier, such as a warrior-king (Gen 10:8; Isa 9:5), and it is also used of elite troops (2 Sam 23:9). It often refers to the main body of the army (2 Sam 20:7; 2 Chr 17:13-14). In the Iron Age, the heavy infantry composed the backbone of the army. It was composed of citizens who were prosperous enough to afford the equipment of a heavy infantryman; typically, these soldiers were from the landed yeoman farmers. By analogy, yeoman farmers made up the Athenian hoplite corps and the legions of the Roman republic (see also *ABD*, "Military Organization in Mesopotamia). Poorer citizens often made up the light infantry, who served as skirmishers and peltasts, and the truly well-off served as cavalry (as they could afford horses). Heavy infantry stood in ranks, wore heavy armor, and bore the brunt of the serious fighting. In this context, set opposite the archers, the "swift of foot," and the cavalry, the גִּבּוֹר is probably the heavy infantryman.

לֹא־יְמַלֵּט. Piel *yiqtol* 3 m s of מלט with negative.

נַפְשׁוֹ. Direct object with 3 m s suffix.

Line Dd: The colon-marker is *zaqeph qaton* and the constraints are: 1 predicator, 2 constituents, and 3 units.

וְתֹפֵשׂ הַקֶּשֶׁת. Qal active participle of תפשׂ ("hold") in construct with הַקֶּשֶׁת (an objective genitive relationship). The participle is not a predicator here. The "holder of the bow" is, of course, an archer.

לֹא יַעֲמֹד. Qal *yiqtol* 3 m s of עמד with negative. The verb here connotes holding one's position in the face of danger during battle.

Line De: The colon-marker is *athnach* and the constraints are: 1 predicator, 3 constituents, and 3 units.

וְקַל. The subject.

בְּרַגְלָיו. Prepositional phrase with בְּ. The phrase "swift on his feet" of itself only connotes someone who can run fast, but in this context it is probably not those who are gifted runners but those whose task in a military formation involves speed. This would be the light infantry, who typically carried wicker shields, hurled missiles at the enemy, and who were used for harassment and swift flanking attacks rather than for frontal assaults, which would be the task of the heavy infantry.

לֹא יְמַלֵּט. Piel *yiqtol* 3 m s of מלט with negative. The direct object נַפְשׁוֹ is implied, as in lines Dc and Df.

Line Df: The colon-marker is *silluq* and the constraints are: 1 predicator, 3 constituents, and 4 units.

וְרֹכֵב הַסּוּס. The subject, a qal active participle of רכב, used substantively in a construct chain with הַסּוּס. These are the cavalry.

לֹא יְמַלֵּט. Piel *yiqtol* 3 m s of מלט with negative.

נַפְשׁוֹ. The direct object.

Line Dg: The colon-marker is *athnach* and the constraints are: 0 predicators, 2 constituents, and 3 units. This line depends on the following line Dh.

וְאַמִּיץ לִבּוֹ. The subject, a construct chain. A man who is "mighty of his heart" is a man of exceptional courage, as in the English expression, "stout of heart."

בַּגִּבּוֹרִים. Prepositional phrase with בְּ, here meaning "among." The גִּבֹּרִים are again the heavy infantrymen. These men, in heavy armor, presenting a wall of shields and standing shoulder-to-shoulder in the line of battle, were expected to withstand a frontal charge from the enemy, and thus were the bravest of the brave. The light infantry and archers, by contrast, were not expected to hold their ground in this manner.

Line Dh: The colon-marker is *tifha* and the constraints are: 1 predicator, 3 constituents, and 4 units. As happens sometimes in Amos, the *tifha* marks the end of a line before an oracle formula.

עָרוֹם. An adjective whose antecedent is the soldier described as אַמִּיץ לִבּוֹ. The adjective is adverbial here, describing the condition in which the soldier will flee. "Naked" could literally mean that he has lost all of his clothing, but it at least refers to his having cast away all his heavy armor and weapons.

יָנוּס. Qal *yiqtol* 3 m s of נוס.

בַּיּוֹם־הַהוּא. Prepositional phrase with בְּ used for a temporal phrase.

Line Di: The colon-marker is *silluq* and the constraints are: 0 predicators, 1 constituent, and 2 units.

נְאֻם־יְהוָה. A divine speech formula.

3:1-15: The Lion Roars

This division is in three parts, with three poems (vv. 4-6; 9-11; 13-15) each headed by a prose section (vv. 1-3; 7-8; 12). Each poem is a single stanza and thus quite short. The governing metaphor of this division is the hunting lion, who appears in the first bicolon of the first poem (v. 4) and in the second and third prose sections (vv. 8 and 12). Essentially, 3:1-15 argues against the misguided faith of the Israelites, who assume that because they are YHWH's people, they are inviolable. This attitude is implied in the claim of v. 2 and in the irony of v. 12. On the basis of this presupposition, moreover, they believe that Amos has no right to prophesy as he does. This chapter therefore is also an apology for Amos' prophetic ministry. Against the misguided faith of Israel, Amos argues, (1) the status of being God's people implies that they will be judged, v. 2; (2) Israel is no longer walking with God, v. 3; (3) looking at the evidence, common sense shows that God has turned against Israel, vv. 4-6; (4) divine compulsion requires Amos to prophesy, vv. 7-8; (5) even the pagans would be appalled at what happens in Samaria, vv. 9-11; and (6) the "deliverance" of Israel will be very different from what they expect, v. 12. Following this, Amos delivers a standard judgment oracle analogous to those given against the nations (vv. 13-15). For an analysis of Amos as a debate between the prophet and his opponents, see Möller (2000). On the rhetoric of this chapter, see Gitay (1980).

1 Hear this word, which YHWH speaks against you, sons of Israel,
against all the clan that I brought up from the land of Egypt: 2 You only do
I know of all the clans of the land. Therefore I will punish you for all your
iniquities. 3 Will two walk together unless they be agreed?

4 Will the lion roar in the forest
When he has no prey?
Will the maned lion give his voice from his lair
If he has not captured anything?
5 Will a bird swoop down on a trap on the earth
If it has no bait?
Will a trap spring up from the ground
And not catch anything at all?
6 Will a shofar sound in a city
And a people not be terrified?
Will there be disaster in a city
And YHWH has not done it?

7 For the Lord YHWH does not do anything unless he reveals his secret
plan to his servants, the prophets. 8 The lion has roared! Who will not fear?
The Lord YHWH has spoken! Who will not prophesy?

[9]Make a proclamation at the citadels of Ashdod
And at the citadels in the land of Egypt!

And say, Gather yourselves upon the hills of Samaria!
And see many outrages in her midst
And oppressive acts within her!

[10]And (see that) they do not know how to do what is right—
The oracle of YHWH—
But treasure up violence and destruction in their citadels.

[11]Therefore thus says Lord YHWH:
An enemy, and all around the land!
And he will bring your strength down from you,
And your citadels will be plundered.

[12]Thus says YHWH: Just as a shepherd might "rescue" from a lion's mouth two legs or a piece of an ear, so shall the people of Israel, who sit in Samaria at the corner of a bed and by a footstool of a couch, be "rescued."

[13]Hear and give testimony against the house of Jacob—
An oracle of Lord YHWH, God of Sabaoth!

[14]For in the day that I punish the transgressions of Israel
Then I will punish the altars of Bethel.
And the horns of the altar will be chopped off
And will fall to the earth.
[15]And I will strike the winter house in addition to the summer house,
And the ivory houses will be lost,
And many houses will be swept away.
The oracle of YHWH.

3:1-3: Prose Exordium: This is a single prose paragraph. The call to hear (v. 1) is followed by two sentences that explain why YHWH is about to give an oracle against Israel (vv. 2-3).

3:1 שִׁמְע֞וּ אֶת־הַדָּבָ֣ר הַזֶּ֗ה אֲשֶׁ֨ר דִּבֶּ֧ר יְהוָ֛ה עֲלֵיכֶ֖ם בְּנֵ֣י
יִשְׂרָאֵ֑ל עַ֚ל כָּל־הַמִּשְׁפָּחָ֔ה אֲשֶׁ֧ר הֶעֱלֵ֛יתִי מֵאֶ֥רֶץ
מִצְרַ֖יִם לֵאמֹֽר׃

This sentence is governed by an initial imperative and thus is volitive in nature. Two relative clauses and two appositional phrases expand upon elements in the sentence, as described below.

Prose Clause: שִׁמְעוּ אֶת־הַדָּבָר הַזֶּה . . . לֵאמֹר

The initial imperative (שִׁמְעוּ, a qal imperative m p of שמע) sets this sentence as an exhortation. The main clause includes לֵאמֹר, the qal infinitive construct of אמר with preposition לְ, and it is interrupted by a series of parenthetical relative and appositional expressions. אֶת־הַדָּבָר הַזֶּה is the direct object, and לֵאמֹר is epexegetical of הַדָּבָר הַזֶּה and, as is normal, introduces a quotation.

Prose Clause: אֲשֶׁר דִּבֶּר יְהוָה עֲלֵיכֶם בְּנֵי יִשְׂרָאֵל

This relative clause with אֲשֶׁר has הַדָּבָר הַזֶּה as its antecedent. דִּבֶּר יְהוָה is a piel *qatal* 3 m s of דבר with יהוה serving as the subject. עֲלֵיכֶם is a prepositional phrase with עַל, which can mean "concerning" but here undoubtedly means "against." It has a 2 m p suffix. בְּנֵי יִשְׂרָאֵל is a vocative in apposition to the 2 m p suffix on עֲלֵיכֶם.

Prose Clause: עַל כָּל־הַמִּשְׁפָּחָה

Prepositional phrase with עַל. It is in apposition to עֲלֵיכֶם. The use of מִשְׁפָּחָה, "clan," to designate the whole nation of Israel is somewhat odd, as מִשְׁפָּחָה is often understood to be a sub-unit of שֵׁבֶט, "tribe." But Amos designates all the nations of earth as מִשְׁפְּחוֹת in v. 3, and thus he does not seem to have any derogatory intent in designating Israel as a מִשְׁפָּחָה.

Prose Clause: אֲשֶׁר הֶעֱלֵיתִי מֵאֶרֶץ מִצְרַיִם

A relative clause in apposition to כָּל־הַמִּשְׁפָּחָה. After the relative אֲשֶׁר comes the verb הֶעֱלֵיתִי (hiphil *qatal* 1 c s of עלה), and finally מֵאֶרֶץ מִצְרַיִם, a prepositional phrase with מִן on a construct chain.

3:2 רַק אֶתְכֶם יָדַעְתִּי מִכֹּל מִשְׁפְּחוֹת הָאֲדָמָה עַל־כֵּן
אֶפְקֹד עֲלֵיכֶם אֵת כָּל־עֲוֹנֹתֵיכֶם׃

This sentence, although lacking any transitional particle such as כִּי, is explanatory, telling the audience why YHWH is speaking against them. The lack of transition is more forceful because the sentence is not formally subordinated. The second clause, headed by עַל־כֵּן, "that is why," marks the sentence as explanatory.

Prose Clause: רַק אֶתְכֶם יָדַעְתִּי מִכֹּל מִשְׁפְּחוֹת הָאֲדָמָה

The matrix clause of this sentence, it has the order object-verb, making the object the most prominent feature of the clause. In addition to having the front position, the direct object אֶתְכֶם has the particle רַק, "only," fixing the reader's attention on the unique status of Israel. יָדַעְתִּי is a qal *qatal* 1 c s of ידע. The prepositional phrase מִכֹּל מִשְׁפְּחוֹת הָאֲדָמָה has a partitive מִן, indicating that Israel has been chosen from among the nations of earth.

Prose Clause: עַל־כֵּן אֶפְקֹד עֲלֵיכֶם אֵת כָּל־עֲוֹנֹתֵיכֶם

This clause is formally the logical conclusion of the preceding clause, but it is paradoxical. One would expect that Israel's special status as the people of God would insulate it from judgment, but that is the very fallacy that Amos is seeking to expose. עַל־כֵּן, literally "upon thus," is idiomatic for "that is why" or "for that reason." The verb אֶפְקֹד (qal *yiqtol* 1 c s of פקד) has an enormous semantic range, including "inspect," "visit," "muster (troops)," "take care of," and "punish." Here, it connotes punishing Israel for their sins, as in Exodus 32:34; 20:5; Jeremiah 6:15; etc. עֲלֵיכֶם a prepositional phrase with עַל and 2 m p suffix, repeats עֲלֵיכֶם from v. 1, suggesting that this explains God's speech against Israel announced there. This use of פקד (with the person punished designated by עַל, and with the sin for which punishment comes being the direct object) is quite common, as in Numbers 14:18 and Isaiah 13:11.

3:3 הֲיֵלְכוּ שְׁנַיִם יַחְדָּו בִּלְתִּי אִם־נוֹעָדוּ׃

This sentence is a rhetorical question with an inverted structure of apodosis before protasis. The presence of an inversion is indicated by בִּלְתִּי אִם in the second clause, which means "if not" or "unless" and marks that clause as the protasis. If it were a declarative statement instead of a rhetorical question, it would read, "Unless they are agreed, two will not walk together." In form, this verse is identical to the bicola of 3:4-6, and thus it is universally assumed that this is the first bicolon of a poem of seven bicola. There are two reasons that this is not correct. First, there is nothing poetic about this sentence. It is of itself a simple rhetorical question; in isolation, there is no reason anyone would regard it as poetry; it is in fact a proverb. In 3:4-6, by contrast, this rhetorical question pattern *is converted into poetry* by virtue of the repeated parallelism, there being three matched pairs. Second, although 3:3 serves as a lead-in for the poem of 3:4-6, it is isolated from that poem by form and content. Formally, it lacks a second, matching bicolon. Often Amos, like other prophets, will terminate a repeated pattern with an element that breaks from the pattern, but it is odd to begin a poem with an element that does not conform to the pattern. More significantly, the content is completely different. Verse 3 speaks of two people walking together, but the bicolon pairs of vv. 4-6 all concern acts of violent entrapment: a lion captures its prey, a snare traps a bird, and city is entrapped by an enemy or YHWH. Verse 3 looks back to vv. 1-2, explaining how it is that Israel, YHWH's chosen people, will especially experience his punishment. Verses 4-6 look forward to vv. 7ff., explaining that because YHWH has spoken, Amos must prophesy and destruction must come. Rhetorically, the structure of v. 3 leads into the poem of vv. 4-6, but it is not part of that poem.

Prose Clause: הֲיֵלְכוּ שְׁנַיִם יַחְדָּו

This is the apodosis of the rhetorical question. הֲיֵלְכוּ is a qal *yiqtol* 3 m p of הלך with interrogative ה. The sense of הלך here is probably not "walk together" in the sense of a casual stroll but "go together" in the sense of having a common purpose and destination, and of looking upon one another as partners in a metaphorical journey. The subject (שְׁנַיִם) is followed by an adverb (יַחְדָּו) modifying הלך.

Prose Clause: בִּלְתִּי אִם־נוֹעָדוּ

This, as described above, is the protasis in a rhetorical question. The phrase בִּלְתִּי אִם is adverbial, meaning "unless." The verb נוֹעָדוּ is a niphal *qatal* 3 c p of יעד. This verb is the *crux* of the verse. Shalom Paul argues that it "here means merely 'to meet' without any overtones of by plan or by design" (Paul 1991, 109). He argues that people often walk together when they have met by chance, and that it is not correct to say that people never walk together except by appointment. Against this, the Niphal of יעד does signify coming together at a designated place and time (as in Num 10:3; 14:35; 16:11; Ps 48:4 [E = 5]; Neh 6:2), and no occurrence of the verb connotes a chance meeting. Also, as mentioned above, the sense of הלך here is almost certainly not of two people who accidentally meet and walk in the same direction for a few minutes before parting. It is true that "they have made an appointment" is not the best translation for this verb here, if by that one imagines something analogous to synchronizing appointment books for a planned meeting. In this context, the verb connotes a metaphorical coming together by design, and thus actually means that they have come to terms with one another and can consider themselves to be in a partnership. The point, therefore, is that two will not be partners if they have not come to terms with each other. In addition, the verbal root יעד recalls the אֹהֶל מוֹעֵד, the "tent of meeting" of Israel's wilderness sojourn. This is the place where YHWH would come together (Niphal of יעד) with Israel as they journeyed together (see Exod 25:22; 29:42-43; 30:6). The implication is that fundamental differences now exist between YHWH and Israel, such that he can no longer journey with them and must turn against them. Thus, the verse further explains 3:1, that YHWH is now issuing an oracle against them.

3:4-6: First Poem (An Epigram): This is a short epigram (one stanza) in three strophes, with each strophe containing four lines (consisting of two rhetorical questions of two lines each). Every rhetorical question introduced by an interrogative particle (הֲ in 3:4-5 and אִם in 3:6), with the first line of each question being an apodosis and the second line being a protasis, as in 3:3. The protasis is always negated (with אֵין in 1b and 2b, בִּלְתִּי in 1d, and לֹא in 2d, 3b, and 3d). Each rhetorical question is an implied declarative. The implied declarative for the first question (3:4a), for example, is: "Unless the lion has prey, he will not roar," or conversely, "Since the lion has roared, he must have prey." Since every strophe follows the same pattern, they are not given separate introductions below.

An epigram in Hebrew poetry is a short wisdom poem typically employing a single poetic device and giving several examples of a single lesson. Proverbs 6:16-19, an epigram giving the things God hates, illustrates the pattern. Here in Amos, the first strophe concerns the hunting lion, the second strophe concerns the entrapment of a bird, and the third concerns calamity in a city. The question-and-answer motif is in keeping with the roots of the epigram in wisdom literature. The climax of this sequence is the sixth question (3:6b). The point is that recent disasters that have overtaken Samaria, such as described in 4:6-11, are proof that YHWH is against Samaria. This in turn forces YHWH's prophet, Amos, to prophesy against Samaria, as indicated in the following text, 3:7-8. The function of the epigram is to vindicate Amos' claims against Israel, arguing that, given all that has happened, it is only common sense that to conclude that God has turned against Israel.

3:4 1a הֲיִשְׁאַ֤ג אַרְיֵה֙ בַּיַּ֔עַר
1b וְטֶ֖רֶף אֵ֣ין ל֑וֹ
1c הֲיִתֵּ֨ן כְּפִ֤יר קוֹלוֹ֙ מִמְּעֹ֣נָת֔וֹ
1d בִּלְתִּ֖י אִם־לָכָֽד׃

Line 1a: The colon-marker is *zaqeph qaton* and the constraints are: 1 predicator, 3 constituents, and 3 units.

הֲיִשְׁאַג. Qal *yiqtol* 3 m s of שׁאג with interrogative ה. It may be that the lion is roaring in the forest to paralyze its prey with fear.

אַרְיֵה. The subject. In 3:7 and elsewhere in the prophets YHWH is metaphorically a lion (Amos 1:2; Hos 5:14). Beginning the epigram with this metaphor already suggests that YHWH is roaring with anger and is about to kill.

בַּיַּעַר. Prepositional phrase with locative בְּ and definite article. The definite article represents forest as a representative example; it does not refer to some specific forest.

Line 1b: The colon-marker is *athnach* and the constraints are: 1 predicator, 3 constituents, and 3 units.

וְטֶרֶף. The subject.

אֵין. Negative existential particle serving as the predicator.

לוֹ. Prepositional phrase with לְ, here used for possession.

Line 1c: The colon-marker is *zaqeph qaton* and the constraints are: 1 predicator, 4 constituents, and 4 units.

הֲיִתֵּן. Qal *yiqtol* 3 m s of נתן with interrogative ה.

כְּפִיר. The subject. It is difficult to know whether or in what way the כְּפִיר is different from the אַרְיֵה, the אֲרִי, and the לָבִיא. All mean "lion"; כְּפִיר is traditionally translated as "young lion," but that may well be incorrect. According to *NIDOTTE* (at אֲרִי), both the אֲרִי and אַרְיֵה are African lions, but the לָבִיא is an Asiatic lion. *HALOT* כְּפִיר suggests that כְּפִיר is "distinguishable by his mane" and thus would indicate a male lion that has reached maturity.

קוֹלוֹ. The direct object. נתן קול is used of YHWH in 1:2.

מִמְּעֹנָתוֹ. Prepositional phrase with מִן. A מְעֹנָה is a dwelling place, primarily the den or lair of a wild beast (Nah 2:13 [E 12]; Ps 104:22; Job 37:8). It may be that the lion here gives a growl of satisfaction from his den, having killed and eaten prey.

Line 1d: The colon-marker is *silluq* and the constraints are: 1 predicator, 2 constituents, and 2 units.

בִּלְתִּי אִם־. Adverbial, meaning "unless."

לָכָד. Qal *qatal* 3 m s of לכד. The object, "prey," is implied.

3:5 2a הֲתִפֹּל צִפּוֹר עַל־פַּח הָאָרֶץ
2b וּמוֹקֵשׁ אֵין לָהּ
2c הֲיַעֲלֶה־פַּח מִן־הָאֲדָמָה
2d וְלָכוֹד לֹא יִלְכּוֹד׃

Line 2a: The colon-marker is *zaqeph qaton* and the constraints are: 1 predicator, 3 constituents, and 4 units.

הֲתִפֹּל. Qal *yiqtol* 3 f s of נפל with interrogative ה. The verb here has the sense of "swoop down upon" something in order to eat it.

צִפּוֹר. The subject.

עַל־פַּח הָאָרֶץ. Prepositional phrase with עַל. The construct chain פַּח הָאָרֶץ refers to a trap that is on the ground as opposed to, for example, one located in a tree. The image of the trap may suggest that Israel is entrapping herself due to her senseless greed.

Line 2b: The colon-marker is *athnach* and the constraints are: 1 predicator, 3 constituents, and 3 units.

וּמוֹקֵשׁ. The subject. The word here clearly does not mean "snare," which makes no sense in context, but "bait."

אֵין. Negative existential particle serving as the predicator.

לָהּ. Prepositional phrase with לְ, here used for possession.

Line 2c: The colon-marker is *zaqeph qaton* and the constraints are: 1 predicator, 3 constituents, and 3 units.

הֲיַעֲלֶה. Qal *yiqtol* 3 m s of עלה with interrogative ה. The verb represents a trap springing up to catch a bird. The motion of the trap (עלה) contrasts with the motion of the bird (נפל).

פַּח. The subject.

מִן־הָאֲדָמָה. Prepositional phrase with מִן.

Line 2d: The colon-marker is *silluq* and the constraints are: 1 predicator, 1 constituent, and 2 units.

וְלָכוֹד לֹא יִלְכּוֹד. Qal infinitive absolute used adverbially with negated qal *yiqtol* 3 m s of **לכד**. The meaning of a finite verb with cognate infinitive absolute varies by context. Here, it means, "and not catch anything at all."

3:6 3a אִם־יִתָּקַע שׁוֹפָר בְּעִיר
3b וְעָם לֹא יֶחֱרָדוּ
3c אִם־תִּהְיֶה רָעָה בְּעִיר
3d וַיהוָה לֹא עָשָׂה׃

Line 3a: The colon-marker is *zaqeph qaton* and the constraints are: 1 predicator, 3 constituents, and 3 units.

אִם־יִתָּקַע. Niphal *yiqtol* 3 m s of **תקע** with interrogative particle **אִם**. The change of particle indicates that this is the last strophe.

שׁוֹפָר. The subject. The shofar was used for various purposes (such as to signal the onset of a holy season), but here it is an alarm.

בְּעִיר. Prepositional phrase with locative **בְּ**.

Line 3b: The colon-marker is *athnach* and the constraints are: 1 predicator, 2 constituents, and 2 units.

וְעָם. The subject, with conjunction. The term here refers to the whole population of a city.

לֹא יֶחֱרָדוּ. Negated qal *yiqtol* 3 m p of **חרד**, to "tremble" or "be frantic." Although formally merely another example in the series of rhetorical questions making the point that "if A is true, then B is true," this example invokes the judgment that Amos has already pronounced in 2:14-16, that Israel will suffer calamitous military defeat.

Line 3c: The colon-marker is *zaqeph qaton* and the constraints are: 1 predicator, 3 constituents, and 3 units.

אִם־תִּהְיֶה. Qal *yiqtol* 3 f s of **היה** with interrogative particle **אִם**.

רָעָה. The subject. This is the feminine singular of the adjective רַע, "bad," but it is used substantively to mean "a bad thing." The way in which something is "bad" varies by context. It may be moral badness ("wickedness"), but often it is a bad situation ("distress, calamity, disaster" etc.). It has the latter sense here, and more specifically refers to a city being pillaged by an enemy.

בְּעִיר. Prepositional phrase with locative בְּ.

Line 3d: The colon-marker is *silluq* and the constraints are: 1 predicator, 2 constituents, and 2 units.

וַיהוָה. The subject.

לֹא עָשָׂה. Negated qal *qatal* 3 m s of עשׂה. Amos does not shy away from the implications of divine sovereignty, specifically from the idea that if God is all-powerful, he is ultimately responsible for al that happens in the world. In this case, however, Amos' main concern is not to deal with issues of theodicy but to assert that recent calamities in Israel (see 4:6-11) are proof that YHWH is acting against Israel. This last question is the main point of the entire epigram; the other questions simply make that point that certain evidence renders certain conclusions unavoidable. In addition, the violent nature of all six questions naturally suggests that God has turned against Israel.

3:7-8: First Prose Commentary: This prose commentary both concludes the first poem and leads into the second, thus serving as a transition. The first sentence (3:7) contains two clauses in the pattern of another inverted protasis-apodosis statement (i.e., the apodosis comes first). This is followed in 3:8 by two brief assertions (two words each in Hebrew), each followed by a short, one-clause rhetorical question introduced by מִי. As with 3:3, 3:8 is widely believed to be poetry, and it is generally assumed to be the end of the preceding poem (widely considered to be 3:3-8). Reasons for believing 3:3 to be prose, and separate from 3:4-6, are described above. Here, there is an enormous problem confronting those who wish to connect 3:8 to 3:4-6: verse 7 is indisputably prose, and scanning it as poetry would be forced and unpersuasive. But it is highly peculiar to have a poem with a prose sentence inserted inside it. Indeed, that evidence alone is sufficient to demonstrate that 3:8 cannot be part of the epigram in 3:4-6. H. W. Wolff avoids this problem by arguing that v. 7 is a later redactional insertion within a poem that was originally 3:3–6:8 (Wolff 1977, 180–81), but that only removes the difficulty by postulating the existence of a redactor who was so inept that he inserted a line of prose inside of a poem. In addition, there is little compelling evidence for reading v. 8 as poetry. It does contain parallelism, but parallelism within such a short text is scarcely compelling. Parallelism is neither the essential feature of Hebrew poetry nor absent from Hebrew prose. There is no reason to think that v. 8 cannot be a continuation of the prose of 3:7, to which it is obviously connected.

Verse 7 comments on 3:6b, which spoke of YHWH acting (עשׂה) in judgment, and argues that YHWH will not act (עשׂה) without telling the prophets. Verse 8, with its assertion that the lion has roared, comments on the beginning of the epigram (אַרְיֵה שָׁאָג; cf. הֲיִשְׁאַג אַרְיֵה in 3:2). Thus, it is correct that 3:7-8 refers back to 3:4-6. On the other hand, 3:7-8 also looks forward to the prophetic message in 3:9-11. Verse 7 asserts that divine judgment is preceded by prophecy. In 3:8b, if the verse were only a conclusion to 3:4-6, we might expect to read something like, יהוה עָשָׂה מִי לֹא יֶחֱרָדוּ ("YHWH has acted, who will not be terrified?"). Instead, we read, "YHWH has spoken, who will not prophesy?" This plainly looks forward to the prophetic proclamation of 3:9-11 that begins with הַשְׁמִיעוּ, "Make it heard!"

3:7 כִּי לֹא יַעֲשֶׂה אֲדֹנָי יְהוִה דָּבָר כִּי אִם־גָּלָה סוֹדוֹ אֶל־
עֲבָדָיו הַנְּבִיאִים׃

Prose Clause: כִּי לֹא יַעֲשֶׂה אֲדֹנָי יְהוִה דָּבָר

This is the apodosis of the sentence; the condition is in the next clause, "unless he reveals. . . ." The inversion of the normal order follows the pattern set in vv. 3-6 and here makes the apodosis more prominent. כִּי is here explanatory, meaning "because." לֹא יַעֲשֶׂה is a negated qal *yiqtol* 3 m s of עשׂה, with אֲדֹנָי יְהוִה as the subject. דָּבָר, the direct object, here means a "thing" and with the negative, "anything."

Prose Clause: כִּי אִם־גָּלָה סוֹדוֹ אֶל־עֲבָדָיו הַנְּבִיאִים

The protasis, this asserts that prophetic warnings are an essential precursor to divine judgment. כִּי אִם, "unless," gives the condition. גָּלָה is a qal *qatal* 3 m s of גלה. The noun סוֹדוֹ, the direct object, has a 3 m s suffix. It refers to secret plans or a confidential discussion. אֶל־עֲבָדָיו is a prepositional phrase with אֶל, here marking the indirect object. הַנְּבִיאִים is in apposition to עֲבָדָיו. It appears that Amos is defending his prophetic credentials in much the same manner as Paul defended his apostolic credentials.

3:8 אַרְיֵה שָׁאָג מִי לֹא יִירָא אֲדֹנָי יְהוִה דִּבֶּר מִי לֹא יִנָּבֵא׃

Prose Clause: אַרְיֵה שָׁאָג

The fronting of the subject (אַרְיֵה) instead of the verb (שָׁאָג, a qal *qatal* 3 m s of שׁאג) makes the subject more prominent. The *qatal* clause is here is offline. It is the setting or background information for the question that follows. Although the roaring lion obviously relates to 3:4, the function here is different. In the former case, it was evidence for the lion's capture of prey; here, it is a sound that provokes terror.

Prose Clause: מִי לֹא יִירָא

The word order here, interrogative + negative + verb, is fixed in biblical Hebrew and invariable; thus, nothing significant is implied by it.

Prose Clause: אֲדֹנָי יְהוִה דִּבֶּר

The verb (דִּבֶּר) is a piel *qatal* 3 m s of דבר. The clause structure is the same as in אַרְיֵה שָׁאָג. The roaring of the lion is thus the analogue to divine speech. This suggests that the prophetic message is itself terrifying.

Prose Clause: מִי לֹא יִנָּבֵא

The verb (יִנָּבֵא) is a niphal *yiqtol* 3 m s of נבא. The clause structure is the same as in מִי לֹא יִירָא.

3:9-11: Second Poem: A Prophetic Accusation: This poem, like 3:4-6, is a single stanza in twelve lines. It has four strophes. In form, this is an accusation in which witnesses are called in to adjudicate. Against 3:2, the significance of calling in pagan nations as the jury is clear: Israel is relying on her special status as YHWH's chosen people to protect and vindicate her, but in fact her offenses are so extreme that even Gentiles are (metaphorically) qualified to sit in judgment on her.

3:9a: First Strophe. Two lines, with the verb הַשְׁמִיעוּ governs both lines (gapping). The strophe is a call for heralds to go out to pagan lands and summon them to witness the moral chaos within Israel. This is a rhetorical device; Amos is not literally sending heralds to these lands.

הַשְׁמִ֙יעוּ֙ עַל־אַרְמְנ֣וֹת בְּאַשְׁדּ֔וֹד	1a	3:9a
וְעַל־אַרְמְנ֖וֹת בְּאֶ֣רֶץ מִצְרָ֑יִם	1b	

Line 1a: The colon-marker is *zaqeph qaton* and the constraints are: 1 predicator, 3 constituents, and 3 units.

הַשְׁמִ֙יעוּ֙. Hiphil imperative m p of שמע.

עַל־אַרְמְנ֣וֹת. Prepositional phrase with עַל. Here, the preposition is a locative "at" and does not mean "against," as it does in 3:1.

בְּאַשְׁדּ֔וֹד. Prepositional phrase with locative בְּ. The LXX reads Ἀσσυρίοις, "Assyria," here for "Ashdod." The argument in favor of this reading is that it seems odd to pair the Philistine city with the great nation of Egypt; Assyria would seem to be a better counterpart. Against this, both Ashdod (as a representative of Philistia) and Egypt had already been major oppressors of Israel, but Assyria as of yet had not. Reference to Assyria is in fact conspicuously absent from Amos. Also, it is difficult to see how later scribes, after the fall of Samaria to Assyria, would substitute Ashdod for Assyria. It may be that Egypt's and Ashdod's history of oppressing Israel ironically makes them expert witnesses (Paul 1991, 115). Snyman (1994) argues that Ashdod represents the conquest and Egypt represents the exodus. It is also possible that אַשְׁדּוֹד is here a wordplay on שֹׁד ("destruction") in 3:10.

Line 1b: The colon-marker is *athnach* and the constraints are: 0 predicators, 2 constituents, and 3 units. This line employs both gapping (with the verb) and matching (with the prepositions).

וְעַל־אַרְמְנוֹת. Prepositional phrase with עַל. Here again, the preposition is a locative and does not mean "against."

בְּאֶרֶץ מִצְרָיִם. Prepositional phrase with locative בְּ. It may be that מִצְרַיִם is a wordplay on הָאוֹצְרִים in 3:10.

3:9b: Second Strophe. Three lines. Instead of a separate divine speech formula, there is a one-word imperative (וְאִמְרוּ, analogous to הַשְׁמִיעוּ in line 1a) directed at the implied heralds, with the rest of the strophe being the content of what the heralds are to say to the nations. The heralds' speech to the nations goes at least through line 2c, but it probably includes lines 3a-4d as well.

3:9b	2a	וְאִמְרוּ הֵאָסְפוּ עַל־הָרֵי שֹׁמְרוֹן
	2b	וּרְאוּ מְהוּמֹת רַבּוֹת בְּתוֹכָהּ
	2c	וַעֲשׁוּקִים בְּקִרְבָּהּ׃

Line 2a: The colon-marker is *zaqeph qaton* and the constraints are: 2 predicators, 3 constituents, and 4 units.

וְאִמְרוּ. Qal imperative m p of אמר with conjunction. The subject is the implied heralds who address the nations.

הֵאָסְפוּ. Niphal imperative m p of אסף. The subject is the nations, who are commanded to gather together.

עַל־הָרֵי שֹׁמְרוֹן. Prepositional phrase with עַל. The image has a double purpose. On the one hand it suggests a gathering of armies in camps preparing to lay siege to Samaria, but on the other hand, within the rhetorical metaphor, the nations are seated as jury members upon the hills, observing the evidence and preparing to give a verdict.

Line 2b: The colon-marker is *zaqeph qaton* and the constraints are: 1 predicator, 3 constituents, and 4 units.

וּרְא֞וּ. Qal imperative m p of ראה with conjunction.

מְהוּמֹ֤ת רַבּוֹת֙. The direct object. The word מְהוּמָה implies panic or turmoil, and again there is a double meaning. The panic is the coming panic of Samaria when it is under siege, but it is also the moral turmoil brought about by widespread oppression within the city. It is the latter that the nations are to observe and render a verdict on.

בְּתוֹכָ֔הּ. Prepositional phrase with בְּ (used in a locative sense) and a 3 f s suffix (the antecedent is Samaria). A city is understood to be feminine.

Line 2c: The colon-marker is *silluq* and the constraints are: 0 predicators, 2 constituents, and 2 units. There is gapping, with וּרְא֞וּ governing this line.

וַעֲשׁוּקִ֖ים. The direct object. The noun עֲשׁוּקִים ("acts of oppression") is found only here and in Job 35:9. It is related to the abstract noun עֹשֶׁק ("extortion, oppression").

בְּקִרְבָּֽהּ. Prepositional phrase with בְּ (used in a locative sense) and a 3 f s suffix.

3:10: Third Strophe. Three lines. These lines have a single main clause (3a) followed by a divine speech formula (3b) and participial relative clause (3c).

3:10 3a וְלֹֽא־יָדְע֥וּ עֲשׂוֹת־נְכֹחָ֖ה
3b נְאֻם־יְהוָ֑ה
3c הָאֽוֹצְרִ֛ים חָמָ֥ס וָשֹׁ֖ד בְּאַרְמְנוֹתֵיהֶֽם׃ פ

Line 3a: The colon-marker is *tifha* and the constraints are: 1 predicator, 3 constituents, and 3 units.

וְלֹא־יָֽדְעוּ. Negated qal *qatal* 3 c p of ידע with conjunction. The subject is the Israelite people, and the conjunction relates to the turmoil and oppression that the nations are called on to witness. Thus, the implication is that the command for the nations to "see" what happens in Israel governs this line also.

עֲשׂוֹת. Qal infinitive construct of עשׂה used as a complement to יָדְעוּ. It is not a predicator. The idiom ידע + infinitive normally means to "know how to do" a thing.

נְכֹחָה. The direct object. נָכֹחַ appears to be an adjective meaning "straight," but it is routinely used substantively to mean "proper behavior" or "uprightness." The word often has a feminine form, but the singular, as here, is used more abstractly, while the plural, as in Isa 30:10, seems to refer more concretely to "right things."

Line 3b: The colon-marker is *athnach* and the constraints are: 0 predicators, 1 constituent, and 2 units.

נְאֻם־יְהוָה. A divine speech formula.

Line 3c: The colon-marker is *silluq* and the constraints are: 1 predicator, 3 constituents, and 4 units.

הָאֽוֹצְרִים. Qal active participle m p of אצר with definite article. The participle serves as a relative clause whose antecedent is the implied subject of יָדְעוּ, the people of Samaria. As elsewhere in Amos, the plural participle is joined to a finite verb in a preceding line within the same strophe.

חָמָס וָשֹׁד. A compound direct object of two nouns joined by the conjunction. It may be that חָמָס, "violence," speaks especially of crimes against persons while שֹׁד, "destruction," speaks of crimes against property and property rights, but both include the idea of violence.

בְּאַרְמְנוֹתֵיהֶֽם. Prepositional phrase with בְּ (used here in a locative sense).

3:11: Fourth Strophe. Four lines. This is a judgment strophe, proclaiming the punishment that will come to Israel for all the outrages that occur within her. The language is reminiscent of the minimal judgment strophes against Tyre (1:10), Edom (1:12), and Judah (2:5) in that it speaks of destruction coming upon the citadels (אַרְמְנוֹת) of Samaria.

3:11	4a	לָכֵ֗ן כֹּ֤ה אָמַר֙ אֲדֹנָ֣י יְהוִ֔ה
	4b	צַ֖ר וּסְבִ֣יב הָאָ֑רֶץ
	4c	וְהוֹרִ֤ד מִמֵּךְ֙ עֻזֵּ֔ךְ
	4d	וְנָבֹ֖זּוּ אַרְמְנוֹתָֽיִךְ׃

Line 4a: The colon-marker is *zaqeph qaton* and the constraints are: 1 predicator, 3 constituents, and 4 units. In form, this could be prose (as a number of divine speech formulas appear to be), but 3:11 is a continuation of the poem and this line, therefore, must be scanned as poetry.

לָכֵ֗ן. This references the sins described in strophes two and three as the reasons for the punishment described here.

כֹּ֤ה אָמַר֙. Qal *qatal* 3 m s with an adverb.

אֲדֹנָ֣י יְהוִ֔ה. The subject.

Line 4b: The colon-marker is *athnach* and the constraints are: 0 predicators, 2 constituents, and 3 units. As it stands in the MT, this line is an exclamation rather than a declarative statement. Thus, there is no predicator, although a predicated sentence is implied. "An enemy! And all around the land!" implies, "There is an enemy all around the land!"

צַ֖ר. This noun may mean "distress," as in Job 15:24, but it often means "enemy." Either is possible here, but line 4c implies that "enemy" is the meaning here. The LXX has Τύρος, "Tyre (צֹר)," which is certainly wrong.

וּסְבִ֣יב הָאָ֑רֶץ. Prepositional phrase with סְבִיב and the conjunction. Many emend to יְסוֹבֵב, the polal *yiqtol* 3 m s of סבב, "an enemy shall surround the land," on the basis of the Vulgate (see BHS apparatus). But the full Vulgate reading is *tribulabitur et circumietur terra*, "the land shall be distressed and surrounded," making it difficult to assess what the Vulgate's *Vorlage* was and whether it actually supports the proposed emendation. The MT is intelligible and should be left as is.

Line 4c: The colon-marker is *zaqeph qaton* and the constraints are: 1 predicator, 3 constituents, and 3 units.

וְהוֹרִד. Hiphil *weqatal* 3 m s of ירד. The subject is צַר from 4b. As in earlier judgment strophes, the *weqatal* form is the primary finite verb conjugation employed to describe a series of pending disasters that will come as divine judgment on a nation.

מִמֵּךְ. Prepositional phrase with מִן and a 2 f s suffix. The antecedent of the suffix is the city of Samaria, metaphorically a woman.

עֻזֵּךְ. The direct object with a 2 f s suffix.

Line 4d: The colon-marker is *silluq* and the constraints are: 1 predicator, 2 constituents, and 2 units.

וְנָבֹזּוּ. Niphal *weqatal* 3 c p of בזז. Unlike the prior judgments on the nations, where the citadels were burned down, here they are plundered. This is apropos, considering that a major crime of the Israelite leadership was a plundering of their own people.

אַרְמְנוֹתָיִךְ. The direct object with a 2 f s suffix.

3:12: Second Prose Commentary: This commentary serves as a transition between the second and third poems. Looking back, it comments on 3:11 by describing with the illustration of the lamb how thorough the destruction of Samaria will be. Looking forward, it anticipates the description of the arrogant luxury of the upper classes in Samaria in 3:14-15.

3:12 כֹּ֚ה אָמַ֣ר יְהוָ֔ה כַּאֲשֶׁר֩ יַצִּ֨יל הָרֹעֶ֜ה מִפִּ֧י הָאֲרִ֛י שְׁתֵּ֥י
כְרָעַ֖יִם א֣וֹ בְדַל־אֹ֑זֶן כֵּ֣ן יִנָּצְל֞וּ בְּנֵ֣י יִשְׂרָאֵ֗ל הַיֹּֽשְׁבִים֙
בְּשֹׁ֣מְר֔וֹן בִּפְאַ֥ת מִטָּ֖ה וּבִדְמֶ֥שֶׁק עָֽרֶשׂ׃

Prose Clause: כֹּה֮ אָמַ֣ר יְהוָה֒

A divine speech formula with a qal *qatal* 3 m s of אמר and the particle כֹּה.

Prose Clause: כַּאֲשֶׁר֩ יַצִּ֨יל הָרֹעֶ֜ה מִפִּ֣י הָאֲרִ֗י שְׁתֵּ֥י כְרָעַ֛יִם א֥וֹ בְדַל־אֹ֖זֶן

כַּאֲשֶׁר. introduces the first part of a two-part comparison, in which כַּאֲשֶׁר marks the protasis and is equivalent to "just as" and כֵּן, marking the apodosis, is equivalent to "even so." יַצִּיל is a hiphil *yiqtol* 3 m s of נצל. The *yiqtol* represents possible activity and could be rendered "might snatch." However, this verb often has the connotation of deliverance, and it is here used ironically, as is clear from the use of נצל in the second clause of this verse. הָרֹעֶה is the subject. The definite article represents a class rather than a specific example, and thus it could be translated as "a shepherd" rather than "the shepherd." מִפִּי הָאֲרִי is a prepositional phrase with מִן, "from," on a construct chain. Again, the definite article represents a class, and so it could be translated as "from a lion's mouth." The phrase שְׁתֵּי כְרָעַיִם אוֹ בְדַל־אֹזֶן is two direct objects separated by אוֹ, "or." It means, "two legs or a piece of an ear." The כֶּרַע is the bony lower leg of an animal. The snatching of the lower legs or of a piece of ear from a lion's mouth is indicative of how thoroughly the lamb has been destroyed. Some interpreters see here an allusion to the legal requirement that a hired shepherd snatch a piece of a slain sheep from a beast so that he might show the piece to the owner as evidence that the sheep was slain by an animal and that the shepherd did not simply lose the sheep (Exod 22:12 [E 13]; see Paul 1991, 119). But even if such a legal tradition might explain to us why a shepherd would grab a piece of a lamb from a lion's mouth, we should not make too much of that in interpreting this text. The notion of snatching bits of the lamb away to provide evidence exonerating a shepherd is never developed in the text. There is no counterpart to the hired shepherd in the passage, and there is no reason to suppose Amos wants his reader to think that exoneration of the shepherd is the point of the passage. In short, focusing on this supposed cultural background to the shepherd's action does more to cloud the meaning of the passage than to illuminate it. The main point of the image here is that the sheep has been absolutely destroyed.

Prose Clause: כֵּ֤ן יִנָּצְל֙וּ בְּנֵ֣י יִשְׂרָאֵ֔ל

This is the apodosis of the comparison begun in the prior clause. The particle כֵּן marks the apodosis with יִנָּצְלוּ, a niphal *yiqtol* 3 m p of נצל. The irony here counteracts the casual confidence of the people of Samaria that if they are attacked, YHWH will "deliver" (נצל) them. בְּנֵי יִשְׂרָאֵל is the subject. The phrase represents the Israelite nation and, in the metaphor of the protasis, the main point is that the nation will be utterly destroyed. There is no idea of a remnant here. The metaphor of snatching a piece of an ear from a lion's mouth means that the sheep is dead, not that part has survived.

Prose Clause: הַיֹּֽשְׁבִים֙ בְּשֹׁ֣מְר֔וֹן בִּפְאַ֥ת מִטָּ֖ה וּבִדְמֶ֥שֶׁק עָֽרֶשׂ

This is participial expression used as a relative clause in apposition to בְּנֵי יִשְׂרָאֵל. The word הַיֹּשְׁבִים is a qal active participle of ישב m p with the definite article used as a relative clause; the antecedent is בְּנֵי יִשְׂרָאֵל.

בְּשֹׁמְרוֹן בִּפְאַת מִטָּה וּבִדְמֶשֶׁק עָרֶשׂ are three coordinated prepositional phrases, each with בְּ and dependent on ישב. These words are notoriously difficult, but attempts to resolve the difficulty of this text by cutting the Gordian Knot and emending (e.g., Rabinowitz 1961; Zalcman 2002) are too speculative to be compelling. The first issue is the meaning of ישב with בְּ. Shalom Paul vigorously denies that בְּ can be used with ישב to mean "on," and so he argues that the people are not sitting "on" beds. He thus, like many others, argues that בִּפְאַת מִטָּה and following has no relationship to הַיֹּשְׁבִים but rather modifies יִנָּצְלוּ. The whole sentence therefore means that "those who dwell" (הַיֹּשְׁבִים) "in" (בְּ) Samaria will be "rescued/snatched away" (יִנָּצְלוּ) "with" (בְּ) pieces of a bed. That is, they will be refugees and the only possessions they will be able to retrieve from the ruins of their city will be parts of their beds (Paul 1991, 120). This interpretation is reflected in a number of versions, such as the ESV, which has, "so shall the people of Israel who dwell in Samaria be rescued, with the corner of a couch and part of a bed." This misunderstands the text on several levels.

First, it assumes that the main point of the verse is that some Israelites will "be rescued" from slaughter and survive as refugees. To the contrary, as argued above, the point of the analogy is not the survival of some but the utter destruction of the nation.

Second, it implies that the pieces of furniture are snatched away in a manner analogous to the snatching away of the pieces of the slain lamb. To the contrary, the analogy is not between the legs and ear of the lamb and the pieces of Israelite furniture, it is between the lamb itself and the whole population, the בְּנֵי יִשְׂרָאֵל. Again, it does not assert that some refugees will get away alive but the nation as a whole will be killed.

Third, it is true that ישב with בְּ normally means to reside or sit "at" a location rather than "on" an object. However, the use of בְּ in בִּפְאַת מִטָּה and in וּבִדְמֶשֶׁק עָרֶשׂ may be by attraction to the use of בְּ in בְּשֹׁמְרוֹן. More importantly, we really have little idea what the nouns פֵּאָה and דְּמֶשֶׁק in this context mean and we are thus in no position to assert that the expression ישב בִּפְאַת מִטָּה וּבִדְמֶשֶׁק עָרֶשׂ is impossible. פֵּאָה normally means "corner" or "edge," and that may be its meaning here (Paul [1991, 121] suggests that it is the "head of the bed," like a headboard, but that is speculative). דְּמֶשֶׁק has been taken to mean something like "sheets" or a "footstool" in this context (see *HALOT* דְּמֶשֶׁק; Paul [1991, 121–22] argues that it is the "foot" of a bed, but this is also speculative). The important point is that בְּ with ישב can still be locative but need not mean to sit "on" a couch or bed. It could mean to sit "at" the corner of a bed and "with" a footstool of a couch.

Fourth, the absurdity of this interpretation speaks against it (cf. Hammershaimb 1970, 62). We are asked to suppose that refugees fleeing their city as it goes up in flames before an invading enemy would, of all things, grab a headboard or some other part of a bed as the one item they snatch from the flames. This is far-fetched. People in such a situation might grab their children, gold, or jewels, but would not burden themselves with broken pieces of furniture.

Fifth, Amos 6:4-7 indicates that Israelites lounging on couches and beds is exactly what the prophet has in mind.

3:13-15: Third Poem: This two-strophe poem (one stanza) pronounces the divine judgment on Israel. The first strophe in two lines is a call to listen, and the second in eight lines gives the details of the judgment.

3:13: First Strophe. Two lines. Line 1a is unusual in Amos for having two predicators, and line 1b is an unusually fulsome formula of divine speech. This is therefore an exaggerated call to listen; its extravagance is accounted for by the fact that it introduces a major judgment speech in the following strophe.

3:13 1a שִׁמְעוּ וְהָעִידוּ בְּבֵית יַעֲקֹב
1b נְאֻם־אֲדֹנָי יְהוִה אֱלֹהֵי הַצְּבָאוֹת׃

Line 1a: The colon-marker is *athnach* and the constraints are: 2 predicators, 3 constituents, and 4 units (3 units if בֵּית יַעֲקֹב is regarded as a proper name).

שִׁמְעוּ. Qal imperative m p of שׁמע. The addressees are the jury imagined to be gathered from Egypt and Ashdod.

וְהָעִידוּ. Hiphil imperative m p of עוד. The verb can mean either to give testimony or to admonish; the pagan jury is called to inform Samaria that the charges that YHWH brings against the city are just.

בְּבֵית יַעֲקֹב. Prepositional phrase with בְּ, which is here adversative ("against"), on a construct chain.

Line 1b: The colon-marker is *silluq* and the constraints are: 0 predicators, 1 constituent, and 5 units.

נְאֻם־אֲדֹנָי יְהוִה אֱלֹהֵי הַצְּבָאוֹת. YHWH is here described as the sovereign (אֲדֹנָי serves as a title) and as God of the heavenly assembly (אֱלֹהֵי הַצְּבָאוֹת is in apposition to יהוה).

3:14-15: Second Strophe. Eight lines. A judgment speech, describing the punishment due to Israel, it is modeled on the judgment speeches against Damascus (1:4-5), Gaza (1:7-8), Ammon (1:14-15) and Moab (2:2-3). After line 2a, which introduces the judgments, like those oracles it has seven lines, is dominated by the *weqatal* verb, and ends in a divine speech formula. Structurally, this strophe is in three parts: a protasis (line 2a), an apodosis (lines 2b-g), and the divine speech formula (line 2h). Amos gives three lines to the punishment upon the shrines (2b-d) and three lines to punishment upon the luxurious houses of the rich (2e-g). In this, he neatly summarizes the two main objects of God's wrath: a religious zeal without true fear of God and the arrogant, oppressive behavior of the wealthy.

3:14 2a כִּ֗י בְּי֛וֹם פָּקְדִ֥י פִשְׁעֵֽי־יִשְׂרָאֵ֖ל עָלָ֑יו
2b וּפָקַדְתִּי֙ עַל־מִזְבְּח֣וֹת בֵּֽית־אֵ֔ל
2c וְנִגְדְּעוּ֙ קַרְנ֣וֹת הַמִּזְבֵּ֔חַ
2d וְנָפְל֖וּ לָאָֽרֶץ׃
3:15 2e וְהִכֵּיתִ֥י בֵֽית־הַחֹ֖רֶף עַל־בֵּ֣ית הַקָּ֑יִץ
2f וְאָבְד֞וּ בָּתֵּ֣י הַשֵּׁ֗ן
2g וְסָפ֛וּ בָּתִּ֥ים רַבִּ֖ים
2h נְאֻם־יְהוָֽה׃ ס

Line 2a: The colon-marker is *athnach* and the constraints are: 1 predicator, 3 constituents, and 5 units.

כִּ֗י בְּי֛וֹם פָּקְדִ֥י. The subordinating particle כִּי followed by the temporal prepositional phrase בְּיוֹם attached to the Qal infinitive construct of פקד with a 1 c s suffix. This creates a temporal clause which is the protasis for lines 2b-g.

פִּשְׁעֵי־יִשְׂרָאֵל. A construct chain, the direct object of the verb.

עָלָיו. Prepositional phrase with עַל and a 3 m s suffix. The idiom "to visit (פקד) X upon (עַל) Y" means to "punish Y for X."

Line 2b: The colon-marker is *zaqeph qaton* and the constraints are: 1 predicator, 2 constituents, and 3 units.

וּפָקַדְתִּי. Qal *weqatal* 1 c s of פקד. The *weqatal* is both marking an apodosis and indicating future events.

עַל־מִזְבְּחוֹת בֵּית־אֵל. Prepositional phrase with עַל on a construct chain. The altars are synecdoche for the shrine of Bethel, and the point is that the shrine will come under especially severe punishment.

Line 2c: The colon-marker is *zaqeph qaton* and the constraints are: 1 predicator, 2 constituents, and 3 units.

וְנִגְדְּעוּ. Niphal *weqatal* 3 c p of גדע. The verb means to "chop off."

קַרְנוֹת הַמִּזְבֵּחַ. The direct object. It is a construct chain, "the horns of the altar." The horns were the locus of the altar's holiness; they were where the blood of atonement was smeared. Also, a refugee would seek sanctuary by clinging to the horns of an altar. The point is that sacredness of the location would be destroyed.

Line 2d: The colon-marker is *silluq* and the constraints are: 1 predicator, 2 constituents, and 2 units.

וְנָפְלוּ. Qal *weqatal* 3 c p of נפל. The subject is קַרְנוֹת הַמִּזְבֵּחַ in the previous line.

לָאָרֶץ. Prepositional phrase with לְ indicating direction. The image of the horns of the altar falling into the dirt bespeaks the profanation of the site.

Line 2e: The colon-marker is *athnach* and the constraints are: 1 predicator, 3 constituents, and 5 units. Here, Amos turns from the destruction of holy sites to the destruction of places that display the wealth of the upper classes, their homes.

וְהִכֵּיתִ֥י. Hiphil *weqatal* 1 c s of נכה.

בֵּית־הַחֹ֖רֶף. The direct object; a construct chain.

עַל־בֵּ֣ית הַקָּ֑יִץ. Prepositional phrase with עַל, which here introduces a second direct object and means "in addition to" (see *HALOT* definition 6b, c, d). The existence of both summer and winter homes for very wealthy people is documented in the Bible (Jer 36:22) and elsewhere (Paul 1991, 125–26).

Line 2f: The colon-marker is *revia* and the constraints are: 1 predicator, 2 constituents, and 3 units.

וְאָבְד֞וּ. Qal *weqatal* 3 c p of אבד. The verb here means to be "lost" or "ruined."

בָּתֵּ֣י הַשֵּׁ֗ן. Another direct object construct chain. The phrase of course does not mean that the houses were constructed of ivory but that they were amply decorated with ivory pieces of art. Many examples of such pieces have survived from Samaria itself (most of it from the ninth century B.C.), but other pieces have been found from late bronze Megiddo and from a stash of ivory works (some apparently taken from Israel) from Assyrian Nimrud.

Line 2g: The colon-marker is *tifha* and the constraints are: 1 predicator, 2 constituents, and 3 units.

וְסָ֛פוּ. Qal *weqatal* 3 c p of ספה. The third plural form here, although it implies that some unnamed people will sweep away these houses, is really used impersonally and can be translated as a passive.

בָּתִּ֥ים רַבִּ֖ים. The direct object with an adjective. This can be translated as the subject of a passive verb.

Line 2h: The colon-marker is *silluq* and the constraints are: 0 predicators, 1 constituents, and 2 units.

נְאֻם־יְהוָֽה. The divine speech formula.

4:1-13: Cruelty and Hollow Religion I

This division is the first of two large indictments against Israel (4:1-13; 5:1–6:14) that focus on the oppressive cruelty and hollow religion of the people and especially of its leaders. Amos 4:1-13 is itself in two major sections, and each of these are in two parts. The first section, 4:1–5, is a poetic oracle against the women of Samaria (4:1-3), to which an ironic benediction is added (4:4-5). The second section, 4:6-13, is a prose recitation of YHWH's futile attempts to bring Israel repentance (4:6-12), to which a doxology is added (4:13). The religious language of vv. 4-5 and 13 binds this division together and makes the point that Israel's sin is fundamentally theological. They wrongly assume that an active religious life is sufficient to appease God, and they fail to comprehend the significance of the divine majesty and thus what an encounter with actually God entails.

> [1]*Hear this word,*
> *Cows of Bashan who are on the hill of Samaria,*
> *Who oppress the poor,*
> *Who crush the impoverished,*
> *Who say to their lords,*
> *"Bring us something to drink!"*
>
> [2]*Lord YHWH has sworn by his holiness:*
> *Behold, days are coming upon you*
> *When you people shall be hoisted up with (meat) hooks,*
> *And the rest of you women (shall be hoisted up) with hooks.*
>
> [3]*And you shall go out by the breaches one after another,*
> *And you shall be cast on the dunghill. <emended text>*
> *The oracle of YHWH.*
>
> [4]*Go to Bethel in order to transgress!*
> *At (go) to Gilgal in order to multiply transgression!*
> *And offer your morning sacrifices*
> *and your three-day tithes!*
> [5]*Send up a leavened thanksgiving offering in smoke!*

And proclaim (your) freewill offerings! Make them heard!
For that is what you love to do, sons of Israel.
An oracle of Lord YHWH.

6And even though I gave you cleanness of teeth in all your cities and a lack of food in all your locales, yet you have not returned to me. The oracle of YHWH.

7And even though I withheld the rain from you while it was still three months until the harvest—although I would send rain on a given city, but on another city I would not send rain; a certain field would get rain,
but a field on which it did not rain would dry up. 8And two or three cities
would wander to one city to drink water but were not satisfied. Yet you have not returned to me. The oracle of YHWH.

9I struck you with blight and rust in abundance; locusts have been eating your gardens, your vineyards, your fig trees and your olive trees. Yet you have not returned to me. The oracle of YHWH.

10I sent against you plagues of the Egyptian sort. I slew your young men by the sword as your horses were captured, and I raised up the stench of your army, and that right in your nose! Yet you have not returned to me. The oracle of YHWH.

11I overturned some of you in the way God overturned Sodom and Gomorrah, and you were like a burning stick snatched from a fire. Yet you have not returned to me. The oracle of YHWH.

12Therefore, I will continue to do the same to you, Israel! Because I will
do this to you, prepare to meet your God, Israel! 13For consider:

He fashions mountains and creates the wind!
And he declares to humans what is his grievance!
He makes dawn into darkness,
And treads upon the high places of earth!
His name is YHWH God of Sabaoth!

4:1-5: The Women of Samaria and an Ironic Benediction

This poem is in two stanzas. The first stanza has two strophes (4:1 and 4:2-3), and the second, the ironic blessing, has one (4:4-5).

4:1-3: First Stanza. This follows the normal pattern of accusation and judgment set in chapters 1–2. Here, the women of Samaria are accused in the first strophe (4:1), and their judgment is pronounced in the second (4:2-3). The judgment strophe, like those against Damascus, Gaza, Ammon, and Moab, is in seven lines.

4:1: First Strophe. Six lines. After the initial call to hear (A1a), the addressees are named (A1b) and described in four relative clauses. The first relative clause (A1b) is introduced by אֲשֶׁר and the other three (A1c-e) are participles. This strophe is similar to the accusations against the nations except that these accusations are not governed by עַל. There is chiastic assonance between A1a and A1b with שִׁמְעוּ הַדָּבָר and בְּהַר שֹׁמְרוֹן. All three lines in A1c-e begin with qal active participles, and the strophe begins and ends with lines headed by imperatives.

4:1 A1a שִׁמְע֞וּ הַדָּבָ֣ר הַזֶּ֗ה
A1b פָּר֤וֹת הַבָּשָׁן֙ אֲשֶׁ֙ר בְּהַ֣ר שֹׁמְר֔וֹן
A1c הָעֹשְׁק֣וֹת דַּלִּ֔ים
A1d הָרֹצְצ֖וֹת אֶבְיוֹנִ֑ים
A1e הָאֹמְרֹ֥ת לַאֲדֹנֵיהֶ֖ם
A1f הָבִ֥יאָה וְנִשְׁתֶּֽה׃

Line A1a: The colon-marker is *revia* and the constraints are: 1 predicator, 2 constituents, and 3 units.

שִׁמְע֞וּ. Qal imperative m p of שׁמע.

הַדָּבָ֣ר הַזֶּ֗ה. The direct object, a definite noun with demonstrative pronoun.

Line A1b: The colon-marker is *zaqeph qaton* and the constraints are: 1 predicator, 3 constituents, and 5 units. The line contains a vocative (the predicator) and a modifying relative clause.

פָּרוֹת הַבָּשָׁן. A construct chain vocative; Hebrew vocatives are generally definite, as is the case here (*GKC* §126e). Bashan was the area to the north of the Yarmuk River, east and northeast of the Sea of Galilee; the name always has the definite article in Hebrew. It had lush pastureland and thus famously raised healthy cattle and sheep (Deut 32:14; Ezek 39:18). The epithet "cows of Bashan" here refers to the upper-class women of Samaria who, like those cows, live among great abundance. But the term is not necessarily derisive of itself. Ancient poets regularly employed pastoral imagery to refer to beautiful women, as Song 4:1 does in describing a woman's hair as like a flock of goats. In Greek texts, a regular epithet for Hera is the "cow-eyed (βοῶπις) goddess."

אֲשֶׁר. Relative pronoun; the antecedent is פָּרוֹת.

בְּהַר שֹׁמְרוֹן. Prepositional phrase with בְּ used as a locative. The women called "cows of Bashan" are not actually from Bashan; they are from Samaria.

Line A1c: The colon-marker is *zaqeph qaton* and the constraints are: 1 predicator, 2 constituents, and 2 units. The participle serves as a relative clause and as predicator.

הָעֹשְׁקוֹת. Qal active participle f p of עשׁק with the definite article. The verb means to "oppress" or financially "exploit." Its meaning is well-illustrated by the apologia of Samuel in 1 Samuel 12:3: "Whose ox have I taken? Or whose donkey have I taken? Or whom have I exploited? (וְאֶת־מִי עָשַׁקְתִּי)."

דַּלִּים. The direct object of the preceding participle.

Line A1d: The colon-marker is *athnach* and the constraints are: 1 predicator, 2 constituents, and 2 units. The participle serves as a relative clause and as predicator.

הָרֹצְצוֹת. Qal active participle f p of רצץ with the definite article. רצץ means to "mistreat" or, in the Piel, to "strike down," but the verbs עשׁק and רצץ regularly appear together as a kind of hendiadys (see Deut 28:33; Hos 5:11). In 1 Samuel 12:3, after asking וְאֶת־מִי

עָשַׁקְתִּי, Samuel asks, "Whom have I mistreated? (אֶת־מִי רַצּוֹתִי)."

אֶבְיוֹנִים. The direct object of the preceding participle.

Line A1d: The colon-marker is *tifha* and the constraints are: 1 predicator, 2 constituents, and 2 units. Lines A1d and A1e should not be joined as a single line, since that would create a line of three predicators and a noun. As a rule, a line with three predicators will have nothing else.

הָאֹמְרֹת. Qal active participle f p of אמר with the definite article.

לַאֲדֹנֵיהֶם. The indirect object; the noun אָדוֹן with the 3 m p suffix and the preposition לְ. Because of the masculine suffix, one might argue that the "cows of Bashan" are actually men and that Amos is not specifically attacking the women of Samaria. But Hebrew is not consistent about using the feminine plural pronominal suffixes for feminine antecedents (cf. Ruth 1:8). The noun אָדוֹן here must mean "husband" (as in Gen 18:12), because no other interpretation makes sense. The "cows of Bashan" are therefore women. The noun אָדוֹן is here used for "husband" instead of the more common אִישׁ or בַּעַל as an ironic counterpoint to the title אֲדֹנָי, which is applied to YHWH in line A2a in the next strophe. The Samarian women arrogantly treat their "lords" as household slaves and command them to bring drinks, but "Lord YHWH" has sworn to bring destruction upon them.

Line A1e: The colon-marker is *silluq* and the constraints are: 2 predicators, 2 constituents, and 2 units.

הָבִיאָה. Hiphil imperative m s of בוא with paragogic ה.

וְנִשְׁתֶּה. Qal *weyiqtol* 1 c p of שתה. The *weyiqtol* here implies purpose, "so that we may drink."

4:2-3: Second Strophe. Like the judgment strophe on Damascus (1:3-5) and others, it has seven lines and employs *weqatal* verbs to describe a coming punishment.

4:2 A2a נִשְׁבַּ֨ע אֲדֹנָ֤י יְהוִה֙ בְּקָדְשׁ֔וֹ
A2b כִּ֛י הִנֵּ֥ה יָמִ֖ים בָּאִ֣ים עֲלֵיכֶ֑ם
A2c וְנִשָּׂ֤א אֶתְכֶם֙ בְּצִנּ֔וֹת
A2d וְאַחֲרִיתְכֶ֖ן בְּסִיר֥וֹת דּוּגָֽה׃
4:3 A2e וּפְרָצִ֥ים תֵּצֶ֖אנָה אִשָּׁ֣ה נֶגְדָּ֑הּ
A2f וְהִשְׁלַכְתֶּ֥נָה הַהַרְמ֖וֹנָה
A2g נְאֻם־יְהוָֽה׃

Line A2a: The colon-marker is *zaqeph qaton* and the constraints are: 1 predicator, 3 constituents, and 4 units.

נִשְׁבַּ֨ע. Niphal *qatal* 3 m s of שׁבע.

אֲדֹנָ֤י יְהוִה֙. The subject.

בְּקָדְשׁ֔וֹ. Prepositional phrase with בְּ, here used in an oath formula to signify that by which the oath is taken. קָדוֹשׁ here has the 3 m s suffix and is probably both representative of God's character as the basis for his oath and also metonymy for his whole being; that is, God swears by himself, the supremely holy being.

Line A2b: The colon-marker is *athnach* and the constraints are: 1 predicator, 4 constituents, and 4 units.

כִּ֛י הִנֵּ֥ה. The particle כִּי here indicates the content of the oath and הִנֵּה indicates that a divine decree is being given, as in Genesis 1:29.

יָמִ֖ים. The subject.

בָּאִ֣ים. Qal active participle m p of בּוֹא and the predicate of יָמִים.

עֲלֵיכֶ֑ם. Prepositional phrase with עַל ("against") and a 2 m p suffix.

Line A2c: The colon-marker is *zaqeph qaton* and the constraints are: 1 predicator, 3 constituents, and 3 units.

וְנִשָּׂא. Piel *weqatal* 3 m s of נשׂא. The form is used impersonally and is here virtually passive in meaning. The *weqatal* is the apodosis to the previous line. Through gapping, the verb governs line A2d as well. The piel literally means to "raise up" (2 Sam 5:12). It usually has a positive meaning, to "support" or "supply," as in 1 Kings 9:11; Isaiah 63:9; Esther 5:11; Ezra 1:4. Here, however, the literal meaning of "raise up" is more probable.

אֶתְכֶם. The direct object. The masculine pronoun here as well as in line A2b may imply that the judgment described here pertains to all the people and not to the women alone.

בְּצִנּוֹת. Prepositional phrase with instrumental בְּ. The interpretation of צֵן here is much debated; see the discussion of סִירָה in the next line.

Line A2d: The colon-marker is *silluq* and the constraints are: 0 predicators, 2 constituents, and 3 units. There is gapping, with this line governed by וְנִשָּׂא in A2c.

וְאַחֲרִיתְכֶן. The noun אַחֲרִית (here with 2 f p suffix) means "end." From that, it can mean "destiny" or "fate," or conversely, the "remainder" of a previously larger group. With a suffix, it often means "fate," as in Numbers 20:25, וְאַחֲרִיתוֹ עֲדֵי אֹבֵד ("and his fate [moves] toward ruin"). Similar usage appears in Deuteronomy 32:20, 29; Isaiah 41:22; Jeremiah 5:31; 12:4; Psalm 73:17; etc. If that were the sense here, the line would mean, "Your fate will be in סִירוֹת דּוּגָה," but that is unlikely. The suffixed form of אַחֲרִית is used also for describing the slaughtering of what is left of a people (Ezek 23:25 and Amos 9:1). In Proverbs it often refers to the final outcome of an action or way of life (Prov 5:4, 11; 14:12, 13; 16:25; etc.). The usage in Amos 8:10 (וְאַחֲרִיתָהּ) is similar to the usage in Proverbs, where the "outcome" of the Israelite feasting will be a bitter day. Here in Amos 4:2, it could refer to the back sides of the metaphorical cows (as suggested in *HALOT*, "אַחֲרִית"), but one would expect to see אַחַר if that were the meaning. Within Amos, the closest analogy to the usage here is in

9:1, where God kills "the rest of them" (וְאַחֲרִיתָם) with a sword. This is probably the meaning here.

בְּסִירוֹת דּוּגָה. Prepositional phrase with instrumental בְּ on a construct chain. The phrase is commonly translated as "with fish-hooks," but it is not clear that fishhooks were widely used in eighth century B.C. Israel or Mesopotamia (fishing was commonly done at this time with nets or gigs). We do not know what a סִירַת דּוּגָה is or how it got its name. Although דּוּגָה possibly is related to the word דָּג, "fish," this does not mean that סִירוֹת דּוּגָה are tools used in fishing, whether it be fishhooks, fishing poles, or fish baskets, all of which have been suggested. In the terminology of a trade, a thing may be named for some superficial reason, such as its appearance, and not literally according to function. By analogy, if a truck driver says that he began to "fishtail," he is not describing anything that has to do with literal fish or fishing. An enormous range of interpretations has been applied to the words צִנּוֹת and סִירוֹת דּוּגָה in A2c and A2d (see Paul 1978 and Paul 1991, 130–35). Briefly, they are as follows:

Interpretation 1: Shields, or alternatively boats, on which the women are carried away. The Aramaic Targum has this interpretation (see Cathcart and Gordon 1989, 82). This is lexicographically and historically unlikely.

Interpretation 2: Pots or baskets in which fish are carried to market (סִיר can mean a "pot" for cooking). This may represent either taking the women into captivity (Paul 1991, 134) or carting off the dead bodies like fish in baskets after a slaughter (Hayes 1988, 140–41). Neither is persuasive because the change in metaphor is too abrupt. Up to this point, the women are metaphorically cattle; nothing has prepared the reader for thinking of them as fish. To suddenly introduce this image without telling the reader that the women are like caught fish is a poetic non-sequitur, and the reader is left with a bewildering picture of women (or cattle!) being carried in pots and fish-baskets.

Interpretation 3: צִנּוֹת has been interpreted as "ropes," but this is linguistically implausible (Paul 1991, 131).

Interpretation 4: Thorns, probably here meaning hooks, and fishhooks (סִירוֹת דּוּגָה), which are hooked into the women to pull them along. This is a common interpretation (e.g., Markert 1977, 106; Hammershaimb 1970, 66; de Waard and Smalley 1979, 79). Perhaps the women are literally to be pulled into exile with fishhooks, or perhaps they are metaphorical cattle being pulled with fishhooks, Whatever the case, this interpretation has significant problems. First, it is unlikely that the piel of נשׂא ("raise high, carry aloft") would be used for pulling cattle (or people). Second, as mentioned above, use of fishhooks appears to have been little practiced in the Levant at this time (see Paul 1991, 132–33). Third, if the women are still thought of as metaphorical cattle, it would be dangerous to both owner and beast, and very strange, to try to pull cattle with fishhooks. 2 Kings 19:28 does speak of leading away Assyria with what is often translated as "hooks," but the word there (חָח) is more properly taken to be the nose-rings, such as are used with cattle, rather than as "hooks" (cf. Exod 35:22). חָח is never used in parallel with either צִנּוֹת or סִירוֹת דּוּגָה. It is not impossible that the text represents the women as being led into captivity like cattle with rings through their noses (thus Kleven 1996), but linguistic support for this interpretation is weak, and the verb נשׂא seems to rule it out.

Interpretation 5: The words צִנּוֹת and סִירוֹת דּוּגָה may refer to fishhooks, and the women are conceived of as fish caught with hooks. If so, it is again an abrupt and unannounced change of metaphor from cattle to fish. And again, it may be anachronistic to take this as a metaphor of angling.

Interpretation 6: It is possible that צִנּוֹת and סִירוֹת דּוּגָה are technical terms used by shepherds and ranchers for tools of their trade. If so, then צִנּוֹת and סִירוֹת דּוּגָה are perhaps some kind of prods for driving cattle. On the basis of Proverbs 22:5, it appears that צֵן refers to some kind of spiked object (in that text the noun is masculine and may be either briars or a kind of spiked trap). Here, it may be barbed prods. The main problem with this interpretation is that the piel of נשׂא is an odd verb to use for driving cattle (although of course there could have been an idiomatic usage of נשׂא among cattlemen).

Interpretation 7: It is possible that "hooks" is the meaning of צִנּוֹת and סִירוֹת דּוּגָה if the metaphor is one of butchered cattle, with the meat hanging on hooks (cf. Stuart 1987, 327). This requires taking אֶתְכֶם and וְאַחֲרִיתְכֶן to refer the meat of slaughtered, metaphorical cattle. Given the limitations of our knowledge, interpretation 7 may be the best. The Assyrian practice of actually impaling people on hooks gives some credibility to this view.

Line A2e: The colon-marker is *athnach* and the constraints are: 1 predicator, 4 constituents, and 4 units.

וּפְרָצִים. A preposition בְּ is implied. Thus, it means "(by the) breaches" (that are in the walls) after the city has fallen. Hayes (1988, 141) takes פֶּרֶץ here to refer to bloated corpses that are carried out of the city. His evidence for this interpretation is weak, however, and the verb תֵּצֶאנָה would seem to refer to people who leave under their own power.

תֵּצֶאנָה. Qal *yiqtol* 2 f p of יצא.

אִשָּׁה. The noun is here used distributively to mean "each."

נֶגְדָּהּ. Prepositional phrase with נֶגֶד and a 3 f s suffix. Literally, "each woman before her," it here means, "one behind the other," as in Joshua 6:20.

Line A2f: The colon-marker is *tifha* and the constraints are: 1 predicator, 2 constituents, and 2 units.

וְהִשְׁלַכְתֶּנָה. Hiphil *weqatal* 2 f p of שׁלך with paragogic ה. A paragogic ה on a *weqatal* is odd and may be a scribal error—perhaps dittography from the following word. The hiphil, to "throw," is difficult to make sense of here. On the basis of the LXX (ἀπορριφήσεσθε), one might emend to the hophal וְהָשְׁלַכְתֶּן, "and you shall be thrown."

הַהַרְמוֹנָה. The meaning of this word is entirely lost to us, although it possibly ends with a directive ה. It may be a proper name ("to Harmon," or if repointed to read, "to Hermon," it could refer to the mountain northeast of Dan and refer generally to an exile to the north [Wolff 1977, 207; see also Williams 1979]). It may be a proper name with הַר (such as “to the mountain of Remman” [LXX: εἰς τὸ ὄρος τὸ Ρεμμαν], perhaps referring to Armenia?). Or it may be a common noun (such as “to the citadel” [emending to אַרְמוֹן] or “to the dung” [emending to דֹּמֶן]. It may be that the unemended line is another idiom from the vocabulary of the shepherd and rancher. All of these interpretations are highly speculative. Amos does, however, tend to repeat himself a good deal, and at 8:3 השליך clearly refers to dead bodies being cast away. Thus, one may suggest that the emendation to דֹּמֶן is the best we can do.

Line A2g: The colon-marker is *silluq* and the constraints are: 0 predicators, 1 constituent, and 2 units.

נְאֻם־יְהוָה. A construct chain divine speech formula.

4:4-5: Second Stanza. This stanza (one strophe) is an ironic pilgrimage benediction in eight lines (cf. Dell 1995, 55–56). It is appended to the oracle against the women of Samaria as a parallel to the doxology of 4:13, which is appended to a prose recitation. This ironic benediction does not directly relate to the women of Samaria or to their sin, except for the fact that all the people of Samaria are guilty of supposing that an active religious life, here characterized by regular pilgrimages, vindicates their lives. It may be, however, that the upper class women were especially zealous about making these pilgrimages. A more positive illustration of the ideal of the pilgrimage for the Israelite woman is found in the religious life of Hannah, mother of Samuel (1 Sam 1).

בֹּאוּ בֵית־אֵל֙ וּפִשְׁע֔וּ Ba 4:4
הַגִּלְגָּ֖ל הַרְבּ֣וּ לִפְשֹׁ֑עַ Bb
וְהָבִ֤יאוּ לַבֹּ֙קֶר֙ זִבְחֵיכֶ֔ם Bc
לִשְׁלֹ֥שֶׁת יָמִ֖ים מַעְשְׂרֹתֵיכֶֽם׃ Bd
וְקַטֵּ֤ר מֵחָמֵץ֙ תּוֹדָ֔ה Be 4:5

וְקִרְאוּ נְדָבוֹת הַשְׁמִיעוּ Bf
כִּי כֵן אֲהַבְתֶּם בְּנֵי יִשְׂרָאֵל Bg
נְאֻם אֲדֹנָי יְהוִה׃ Bh

Line Ba: The colon-marker is *zaqeph qaton* and the constraints are: 2 predicators, 3 constituents, and 3 units. When there are two imperatives in a line, and the second has the conjunction, the second imperative often to some degree connotes purpose.

בֹּאוּ. Qal imperative m p of בּוֹא.

בֵית־אֵל. A proper name, "Bethel." A directional particle, such as the preposition אֶל or the directional ה, is often omitted in poetry.

וּפִשְׁעוּ. Qal imperative m p of פשׁע with conjunction.

Line Bb: The colon-marker is *athnach* and the constraints are: 1 predicator, 2 constituents, and 3 units. There is gapping of בֹּאוּ from line Ba.

הַגִּלְגָּל. A proper name, "Gilgal," with definite article. Gilgal is usually but no always written with the article. A locative marker, such as the preposition בְּ or the directional ה, is again omitted but implied.

הַרְבּוּ לִפְשֹׁעַ. Hiphil imperative m p of רבה with qal infinitive construct of פשׁע (with לְ) as an auxiliary. Literally, "Make abundant to sin," this must be rendered with something like, "Sin abundantly!" It is obviously sarcasm.

Line Bc: The colon-marker is *zaqeph qaton* and the constraints are: 1 predicator, 3 constituents, and 3 units.

וְהָבִיאוּ. Hiphil imperative m p of בּוֹא, here used for the bringing of a sacrifice, with conjunction.

לַבֹּקֶר. Prepositional phrase with לְ used for reference, as "for the morning."

זִבְחֵיכֶם. The direct object with a 2 m p suffix. With לַבֹּקֶר, this means, "your morning sacrifices." A זֶבַח is a blood-sacrifice (an animal offering rather than a grain offering).

Line Bd: The colon-marker is *silluq* and the constraints are: 0 predicators, 2 constituents, and 3 units. There is gapping of וְהָבִיאוּ from the previous line.

לִשְׁלֹשֶׁת יָמִים. In parallel with לַבֹּקֶר in line Bc, this is a referential use of the preposition לְ meaning "for a three-day period" or "after three days."

מַעְשְׂרֹתֵיכֶם. The direct object with a 2 m p suffix. In parallel with line Bc and with לִשְׁלֹשֶׁת יָמִים, this must mean, "your three-day tithes." Perhaps pilgrims were expected to make a tithe gift on the third day (two days after their arrival at a shrine). We have no evidence elsewhere for such a practice, but our knowledge of cultic worship at these shrines is very sparse. There is a provision for a three-year tithe in Deuternomy 14:28, but this is probably not meant here.

Line Be: The colon-marker is *zaqeph qaton* and the constraints are: 1 predicator, 3 constituents, and 3 units.

וְקַטֵּר. Piel imperative m p with conjunction. The verb means to send an offering up in smoke, whether it is the burning of incense or of some other offering.

מֵחָמֵץ. Prepositional phrase with מִן used partitively. An offering with leavened bread was forbidden in Torah for certain sacrifices, but it could be offered with the thank offering (Lev 7:12). Elsewhere in this text, Amos is attacking faith in the automatic efficacy of pilgrimages to the shrines rather than illicit practices at the shrines, so it is doubtful that here he is asserting that the offerings are unlawful.

תּוֹדָה. The direct object. The thank offering of Leviticus 7:12 is called הַתּוֹדָה.

Line Bf: The colon-marker is *athnach* and the constraints are: 2 predicators, 3 constituents, and 3 units.

וְקִרְאוּ. Qal imperative m p of קרא with conjunction.

נְדָבוֹת. The direct object. The freewill offerings would be proclaimed aloud because they were given in fulfillment of vows.

הַשְׁמִיעוּ. Hiphil imperative m p of שׁמע. The asyndeton with this second, redundant imperative gives it the sense of ironic encouragement.

Line Bg: The colon-marker is *zaqeph qaton* and the constraints are: 2 predicators (including the vocative), 2 constituents, and 2 units.

כִּי כֵן אֲהַבְתֶּם. Qal *qatal* 2 m p with the particles כִּי (used in an explanatory sense) and כֵּן (used adverbially, "that is how").

בְּנֵי יִשְׂרָאֵל. A construct chain vocative.

Line Bh: The colon-marker is *silluq* and the constraints are: 0 predicators, 1 constituent, and 3 units.

נְאֻם אֲדֹנָי יְהוִה. A divine speech formula.

4:6-13: Blindness to YHWH's Warnings and a Doxology of Dread

This section, like the previous, is in two parts except that the first part (vv. 6-12) is prose. Just as 4:4-5 is an ironic benediction on the pilgrims to the shrines, so also v. 13 is ironic in that it is a doxology but it prompts only terror and not joy or worship. In addition, the constant complaint of this text, that the Israelites have not returned to YHWH, is set against the sarcastic encouragement to go to the shrines.

4:6-12: Unheeded Warnings: This is a lengthy prose text in which YHWH details his vain efforts to bring Israel to repentance by means of various afflictions. Behind this passage stand the warnings of Deuteronomy 28:15-68, which tell the Israelites that if they refuse to obey the laws of the covenant, they will be beset with disease, drought, crop failure, and military defeat in increasing severity. Although some clauses could be scanned as poetry, other clauses are too long and the grammar of the sentences is too complex to analyze this text convincingly as a poem.

4:6 וְגַם־אֲנִי נָתַתִּי לָכֶם נִקְיוֹן שִׁנַּיִם בְּכָל־עָרֵיכֶם וְחֹסֶר
לֶחֶם בְּכֹל מְקוֹמֹתֵיכֶם וְלֹא־שַׁבְתֶּם עָדַי נְאֻם־יְהוָה׃

This verse is a sentence of three clauses, the first being a concessive protasis and the second being the apodosis. The third clause is the divine speech formula.

Prose Clause: וְגַם־אֲנִי֩ נָתַ֨תִּי לָכֶ֜ם נִקְי֤וֹן שִׁנַּ֙יִם֙ בְּכָל־עָ֣רֵיכֶ֔ם וְחֹ֣סֶר לֶ֔חֶם בְּכֹ֖ל מְקוֹמֹתֵיכֶ֑ם

A concessive clause (introduced by וְגַם) serving as a protasis, it has a transitive verb (נָתַתִּי, a qal *qatal* 1 c s of נתן) and two conjoined and parallel construct chain direct objects (נִקְיוֹן שִׁנַּיִם ["cleanness of teeth"] and וְחֹסֶר לֶחֶם ["and lack of bread"]). Each direct object has a phrase with locative בְּ appended to it (בְּכָל־עָרֵיכֶם and בְּכֹל מְקוֹמֹתֵיכֶם). Parallelism is a feature of rhetoric; it is not unique to poetry. "Cleanness of teeth" (נִקְיוֹן שִׁנַּיִם) obviously refers to a food shortage.

Prose Clause: וְלֹֽא־שַׁבְתֶּ֥ם עָדַ֖י

The conjunction on וְלֹא marks the apodosis. שַׁבְתֶּם is a qal *qatal* 2 m p of שׁוּב, which signifies repentance when used of persons "returning" to God. The *qatal* could be translated with a past tense or a perfect or even present tense.

Prose Clause: נְאֻם־יְהוָֽה

A divine speech formula.

4:7 וְגַ֣ם אָנֹכִי֩ מָנַ֨עְתִּי מִכֶּ֜ם אֶת־הַגֶּ֗שֶׁם בְּעוֹד֩ שְׁלֹשָׁ֤ה
חֳדָשִׁים֙ לַקָּצִ֔יר וְהִמְטַרְתִּי֙ עַל־עִ֣יר אֶחָ֔ת וְעַל־עִ֥יר
אַחַ֖ת לֹ֣א אַמְטִ֑יר חֶלְקָ֤ה אַחַת֙ תִּמָּטֵ֔ר וְחֶלְקָ֛ה
אֲשֶׁר־לֹֽא־תַמְטִ֥יר עָלֶ֖יהָ תִּיבָֽשׁ׃

This verse is a series of six clauses, all of which are part of a concessive protasis to the apodosis at the end of 4:8.

Prose Clause: וְגַ֣ם אָנֹכִי֩ מָנַ֨עְתִּי מִכֶּ֜ם אֶת־הַגֶּ֗שֶׁם בְּעוֹד֩ שְׁלֹשָׁ֤ה חֳדָשִׁים֙ לַקָּצִ֔יר

וְגַם with the verb מָנַעְתִּי (qal *qatal* 1 c s of מנע) again marks a concessive protasis. מִכֶּם (the preposition מִן ["from"] with a 2 m p suffix) is an indirect object complement to מָנַעְתִּי (the direct object being אֶת־הַגֶּשֶׁם ["the rain"]). The prepositional phrase with בְּ on the adverb עוֹד is idiomatic for "while still." The לְ on לַקָּצִיר ("to the harvest") illustrates how sometimes this preposition can be translated as "from" or "until." To have no rain so long before harvest was obviously a calamity.

Prose Clause: וְהִמְטַרְתִּי עַל־עִיר אֶחָת

וְהִמְטַרְתִּי, a hiphil *weqatal* 1 c s of מטר here functions imperfectively, "and I would send rain," in contrast to the simple past meaning a *wayyiqtol* would convey. This clause is epexegetical of "and I withheld rain" in the first clause (it is offline relative to context; it is also concessive here and could be rendered as "although"). The word אֶחָת in the prepositional phrase עַל־עִיר אֶחָת ("upon one city") functions indefinitely like "a given" or "a certain."

Prose Clause: וְעַל־עִיר אַחַת לֹא אַמְטִיר

The ו + [x] + *yiqtol* pattern (with אַמְטִיר, a hiphil *yiqtol* 1 c s of מטר), following the previous *weqatal*, binds the two contrasting clauses together and indicates that the action of the two is conceptually simultaneous.

Prose Clause: חֶלְקָה אַחַת תִּמָּטֵר

This line has Ø conjunction (asyndeton), indicating that it is an offline commentary on the previous clauses. תִּמָּטֵר (niphal *yiqtol* 3 f s of מטר) is imperfective. חֶלְקָה, literally a "share," here refers to a plot of arable land.

Prose Clause: וְחֶלְקָה . . . תִּיבָשׁ

This clause is interrupted by a relative clause (thus the ellipsis). The ו + [x] + *yiqtol* joins this clause to the previous offline clause as a parallel but contrasting event.

Prose Clause: אֲשֶׁר־לֹא־תַמְטִיר עָלֶיהָ

This is a relative clause inserted in the previous clause; its antecedent is וְחֶלְקָה. There is a resumptive pronoun pattern in . . . אֲשֶׁר עָלֶיהָ, meaning "upon which." The *yiqtol* verb in תַמְטִיר (hiphil *yiqtol* 3 f s) is imperfective, implying a prolonged period with no rain. The 3 f s is surprising; some manuscripts, with the LXX and Vulgate, have a 1 c s. But the 3 f s may be impersonal, like the English, "it rained."

4:8 וְנָעוּ שְׁתַּיִם שָׁלֹשׁ עָרִים אֶל־עִיר אַחַת לִשְׁתּוֹת מַיִם
וְלֹא יִשְׂבָּעוּ וְלֹא־שַׁבְתֶּם עָדַי נְאֻם־יְהוָה׃

This verse is made of four clauses. The first two continue the protasis from v. 7, the third is the apodosis, and the fourth is the oracle formula.

Prose Clause: וְנָעוּ שְׁתַּיִם שָׁלֹשׁ עָרִים אֶל־עִיר אַחַת לִשְׁתּוֹת מַיִם

The *weqatal* וְנָעוּ (qal *weqatal* 3 c p of נוע) resumes the series of concessive clauses that make up the protasis. The asyndeton with שְׁתַּיִם שָׁלֹשׁ means, "two or three." עָרִים ("cities") is here synecdoche for the people of those cities. לִשְׁתּוֹת, a qal infinitive construct of שתה with לְ, here expresses purpose as a complement to the main verb. מַיִם is the direct object.

Prose Clause: וְלֹא יִשְׂבָּעוּ

The וְ + לֹא + *yiqtol* (יִשְׂבָּעוּ, a qal *yiqtol* 3 m p of שׂבע) here implies a negation of a result one might have desired or expected on the basis of the previous clause. It could be translated as "but were not satisfied." Cf. the ו + לֹא + *yiqtol* in Genesis 2:25: וַיִּהְיוּ שְׁנֵיהֶם עֲרוּמִּים הָאָדָם וְאִשְׁתּוֹ וְלֹא יִתְבֹּשָׁשׁוּ ("and the two of them, the man and his woman, were naked but not ashamed").

Prose Clause: וְלֹא־שַׁבְתֶּם עָדַי

The וְ + לֹא + *yiqtol* (שַׁבְתֶּם, a qal *yiqtol* 2 m p of שׁוּב) is here the apodosis of the preceding lengthy protasis. Notice that in structure it is identical to the preceding clause, but that it serves an entirely different syntactical function. The change in subject from third to second person is the only signal that this clause plays a different role in the sentence-level structure.

Prose Clause: נְאֻם־יְהוָ֑ה

A divine speech formula.

4:9 הִכֵּ֣יתִי אֶתְכֶם֮ בַּשִּׁדָּפ֣וֹן וּבַיֵּרָקוֹן֒ הַרְבּ֞וֹת גַּנּוֹתֵיכֶ֧ם
וְכַרְמֵיכֶ֛ם וּתְאֵנֵיכֶ֥ם וְזֵיתֵיכֶ֖ם יֹאכַ֣ל הַגָּזָ֑ם וְלֹֽא־שַׁבְתֶּ֥ם
עָדַ֖י נְאֻם־יְהוָֽה׃ ס

This verse is made of four clauses. The first three are another concessive protasis-apodosis pattern and the fourth is the oracle formula.

Prose Clause: הִכֵּ֣יתִי אֶתְכֶם֮ בַּשִּׁדָּפ֣וֹן וּבַיֵּרָקוֹן֒ הַרְבּ֞וֹת

הִכֵּ֣יתִי is a hiphil *qatal* 1 c s of נכה. This clause, unlike 4:6-7, lacks the particle וְגַם, but the similarities to those verses indicate that the syntax of the sentence is the same. Having the *qatal* alone (where the previous verses have the particle and a pronoun) is rhetorically more dramatic. שִׁדָּפוֹן, often translated "blight," is literally a drying out or scorching (see *HALOT*, שִׁדָּפוֹן). יֵרָקוֹן, literally "paleness," is a plant affliction and is often translated as "rust" or "mildew." The two terms regularly appear as a pair (Deut 28:22; 2 Chr 6:28; Hag 2:17) and may be hendiadys. This clause perhaps alludes to Deuteronomy 28:22 (יַכְּכָה יְהוָה בַּשַּׁחֶפֶת . . . וּבַשִּׁדָּפוֹן וּבַיֵּרָקוֹן ["YHWH will strike you with consumption . . . and with blight and mildew"]). הַרְבּוֹת, the hiphil infinitive absolute of רבה, here as elsewhere is adverbial ("much" or "abundantly"). The MT gives the word the conjunctive *azla*, apparently linking it to the following words, but that is probably incorrect.

Prose Clause: גַּנּוֹתֵיכֶ֧ם וְכַרְמֵיכֶ֛ם וּתְאֵנֵיכֶ֥ם וְזֵיתֵיכֶ֖ם יֹאכַ֣ל הַגָּזָ֑ם

The Ø + [x] + *yiqtol* pattern indicates that this is an offline, imperfective clause here serving as epexegesis for the previous clause. That is, the conditions that favored the development of blight and mildew also favored the development of insect vermin. The fronting of the direct object in a compound phrase of four nouns (גַּנּוֹתֵיכֶם וְכַרְמֵיכֶם וּתְאֵנֵיכֶם וְזֵיתֵיכֶם) indicates that destruction of the gardens—especially the variety and quantity of what was lost—is the focus here. The agent of destruction, the locusts, is not the focus. The verb יֹאכַל (qal *yiqtol* 3 m s of אכל) is imperfective and could be rendered, "have been eating."

Prose Clause: וְלֹֽא־שַׁבְתֶּ֥ם עָדַ֖י

See 4:6, 8.

Prose Clause: נְאֻם־יְהוָֽה

A divine speech formula.

4:10 שִׁלַּ֨חְתִּי בָכֶ֥ם דֶּ֙בֶר֙ בְּדֶ֣רֶךְ מִצְרַ֔יִם הָרַ֤גְתִּי בַחֶ֙רֶב֙
בַּחוּרֵיכֶ֔ם עִ֖ם שְׁבִ֣י סוּסֵיכֶ֑ם וָאַעֲלֶ֞ה בְּאֹ֤שׁ מַחֲנֵיכֶם֙
וּֽבְאַפְּכֶ֔ם וְלֹֽא־שַׁבְתֶּ֥ם עָדַ֖י נְאֻם־יְהוָֽה׃

This verse is made of five clauses. The first four are another concessive protasis-apodosis pattern and the fifth is the oracle formula. In contrast to 4:7-8, the verbs in the first two clauses here are *qatal*, indicating that they are two distinct actions and are not imperfective in aspect.

Prose Clause: שִׁלַּ֨חְתִּי בָכֶ֥ם דֶּ֙בֶר֙ בְּדֶ֣רֶךְ מִצְרַ֔יִם

Again, וְגַם is implied on the basis of 4:6, 7, and fronting of the *qatal* verb (שִׁלַּחְתִּי, a piel *qatal* 1 c s of שלח) is rhetorically dramatic. The preposition בְּ in בָכֶם may either mean "among" or be used in a hostile sense, "against" (see the use of שלח בְּ in Gen 37:22). דֶּבֶר ("plague") is the direct object, and דֶּרֶךְ in בְּדֶרֶךְ means "way" or "manner," as in Genesis 31:35, and it here refers to the manner in which God struck Egypt with plagues. Israel had evidently recently gone through a series of natural calamities analogous to those that befell Egypt at the exodus.

Prose Clause: הָרַ֨גְתִּי בַחֶ֜רֶב בַּחֽוּרֵיכֶ֗ם עִ֚ם שְׁבִ֣י סֽוּסֵיכֶ֔ם

A second protasis clause headed by *qatal*, this is a second example in this series; it is analogous to the action of the first clause but is separate and distinct. Here הָרַגְתִּי בַחֶרֶב indicates death in battle. הָרַגְתִּי is a qal *qatal* 1 c s. בַּחוּרֵיכֶם, "your young men," is the direct object and refers to the rank and file soldiers. עִם שְׁבִי סוּסֵיכֶם, "with the captivity of your horses," is sometimes emended to read צְבִי ("pomp") instead of שְׁבִי on the grounds that שְׁבִי normally refers to the capture of humans (e.g., Wolff 1977, 210 note q). But this is unnecessary. The point is that the Israelites have suffered the double loss of having their troops killed in battle and their war-horses captured.

Prose Clause: וָאַעֲלֶ֞ה בְּאֹ֤שׁ מַֽחֲנֵיכֶם֙ וּֽבְאַפְּכֶ֔ם

The *wayyiqtol* verb (וָאַעֲלֶה, hiphil *wayyiqtol* 1 c s of עלה) joins this clause to the previous and indicates that the two refer to a sequence of events within a single episode, the defeat of an Israelite army and subsequent rotting of the dead bodies. בְּאֹשׁ, "stench," is sometimes emended to בְּאֵשׁ, "with fire," on the basis of the LXX ἐν πυρὶ, but this does not yield a better sense. וּבְאַפְּכֶם ("and in your nose") is also considered suspect, or at least surprising, for having the conjunction. This is the *waw explicativum* (GKC §154a, note 1b). It might be rendered, "and right in your nose!" The point is that the defeat did not occur far away, where they could only hear news of it from a distance, but right in their midst, where they could smell it. Amos may here be referring to defeats suffered under Hazael.

Prose Clause: וְלֹֽא־שַׁבְתֶּ֥ם עָדַ֖י

See 4:6, 8.

Prose Clause: נְאֻם־יְהוָֽה

A divine speech formula.

4:11 הָפַכְתִּי בָכֶם כְּמַהְפֵּכַת אֱלֹהִים אֶת־סְדֹם וְאֶת־
עֲמֹרָה וַתִּהְיוּ כְּאוּד מֻצָּל מִשְּׂרֵפָה וְלֹא־שַׁבְתֶּם עָדַי
נְאֻם־יְהוָה׃ ס

This verse is made of four clauses. The first three are another concessive protasis-apodosis pattern and the fourth is the oracle formula. Sodom and Gomorrah represent God's ultimate judgment, the complete eradication of a people, and thus this is the last in this series of references to recent calamities. The first clause seems to say that Israel suffered this judgment (which, if true, would mean that Amos would have no Israel to address), but the second clause draws back from this inference, asserting that Israel just barely survived this experience. It probably refers to the near collapse of Israel prior to the rise of Jeroboam II.

Prose Clause: הָפַכְתִּי בָכֶם כְּמַהְפֵּכַת אֱלֹהִים אֶת־סְדֹם וְאֶת־עֲמֹרָה

Again, וְגַם is implied, and fronting of the *qatal* verb (הָפַכְתִּי, a qal *qatal* 1 c s of הפך) is rhetorically dramatic. The preposition בְּ in בָכֶם may be partitive, "some of you," indicating that some but not all of the cities of Israel were annihilated in the manner of Sodom. The prepositional phrase כְּמַהְפֵּכַת אֱלֹהִים, where כְּ and the noun מַהְפֵּכָה (an "overturning") function like an infinitive construct phrase used as a finite verb. Thus it takes the direct objects אֶת־סְדֹם וְאֶת־עֲמֹרָה.

Prose Clause: וַתִּהְיוּ כְּאוּד מֻצָּל מִשְּׂרֵפָה

The *wayyiqtol* verb (וַתִּהְיוּ, qal *wayyiqtol* 2 m p of היה) joins this clause to the previous and indicates that the two refer to a single episode, the near annihilation but subsequent survival of Israel. Rhetorically, the prepositional phrase with כְּ parallels כְּמַהְפֵּכַת in the previous clause and sets up a contrast. אוּד is a burning stick in a bonfire; cf. Zech 3:2. מֻצָּל is a hophal participle m s from נצל, "snatched." A שְׂרֵפָה is a very hot fire meant to either harden something (like firing clay in a kiln; Gen 11:3) or incinerate it (such as the fire for incinerating the red heifer; Num 19:6).

Prose Clause: וְלֹא־שַׁבְתֶּם עָדַי

See 4:6, 8.

Prose Clause: נְאֻם־יְהוָה

A divine speech formula.

4:12 לָכֵן כֹּה אֶעֱשֶׂה־לְּךָ יִשְׂרָאֵל עֵקֶב כִּי־זֹאת אֶעֱשֶׂה־לָּךְ הִכּוֹן לִקְרַאת־אֱלֹהֶיךָ יִשְׂרָאֵל׃

This verse concludes the prose recitation. It is pregnant in that judgment is threatened but not expressly or specifically described; the reader is left to imagine what may come next. In light of how the series of judgments has progressed to this point, the reasonable conclusion is that the ultimate decree of judgment, the annihilation of Israel, is coming. A number of scholars believe that the first two clauses fit together awkwardly and that the present text is a conflation of variant readings (see Paul 1991, 150). This is unnecessary; the two clauses have entirely different functions and are in fact in different sentences, as described below.

Prose Clause: לָכֵן כֹּה אֶעֱשֶׂה־לְּךָ יִשְׂרָאֵל

אֶעֱשֶׂה, a qal *yiqtol* 1 c s of עשׂה (used here for future action), is followed by an indirect object (לְּךָ) and a vocative (יִשְׂרָאֵל). The key to understanding the clause is the particle כֹּה, which here means, "in the same manner." Shalom Paul appropriately compares this to the oath formula in 1 Kings 2:23, כֹּה יַעֲשֶׂה־לִּי אֱלֹהִים וְכֹה יוֹסִיף, "May God do the same to me and may he do more of the same!" (Paul 1991, 150). This clause therefore looks back over all of the preceding and asserts that God will continue to afflict Israel in the same manner.

Prose Clause: עֵקֶב כִּי־זֹאת אֶעֱשֶׂה־לָּךְ

עֵקֶב means "back, end," and from that means "result" or "wages," with עֵקֶב כִּי idiomatically meaning "because." זֹאת is the direct object of אֶעֱשֶׂה (qal *yiqtol* 1 c s of עשׂה), and its antecedent is the implied judgment of the previous clause. This clause is the causal protasis of the next clause. It in fact begins an entirely new sentence and is separate from the preceding clause.

Prose Clause: הִכּוֹן לִקְרַאת־אֱלֹהֶיךָ יִשְׂרָאֵל

This is the apodosis of the previous clause. הִכּוֹן is a niphal imperative m s of כּוּן (cf. Ezek 38:7, where the niphal imperative implies preparation for combat). לִקְרַאת is a qal infinitive construct of קרא II ("meet") and, against Youngblood (1971), not קרא I ("call"). אֱלֹהֶיךָ is the direct object. The repetition of the vocative יִשְׂרָאֵל (also found in the first clause), indicates again that there are two sentences in this verse (since it is peculiar to repeat a vocative in two separate places in one sentence).

4:13: Doxology: This poem is a doxology in five lines (one stanza and one strophe). The doxology concludes this section and appears abruptly; the reader is not expecting such language. Its presence heightens the suspense created by the pregnant threat of judgment in v. 12. The doxology describes the kind of God that Israel must be ready to meet (viz., an all-powerful God). It may also be adapted from one of the hymns sung at the Israelite shrines. The doxology consists of four lines giving descriptions of YHWH's power, with the fifth line naming him. The whole doxology is thus a kind of implied question and answer, with lines a-d implicitly asking, "Who is the fashioner of hills and creator of wind . . .?" and line e giving the answer. The logic of the first four lines is that YHWH is first maker of heaven and earth (here represented by mountains and wind; line a), he secondly is judge of all the earth, bringing accusations against humanity (line b), and he thirdly comes in apocalyptic terror (lines c-d).

כִּ֞י הִנֵּ֠ה 4:13a

The first two words (כִּי הִנֵּה) are a prose introduction to the doxology. They call the reader's attention to the doxology and encourage meditation over its significance.

4:13b a יוֹצֵר הָרִים וּבֹרֵא רוּחַ
b וּמַגִּיד לְאָדָם מַה־שֵּׂחוֹ
c עֹשֵׂה שַׁחַר עֵיפָה
d וְדֹרֵךְ עַל־בָּמֳתֵי אָרֶץ
e יְהוָה אֱלֹהֵי־צְבָאוֹת שְׁמוֹ׃ ס

Line a: The colon-marker is *revia* and the constraints are: 2 predicators, 2 constituents, and 4 units.

יוֹצֵר הָרִים. A construct chain with the qal active participle m s of יצר used in a periphrastic construction with the implied subject "he" (הוּא). הָרִים is an objective genitive.

וּבֹרֵא רוּחַ. Another construct chain, with the qal active participle m s of ברא used periphrastically before an objective genitive.

Line b: The colon-marker is *zaqeph qaton* and the constraints are: 1 predicator, 4 constituents, and 4 units.

וּמַגִּיד. Hiphil participle m s of נגד with conjunction in a periphrastic construction.

לְאָדָם. Prepositional phrase with לְ indicating addressee.

מַה. The pronoun is the direct object of וּמַגִּיד and introduces an indirect question.

שֵּׂחוֹ. The noun שֵׂחַ is *hapax legomenon*. שֵׂחַ is often translated as "thought" in Amos, but there is confusion regarding the 3 m s suffix. Is God declaring his own thoughts, or is he telling the man what the man is thinking? There are no grounds for translating it as "plan," as is sometimes done (Stuart 1987, 335). שֵׂחַ is apparently a by-form of שִׂיחַ II, "meditation, lament" ("In Samaria diphthongs were monophthongized"; Paul 1991, 254). In 1 Kings 18:27 Elijah mockingly says that Baal has a שִׂיחַ, but the meaning of שִׂיחַ in that text is disputed. שיח appears a number of times in the Hebrew of Sirach, as at 13:11: ואל תאמן לרב שיחו ("and do not believe his abundant speech"). Elsewhere, שִׂיחַ is almost always used for a complaint (1 Sam 1:16; Ps 55:3 [E = 2]; 142:3 [E = 2]; Job 7:13; 9:27; 10:1; etc.). Normally, of course, a person pours out his complaint to God. Here, however, it is very strange to treat the 3 m s suffix as referring to the man, as that would mean that God was telling a man what is that man's complaint. Thus, the suffix must refer to God. The use of שֵׂחַ here is close to Job's use of שִׂיחַ, where it is a formal complaint or accusation, analogous to רִיב. Sirach 11:8, in a context of adjudicating a dispute, has ובתוך שיחה אל תדבר ("and do not speak while [another] makes his case"). Thus, God is making known his charge or grievance against a man, or, more probably, against humanity (so understanding אָדָם).

Line c: The colon-marker is *zaqeph qaton* and the constraints are: 1 predicator, 2 constituents, and 3 units.

עֹשֵׂה שַׁחַר. A construct chain with qal active participle of עשׂה and an objective genitive.

עֵיפָה. A secondary object, the outcome of what God makes of שַׁחַר. This line is often translated, "who makes the dawn into darkness," with the understanding that this is an apocalyptic darkening of the heavens. Shalom Paul, however, understands the meaning of the words to be reversed, so that it actually means, "who makes gloom into shining dawn" (Paul 1991, 155). At issue is whether עֵיפָה is derived from עוּף, to be dark, or יעף, to shine. On balance and against Paul, it is more likely that it is derived from עוּף (see *NIDOTTE* עוּף II).

Line d: The colon-marker is *athnach* and the constraints are: 1 predicator, 2 constituents, and 3 units.

וְדֹרֵךְ. Qal active participle of דרךְ with conjunction.

עַל־בָּמֳתֵי אָרֶץ. Prepositional phrase with locative עַל. The language of this verse has several analogies in the Bible. In Deuteronomy 33:29 Israel treads on (דרך עַל) the backs (בָּמָה) of their enemies. In Habakkuk 3:19 the psalmist asserts that God made his feet as swift as a deer's, so that he can tread on (דרך עַל) hills (בָּמָה). In Micah 1:3, YHWH comes forth as a warrior and tramples (דרך עַל) the hills (בָּמָה) so that they melt under him, and in Job 9:8 God steps across (דרך עַל) the waves (בָּמָה) of the sea. The significance of בָּמָה here is debated. Interpretations include: (1) YHWH is like a gigantic figure stepping from hilltop to hilltop. (2) YHWH is like a vigorous man who walks up and down hills with ease. (3) YHWH is treading on (i.e., crushing) the cultic high places of Canaan. Amos probably implies a combination of ideas, that YHWH is vigorous, that he is a cosmic figure stepping across the earth, and that he is a warrior before whom nothing can stand (the parallel to Mic 1:3 is especially telling). The notion of God stamping on cultic high places may also be implied as a reflection on 4:4-5. (See also Crenshaw 1972, 42–44).

Line e: The colon-marker is *silluq* and the constraints are: 0 predicators, 2 constituents, and 4 units.

יְהוָה אֱלֹהֵי־צְבָאוֹת. The predicate in a verbless clause.

שְׁמוֹ. Noun with 3 m s suffix; the subject.

5:1–6:14: Cruelty and Hollow Religion II

With 4:1-13, this is the second of two indictments against Israel for its oppression and its empty religion. The opening call for Israel to listen to a lament (5:1) misleads some readers to suppose that the entire section that follows, often defined as including at least all of chapter 5, is formally a lamentation. This is not correct. The lament proper is only 5:2; verses subsequent to that are a mixture of oracles and exhortations of various kinds in both prose and poetry. On the other hand, the lamentation motif does provide important structure for this passage. Three times the motif of lamentation is prominent: first, in a lament poem (5:2); second, in a prediction that people will call for mourners (5:16-17); and third, in an account of a scene in which typically there would be wailing and lamentation but ironically lamentation is absent (6:9-10). The full text of 5:1–6:14 is bounded by an inclusion (see discussion at 6:14). In structure, this division has an introduction (5:1-3) followed by a series of accusations and warnings (5:4–6:8a), after which there is a judgment oracle introduced by a long and solemn divine speech formula (6:8b-11). Finally, there is a summarizing conclusion (6:12-14). There are numerous parallel elements, especially in sections I, II and III, as is apparent in the outline below. A motif of this text, brought out clearly in the proverb that opens the concluding summary (6:12a), is Israel's perversity, the idea that the nation behaves in a way that is absurdly wrongheaded. The structure is:

I. Introduction: (5:1-3)

- A: The Call to Hear (5:1)
- B: The Lament Poem (5:2)
- C: The Oracle of Doom (5:3)

II: Accusations, Warnings, and Exhortations (5:4–6:8a)

- A: First Series (5:4-15)
    - 1: Accusation: Religious Arrogance (5:4-7)
    - 2: Doxology: YHWH Made the Heavens (5:8-9)
    - 3: Accusation: No Respect for Poor (5:10-15)
- B: Doom Oracle Predicting Lamentation (5:16-17)
- A': Second Series (5:18–6:8a)
    - 1': Accusation: Religious Arrogance (5:18-24)
    - 2': Question and Oracle: Sky Gods (5:25-27)
    - 3': Accusation: Arrogant Luxuries (6:1-8a)

III. Judgment on the Houses of Samaria (6:8b-11)

- A: Oracle of Doom (6:8b)
- B: A Mass-Funeral without Lamentation (6:9-10)
- A': Oracle of Doom: (6:11)

IV. Summary (6:12-14)

A: Proverb (6:12a)

B: Proverb Exposition and Accusation (6:12b-13)

C: Oracle of Doom (6:14)

Looking at the data in a slightly different manner, this text can be seen as a pair of linked chiastic structures with a summarizing conclusion. The first chiasmus is 5:1-17 (A: doom [1-3], B: accusation [4-7], C: doxology [8-9], B': accusation [10-15], A': doom [16-17]), and the second chiasmus is 5:16–6:11 (A: doom [5:16-17], B: accusation [5:18-24], C: sky gods [5:25-27], B': accusation [6:1-8a], and A': doom [6:8b-11]). On the chiasmus of 5:1-17, see also de Waard (1977).

1Hear this word that I am raising against you as a lament, house of Israel!
2She has fallen never to rise again—
The Virgin Israel—
She is abandoned on her land with no one to raise her!

3For thus says the Lord YHWH:

The city that sends out a thousand will have a hundred left,
And the one that sends out a hundred will have ten left in the house of Israel.

4For thus says YHWH to the house of Israel:

Seek me that you may live!
5Do not seek Bethel!
And do not go to Gilgal!
And do not cross over to Beersheba!
For Gilgal will certainly go into exile,
And Bethel will become a disaster!
6Seek YHWH that you may live!

Lest he rush upon the House of Joseph like a fire,
And it consume without anyone at Bethel to put it out,

7*Where they turn justice to wormwood*
And lay righteousness in the dirt.

8*He is the maker of Pleiades and Orion!*
And he turns deep darkness to morning
And darkens daylight at night!
He calls to the waters of the sea
And then pours them out on the surface of the earth!
His name is YHWH!

9*He smiles destruction upon the strong*
And destruction comes upon the fortress!

10*At the gate, they hate a reprover*
And they abhor an honest speaker.

11*Therefore, because you impose a grain tax upon the poor*
And you take a grain-duty from them,
You build houses of ashlar
But you will not dwell in them.
You build pleasant vineyards
But you will not drink their wine.

12*For I know that your transgressions are many,*
(I know) that your sins are strong.

They attack a righteous man! They take bribes!
And they turn aside poor people at the gate.
13*Therefore the prudent man is silent in such a time as this;*
It is indeed an evil time.

14*Seek good and not evil*
So that you may live
And it may be true: 'YHWH, God of Sabaoth be with you!'
Just as you say.

15*Hate evil and love good,*
And establish justice at the gate!
Perhaps YHWH, God of Sabaoth, will favor
The remnant of Joseph.

[16]Therefore, thus says YHWH, God of Sabaoth, the Lord:
In all plazas, (there will be) lamentation!
And in all streets, they will say, "Woe! Woe!"
And they will call farmers to mourning
And (will call for) lamentation to those skilled in wailing!
[17]And in all vineyards there will be lamentation!
For I will pass over in the midst of you,
Says YHWH.

[18]Woe to those who desire the day of YHWH!
Why is the day of YHWH this to you?
It will be darkness and not light!
[19]Just as though a man were to flee from a lion
And a bear met him.
Or he went home
And leaned his hand on the wall,
And a snake bit him.
[20]Isn't the day of YHWH darkness—not light—
And gloom without any brightness in it?
[21]I hate, I despise your festivals,
And I will not show favor to your assemblies.
[22]For even if you were to offer whole offerings to me,
I would neither be pleased with your gifts
Nor would I favorably look upon your peace offerings of fatted calves.
[23]Get the noise of your songs away from me!
And I will not listen to the music of your lyres.
[24]But let justice roll like water,
And (let) righteousness (roll) like a perennial stream!

[25]Did you bring me sacrifices and offering for forty years in the wilder-
ness, house of Israel, [26]while you were carrying Sikkuth, your king, and
Kiyyun—your images, your astral deities that you made for yourselves?

[27]But I shall exile you beyond Damascus,
Says YHWH, whose name is "God of the Heavenly Hosts."

[6:1]Alas! The carefree in Zion,
And those confident in the acropolis of Samaria!
They are marked as "the best of the nations"
And the house of Israel comes to them.

[2]Cross over to Calneh and see!
And go from there to Great Hamath!
And go down to Gath of the Philistines!

Are you better than these kingdoms,
Or is their territory bigger than your territory?

[3]They push away the evil day
And bring near the habitation of violence.

[4]They lie on beds of ivory
And recline on their couches
And eat lambs from the flock
And calves from the midst of the stall!
[5]They strum at the mouth of the lyre;
Like David they improvise for themselves upon musical instruments!

[6]They drink with wine-bowls
And anoint (themselves) with the best of oils.
And they feel no distress over the breakup of Joseph.

[7]Therefore, they will now go into exile at the head of the exiles
And the symposium of the reclining (revelers) will come to an end,
[8]Swears the Lord YHWH by himself.

The oracle of YHWH, God of Sabaoth.
I abhor the pride of Jacob
And I hate his citadels,
And I will hand the city and the people who fill it over (to exile).

[9]And it shall be that if ten persons are left in one household, they will die. [10]And their Uncle Undertaker will take them up to remove the bodies from the household, and he will say to the one who is in the back chamber

of the house, "Any more with you?" And (the one at the back) will say, "That's it!" And (Uncle Undertaker) will say, "Hush! For it is not right to invoke YHWH's name!"

[11]For behold YHWH is issuing a command,
And he will knock the great house to pieces
And the small house to rubble.

[12]Do horses run upon a rocky crag?
Or does one plow (a rocky crag) with oxen?
Well, you turn justice into the poisonous Rosh plant,
And the "righteousness plant" into bitter wormwood.
[13](You, who) rejoice at Lo-debar
And say,
"Didn't we take Karnaim for ourselves by our own strength?"

[14]For behold, House of Israel, I am raising up against you—the oracle of YHWH, God of Sabaoth—a nation, and it will push you out (of the land that stretches) from Lebo-Hamath to the Brook of the Arabah.

5:1-3: Introduction

This text begins with a prose call to listen to a lament (v. 1), followed by the lament itself in v. 2. The lament, as is customary, is poetic in form. It has one strophe of three lines. This is followed by an oracle that explains what prompts this lament.

5:1: Call to Hear: A formal summons for Israel to listen to the prophet, in prose, announces a lament.

5:1 שִׁמְעוּ אֶת־הַדָּבָר הַזֶּה אֲשֶׁר אָנֹכִי נֹשֵׂא עֲלֵיכֶם
קִינָה בֵּית יִשְׂרָאֵל׃

Prose Clause: שִׁמְעוּ אֶת־הַדָּבָר הַזֶּה . . . בֵּית יִשְׂרָאֵל

שִׁמְעוּ. the qal imperative m p of שׁמע, opens major divisions of Amos at 3:1; 4:1; here at 5:1; and 8:4. אֶת־הַדָּבָר הַזֶּה is the direct object and בֵּית יִשְׂרָאֵל is a vocative construct chain.

Prose Clause: אֲשֶׁר אָנֹכִ֜י נֹשֵׂ֥א עֲלֵיכֶ֛ם קִינָ֖ה

A relative clause headed by אֲשֶׁר, this interrupts the previous clause. The antecedent of אֲשֶׁר is הַדָּבָר הַזֶּה, and the relative is the direct object of נֹשֵׂא (qal active participle of נשא with אָנֹכִי as the subject). The prepositional phrase עֲלֵיכֶם is a complement meaning "concerning you" or "against you." קִינָה, "lament," is in apposition to אֲשֶׁר.

5:2: The Lament Poem: The lament proper is made of a single stanza (one strophe of three lines). It serves to introduce the accusation, exhortations, and judgments that follow. There is an inclusion construction in that lines a and c both begin with a *qatal* 3 f s and both start with נ, and both lines end with the root קום.

5:2 a נָֽפְלָה֙ לֹֽא־תוֹסִ֣יף ק֔וּם
b בְּתוּלַ֖ת יִשְׂרָאֵ֑ל
c נִטְּשָׁ֥ה עַל־אַדְמָתָ֖הּ אֵ֥ין מְקִימָֽהּ׃

Line a: The colon-marker is *zaqeph qaton* and the constraints are: 2 predicators, 2 constituents, and 3 units.

נָֽפְלָה֙. Qal *qatal* 3 f s of נפל.

לֹֽא־תוֹסִ֣יף ק֔וּם. Negated hiphil *yiqtol* 3 f s of יסף with qal infinitive construct of קוּם as an auxiliary. The verb יסף (hiphil stem), when negated, often takes an infinitive as its auxiliary to mean, "shall not do (X) anymore." The asyndeton with a negated *yiqtol* after a *qatal* also makes this clause effectively adverbial after נָפְלָה; it could be translated as "never to rise again."

Line b: The colon-marker is *athnach* and the constraints are: 0 predicators, 1 constituents, and 2 units.

בְּתוּלַת יִשְׂרָאֵל. The subject of the two prior verbs is not named until the second line and is set by itself between the two lines of the inclusion. This makes the naming of Israel as the object of lament more prominent. Describing a nation as a "virgin" suggests that it ought to be impregnable; it is not a statement about the moral quality of the citizens.

Line c: The colon-marker is *silluq* and the constraints are: 2 predicators, 4 constituents, and 4 units. Like line a, this line has two clauses with asyndeton.

נִטְּשָׁה. Niphal *qatal* 3 f s of נטשׁ. The root means to leave something alone (such as leaving ground fallow, Exod 23:11), or to abandon something. That which is abandoned in this manner (niphal stem of נטשׁ) may run rampant, as there is nothing to restrain it (Judg 15:9; Isa 16:8), or it may be left desolate and without help, as is the case here.

עַל־אַדְמָתָהּ. Prepositional phrase with locative עַל on the noun אֲדָמָה with a 3 f s suffix (בְּתוּלַת יִשְׂרָאֵל is the antecedent of the suffix).

אֵין. The second predicator. Again there is asyndeton after a *qatal* form, and again this could be rendered adverbially, "without anyone to raise her."

מְקִימָהּ. Hiphil participle m s of קום with 3 f s suffix. With אֵין, this forms one predicator, a periphrastic construction.

5:3: Oracle: A prophecy of military disaster explains why the lament is necessary. After a prose divine speech formula introducing the oracle, the oracle itself is a two-line poem. The oracle asserts that Israel will suffer very high casualties (90 percent if taken literally) in a coming conflict.

כִּי כֹה אָמַר אֲדֹנָי יְהוִה 5:3a

The above is a divine speech formula in prose with אָמַר, a qal *qatal* 3 m s of אמר.

5:3b: Judgment Poem: Two lines. This could be called an oracle of doom, describing as it does a military disaster (oracular statements can be very short poems). It looks back to the initial judgment against Israel in 2:14-16.

a 5:3b הָעִיר הַיֹּצֵאת אֶלֶף תַּשְׁאִיר מֵאָה
b וְהַיּוֹצֵאת מֵאָה תַּשְׁאִיר עֲשָׂרָה לְבֵית יִשְׂרָאֵל׃ ס

Line a: The colon-marker is *athnach* and the constraints are: 2 predicators, 3 constituents, and 5 units.

הָעִיר הַיֹּצֵאת אֶלֶף. Both הַיֹּצֵאת (qal active participle f s of יצא) and the numeral אֶלֶף are in apposition to הָעִיר. The "city" here by synecdoche represents the military men of that city. The participle forms a relative clause.

תַּשְׁאִיר. Hiphil *yiqtol* 3 f s of שׁאר. The *yiqtol* here is a simple future indicative; this is a predictive text.

מֵאָה. is a complement to the verb and has the phrase הָעִיר הַיֹּצֵאת אֶלֶף as its antecedent.

Line b: The colon-marker is *silluq* and the constraints are: 2 predicators, 4 constituents, and 5 units (as a proper name, בֵית יִשְׂרָאֵל can be counted as a single unit).

וְהַיּוֹצֵאת מֵאָה. There is gapping of הָעִיר from line a. This participle phrase serves as another relative clause.

תַּשְׁאִיר. Hiphil *yiqtol* 3 f s of שׁאר.

עֲשָׂרָה. functions the same as מֵאָה in line a.

לְבֵית יִשְׂרָאֵל. Prepositional phrase with לְ, which is here properly possessive in meaning although it might be translated, "in the house of Israel."

5:4-15: First Series of Accusations, Warnings, and Exhortations

This series, as described above, is in three parts: an accusation that focuses on religious arrogance (5:4-7); a doxology to YHWH, maker and governor of the Heavens (5:8-9); and a second accusation focusing on how the poor are abused before the courts (5:10-15). The overall message is that this is a topsy-turvy world, in which wrong behavior and concepts about God are substituted for what is right.

5:4-7: Accusation Concerning Religious Arrogance: The poem, after a prose divine speech formula, is in two strophes. There is a chiastic structure in the first strophe, as follows:

A: Seek and live (line 1a)

B: Bethel (line 1b)

C: Gilgal (line 1c)

D: Beersheba (line 1d)

C': Gilgal (line 1e)

B': Bethel (line 1f)

A': Seek and live (line 1g).

This chiasmus is followed by a second strophe, a warning introduced by פֶּן (lines 2a-2d).

5:4a כִּ֣י כֹ֤ה אָמַ֣ר יְהוָ֔ה לְבֵ֖ית יִשְׂרָאֵ֑ל

A prose divine speech formula preceded by כִּי, which here is probably explanatory ("for"), with **אָמַר**, a qal *qatal* 3 m s of **אמר**. The prepositional phrase לְבֵית יִשְׂרָאֵל names the poem's addressee.

5:4b-6a: First Strophe. Seven lines. The initial imperative marks this as a directive text-type, as the poem uses commands, purpose clauses, prohibitions, and explanatory clauses to make its exhortation.

דִּרְשׁ֖וּנִי וִֽחְיֽוּ׃ 1a 5:4b
וְאַל־תִּדְרְשׁוּ֙ בֵּֽית־אֵ֔ל 1b 5:5
וְהַגִּלְגָּל֙ לֹ֣א תָבֹ֔אוּ 1c
וּבְאֵ֥ר שֶׁ֖בַע לֹ֣א תַעֲבֹ֑רוּ 1d
כִּ֤י הַגִּלְגָּל֙ גָּלֹ֣ה יִגְלֶ֔ה 1e
וּבֵֽית־אֵ֖ל יִהְיֶ֥ה לְאָֽוֶן׃ 1f
דִּרְשׁ֥וּ אֶת־יְהוָ֖ה וִֽחְי֑וּ 1g 5:6a

Line 1a: The colon-marker is *silluq* and the constraints are: 2 predicators, 2 constituents, and 2 units.

דִּרְשׁ֖וּנִי. Qal imperative m p of דרשׁ with 1 c s suffix and energic נ. See *GKC* §58i.

וִֽחְיֽוּ. Qal imperative m p of חיה. Although it may be translated simply as "and live," it probably is implying purpose ("so that you may live"). See the parallel to this verb in Amos 5:14, לְמַעַן תִּחְיוּ, and cf. וֶהְיֵה בְּרָכָה ("so that you may be a blessing") in Genesis 12:2.

Line 1b: The colon-marker is *zaqeph qaton* and the constraints are: 1 predicator, 2 constituents, and 2 units.

וְאַל־תִּדְרְשׁוּ֙. Negated qal *yiqtol* 2 m p of דרשׁ (used for a prohibition). The negative אַל rather than לֹא may have been used here as a play on the name בֵּית־אֵל. Contrast the use of לֹא in lines 1c and 1d, and note the inclusion structure formed by אל at the beginning and end of this line.

בֵּֽית־אֵ֔ל. The direct object. The shrine here is synecdoche for the religious leadership there. Set up as a rival shrine to the Jerusalem temple, it is also implicitly a rival to God.

Line 1c: The colon-marker is *zaqeph qaton* and the constraints are: 1 predicator, 2 constituents, and 2 units. This line has a chiastic structure with line 1b.

וְהַגִּלְגָּל. One might expect a directive ה or preposition אֶל here, but omitting it makes for a better parallel to בֵּית־אֵל. Gilgal was on the west side of the Jordan near Jericho (Josh 4:19). As the first ground occupied by Israel west of the Jordan and as the spot where the disgrace of an uncircumcised generation was removed (Josh 5:2-9), Gilgal became a major cultic site. Samuel visited it annually, along with Bethel and Mizpah, in the circuit of his ministry (1 Sam 7:16), and the site appears repeatedly in the Samuel narrative.

לֹא תָבֹאוּ. Negated qal *yiqtol* 2 m p of בּוֹא used for a prohibition. As a general rule, אַל often marks a temporary or specific prohibition while לֹא marks a permanent or general one, but this is not always the case, as it clearly is not here. Amos is not saying that no one should ever go to Gilgal.

Line 1d: The colon-marker is *athnach* and the constraints are: 1 predicator, 2 constituents, and 2 units. This line is syntactically parallel to 1c, and thus it, too, is bound to 1b. Lines 1b-d are thus a single set of prohibitions.

וּבְאֵר שֶׁבַע. It is surprising that the people of Samaria would cross Judah to make a pilgrimage to Beersheba, but the site is important in the stories of Abraham. A dismantled altar was found in layer III–II of Beersheba (Tell es-Seba), suggesting that a cult flourished their during the divided monarchy period. The altar may have been dismantled as part of the reforms of Hezekiah (see *ABD*, "Beer-Sheba").

לֹא תַעֲבֹרוּ. Negated qal *yiqtol* 2 m p of עבר used for a prohibition. The use of עבר reflects the fact that the pilgrims had to cross through Judahite territory. There is assonance of וּבְאֵר at the beginning of the line with תַעֲבֹרוּ at the end with the repetition of ב and ר.

Line 1e: The colon-marker is *zaqeph qaton* and the constraints are: 1 predicator, 2 constituents, and 3 units.

כִּי הַגִּלְגָּל. The כִּי is explanatory. There is obviously assonance between הַגִּלְגָּל and the following גָּלֹה יִגְלֶה.

גָּלֹה יִגְלֶה. Qal infinitive absolute of גלה with the qal *yiqtol* 3 m s of the same root here expresses certainty.

Line 1f: The colon-marker is *silluq* and the constraints are: 1 predicator, 3 constituents, and 3 units.

וּבֵית־אֵל. In the chiastic structure, Bethel heads and concludes the list of towns, attesting to its prominence in the religious life of Israel.

יִהְיֶה. Qal *yiqtol* 3 m s of היה. Used with לְ, it often means "become" (*HALOT* היה Qal 7c).

לְאָוֶן. The use of אָוֶן (here meaning "disaster" or "nothingness"; cf. Paul 1991, 164) as a wordplay on the name בֵּית־אֵל is taken up in Hosea 4:15; 5:8. That is, instead of being the "House of God" (אֵל) it is the "House of Nothingness" (אָוֶן).

Line 1g: The colon-marker is *athnach* and the constraints are: 2 predicators, 3 constituents, and 3 units.

דִּרְשׁוּ. Qal imperative m p of דרשׁ.

אֶת־יְהוָה. In contrast to line 1a, which has "seek me," the parallel here has the divine name.

וִחְיוּ. Again, the qal imperative m p of חיה probably connotes purpose (see line 1a).

5:6b-7: Second Strophe. Four lines in two bicola. Because of the close connection between הַהֹפְכִים in 2c and לְבֵית־אֵל in 2b, these lines should not be separated into two different strophes (see comments on line 2c below).

5:6b 2a פֶּן־יִצְלַח כָּאֵשׁ בֵּית יוֹסֵף

2b וְאָכְלָה וְאֵין־מְכַבֶּה לְבֵית־אֵל׃

5:7 2c הַהֹפְכִים לְלַעֲנָה מִשְׁפָּט

2d וּצְדָקָה לָאָרֶץ הִנִּיחוּ׃

Line 2a: The colon-marker is *zaqeph qaton* and the constraints are: 1 predicator, 3 constituents, and 3 units. This treats בֵּית יוֹסֵף as a proper name and therefore a single unit.

פֶּן־יִצְלַח. The use of פֶּן to begin a strophe may seem unusual, but cf. Ps 7:3 (E 2); Job 32:13; Prov 5:9. פֶּן also begins a sentence at Deuteronomy 8:12. The qal *yiqtol* 3 m s of צלח is somewhat enigmatic, as that root often means to "be successful" (Isa 54:17) or "be useful" (Jer 13:10; Ezek 15:4). However, the verb can also mean to "rush upon" (Judg 14:6), where the subject is the רוּחַ יהוה. Here, YHWH rushes upon the House of Joseph as an enemy.

כָּאֵשׁ. Prepositional phrase with כְּ used for a simile. Note that YHWH, not the fire, is the actual subject of the verb יִצְלַח.

בֵּית יוֹסֵף. A construct chain direct object.

Line 2b: The colon-marker is *silluq* and the constraints are: 2 predicators, 4 constituents, and 4 units.

וְאָכְלָה. Qal *weqatal* 3 f s of אכל. The simile of the fire is extended here.

וְאֵין. Although אֵין is a second predicator in the Hebrew grammar of this line, it can be translated adverbially as a circumstantial clause, "without there being."

מְכַבֶּה. The piel participle m s of כבה is here used periphrastically with וְאֵין.

לְבֵית־אֵל. The preposition לְ may express either advantage ("for the sake of") or possession. The latter is probably preferable, and it here could be translated as "at."

Line 2c: The colon-marker is *athnach* and the constraints are: 1 predicator, 3 constituents, and 3 units.

הַהֹפְכִים. Qal participle m p of הפך with definite article, here serving as a relative clause. What is the antecedent of this participle? Clearly this cannot be linked to the following verse, a doxology to YHWH. The verb הִנִּיחוּ in line 2d is third person (and lines 2c and

2d are obviously bound together), which indicates that the antecedent to הַהֹפְכִים is not the implied second person "you" of דִּרְשׁוּ in line 1g. This means that the common translation, "you that turn justice to wormwood" (thus the NRSV; the ESV and NIV are similar) cannot be correct. The antecedent can only be the implied people at Bethel from line 2b, and is most likely the priests and other officials of that shrine. The participle is therefore implicitly explanatory, asserting that Israel should not go to Bethel because the priests there turn justice to wormwood. To bring out this connection to Bethel, one can render the participle as "where they turn," as is done in the above translation.

לְלַעֲנָה. After הפך, the preposition לְ points to the thing into which something is changed.

מִשְׁפָּט. The direct object. The point is that the priests and officials at Bethel and the other shrines give teachings and rulings that are perverse.

Line 2d: The colon-marker is *silluq* and the constraints are: 1 predicator, 3 constituents, and 3 units. This line is bound to 2c in a chiasmus, indicating that the two lines describe a single event or circumstance.

וּצְדָקָה. The direct object. The conjunction binds this line to the previous. צְדָקָה here stands for the precepts of right religion.

לָאָרֶץ. The preposition לְ is here directional. אֶרֶץ is here better translated as "dirt" than "land" or "earth."

הִנִּיחוּ. Hiphil *qatal* 3 c p of נוּחַ. The hiphil of this root has two different forms, with the one (הֵנִיחַ) generally having a meaning of "giving repose" to something or "satisfying" it, and the other (הִנִּיחַ) meaning to "lay down" or "leave behind" (see *HALOT*). This is the second form.

5:8-9: Doxology: YHWH, Ruler of the Skies: The following poem is one stanza in two strophes. It has one unusual feature: the nominal clause יְהוָה שְׁמוֹ in line 1f suggests that the doxology ends here (see 4:13; 9:6). However, lines 2a-b seem to function as a dark and unexpected afterthought; the cosmic deity YHWH, who controls days and seasons and rains, is bringing his power against human institutions. It may be that Amos has added 5:9 to an already familiar doxology in 5:8. The insertion of this doxology at this point seems arbitrary, but it serves two purposes. First, by proclaiming the cosmic power of YHWH, it rebukes the attempts to domesticate him, treating him as a god of the shrines who can be appeased by pilgrimages and offerings. Second, it sets up a contrast to the Israelite adoration of sky deities in 5:25-27.

5:8: First Strophe. Six lines. There is an inclusion with a nominal clause at each end of the poem (lines 1a and 1f). Within that, there are two couplets (1b-c and 1d-e), each having a periphrastic participle in the first line and a finite verb in the second line. The focus is on YHWH's powers over the sky and seas, as he is both maker and governor of the heavenly bodies and the one who sends rain. There is nothing threatening in this picture of YHWH; it is made threatening by added second strophe.

5:8 1a עֹשֵׂ֨ה כִימָ֜ה וּכְסִ֗יל
1b וְהֹפֵ֤ךְ לַבֹּ֙קֶר֙ צַלְמָ֔וֶת
1c וְי֖וֹם לַ֣יְלָה הֶחְשִׁ֑יךְ
1d הַקּוֹרֵ֣א לְמֵי־הַיָּ֗ם
1e וַֽיִּשְׁפְּכֵ֛ם עַל־פְּנֵ֥י הָאָ֖רֶץ
1f יְהוָ֥ה שְׁמֽוֹ׃ ס

Line 1a: The colon-marker is *revia* and the constraints are: 0 predicators, 2 constituents, and 3 units.

עֹשֵׂ֨ה. Qal active participle m s construct of עשׂה. On the syntax of the participle, see line 1b.

כִימָ֜ה וּכְסִ֗יל. These are widely regarded as respectively the Pleiades and Orion. These constellations are associated with the New

Year and the change from winter to summer, and thus their mention here implies that YHWH governs the seasons (Paul 1991, 168).

Line 1b: The colon-marker is *zaqeph qaton* and the constraints are: 1 predicator, 3 constituents, and 3 units.

וְהֹפֵךְ. Qal active participle m s of הפך functioning as a periphrastic predicator. There are two possible interpretations of this and the previous participle. They could be substantival in verbless clauses, as in "(he is) maker of the Pleiades and Orion." Or, they could periphrastic, as in, "and (he) turns darkness to morning." In fact, it appears that, notwithstanding the formal similarity between lines 1a and 1b, עֹשֵׂה is substantival and וְהֹפֵךְ is periphrastic. Line 1a refers to a single event in the past and not to ongoing activity, but line 1b refers to ongoing activity. Also, line 1b is bound in a chiasmus to the finite verb in line 1c, which implies that וְהֹפֵךְ is verbal and not substantival.

לַבֹּקֶר. There is probably some intended irony in the repetition of the idiom הפך לְ here after its usage in 5:7.

צַלְמָוֶת. The direct object.

Line 1c: The colon-marker is *athnach* and the constraints are: 1 predicator, 3 constituents, and 3 units.

וְיוֹם. The direct object.

לַיְלָה. We might have expected the preposition לְ, meaning "into night." The lack of the preposition suggests that לַיְלָה is here temporal, "at night." But it should not be taken apocalyptically (as, "he makes day as dark as night") since everything else in lines a-f relates to the normal functioning of the cosmos and not to an apocalyptic calamity.

הֶחְשִׁיךְ. Hiphil *qatal* 3 m s of חשך. The change from participle in line 1b to the pattern וְ + [X] + *qatal* here creates contrastive matching for the two lines (i.e., it is conceptually a single event that goes through cycles of day and night).

Line 1d: The colon-marker is *revia* and the constraints are: 1 predicator, 2 constituents, and 3 units.

הַקּוֹרֵא. Qal active participle m s of קרא with definite article and forming a periphrastic relative clause.

לְמֵי־הַיָּם. The preposition לְ here marks the addressee.

Line 1e: The colon-marker is *tifha* and the constraints are: 1 predicator, 2 constituents, and 3 units.

וַיִּשְׁפְּכֵם. Qal *wayyiqtol* 3 m s of שפך with 3 m p suffix. The *wayyiqtol* is used here because the *wayyiqtol* more clearly suggests the idea of sequential action (rather than the cyclic pattern of lines 1b-c). The idea of sequence may be included in the translation with the English word "then," as is done above.

עַל־פְּנֵי הָאָרֶץ. Prepositional phrase with עַל on a construct chain. The preposition is directional, marking motion from above.

Line 1f: The colon-marker is *silluq* and the constraints are: 0 predicators, 2 constituents, and 2 units. It is impossible to tell with certainty which noun in this nominal clause is the subject and which is the predicate. Probably the suffixed noun is the subject and the predicate, יְהוָה, is fronted as the focus of the clause.

יְהוָה. Proper name as predicate (or subject).

שְׁמוֹ. Suffixed noun as subject (or predicate).

5:9: Second Strophe. Two lines. As described above, this comes as an unexpected amendment to the doxology after line 1f. Praised as a deity of sky and sea, YHWH seems safely distant. Suddenly, he is threateningly close.

5:9 2a הַמַּבְלִיג שֹׁד עַל־עָז
2b וְשֹׁד עַל־מִבְצָר יָבוֹא׃

Line 2a: The colon-marker is *athnach* and the constraints are: 1 predicator, 3 constituents, and 3 units.

הַמַּבְלִיג. Hiphil participle m s of בלג with definite article. The hiphil of בלג elsewhere means to "smile" (Ps 39:14 [E = 13]; Job 9:27;

10:20). Some resolve the problem by emending the text (e.g., Mays 1969, 95, reads הַמַּפִּיל. "who sends down"; Wolff 1977, 229, reads הַמַּבְדִּיל, supposedly "who appoints," on the basis of the LXX (ὁ διαιρῶν). For discussion of other proposed emendations, see Zalcman (1981). But such emendation is guesswork and hardly persuasive. Some take "smile" to connote a shining or flashing countenance, and thus translate the word here as "flash forth," but others are dubious of this (e.g., Paul 1991, 169). It may be that הַמַּבְלִיג connotes mocking or laughing at, as do שׂחק and לעג in Psalm 2:4. The beneficent management of the cosmos in lines 1a-f is therefore ironically reversed. God's power over the world is such that he smiles, but not benevolently, on the human power that opposes him, and he uses his cosmic power to bring destruction upon them.

שֹׁ֖ד. Although the hiphil of בלג is elsewhere intransitive (Ps 39:14 [E 13]; Job 9:27; 10:20), שׁד appears to be a direct object. The resultant oxymoron, "he smiles destruction," is probably as peculiar in Hebrew as it is in English, but it is intelligible in context.

עַל־עָ֑ז. In light of the verb used here, the preposition may speak of a potential or imminent destruction hanging above the strong, and the adjective is used substantively.

Line 2b: The colon-marker is *silluq* and the constraints are: 1 predicator, 3 constituents, and 3 units.

וְשֹׁ֖ד. Neither this nor the previous occurrence of שׁד should be emended, as the repetition connotes the fulfillment of a process: God conceives of and "smiles destruction" upon the mighty, and then that destruction does in fact come. Note that the pattern of line 3a is: participle + שׁד + preposition עַל, while the pattern of line 3b is: שׁד + preposition עַל + *yiqtol*. That is, the two lines are paired in a manner analogous to that of lines 1b-c and lines 2a-b, only here the pattern is one of anticipation and fulfillment. That is, line 3a suggests divine intent, and line 3b suggests the fulfillment, in a negative counterpart to the word-creation sequence seen in Genesis 1. Thus it is here, and not in strophe 1, that there is an apocalyptic element. The benevolent creator God of strophe 1 becomes the destructive, apocalyptic God in strophe 2.

עַל־מִבְצָר. The preposition עַל again is directional, marking motion from above.

יָבוֹא. Qal *yiqtol* 3 m s of בוֹא.

5:10-15: Accusation: No Respect for the Poor: The fundamental accusation here is that the powerful class exploits the poor by imposing severe taxes on their grain harvests and then, by means of its control of the court system, thwarts any efforts by the poor to get justice. Since its control of the courts is the key to its ability to fleece the poor, the aristocracy is openly hostile to anyone who feels obliged to deal honestly and fairly with legal cases. Thus, honest men are silenced. The structure of this poem is as follows. The first two strophes are bound by a chiastic pattern (third person / second person // second person / third person). The third strophe is an exhortation that follows from the accusations.

Stanza 1: First accusation pair (5:10-11)

Strophe 1: Accusation in third person (5:10)

Strophe 2: Protasis-Apodosis; accusation and judgment in second person (5:11)

Stanza 2: Second accusation pair (5:12-13)

Strophe 1: Accusation in second person (5:12a)

Strophe 2: Protasis-Apodosis; accusation and social consequence in third person (5:12b-13)

Stanza 3: Exhortation (5:14-15)

Strophe 1: "Seek good and not evil" (5:14)

Strophe 2: "Hate evil and love good" (5:12b-13)

5:10-11: First Stanza. Two strophes respectively of two and six lines. The first strophe makes a general accusation about the antagonism displayed toward honest people who take part in judicial proceedings. By itself, this is difficult for the reader to understand as it has no context. However, the second strophe explains why men of integrity are unwelcome at court.

5:10: First Strophe. Two lines in chiastic parallelism.

5:10 A1a שָׂנְאוּ בַשַּׁעַר מוֹכִיחַ
A1b וְדֹבֵר תָּמִים יְתָעֵבוּ׃

Line A1a: The colon-marker is *athnach* and the constraints are: 1 predicator, 3 constituents, and 3 units.

שָׂנְאוּ. Qal *qatal* 3 c p of שׂנא. The *qatal* here connotes gnomic or typical action.

בַשַּׁעַר. The preposition בְּ is locative, and the gate represents the law courts.

מוֹכִיחַ. Hiphil participle m s of יכח (used substantively and not as a predicator here). This is a person who openly criticizes corrupt practices during court proceedings. A modern counterpart would be a "whistle-blower."

Line A1b: The colon-marker is *silluq* and the constraints are: 1 predicator, 2 constituents, and 3 units.

וְדֹבֵר תָּמִים. Qal active participle m s of דבר with conjunction and the adjective תָּמִים. This is a person who testifies honestly in a court case. The participle is substantival.

יְתָעֵבוּ. Piel *yiqtol* 3 m p of תעב. Both the *qatal* and the *yiqtol* can be used for gnomic action.

5:11: Second Strophe. Six lines, including a protasis (lines A2a-b) and an apodosis (lines A2c-f). The apodosis is a loose citation of Deuteronomy 28:30. The punishment fits the crimes, but being an allusion to Deuteronomy 28:30, it also implies that the curses of Deuteronomy 28 have fallen upon Israel. This apodosis, moreover, is itself made of two bicola (A2c-d and A2e-f), each one a protasis-apodosis construction. Thus the text has a complex protasis-apodosis structure, as follows:

<table>
<tr><td rowspan="2">Major protasis</td><td>Line A2a</td><td></td></tr>
<tr><td>Line A2b</td><td></td></tr>
<tr><td rowspan="4">Major apodosis</td><td>Line A2c</td><td>Minor protasis 1</td></tr>
<tr><td>Line A2d</td><td>Minor apodosis 1</td></tr>
<tr><td>Line A2e</td><td>Minor protasis 2</td></tr>
<tr><td>Line A2f</td><td>Minor apodosis 2</td></tr>
</table>

5:11 A2a לָכֵ֗ן יַ֣עַן בּוֹשַׁסְכֶ֞ם עַל־דָּ֗ל
A2b וּמַשְׂאַת־בַּר֙ תִּקְח֣וּ מִמֶּ֔נּוּ
A2c בָּתֵּ֥י גָזִ֛ית בְּנִיתֶ֖ם
A2d וְלֹא־תֵ֣שְׁבוּ בָ֑ם
A2e כַּרְמֵי־חֶ֣מֶד נְטַעְתֶּ֔ם
A2f וְלֹ֥א תִשְׁתּ֖וּ אֶת־יֵינָֽם׃

Line A1a: The colon-marker is *revia* and the constraints are: 1 predicator, 3 constituents, and 3 units.

לָכֵן. The word לָכֵן has been moved up into the protasis and away from its normal place in the apodosis. This placing of לָכֵן makes the apodosis rhetorically stronger, as it does not begin with a transitional adverb.

יַ֣עַן בּוֹשַׁסְכֶ֞ם. This is the only place in the Hebrew Bible where יַ֣עַן ("because") immediately follows לָכֵן; it is יַעַן that marks this line as the protasis. The verb בּוֹשַׁסְכֶם is often regarded as a poel infinitive construct of בּוּס, to "trample," but it more probably is a cognate of Akkadian *šabāšu sĭbsa*, "to extract a grain tax" (*HALOT* בשׁס). In Hebrew, the שׁ and בּ metathesized (Paul 1991, 173, suggests that it should here be pointed as a Qal infinitive construct with 2 m p suffix as בָּשְׁסְכֶם). Officials of the royal government apparently taxed the peasants exorbitantly for their crops and also skimmed off some for themselves.

עַל־דָּל. Prepositional phrase with עַל. The preposition suggests that the tax is a burden upon the poor.

Line A1b: The colon-marker is *zaqeph qaton* and the constraints are: 1 predicator, 3 constituents, and 4 units.

וּמַשְׂאַת־בַּר. A construct chain used as the direct object. This is another tax or duty imposed on the yeomen and paid in kind with grain.

תִּקְחוּ. Qal *yiqtol* 2 m p from לקח. The shift from the more abstract third person in A1a-b to the more direct second person in A2a-f is striking; the first bicolon is a general statement about the current state of moral perversity in the land, while the second is a direct accusation and leads into a pronouncement of doom.

מִמֶּנּוּ. The 3 m s suffix on מִן has דָּל in A2a as its antecedent.

Line A2c: The colon-marker is *tifha* and the constraints are: 1 predicator, 2 constituents, and 3 units. This is the first minor protasis (having A2d as its apodosis), but it is unmarked, having no particle such as יַעַן to indicate that it is a protasis. This creates momentary suspense, as the reader does not yet know why Amos mentions that they build ashlar houses.

בָּתֵּי גָזִית. Houses built of ashlar (cut stone) would be of the highest quality and extremely expensive. Because the accused enriched themselves by exploiting the farmers they can afford such extravagance.

בְּנִיתֶם. Qal *qatal* 2 m p of בנה. This should not be translated as a past tense but a present, since it would not make sense to suppose that they had already built such houses but were not inhabiting them.

Line A2d: The colon-marker is *athnach* and the constraints are: 1 predicator, 2 constituents, and 2 units.

וְלֹא־תֵשְׁבוּ. Qal *yiqtol* 2 m p of ישב with לֹא and conjunction serving to mark the first minor apodosis. The conjunction here is adversative.

בָּם. Preposition בְּ with 3 m p suffix; the antecedent is בָּתֵּי.

Line A2e: The colon-marker is *zaqeph qaton* and the constraints are: 1 predicator, 2 constituents, and 3 units. This is the second minor protasis, and it, too, is unmarked.

כַּרְמֵי־חֶמֶד. A construct chain direct object in which the absolute noun is used adjectivally. Thus, "vineyards of pleasure" means "pleasant vineyards."

נְטַעְתֶּם. Qal *qatal* 2 m p of נטע.

Line A2f: The colon-marker is *silluq* and the constraints are: 1 predicator, 2 constituents, and 2 units.

וְלֹא תִשְׁתּוּ. Qal *yiqtol* 2 m p of שׁתה with לֹא and conjunction serving to mark the second minor apodosis.

אֶת־יֵינָם. The direct object; the 3 m p suffix has כַּרְמֵי־חֶמֶד as its antecedent.

5:12-13: Second Stanza. Two strophes of two and four lines. It mirrors the first stanza, except that it has the first strophe in the second person and the second strophe in the third.

5:12a: First Strophe. Two lines. Another accusation, in which the crimes of Israel are grammatically governed by יָדַעְתִּי, rhetorically implying that these crimes are undeniable by virtue of being objects of divine knowledge.

כִּי יָדַעְתִּי רַבִּים פִּשְׁעֵיכֶם B1a 5:12a
וַעֲצֻמִים חַטֹּאתֵיכֶם B1b

Line B1a: The colon-marker is *zaqeph qaton* and the constraints are: 1 predicator, 3 constituents, and 3 units. After the predicator יָדַעְתִּי, the words רַבִּים פִּשְׁעֵיכֶם are a subordinate verbless clause describing the content of what YHWH knows.

כִּי יָדַעְתִּי. Qal *qatal* 1 c s of ידע with an explanatory כִּי, indicating that this is justification for the aforementioned punishment.

רַבִּים. A predicate adjective.

פִּשְׁעֵיכֶם. Definite by virtue of the pronoun suffix, this is the subject of the two-word verbless clause רַבִּים פִּשְׁעֵיכֶם.

Line B1b: The colon-marker is *athnach* and the constraints are: 0 predicators, 2 constituents, and 2 units. There is gapping, with יָדַעְתִּי in line B1a governing both lines.

וַעֲצֻמִים. A predicate adjective.

חַטֹּאתֵיכֶם. Definite by virtue of the pronoun suffix, this is the subject of another two-word verbless clause.

5:12b-13: Second Strophe. Four lines. The two lines of 5:12b belong with 5:13 and not with 5:12a. This is because, first, the abstract accusation of 5:12a contrasts with the specific details of 5:12b in a manner analogous to the two strophes of 5:10-11. Second, 5:12a is in second person, while 5:12b is third person (see הִטּוּ in line B2b). Third, the muted response of the prudent man in 5:13 makes sense in the context of the perversion of justice going on in the court proceedings at the gate.

5:12b B2a צֹרְרֵי צַדִּיק לֹקְחֵי כֹפֶר
B2b וְאֶבְיוֹנִים בַּשַּׁעַר הִטּוּ׃
5:13 B2c לָכֵן הַמַּשְׂכִּיל בָּעֵת הַהִיא יִדֹּם
B2d כִּי עֵת רָעָה הִיא׃

Line B2a: The colon-marker is *zaqeph qaton* and the constraints are: 2 predicators, 2 constituents, and 4 units. The two participles are in construct form. They are predicators by virtue of being coordinated with the finite verb of line B2b. This pattern, one or more participles in a series of clauses that concludes in a finite verb, is frequent in Amos. The two participles here are predicates to the implied subject in line B2b and therefore should be translated as third person verbs.

צֹרְרֵי צַדִּיק. Qal participle m p construct of צרר II ("attack") with the absolute noun צַדִּיק serving as an objective genitive. In this context, a צַדִּיק is a man whose case before the court is right.

לֹקְחֵי כֹפֶר. Qal participle m p construct of לקח with the absolute noun כֹּפֶר serving as an objective genitive.

Line B2b: The colon-marker is *silluq* and the constraints are: 1 predicator, 3 constituents, and 3 units. When the poor go to court to complain of the injustice done to them, they are turned away.

וְאֶבְיוֹנִים. The direct object. The word אֶבְיוֹן, "poor," is derived from אבה, to "need," and often connotes financial poverty. In Psalm 49:3 (E 2), it is the polar opposite of "rich" (עָשִׁיר וְאֶבְיוֹן) in a merism.

בַּשַּׁעַר. Prepositional phrase with locative בְּ.

הִטּוּ. Hiphil *qatal* 3 m p of נטה. The verb here means to "turn away." Similar usage is found, for example, in Psalm 27:9, אַל־תַּט־בְּאַף עַבְדֶּךָ ("Do not turn away your servant away in anger").

Line B2c: The colon-marker is *athnach* and the constraints are: 1 predicator, 4 constituents, and 5 units.

לָכֵן. The particle ("therefore") leads into the consequence of the aforementioned situation. The widespread corruption in the courts has silenced men of integrity; they cannot openly oppose such a system for fear of reprisal and because no one in power will listen.

הַמַּשְׂכִּיל. Hiphil participle m s of שׂכל with definite article; it is substantive and is not a predicator. The hiphil participle of שׂכל (used either as a substantive, הַמַּשְׂכִּיל, or without the article as an attributive or predicate adjective) regularly implies positive moral qualities. A person so described is prudent and seeks God (Ps 14:2; 53:3 [E 2]), gives thought to the poor (Ps 41:2 [E 1]), is diligent (Prov 10:5), controls his tongue (Prov 10:19), and is intelligent and of good character (Dan 1:4). Even where the person called מַשְׂכִּיל is described as having success, the implication that he has prudence or piety is also present (1 Sam 18:14-15; Prov 14:35; 17:2). Against Smith (1988), the word does not refer to wealthy but unscrupulous individuals who by their silence join in the oppression of the poor.

בָּעֵ֥ת הַהִ֖יא. Prepositional phrase with בְּ. This expression, analogous to the English "in such a time as this," marks exasperation over the current moral climate.

יִדֹּ֑ם. Qal *yiqtol* 3 m s of דמם, "be silent." Many geminate qal *yiqtol* verbs have a morphology that seems to follow that of the root I-נ (such as נפל, with the *yiqtol* יִפֹּל).

Line B2d: The colon-marker is *silluq* and the constraints are: 0 predicators, 2 constituents, and 3 units.

כִּ֛י עֵ֥ת רָעָ֖ה. The predicate עֵת is modified by the adjective רָעָה. The particle כִּי introduces this second comment on the nature of the time, that society is so corrupt that this era can simply be called "evil."

הִֽיא. A neutrum, this is the subject of the nominal clause of this line.

5:14-15: Third Stanza. This stanza is made up of two strophes that recall 5:4b-7 and also closely reflect one another. Each is in four lines, and in both a protasis exhorts Israel to seek good and not evil, and then an apodosis offers a potential benefit to them for doing so.

5:14: First Strophe. Four lines in protasis-apodosis structure, with C1a being the protasis, and C1b-c being the apodosis. Line C1d comments on the apodosis, declaring that the condition it describes is what Israel desires.

5:14 C1a דִּרְשׁוּ־ט֥וֹב וְאַל־רָ֖ע
C1b לְמַ֣עַן תִּֽחְי֑וּ
C1c וִיהִי־כֵ֞ן יְהוָ֧ה אֱלֹהֵי־צְבָא֛וֹת אִתְּכֶ֖ם
C1d כַּאֲשֶׁ֥ר אֲמַרְתֶּֽם׃

Line C1a: The colon-marker is *tifha* and the constraints are: 1 predicator, 3 constituents, and 3 units.

דִּרְשׁוּ. Qal imperative m p of דרשׁ.

טוֹב. The direct object. One may wonder to what specifically טוֹב refers. Is it God himself, or right behavior, or "true religion" (as described in James 1:26-27)? It probably includes all of these.

וְאַל־רָע. Negated direct object. The specific content of רַע would be the reverse of טוֹב above.

Line C1b: The colon-marker is *athnach* and the constraints are: 1 predicator, 1 constituents, and 2 units.

לְמַעַן תִּחְיוּ. A purpose clause with a qal *yiqtol* 2 m p of חיה giving the expected result of following the command in C1a, the protasis. חיה includes avoidance of the military calamity predicted in 5:3 and more broadly invokes all the blessings promised in Deuteronomy (e.g., 4:1; 5:33; 8:1; 16:20; 30:16).

Line C1c: The colon-marker is *tifha* and the constraints are: 1 predicator, 3 constituents, and 5 units. The particle כֵּן is not a unit. The verbless clause יְהוָה אֱלֹהֵי־צְבָאוֹת אִתְּכֶם is apparently a conventional blessing used at the shrines, which Amos cites with the hope that it may one day come true.

וִיהִי־כֵן. Qal *weyiqtol* 3 m s expressing purpose, with כֵּן, which here means "true."

יְהוָה אֱלֹהֵי־צְבָאוֹת. The name YHWH is here given with one of his titles, as is appropriate for a formal benediction.

אִתְּכֶם. The predicate of the benediction.

Line C1d: The colon-marker is *silluq* and the constraints are: 1 predicator, 1 constituent, and 2 units.

כַּאֲשֶׁר אֲמַרְתֶּם. Qal *qatal* 2 m p of אמר with כַּאֲשֶׁר, "just as." The context in which this is said is probably in benedictions at the shrines.

5:15: Second Strophe. Four lines. This parallels the previous strophe, indicating again that good will come if they repent.

שִׂנְאוּ־רָע וְאֶהֱבוּ טוֹב C2a 5:15
וְהַצִּיגוּ בַשַּׁעַר מִשְׁפָּט C2b
אוּלַי יֶחֱנַן יְהוָה אֱלֹהֵי־צְבָאוֹת C2c
שְׁאֵרִית יוֹסֵף׃ ס C2d

Line C2a: The colon-marker is *zaqeph qaton* and the constraints are: 2 predicator, 4 constituents, and 4 units.

שִׂנְאוּ. Qal imperative m p of שׂנא.

רָע. The direct object of שִׂנְאוּ. The order of "good" and "evil" is here reversed over against line C1a.

וְאֶהֱבוּ. Qal imperative m p of אהב with conjunction. An imperative may be followed by a *weqatal* with imperatival force when they constitute a sequence of actions. Here, the two imperatives indicate not a sequence but a merism with "hate evil" and "love good," as in the so-called "antithetical parallelism" of Proverbs.

טוֹב. The direct object of וְאֶהֱבוּ.

Line C2b: The colon-marker is *athnach* and the constraints are: 1 predicator, 3 constituents, and 3 units.

וְהַצִּיגוּ. Hiphil imperative m p of יצג, "establish." On roots I-י with י assimilated, see *GKC* §71.

בַשַּׁעַר. Prepositional phrase with בְּ, with שַׁעַר here referring to the courtroom setting.

מִשְׁפָּט. The direct object. "Justice" here refers to a right verdict in the courts, and specifically to one that respects the rights of the poor.

Line C2c: The colon-marker is *tifha* and the constraints are: 1 predicator, 3 constituents, and 5 units.

אוּלַי. Introducing the apodosis with אוּלַי, "perhaps," implies that the suppliant cannot presume upon divine grace. It often appears in contexts of repentance and supplication, as in Isaiah 37:4; Jeremiah 21:2; Jeremiah 36:7; Jonah 1:6; Zephaniah 2:3.

יְחֻנַּן. Qal *yiqtol* 3 m s of חנן, "be gracious."

יְהוָה אֱלֹהֵי־צְבָאוֹת. The title for God here deliberately follows the pleonastic formula used in the shrine benediction cited in C1c.

Line C2d: The colon-marker is *silluq* and the constraints are: 0 predicators, 1 constituent, and 2 units. This line is the direct object of the verb of line C2c. There is dramatic power in ending the stanza with the words, "the remnant of Joseph." It implies that destruction is all but certain but that there is yet hope.

שְׁאֵרִית יוֹסֵף. This phrase occurs only here in the Hebrew Bible. It is also one of the few places where a remnant theology appears in Amos, and it suggests that Amos is thinking more of a future restoration than of an avoidance of the destruction currently looming over Israel. Otherwise, it is odd that he would describe Jeroboam II's Israel, at the height of its powers, as a "remnant."

5:16-17: Lamentation Predicted

The theme of lamentation is resumed not with a lament poem but with a prediction of lamentation to come.

5:16a לָכֵן כֹּה־אָמַר יְהוָה אֱלֹהֵי צְבָאוֹת אֲדֹנָי

The above prose divine quotation formula introduces the following poem. The clause has too many units for it to be considered poetry. The title for God is given as extravagantly as possible, suggesting that what follows is an divine oracle or curse given with full solemnity. Also, if the pleonastic title is also used in the shrine benedictions (5:14), the text tells the reader that the God by whose title they pronounce blessings is in fact cursing Israel.

5:16b-17: Oracle: Seven lines. The poem is not properly a lament but a prophecy that a time of lamentation is coming. It is clearly an oracle, being bounded by an inclusion formed by כֹּה־אָמַר יְהוָה in the prose introduction at 5:16a and אָמַר יְהוָה in line g. It thus takes up the pattern of the long judgment stanzas in the oracles on the nations (e.g., 1:4-5). Repetition of בְּכָל in lines a, b, and e dominates the poem, with lines c and d giving exposition on the nature of the lamentation that will come, and line f giving the reason for the lamentation. This oracle parallels that given 5:3.

בְּכָל־רְחֹבוֹת מִסְפֵּד a 5:16b
וּבְכָל־חוּצוֹת יֹאמְרוּ הוֹ־הוֹ b
וְקָרְאוּ אִכָּר אֶל־אֵבֶל c
וּמִסְפֵּד אֶל־יוֹדְעֵי נֶהִי׃ d
וּבְכָל־כְּרָמִים מִסְפֵּד e 5:17
כִּי־אֶעֱבֹר בְּקִרְבְּךָ f
אָמַר יְהוָה׃ ס g

Line a: The colon-marker is *zaqeph qaton* and the constraints are: 0 predicators, 2 constituents, and 2 units. This is a nominal (verbless) clause; subsequent verbs indicate that it should be regarded as predictive.

בְּכָל־רְחֹבוֹת. Prepositional phrase with locative בְּ serving as the predicate. The plazas referred to here are those within Samaria and the other cities of Israel.

מִסְפֵּד. The subject. The term מִסְפֵּד refers to an outpouring of grief and may refer to a funeral ceremony. Isaiah 22:12, וַיִּקְרָא אֲדֹנָי יְהוִה צְבָאוֹת בַּיּוֹם הַהוּא לִבְכִי וּלְמִסְפֵּד וּלְקָרְחָה וְלַחֲגֹר שָׂק ("In that day YHWH GOD of Sabaoth called to weeping and mourning, to baldness and putting on sackcloth"), illustrates the four acts associated with a public display of grief.

Line b: The colon-marker is *athnach* and the constraints are: 1 predicator, 3 constituents, and 4 units.

וּבְכָל־חוּצוֹת. Matching the previous line, this begins with a prepositional phrase with locative בְּ. Here, however, the prepositional phrase modifies a finite verb.

יֹאמְר֥וּ. Qal *yiqtol* 3 m p of אמר in a predictive (future tense) text.

הוֹ־הֽוֹ. Reported speech; the content of what the people will say.

Line c: The colon-marker is *zaqeph qaton* and the constraints are: 1 predicator, 3 constituents, and 3 units.

וְקָרְא֤וּ. Qal *weqatal* 3 c p of קרא.

אִכָּ֔ר. The direct object indicating which person is addressed. Apparently a massive crop failure is behind the lamentation, and thus the farmer is called upon to mourn.

אֶל־אֵ֕בֶל. Prepositional phrase with אֶל indicating purpose, the task to which the farmer is called. אֵבֶל, like מִסְפֵּד, refers generally to mourning, but אֵבֶל sometimes refers more specifically to a time or ceremony of mourning. See the usage of אֵבֶל and מִסְפֵּד in Genesis 50:10.

Line d: The colon-marker is *silluq* and the constraints are: 0 predicators, 2 constituents, and 3 units. There is gapping, with וְקָרְא֤וּ from line c governing this line as well. Amos' skills as a poet are evident here. Formally, the two lines parallel each other very closely, with each having a anarthrous noun followed by a prepositional phrase with אֶל. Functionally, however, the grammatical slots have reversed roles, with the anarthrous noun being the addressee in line c but the task to which he is called in line d, but with the אֶל phrase being the task in line c but the addressee in line d.

וּמִסְפֵּ֖ד. The direct object.

אֶל־י֥וֹדְעֵי נֶֽהִי. Qal active participle m p construct of ידע in a construct chain with נְהִי (in pausal form) and preposition אֶל. Here, אֶל indicates which persons are addressed. נְהִי is an act of lamentation associated with weeping and bitter wailing; see Jeremiah 9:17 (E 18); Micah 2:4.

Line e: The colon-marker is *athnach* and the constraints are: 0 predicators, 2 constituents, and 2 units. This is a verbless clause with a prepositional phrase as the predicate.

וּבְכָל־כְּרָמִים. Prepositional phrase with locative בְּ. Again, the text indicates that the focus of the mourning is an agricultural calamity.

מִסְפֵּד. The subject.

Line f: The colon-marker is *tifha* and the constraints are: 1 predicator, 2 constituents, and 2 units.

כִּֽי־אֶעֱבֹר. Qal *yiqtol* 1 c s of עבר with explanatory כִּי.

בְּקִרְבְּךָ. The verb עבר with בְּקֶרֶב occurs five times in the Hebrew Bible (Deut 29:15 [E 16]; Josh 1:11; 3:2; 24:17; and here). In all other cases, it refers to a person or group passing through another group of people (in Deut 29:15 and Josh 24:17 it refers to Israel's march during the exodus). In Exod 12:12 (with בְּ, but not בְּקֶרֶב) the word עבר describes YHWH moving through Egypt to slay the firstborn. Exodus also speaks of a great outcry (צְעָקָה) going up from the Egyptians over their dead; Amos uses אֵבֶל and מִסְפֵּד, but not צְעָקָה. It is probable, but not certain, that Amos is alluding to the Exodus 12 event, asserting that the God of the Passover was now creating devastation in Israel itself.

Line g: The colon-marker is *silluq* and the constraints are: 1 predicator, 2 constituents, and 2 units. This is another divine speech formula.

אָמַר. Qal *qatal* 3 m s of אמר.

יְהוָה. The subject.

5:18–6:8: Second Series of Accusations, Warnings and Exhortations

Parallel to 5:4-15, this section is in three major parts: an accusation against perverse religion (5:18-24; compare 5:4-7); a question concerning the sky gods (5:25-27; contrast 5:8-9); an accusation against the upper classes (6:1-8a; compare 5:10-15). In addition, all three parts of this section begin with rhetorical questions (5:18, 25-26; 6:2-3), and the two accusatory poems, 5:18-24 and 6:1-8a, both begin with הוֹי.

5:18-24: Accusation: Perverse Religion. This section begins with הוֹי, an outcry of woe but used here, as in 6:1, to identify in a general way those against whom YHWH has an accusation. The accusation is in two stanzas (vv. 18-20 and 21-24) that describe how Israel's religion is perversely misguided.

5:18-20: First Stanza. This stanza is in three strophes. There is a chiastic structure here, as strophes 1 (v. 18) and 3 (v. 20) both speak of the day of YHWH as darkness and not light, and both employ rhetorical questions. The essence of the religious perversity of Israel here is the assumption that the day of YHWH is salvation for them when it is in fact inescapable doom.

5:18: First Strophe. Three lines. The initial cry of lament, הוֹי, connects this to the lament text that precedes this, but this is not a lamentation, as the subsequent content makes clear.

5:18 A1a הֹ֥וי הַמִּתְאַוִּ֖ים אֶת־י֣וֹם יְהוָ֑ה
A1b לָמָּה־זֶּ֥ה לָכֶ֛ם י֥וֹם יְהוָ֖ה
A1c הוּא־חֹ֥שֶׁךְ וְלֹא־אֽוֹר׃

Line A1a: The colon-marker is *athnach* and the constraints are: 1 predicator, 3 constituents, and 4 units.

הֹ֥וי. An interjection. It is commonly used in the prophets when calling out to an evil people on whom disaster is soon to come (e.g., Isa 1:4; 5:8,11; 10:5; 29:15; 45:9; Jer 23:1; 48:1; Ezek 13:18; Mic 2:1; Hab 2:12; Zeph 2:5), although it sometimes is used of mourning generally without moral condemnation (e.g., Jer 34:5). An interjection, it is distinct from the word אוֹי, which appears to be properly a noun meaning "grief" (cf. Prov 23:29, לְמִי אוֹי ["Who has grief?"]). When used to mean "woe to," אוֹי almost always has the preposition לְ (e.g., Num 21:29; 1 Sam 4:7; Isa 3:9; Ezek 16:23); but הוֹי, a simple particle, never does (Ezek 13:18 being the exception that proves the rule). In an extensive discussion, Wolff (1977, 242–45) argues that the "woe saying" (with הוֹי) arose in circles of clan wisdom and was adopted by Amos, but this is neither persuasive nor helpful.

הַמִּתְאַוִּים. Hithpael participle m p with article. This participle is a periphrastic relative clause and is also vocative, as indicated both by the second person pronoun suffix in line A1b and by the fact that these are the people to whom "woe" is addressed.

אֶת־יוֹם יְהוָה. The direct object of the participle. It would appear that eager anticipation of the day of YHWH had become a standard feature of the Israelite shrines. They probably thought that YHWH would appear as a warrior to defeat Israel's enemies on that day.

Line A1b: The colon-marker is *tifha* and the constraints are: 0 predicators, 4 constituents, and 5 units.

לָמָּה. Interrogative pronoun.

זֶּה. The ז of זֶה often has *daghesh forte* after לָמָּה, as in Genesis 25:22. Also, there is doubling of the first letter of a monosyllable closely connected to a preceding word accented on the penult; see *GKC* §20f. Apparently לָמָּה here is to be considered as accented on the penult. Normally when a demonstrative heads a verbless clause, the nominative that forms the other part of the clause will be the predicate, as in זֶה יוֹם יהוה, "This is the day of YHWH." In this case, however, the demonstrative is the predicate. Grammatical clines that describe greater degrees of definiteness in order to determine predication are not inviolable. The implied antecedent for זֶּה, from A1a, is "an object of desire."

לָכֶם. Prepositional phrase with לְ and 2 m p suffix. The dative expression "to you" here means, "in your estimation." That is, it means, "Why do you regard the day of YHWH as this (a thing to be desired)?"

יוֹם יְהוָה. Subject of verbless clause; a construct chain.

Line A1c: The colon-marker is *silluq* and the constraints are: 0 predicators, 3 constituents, and 3 units.

הֽוּא. The subject. The antecedent is יוֹם יְהוָה.

חֹ֖שֶׁךְ. The predicate in a verbless clause.

וְלֹא־אֽוֹר. A second, negated predicate. The precise significance of the metaphors "darkness" and "light" is not made clear, but probably they respectively represent disaster and salvation.

5:19: Second Strophe. Five lines describing a hypothetical flight from wild beasts as an analogy to how inescapable is the doom of the day of YHWH.

כַּאֲשֶׁ֨ר יָנ֥וּס אִישׁ֙ מִפְּנֵ֣י הָאֲרִ֔י A2a 5:19
וּפְגָע֖וֹ הַדֹּ֑ב A2b
וּבָ֣א הַבַּ֔יִת A2c
וְסָמַ֤ךְ יָדוֹ֙ עַל־הַקִּ֔יר A2d
וּנְשָׁכ֖וֹ הַנָּחָֽשׁ׃ A2e

Line A2a: The colon-marker is *zaqeph qaton* and the constraints are: 1 predicator, 4 constituents, and 4 units.

כַּאֲשֶׁ֨ר. This word generally stands before a finite verb and means "just as." It can be used in a temporal sense (Gen 12:11; Jer 38:28), or it can describe some kind of correspondence, usually either between what was said and what was done, or between two actions thought to be equivalent (Gen 17:23; 21:4; 26:29; 41:13; Exod 1:12; 7:20; 1 Kgs 1:30; Isa 14:24; Ezek 16:59). Here, it is used to introduce an analogy (see Isa 9:2; 29:8; 65:8; Jer 13:11; 43:12; Ezek 1:16; 15:6; Amos 2:13).

יָנ֥וּס. Qal *yiqtol* 3 m s of נוּס. The issue of flight from danger recalls Amos' initial statement of judgment on Israel (2:16). The *yiqtol* here is used for the subjunctive mood, here setting up an unreal, hypothetical condition.

אִישׁ֙. The subject, here a hypothetical man.

מִפְּנֵי הָאֲרִי. Prepositional phrase with מִפְּנֵי. For a second time Amos uses the lion (אֲרִי) as an analogy for the disaster about to overtake Israel; see Amos 3:12.

Line A2b: The colon-marker is *athnach* and the constraints are: 1 predicator, 2 constituents, and 2 units.

וּפְגָעוֹ. Qal *weqatal* 3 m s of פגע ("meet") with 3 m s suffix. The *weqatal* marks the apodosis after the preceding line, a hypothetical situation that forms the protasis.

הַדֹּב. This is the only place where Amos refers to the bear, although Hosea 13:8 uses it for a metaphor of divine wrath. Here, it illustrates futility; a person escapes one disaster only to run headlong into another.

Line A2c: The colon-marker is *zaqeph qaton* and the constraints are: 1 predicator, 2 constituents, and 2 units.

וּבָא. Qal *weqatal* 3 m s of בוֹא. The *weqatal* here could be sequential to the previous episode, as in, "and then he," or it could mark an alternative apodosis, using "or" for the conjunction.

הַבַּיִת. The noun here is equivalent to the English "home" and needs no preposition or directive ה.

Line A2d: The colon-marker is *zaqeph qaton* and the constraints are: 1 predicator, 3 constituents, and 3 units.

וְסָמַךְ. Qal *weqatal* 3 m s of סמך. This is another sequential *weqatal*.

יָדוֹ. The direct object.

עַל־הַקִּיר. Prepositional phrase with locative עַל. The implication is that he thinks he has escaped and can rest a moment.

Line A2e: The colon-marker is *silluq* and the constraints are: 1 predicator, 2 constituents, and 2 units.

וּנְשָׁכוֹ. Qal *weqatal* 3 m s of נשך. Although sequential, it is also the apodosis to lines A2c-d; note also that it is morphologically identical to וּפְגָעוֹ in line A2b.

הַנָּחָשׁ. The biting of the snake (נָחָשׁ and the verb נשׁךְ) is used here and in 9:3 to describe the futility of trying to escape God's wrath. There is more than futility here; there is also irony. The man who tries to escape a lion runs straight to a bear or finds himself bitten by a snake. The irony relates to the absurdity of Israel going to the shrines and thinking that there and in the day of YHWH they have safety.

5:20: Third Strophe. Two lines. Repetition of the homophone *lō* (twice in A3a as לֹא, and twice A3b as לֹא and לוֹ) dominates these lines.

הֲלֹא־חֹשֶׁךְ יוֹם יְהוָה וְלֹא־אוֹר A3a 5:20
וְאָפֵל וְלֹא־נֹגַהּ לוֹ׃ A3b

Line A3a: The colon-marker is *athnach* and the constraints are: 0 predicators, 3 constituents, and 4 units. This is a verbless clause with a compound predicate.

הֲלֹא־חֹשֶׁךְ. Another rhetorical question, this one is introduced by הֲלֹא, implying that the answer should be self-evident. Thus, longing for the day of YHWH is a form of self-delusion.

יוֹם יְהוָה. The subject, with חֹשֶׁךְ being the predicate.

וְלֹא־אוֹר. A second, negated predicate.

Line A3b: The colon-marker is *silluq* and the constraints are: 0 predicators, 3 constituents, and 3 units. There is gapping, with the subject יוֹם יְהוָה from line A3a governing this line.

וְאָפֵל. Another predicate for יוֹם יְהוָה and parallel to חֹשֶׁךְ. The form אָפֵל is found only here; elsewhere the word is אֹפֶל (which itself occurs only eight times [five times in Job]). Another cognate noun, אֲפֵלָה, is more common in the prophets (e.g., Isa 8:22; Joel 2:2). All three cognates mean "darkness."

וְלֹא נֹגַהּ. Another negated, secondary predicate, and in parallel with וְלֹא־אוֹר.

לֹו. Prepositional phrase with possessive לְ. This actually makes for a much stronger statement; line A3a had merely said that it was darkness and not light. With this prepositional phrase, this line says that the day of YHWH possesses no light at all. This suggests hopelessness, analogous to Dante's "Abandon all hope ye who enter here" (*Inferno* III.9).

5:21-24: Second Stanza. Four strophes at vv. 21, 22, 23, and 24. In these strophes YHWH respectively rejects their feasts, sacrifices and sacred music, but then calls on them to fill the land with justice. Each strophe is of a distinct grammatical type: strophe 1 is declarative, strophe 2 is a protasis-apodosis construction, strophe 3 has a second person imperative and an emphatic first person *yiqtol*, and strophe 4 is a third person jussive.

5:21: First Strophe. Two lines. This strophe describes God's disdain for Israel's festivals.

שָׂנֵ֥אתִי מָאַ֖סְתִּי חַגֵּיכֶ֑ם B1a 5:21
וְלֹ֥א אָרִ֖יחַ בְּעַצְּרֹתֵיכֶֽם׃ B1b

Line B1a: The colon-marker is *athnach* and the constraints are: 2 predicators, 3 constituents, and 3 units.

שָׂנֵ֥אתִי. Qal *qatal* 1 c s of שׂנא, "hate."

מָאַ֖סְתִּי. Qal *qatal* 1 c s of מאס, "reject." The anarthrous seconding of the first verb with another, near-synonymous verb eloquently expresses the disgust of someone who is weary of something tedious and irksome.

חַגֵּיכֶ֑ם. The direct object with a 2 m p suffix. Festivals were of course intended to be occasions of celebration, and the triumphalist assumption of the participants is that God is as pleased with the worship as the people themselves are. The suffix subtly suggests that God has nothing to do with religious ceremonies that belong to "you" and not to God.

Line B1b: The colon-marker is *silluq* and the constraints are: 1 predicator, 2 constituents, and 2 units.

וְלֹ֥א אָרִ֖יחַ. Hiphil *yiqtol* 1 c s of רוח. The verb properly means to "smell," but here it connotes God's approving acceptance of sacrifices (cf. Gen 8:21). In Leviticus 26:31, the verb has the preposition בְּ attached to its object: וְלֹא אָרִיחַ בְּרֵיחַ נִיחֹחֲכֶם ("and I will not inhale your pleasing aromas"). But the usage here seems different (see below).

בְּעַצְּרֹתֵיכֶֽם. The noun עֲצָרָה means "assembly" (2 Kgs 10:20; 2 Chr 7:9), which seems an odd object for the verb אָרִיחַ. However, "sacrifices" may be implied as what takes place "in" (בְּ) the sacred assemblies. Note the close association between offerings, incense, and the עֲצָרָה in Isaiah 1:13.

5:22: Second Strophe. Three lines. No amount of extravagance or expense in religious offerings will move YHWH to show them favor.

כִּ֣י אִם־תַּעֲלוּ־לִ֥י עֹל֛וֹת B2a 5:22
וּמִנְחֹתֵיכֶ֖ם לֹ֣א אֶרְצֶ֑ה B2b
וְשֶׁ֧לֶם מְרִיאֵיכֶ֛ם לֹ֥א אַבִּֽיט׃ B2c

Line B2a: The colon-marker is *tevir* and the constraints are: 1 predicator, 3 constituents, and 3 units. The use of the *tevir* for a colon-marker is unusual; by the cantillation marks alone we would treat B2a and B2b together as one line. Here, however, this is peculiar. First, as one line, there would be five constituents. Second, עֹלוֹת and וּמִנְחֹתֵיכֶם do not fit well together on a single line as the compound direct object of תַּעֲלוּ. This is because עֹלוֹת has no suffix but וּמִנְחֹתֵיכֶם does. Note, however, that in the colometry proposed above line B2b is syntactically parallel to B2c (a direct object with 2 m p suffix followed by a negated *yiqtol*). Thus, we propose that line B2a is the protasis and lines B2b and B2c are a parallel, two-line apodosis.

כִּֽי אִם־תַּעֲלוּ. Hiphil *yiqtol* 2 m p of עלה, preceded by כִּי אִם (not the exceptive meanings "unless" or "instead" [*GKC* §163] but the more literal "for if").

לִ֛י. The indirect object.

עֹל֧וֹת. The direct object. As a sacrifice in which the offered beast is entirely consumed in fire, with nothing left for the participants, the whole offering is the most extravagant (and expensive) cultic display of devotion to God. This suggests that this line is really a concessive protasis: "*even if* you were to offer whole offerings to me."

Line B2b: The colon-marker is *athnach* and the constraints are: 1 predicator, 2 constituents, and 2 units.

וּמִנְחֹתֵיכֶם. The direct object. The noun מִנְחָה is here the most general and broad term for offerings made to God, including all kinds of sacrifices, libations, and grain offerings. It thus includes but is not limited to the whole offerings of the previous line. It is odd for a negated apodosis to begin with a conjunction and noun, but this is precisely what Amos does twice in 3:6 (אִם־יִתָּקַע שׁוֹפָר בְּעִיר וְעָם לֹא יֶחֱרָדוּ ["Will a shofar sound in a city / And a people not be terrified?"] and אִם־תִּהְיֶה רָעָה בְּעִיר וַיהוָה לֹא עָשָׂה ["Will there be disaster in a city / And YHWH has not done it?"]). Granted, 3:6 contains rhetorical questions and the present verse does not. On the other hand, the fronting of the two conjoined noun phrases in B2b-c (וּמִנְחֹתֵיכֶם and וְשֶׁלֶם מְרִיאֵיכֶם) suggests that these two items are made prominent in order to set them in contrast with עֹלוֹת in line B2a. The idea is that God would not accept their gifts and peace offerings even if they included whole burnt sacrifices.

לֹ֣א אֶרְצֶ֑ה. Negated qal *yiqtol* 1 c s of רצה.

Line B2c: The colon-marker is *silluq* and the constraints are: 1 predicator, 2 constituents, and 3 units.

וְשֶׁ֥לֶם מְרִיאֵיכֶ֖ם. The direct object in a construct chain with the conjunction.

לֹ֥א אַבִּֽיט. Negated hiphil *yiqtol* 1 c s of נבט. The use of this verb in a cultic setting with the meaning "look favorably upon" is unusual, but the word, when God is the subject, can have such a meaning. Cf. Isaiah 66:2: וְאֶל־זֶה אַבִּיט אֶל־עָנִי וּנְכֵה־רוּחַ ("and to this one I will look [with favor], to the humble and broken-hearted").

5:23: Third Strophe. Two lines. This strophe describes God's disdain for Israel's sacred music.

5:23 B3a הָסֵר מֵעָלַי הֲמוֹן שִׁרֶיךָ
B3b וְזִמְרַת נְבָלֶיךָ לֹא אֶשְׁמָע׃

Line B3a: The colon-marker is *athnach* and the constraints are: 1 predicator, 3 constituents, and 4 units.

הָסֵר. Hiphil imperative m s of סוּר.

מֵעָלַי. Prepositional phrase with מִן and עַל on a 1 c s suffix. The preposition עַל suggests that the music of Israel has become an unbearable burden upon YHWH. It is difficult to convey this in English.

הֲמוֹן שִׁרֶיךָ. The direct object; a construct chain with 2 m s suffix. Here, the absolute noun ("your songs") is adjectival, describing what the construct noun ("noise") consists of. There does not appear to be any significance to the change from plural suffixes in the previous strophe to the singular suffixes used here, except that perhaps it helps to delineate strophic divisions. The noun הָמוֹן generally refers either to a mob of people (Isa 5:13) or to the discordant noise they create (1 Sam 14:19; Isa 31:4). Thus, the worship songs of Israel's singers are regarded as the cacophony of a mob.

Line B3b: The colon-marker is *silluq* and the constraints are: 1 predicator, 2 constituents, and 3 units.

וְזִמְרַת נְבָלֶיךָ. The direct object; a construct chain with 2 m s suffix. This is formally parallel to הֲמוֹן שִׁרֶיךָ in the previous line. The noun וְזִמְרַת, however, does not carry any negative connotations (see Ps 81:3 [E 2]). The important point is that it is not the quality of their playing that makes their songs discordant in God's ears, but their moral and spiritual lives. The נֵבֶל ("lyre") is associated with worship in various contexts (e.g., Ps 144:9). For further discussion on the nature of the instrument, see the comments on 6:5.

לֹא אֶשְׁמָע. Qal *yiqtol* 1 c s of שׁמע and the negative לֹא. The first person *yiqtol* here is not a simple statement of the future but an emphatic refusal to listen, as when an English speaker says, "I will not go!" as an emphatic refusal to go.

5:24: Fourth Strophe. Two lines. YHWH here gives Israel an alternative to trying to please him with sacrifice and song.

5:24 B4a וְיִגַּל כַּמַּיִם מִשְׁפָּט
B4b וּצְדָקָה כְּנַחַל אֵיתָן׃

Line B4a: The colon-marker is *athnach* and the constraints are: 1 predicator, 3 constituents, and 3 units.

וְיִגַּל. Niphal *weyiqtol* 3 m s of גלל. The *weyiqtol* has jussive force and is here contrastive, suggesting that the Israelites should do this rather than sing their praise-songs. גלל is not elsewhere used with מַיִם. The niphal of גלל appears in only one other place, Isaiah 34:4, where heaven is "rolled up like a scroll." Thus the verb here seems to refer to how water rolls over itself in waves. This suggests waters that move with speed and in abundance. Justice should come forth plenteously and not, as it were, in a small trickle.

כַּמַּיִם. Prepositional phrase with כְּ, forming an analogy. Water is refreshing and cleansing, and so is an apt metaphor for justice.

מִשְׁפָּט. The direct object. In context, this would refer to putting an end to the oppression of the poor.

Line B4b: The colon-marker is *silluq* and the constraints are: 0 predicators, 2 constituents, and 3 units. There is gapping, with וְיִגַּל governing this line.

וּצְדָקָה. Parallel to מִשְׁפָּט, this again refers to honesty in the courts and concern for the needs of the poor.

כְּנַחַל אֵיתָן. Prepositional phrase with כְּ and parallel to כַּמַּיִם. The adjective אֵיתָן means "permanent, perennial" and so here refers to a stream that does not run dry.

5:25-27: Question and Oracle: Sky Gods: This text, a prose rhetorical question (5:25-26) with an oracle from YHWH (5:27), is ironically juxtaposed with 5:8-9, a doxology that asserts that YHWH is ruler of the heavens (note also that יְהוָה שְׁמוֹ in 5:8 is answered by אָמַר יְהוָה אֱלֹהֵי־צְבָאוֹת שְׁמוֹ in 5:27). Although YHWH rules heaven and earth, Israel worships minor astral deities! The only possible response to this perverse apostasy is for Israel to go into exile.

5:25-26: This is a prose rhetorical question; it is a single sentence in three clauses.

5:25-26 הַזְּבָחִים וּמִנְחָה הִגַּשְׁתֶּם־לִי בַמִּדְבָּר אַרְבָּעִים
שָׁנָה בֵּית יִשְׂרָאֵל׃ וּנְשָׂאתֶם אֵת סִכּוּת מַלְכְּכֶם
וְאֵת כִּיּוּן צַלְמֵיכֶם כּוֹכַב אֱלֹהֵיכֶם אֲשֶׁר עֲשִׂיתֶם
לָכֶם׃

Prose Clause: הַזְּבָחִים וּמִנְחָה הִגַּשְׁתֶּם־לִי בַמִּדְבָּר אַרְבָּעִים שָׁנָה בֵּית יִשְׂרָאֵל׃

The above, 5:25, is a single clause. Its verb, הִגַּשְׁתֶּם (hiphil *qatal* 2 m p of נגשׁ), here indicates that the text perspective is historical (past tense). The sentence begins with two direct objects (הַזְּבָחִים וּמִנְחָה ["sacrifices and offering"]) pointing to the focus of this paragraph, the religious observances of Israel. Formally, the prefix on הַזְּבָחִים has all the characteristics of a definite article, but it is widely taken to be an interrogative ה (cf. the *pathach* and *daghesh forte* before *shewa* in the interrogative ה of Numbers 13:19, הַבְּמַחֲנִים). If the prefix on הַזְּבָחִים were the article, it would be anomalous that וּמִנְחָה does not have the article. All in all, it appears certain that the prefix is in fact an interrogative ה. The first person indirect object (לִי) indicates the recipient of the sacrifices, YHWH. The locative phrase (בַּמִּדְבָּר) and the temporal phrase (אַרְבָּעִים שָׁנָה) together indicate that the setting for the question is the forty years in the wilderness. A vocative (בֵּית יִשְׂרָאֵל) concludes the clause. The real problem here, of course, is not the grammar of the text but the astonishing inference one draws from it, that Amos here claims that Israel made no sacrifices to God for forty years in the wilderness. A common interpretation is that Amos 5:25, along with Jeremiah 7:22-23, either follows JE against P (Paul 1991, 194) or reflects Deuteronomistic thinking (Wolff 1977, 264–65) when it asserts that the Israelites received little if any cultic instruction in the wilderness. Mays (1974, 111–12) suggests that Amos' words reflect a somewhat strident attitude on his part as a spokesman for the anti-sacrifice party. See also the views expressed in Smith (1998, 253–54); Cripps (1929, 338–48); Andersen and Freedman (1989, 531–37). I am on record for rejecting the documentary hypothesis (Garrett 1991), but this is not the place for entering into such a far-reaching discussion, nor is there room here for dealing either with Jeremiah 7:22-23 or with the reconstruction of Israel's religious history that asserts that the prophets rejected the cult. In my view, the entire discussion of Amos 5:25 is misguided since it fails to reckon with the connection between 5:25 and 5:26 (Andersen and Freedman do see a connection between these verses, but they are not able to work this into an intelligible interpretation and their discussion flounders).

Prose Clause: וּנְשָׂאתֶם אֵת סִכּוּת מַלְכְּכֶם וְאֵת כִּיּוּן צַלְמֵיכֶם כּוֹכַב אֱלֹהֵיכֶם

The single most important grammatical feature of this text is the verb וּנְשָׂאתֶם, a qal *weqatal* 2 m p of נשׂא. Why is the *weqatal* used? It cannot have one of its more common functions here (such as an apodosis, a final clause, or a mainline verb in a predictive or directive text), since all of these interpretations disregard the context. Rather, this is a case where the *weqatal* has imperfective force in a past tense context. This is most often seen where the past tense context is set by a prior *wayyiqtol* verb (Gen 30:40-41; 1 Sam 7:15-16; see *IBHS* §32.2.3), but in this case the context is a rhetorical question, which is naturally headed by a *qatal* rather than a *wayyiqtol.* Translating literally, therefore, וּנְשָׂאתֶם here means, "and you were carrying" or "and you would carry," but putting it into normal English in the context of a past tense rhetorical question, it means, "while you were carrying." Amos is not simply asking if they made sacrifices to YHWH during the forty years, but *whether they made sacrifices while also carrying images of the sky gods from place to place.* He is not denying that Israel sacrificed to YHWH in the wilderness. He is saying that sacrificing to YHWH is fundamentally incompatible with giving reverence to the sky gods, and he is pointing out how absurd it is to imagine the wilderness Israelites under Moses doing such a thing. Also, the "carrying" of the sky gods may allude to festive processions, in which images of astral deities were paraded about, that took place at the shrines in Amos' time. The alternative interpretation, taking וּנְשָׂאתֶם as a future tense that refers to the Israelites carrying their gods into exile, is both grammatically a non sequitur and historically implausible. The grammar of the rest of the sentence is somewhat difficult for having so many nouns one after another. Emending the text, as is proposed by Isbell (1978) on the basis of the LXX, is highly speculative and not persuasive. The best solution is to take סִכּוּת and כִּיּוּן, both proper names, as the direct objects of the verb. Paul (1991, 195–96) has demonstrated that Sikkuth and Kiyyun were ancient deities known in Mesopotamia and Ugarit and that no emendation is necessary. מַלְכְּכֶם is a common noun in apposition to סִכּוּת, while צַלְמֵיכֶם and כּוֹכַב אֱלֹהֵיכֶם both stand in apposition to both proper names. The singular noun כּוֹכַב in כּוֹכַב אֱלֹהֵיכֶם here refers to a plurality and should be rendered as, "the stars of your gods" or more simply, "your astral gods" (cf. the analogous construction in Gen 32:17, בְּיַד־עֲבָדָיו ["in the hands (singular noun representing a plural) of his servants"]). The phrasing אֵת סִכּוּת מַלְכְּכֶם וְאֵת כִּיּוּן צַלְמֵיכֶם may be deliberately constructed as a mocking rhyme.

Prose Clause: אֲשֶׁר עֲשִׂיתֶם לָכֶם

The is a relative clause; the antecedent of אֲשֶׁר is the two proper names Sikkuth and Kiyyun. עֲשִׂיתֶם, a qal *qatal* 2 m p of עשׂה, and לָכֶם, "for yourselves," point out that these deities are man-made and are novelties as far as Israel's religious traditions go. The words אֱלֹהֵיכֶם אֲשֶׁר עֲשִׂיתֶם לָכֶם may also allude to the golden calf episode, suggesting that Israel is fulfilling that one unsavory aspect of the exodus story (cf. Exod 32:1, עֲשֵׂה־לָנוּ אֱלֹהִים ["make gods for us!"]).

5:27: Oracle. Two lines. This is connected to the preceding text by the verb (*weqatal*), but it signals a change by a switch to the first person singular over against the prior second plural verbs. This section scans as a poem, unlike the prior text, and as is appropriate to an oracle it has a divine speech formula.

5:27	a	וְהִגְלֵיתִ֥י אֶתְכֶ֖ם מֵהָ֣לְאָה לְדַמָּ֑שֶׂק
	b	אָמַ֥ר יְהוָ֛ה אֱלֹהֵֽי־צְבָא֖וֹת שְׁמֽוֹ׃ פ

Line a: The colon-marker is *athnach* and the constraints are: 1 predicator, 3 constituents, and 4 units.

וְהִגְלֵיתִ֥י. Hiphil *weqatal* 1 c s of גלה, here functioning as a predictive text. As indicated above, this verb falls within a separate section of the text from the previous *weqatal*, וּנְשָׂאתֶם, and it is also marked by a change in subject. Apart from that, it is not at all unusual for two consecutive *weqatal* verbs to have entirely different syntactical functions.

אֶתְכֶם. The direct object.

מֵהָ֣לְאָה לְדַמָּ֑שֶׂק. The pronoun הָלְאָה ("over there") combines with מִן and לְ to form the preposition מֵהָלְאָה לְ ("beyond"). It is found in Genesis 35:21; Jeremiah 22:19; and here. "Beyond Damascus" suggests Assyrian domains in northern Mesopotamia. This removes the Israelites beyond the expanded domain Israel had achieved under Jeroboam II (see 2 Kgs 14:28).

Line b: The colon-marker is *silluq* and the constraints are: 1 predicator, 4 constituents, and 5 units. There are two clauses: אָמַר יְהוָה

and אֱלֹהֵי־צְבָאוֹת שְׁמוֹ. The conjunctive *merka* in יְהוָה should be disregarded; it makes the line ungrammatical. The second clause is a relative clause with implied אֲשֶׁר.

אָמַר. Qal *qatal* 3 m s of אמר.

יְהוָה. The subject in the divine speech formula אָמַר יְהוָה.

אֱלֹהֵי־צְבָאוֹת. This construct chain is the predicate of the relative clause (אֲשֶׁר) אֱלֹהֵי־צְבָאוֹת שְׁמוֹ.

שְׁמוֹ. This is the subject (with implied אֲשֶׁר) of the relative clause. It means, "whose name (is)."

6:1-8a: Accusation: Perverse Behavior: Four stanzas. Like the first poem of the second complaint (5:18-24), this poem begins with the lament cry הוֹי. It is a complex text of several parts. After the initial cry of woe, identifying the accused (6:1), the text commands the accused to take note of nations that are comparable to their own and draw the relevant lesson (6:2). After this, it presents the aristocrats in Samaria with a detailed list of accusations (6:3-6) and concludes with an oracle of judgment (6:7-8a).

6:1: First Stanza. This stanza is in one strophe of four lines. The Hebrew is somewhat difficult, but neither emending (as in Holladay 1972) nor removing line Ac as a Deuteronomistic gloss (as in Wolff 1977, 270–71) is persuasive. This stanza is two parts. The first, lines Aa-b, is an interjection, a cry of woe against the upper classes. The second, lines Ac-d, is a sentence in two clauses describing the honors given to those classes.

6:1 Aa הוֹי הַשַּׁאֲנַנִּים בְּצִיּוֹן
Ab וְהַבֹּטְחִים בְּהַר שֹׁמְרוֹן
Ac נְקֻבֵי רֵאשִׁית הַגּוֹיִם
Ad וּבָאוּ לָהֶם בֵּית יִשְׂרָאֵל׃

Line Aa: The colon-marker is *zaqeph qaton* and the constraints are: 0 predicators, 3 constituents, and 3 units. This line is an exclamation and lacks any predication.

הוֹי. The initial cry of woe governs lines Aa-b.

הַשַּׁאֲנַנִּים. The adjective שַׁאֲנָן ("self-confident, carefree") with a definite article.

בְּצִיּוֹן. Prepositional phrase with locative בְּ. It is peculiar that Amos, who devotes almost the whole of his book to castigating Samaria and the northern kingdom, should in this brief instance and contrary to context speak against the Jerusalem aristocracy. The LXX here is quite different, taking it as an attack on those who reject Zion theology (οὐαὶ τοῖς ἐξουθενοῦσιν Σιων ["Woe to those who despise Zion"]). But the LXX should not be followed here (it is unreliable as a witness to the Hebrew *Urtext*; see Gelston 2002). Scholars routinely treat this line as an interpolation or seek to emend the text (see Wolff 1977, 269–70). It is better to see this as a place where the humanity of Amos comes through. Amos could not have been unaware of fact that most of the aristocrats in his homeland were no better than those of Samaria, and he probably felt greater bitterness towards the corrupt snobs who mistreated his own people. His commission was to Israel, but he inserts a word of condemnation against similar sinners in Zion. The authenticity of "Zion" here is also attested to by Amos' oblique reference to Jerusalem's domination over Gath in 6:2 (see the discussion at 6:2b).

Line Ab: The colon-marker is *athnach* and the constraints are: 0 predicators, 2 constituents, and 3 units.

וְהַבֹּטְחִים. Qal active participle of בטח with conjunction. It functions adjectivally in parallel with הַשַּׁאֲנַנִּים in line Aa.

בְּהַר שֹׁמְרוֹן. Prepositional phrase with locative בְּ. The term הַר here refers to the acropolis of the city and by extension its fortifications and cultic sites in which people placed their hopes for military and divine protection.

Line Ac: The colon-marker is *zaqeph qaton* and the constraints are: 1 predicator, 1 constituent, and 3 units.

נְקֻבֵי רֵאשִׁית הַגּוֹיִם. A construct chain with a qal passive participle m p construct of נקב ("designate, mark"). It is not grammatically connected to the previous two lines (note the lack of a conjunction), but it is joined to the next line (indicated by the *weqatal* that begins line Ad). For this reason, this line should be translated as a periphrastic clause with the subject ("they," from לָהֶם in the next line) implied. רֵאשִׁית is an appositional genitive and הַגּוֹיִם is a partitive genitive. It ironically speaks to the conceit of the aristocracy of Samaria, who think of themselves as the best people of the best country in the world.

Line Ad: The colon-marker is *silluq* and the constraints are: 1 predicator, 3 constituents, and 3 units (counting בֵּית יִשְׂרָאֵל as a proper name and therefore one unit). This line is exposition on line Ac.

וּבָאוּ. Qal *weqatal* 3 c p of בּוֹא. The *weqatal* functions imperfectively to describe a frequent event.

לָהֶם. Prepositional phrase with directional לְ and a 3 m p suffix.

בֵּית יִשְׂרָאֵל. The subject. The phrase here stands for all the people of Israel, and thus the third plural verb. The meaning is that the aristocracy basks in the glory of having people from all over the nation come to them for advice, help, or to pay homage.

6:2: Second Stanza. This stanza is in two strophes. The first is a tricolon of imperatives and the second is a pair of alternative questions. It points to other nations in order to demonstrate the folly of Samaria's confidence and pride.

6:2a: First Strophe. Three lines, each beginning with an imperative.

6:2a B1a עִבְרוּ כַלְנֵה וּרְאוּ
B1b וּלְכוּ מִשָּׁם חֲמַת רַבָּה
B1c וּרְדוּ גַת־פְּלִשְׁתִּים

Line B1a: The colon-marker is *zaqeph qaton* and the constraints are: 2 predicators, 3 constituents, and 3 units.

עִבְר֞וּ. Qal imperative mp of עבר. The verb here signifies crossing into another nation's territory.

כַלְנֵה֙. Calneh, also called Calno, was located in Syria, in the lower Orontes valley (it is also mentioned in Isa 10:9). On the significance of mentioning Calneh here, see the discussion below at 6:2b.

וּרְא֔וּ. Qal imperative m p of ראה with conjunction; the imperative with conjunction sometimes implies purpose.

Line B1b: The colon-marker is *athnach* and the constraints are: 1 predicator, 3 constituents, and 3 units (taking חֲמַת רַבָּה as a proper name and therefore one unit).

וּלְכ֥וּ. Qal imperative m p of הלך with conjunction.

מִשָּׁ֖ם. Prepositional phrase with מִן.

חֲמַ֣ת רַבָּ֑ה. "Great Hamath," so-called because it contained various smaller states within it. In the text of the Eponym Chronicle, where Tiglath-pileser III mentions his defeat of Calneh, he also refers to the "nineteen districts of Hamath." It was located on the Orontes in Syria.

Line B1c: The colon-marker is *revia* and the constraints are: 1 predicator, 2 constituents, and 2 units.

וּרְד֣וּ. Qal imperative mp of רדה with conjunction.

גַת־פְּלִשְׁתִּ֔ים. The proper name construct chain "Gath of the Philistines." A directive particle such as a preposition אֶל or directive ה is implied. Gath was almost certainly located at Tell es-Safi. According to 2 Kings 12:18 (E 17), Hazael of Damascus seized Gath in the late ninth century. Uzziah of Judah, within whose reign Amos prophesied (Amos 1:1), pulled down the walls of Gath in the early 8th century according to 2 Chronicles 26:6. A major destruction level, together with a major siege trench, dating to Iron Age IIA has been found at Tell es-Safi. Evidence indicates that this siege was carried out by Hazael; Uzziah probably further reduced Gath after the Hazael's departure from the area. For further discussion, see Maeir (2004).

6:2b: Second Strophe. Two lines, each containing a direct question.

6:2b	B2a	הֲטוֹבִים מִן־הַמַּמְלָכוֹת הָאֵלֶּה
	B2b	אִם־רַב גְּבוּלָם מִגְּבֻלְכֶם׃

Line B2a: The colon-marker is *zaqeph qaton* and the constraints are: 0 predicators, 2 constituents, and 3 units. This is a verbless clause, but the subject is not explicit; it is implied to be "you" by the 2 m p suffix in line B2b.

הֲטוֹבִים. Adjective with interrogative ה. In the comparative context, this means "better," which here implies richer, more powerful, or having a larger territory.

מִן־הַמַּמְלָכוֹת הָאֵלֶּה. Prepositional phrase with comparative מִן followed by a noun with demonstrative pronoun. The word מַמְלָכָה refers to the domain, reign or royal power of a king.

Line B2b: The colon-marker is *silluq* and the constraints are: 0 predicators, 3 constituents, and 3 units.

אִם־רַב. The word אִם here means "or." The adjective רַב in conjunction with the following מִן is comparative in force and thus means "larger" or "greater."

גְּבוּלָם. The subject, with 3 m p suffix. This word may mean "boundary" or "territory", and it here focuses on the size of a kingdom's territory as a measure of its greatness.

מִגְּבֻלְכֶם. Prepositional phrase with comparative מִן. These territories, Calneh, Great Hamath, and Gath, are held up as examples before the arrogant people of Samaria. Calneh and Hamath suffered either destruction or subjugation c. 738 B.C. at the hands of Tiglath-pileser III. See *ABD*, "Calneh," and also Rainey and Notley

(2006, 226–27). Hamath was listed among states giving tribute to Tiglath-pileser III in that year, and its territory was reduced (Paul 1991, 202). The problem, however, is that the conquest of Calneh by Tiglath-pileser III was some twenty years after the ministry of Amos, but the text here indicates that the subjugation of these states has already taken place. A number of scholars therefore argue that this section is a later interpolation by a disciple of Amos from the period after Tiglath-pileser III's campaign (see Wolff 1977, 274). There are two possible alternatives to this analysis. (1) It may be that Amos is not at all suggesting that these nations have already been brought down but in fact asserting that they were equally as prosperous as Israel (Paul 1991, 203). The question of line B2b ("Or is their territory bigger than yours?") indicates that in Amos' day these cities were still standing and still fairly robust. Against this interpretation, however, is the mention of Gath, which had lost its power and prestige by the time of Amos (see the discussion at 1:6-8). (2) A better solution is that these three states are mentioned neither because they had been already obliterated by Assyria nor because they were still as prosperous as Israel but because they were under Israelite or Judahite domination. Jeroboam II himself had forced Hamath into submission earlier in his reign (2 Kgs 14:28), and Gath was ruled by Uzziah of Judah (2 Chr 26:6). Nothing certain is known of the situation of Calneh during Amos' ministry. On the other hand, since Jeroboam II had become dominant in the region, it is reasonable to assume that Calneh, too, was in some measure subordinate to Israel. The smugness of the aristocracies in Samaria and Zion was in part due to their domination of these three kingdoms.

6:3-6: Third Stanza. This stanza, giving the details of the accusations against the aristocrats, has eleven lines divided into three strophes. The key to the strophic division is in Amos' tendency to match a participle in an opening line or lines with a finite verb in a closing line or lines. This pattern governs these three strophes (C1a with C1b; C2a-e with C2f; C3a with C3b-c). Throughout the stanza, the participles that lead lines must be regarded as predicators, as in every case they are joined by a conjunction to a concluding finite verb. The stanza ends in 6:6 with two lines governed by finite verbs. The lengthy second strophe, describing the carefree attitude of the aristocrats, is the heart of the stanza. The first strophe introduces the theme by noting that they push back any thought that disaster may be coming, and the third stanza concludes it with a picture of an self-indulgent drinking party. A number of scholars call this text a "woe" passage (see discussion of line C1b). They seem to think that the grammar of having a participle in one line followed by a conjunction and finite verb in the next, the pattern used throughout this text, means that the text is a "woe." This is plainly wrong; in 6:8b this pattern is used with God as the subject, and God is not pronouncing a woe on himself.

6:3: First Strophe. Two lines describing how the wicked have a kind of cognitive dissonance, on the one hand scoffing at the idea that disaster is near but on the other promoting the conditions that guarantee it will come.

6:3 C1a הַֽמְנַדִּ֖ים לְי֣וֹם רָ֑ע
C1b וַתַּגִּישׁ֖וּן שֶׁ֥בֶת חָמָֽס׃

Line C1a: The colon-marker is *athnach* and the constraints are: 1 predicator, 2 constituents, and 3 units.

הַֽמְנַדִּ֖ים. Piel participle m p of נדה with definite article. The root נדה occurs only in the Piel and twice in the Hebrew Bible (here and Isaiah 66:5: אֲחֵיכֶם שֹׂנְאֵיכֶם מְנַדֵּיכֶם, "your brothers [who] hate you [and] push you away"). This interpretation of the verb is supported by the Hebrew of Sirach 6:10 (concerning the false friend): ברעתך יתנדה ממך ("when you are in trouble he separates himself from you"), using the Hithpael. Stuart (1987, 357) argues that this is the Akkadian *nadû*, to "forecast." But, apart from the aforementioned evidence, the antithesis of the piel נדה in this line with the hiphil הגיש ("bring near") in the next is compelling, and an alternative meaning for נדה is not persuasive. Also, the idea that they "push away the evil day" (i.e., dismiss the notion that trouble is near) leads into the next strophe, where they live in careless indulgence.

לְי֣וֹם רָ֑ע. Prepositional phrase with לְ. The use of לְ to mark an accusative is well-attested (*IBHS* §11.2.10g), but we do not have any data for נדה ל apart from this example. יוֹם רַע only occurs here, although we do have יְמֵי רַע in Psalm 49:6 (E 5) and Psalm 94:13. It refers to a time of disaster. The aristocrats of Samaria reject the idea that such a crisis is coming, as illustrated by their words in 9:10.

Line C1b: The colon-marker is *silluq* and the constraints are: 1 predicator, 2 constituents, and 3 units.

וַתַּגִּישׁ֖וּן. Hiphil *wayyiqtol* 2 m p of נגשׁ with conjunction and paragogic נ. The paragogic נ may mark contrast (see *IBHS* §31.7.1b), and contrast is apparent here. The normal meaning of this verb is to "bring close." Stuart (1987, 357) suggests that the verb here means "produce via divination," but such a meaning is unparalleled for this verb. A number of scholars have stated that the second person verb looks peculiar here; Wolff has proposed emending to third person (Wolff 1977, 271–72). This is founded on the notions that this strophe is a "woe" statement, which should be in the third person. But in fact this is a series of accusations; it is not governed by the הוֹי of 6:1; the second stanza (6:2) between 6:1 and 6:3 precludes this possibility (contrary, e.g., to Andersen and Freedman [1989, 544–46, 559–60], who arbitrarily add הוֹי six times in 6:1-6 to create a series of seven woes).

שֶׁ֥בֶת חָמָֽס. The direct object. The meaning of שֶׁבֶת here is debated. It appears to be a noun (or infinitive construct) of the root ישׁב, which would give the meaning "seat / habitation of violence." This is compared to Psalm 94:20, הַיְחָבְרְךָ כִּסֵּא הַוּוֹת ("Can a throne of destruction be joined to you?" i.e., "Can violent rulers be allied with you, [YHWH]?"). Or, שֶׁבֶת could be derived from the root שׁבת and taken to mean "cessation." But "cessation of violence" is surely not the meaning here. Occurrences of שֶׁבֶת in Exodus 21:19; 2 Samuel

23:7; Isaiah 30:7 are themselves quite obscure, but in 1 Kings 10:19 (|| 2 Chr 9:18); Obadiah 3; Lamentations 3:63 it clearly means "seat" or "sitting." In Proverbs 20:3 either "sitting" or "cessation" is possible. Stuart (1987, 357) emends שֶׁבֶת to שַׁבָּת and so translates the verse, "Those who are forecasting a bad day / And divining a harmful week," but this builds speculation on speculation and cannot be followed. For other proposed emendations or interpretations of שֶׁבֶת, see Wolff 1977, 272. On the whole, "habitation of violence" remains the most persuasive option. The bicolon means that they scoff at the notion that disaster is near but make Samaria a place where violent oppression has a home.

6:4-5: Second Strophe. Six lines following the pattern of a participle (lines C2a-e) followed by a finite verb (C2f). Translating these participles into English, it is appropriate to use finite verbs (e.g., "They lie on beds of ivory").

6:4 C2a הַשֹּׁכְבִים֙ עַל־מִטּ֣וֹת שֵׁ֔ן
C2b וּסְרֻחִ֖ים עַל־עַרְשׂוֹתָ֑ם
C2c וְאֹכְלִ֤ים כָּרִים֙ מִצֹּ֔אן
C2d וַעֲגָלִ֖ים מִתּ֥וֹךְ מַרְבֵּֽק׃
6:5 C2e הַפֹּרְטִ֖ים עַל־פִּ֣י הַנָּ֑בֶל
C2f כְּדָוִ֕יד חָשְׁב֥וּ לָהֶ֖ם כְּלֵי־שִֽׁיר׃

Line C2a: The colon-marker is *zaqeph qaton* and the constraints are: 1 predicator, 2 constituents, and 3 units.

הַשֹּׁכְבִים֙. Qal active participle m p of שׁכב with definite article. In context, they are not lying down to sleep but reclining at feasts. The definite article appears with the participle here and in C2e but not in C2b and C2c. This groups the strophe into two parts, C2a-d and C2e-f; see the translation above.

עַל־מִטּ֣וֹת שֵׁ֔ן. Prepositional phrase with עַל on a construct chain (an adjectival genitive). This of course does not mean that the entire bed is made of ivory but that it is decorated with ivory inlay.

Line C2b: The colon-marker is *athnach* and the constraints are: 1 predicator, 2 constituents, and 2 units. The line is semantically parallel to C2a.

וּסְרֻחִים. Qal passive participle m p of סרח with conjunction. The verb סרח appears in the qal *yiqtol* in Exodus 26:12 (תִּסְרַח) where it refers to an excess of tent fabric that hangs over the back of the tent. In the next verse, Exodus 26:13, יִהְיֶה סָרוּחַ ("it shall be overhung"), with the passive participle, is used in a parallel manner. See also Ezekiel 23:15. Used of people, this refers to lounging on a couch (draping one's body over it) in a carefree manner that suggests luxury and arrogance.

עַל־עַרְשׂוֹתָם. Prepositional phrase with locative עַל.

Line C2c: The colon-marker is *zaqeph qaton* and the constraints are: 1 predicator, 3 constituents, and 3 units.

וְאֹכְלִים. Qal active participle m p of אכל with conjunction, implying that the lounging on couches and eating are part of a single event (i.e., a meal while reclining).

כָּרִים. The direct object. The word refers to young rams or lambs, the meat of which would be tender and presumably expensive. In 1 Samuel 15:9, הַכָּרִים are listed among the best of the flock that the people refused to destroy in the *herem* of Agag's possessions.

מִצֹּאן. Prepositional phrase with partitive מִן.

Line C2d: The colon-marker is *silluq* and the constraints are: 0 predicators, 2 constituents, and 3 units. There is gapping of וְאֹכְלִים from the previous line.

וַעֲגָלִים. The direct object. An עֵגֶל is a young bull from which tender cuts of veal would come.

מִתּוֹךְ מַרְבֵּק. Prepositional phrase with מִן, referring to origin. Cattle were confined to stalls in order to fatten them; they would of course be very expensive.

Line C2e: The colon-marker is *athnach* and the constraints are: 1 predicator, 2 constituents, and 3 units.

הַפֹּרְטִים. Qal active participle m p of פרט with definite article. The root is *hapax legomenon*; it is probably onomatopoeic for the sound of strumming on strings.

עַל־פִּי הַנָּבֶל. Prepositional phrase with locative עַל on a construct chain. The נֵבֶל is generally translated "harp" while the כִּנּוֹר is generally translated "lyre." The lyre is bow-shaped with a cross-bar across the top of the bow; strings extend parallel to each other from the bar to the bow, and the longest strings are those at the center. Artistic depictions of symposia on Greek pottery routinely show celebrants holding lyres. The harp, by contrast, is bowed but the strings run parallel to one another from one end of the bow to the other end (like the string on a bow for arrows), and they get progressively longer nearer to the two ends of the bow. A harp may have a cross-bar to strengthen the bow, but strings will not be strung from it. Large harps, such as stand on a pedestal (like the modern harp), are attested in the ancient world. We cannot be sure, however, that these definitions for lyre and harp apply to the כִּנּוֹר and נֵבֶל. The Bible speaks of both a נֵבֶל and of a כִּנּוֹר which was hand-held and thus relatively small (e.g., 1 Sam 10:5; Isa 23:16; 1 Chr 13:8). Josephus, *Antiq.* 7:306 (7.12.3.306) says that the כִּנּוֹר (κινύρα) had ten "strings" (χορδή) and was played with a plectrum but that the נֵבֶל (νάβλα) had twelve "notes" (φθόγγος) and was played with the fingers. If Josephus is correct about how the instruments were played, and if analogies from classical Greece are appropriate, then the נֵבֶל was actually a lyre. Classical depictions of symposia generally have the participants playing the lyre (with the fingers, not a plectrum) and not the harp. The "mouth" (פֶּה) of the lyre would be the open space in the center where the fingers plucked the strings.

Line C2f: The colon-marker is *silluq* and the constraints are: 1 predicator, 4 constituents, and 5 units.

כְּדָוִיד. Prepositional phrase with comparative כְּ.

חָשְׁבוּ. Qal *qatal* 3 c p of חשב. The verb here means "devise," as in Exodus 31:4. In context, it could be translated as "improvise."

לָהֶם. Indirect object with לְ and a 3 m p suffix.

כְּלֵי־שִׁיר. This construct chain appears to be the direct object and to mean "musical instruments," since כְּלִי normally refers to some object, such as pottery, a tool, or a weapon. See also כְּלֵי־שִׁיר in Nehemiah 12:36; 1 Chronicles 15:16; 16:42; 2 Chronicles 7:6; 34:12; where it always means "musical instruments." It seems odd, however, that revelers reclining on couches at a symposium would be busy inventing new musical instruments, and it contradicts the previous line, where they are *playing* instruments and not making them. It is best to assume that כְּלֵי־שִׁיר is not the direct object but is instrumental; it may be that the עַל from line C2e implicitly governs this phrase. The direct object, implied by the term כְּלֵי־שִׁיר, is an unstated שִׁיר ("song"). See also the next line, C3a, which speaks of the vessel with which they drink but does not explicitly state what they drink since the implied direct object with בְּמִזְרְקֵי יַיִן ("with bowls of wine") is יַיִן.

6:6: Third Strophe. Three lines. The end of this stanza is marked by ending the strophe with two finite verbs instead of just one.

6:6 C3a הַשֹּׁתִ֤ים בְּמִזְרְקֵ֣י יַ֔יִן
C3b וְרֵאשִׁ֥ית שְׁמָנִ֖ים יִמְשָׁ֑חוּ
C3c וְלֹ֥א נֶחְל֖וּ עַל־שֵׁ֥בֶר יוֹסֵֽף׃

Line C3a: The colon-marker is *zaqeph qaton* and the constraints are: 1 predicator, 2 constituents, and 3 units.

הַשֹּׁתִ֤ים. Qal active participle m p of שׁתה with the definite article.

בְּמִזְרְקֵ֣י יַ֔יִן. Prepositional phrase with instrumental בְּ. The מִזְרָק is a shallow bowl used for drinking wine and pouring out libations. In Greece, participants in a symposium might drink from a large bowl called a φιάλη, which they passed from one to the other (Plato, *Symposium* 223c: πίνειν ἐκ φιάλης μεγάλης ["to drink from a large bowl"]). Artwork also depicts celebrants drinking from small, shallow, cup-sized bowls held in one hand. In the construct chain, יַיִן is an adjectival genitive.

Line C3b: The colon-marker is *athnach* and the constraints are: 1 predicator, 2 constituents, and 3 units.

וְרֵאשִׁית שְׁמָנִים. A construct chain with conjunction, this is an accusative phrase describing the substance with which they were anointed. The genitive relationship in the construct chain is partitive; they use the best of all available oils.

יִמְשָׁחוּ. Qal *yiqtol* 3 m p of משׁח. The verb usually connotes some kind of ritual anointing, but it can be used for non-ritual purposes (Isa 21:5; Jer 22:14). People generally anointed themselves with oils at dinners and parties; cf. Luke 7:46.

Line C3c: The colon-marker is *silluq* and the constraints are: 1 predicator, 2 constituents, and 3 units.

וְלֹא נֶחְלוּ. Niphal *qatal* 3 c p of חלה. The verb means to be sick or feel pain, and here it refers to emotional distress.

עַל־שֵׁבֶר יוֹסֵף. Prepositional phrase with עַל meaning "concerning." The construct chain here properly means the "breakup of Joseph." The use of "Joseph" as synecdoche for the northern kingdom is fairly rare; it is also found in Ezekiel 37:16, 19; Psalm 80:2 (E 1). שֶׁבֶר can refer to the destruction of a nation by an outside entity (Jer 4:6). This could be the meaning here, but Amos implies that this is something the leaders of society should perceive around them at the present; it is not something in the future that only a prophet can see. It may refer to the split of the nation into factions and divisions. On the one hand, divisions between economic and social classes were widening, and on the other, factions within the aristocracy must have already been apparent. With the death of Jeroboam II, Israel would fall into political chaos if not outright civil war.

6:7-8A: Fourth Stanza. This stanza is in one strophe and has three lines. Interpreters normally take line Dc (the beginning of v. 8) with the rest of v. 8 in accordance with the paragraph division of the MT. However, it is better to read line Dc with v. 7 for two reasons. First, a divine oath normally should be attached to a solemn statement in which God declares what he will or will not do in the future, as in the other instances of נשבע in Amos (4:2 and 8:7). It is peculiar that God would, taking line Dc with v. 8, swear an oath that he hates something. It makes more sense to take the oath with 6:7, a promise that the leading men of Samaria will head off into exile. Second, beginning the next section in 6:8b with נְאֻם־יְהוָה אֱלֹהֵי צְבָאוֹת, as is proposed below, creates an inclusion structure for 6:8 with 6:14, where we have נְאֻם־יְהוָה אֱלֹהֵי הַצְּבָאוֹת.

6:7	Da	לָכֵ֞ן עַתָּ֤ה יִגְלוּ֙ בְּרֹ֣אשׁ גֹּלִ֔ים
	Db	וְסָ֖ר מִרְזַ֥ח סְרוּחִֽים׃ פ
6:8a	Dc	נִשְׁבַּ֨ע אֲדֹנָ֤י יְהוִה֙ בְּנַפְשׁ֔וֹ

Line Da: The colon-marker is *athnach* and the constraints are: 1 predicator, 4 constituents, and 5 units.

לָכֵ֞ן. "Therefore." The previous accusations conclude with the judgment that must logically follow.

עַתָּ֤ה. This word is not merely filler; the literal meaning "now" indicates that the judgment is imminent.

יִגְלוּ֙. Qal *yiqtol* 3 m p of גלה used for future tense.

בְּרֹ֣אשׁ גֹּלִ֔ים. Prepositional phrase with locative בְּ on the qal active participle m s of גלה. Their prior position, according to 6:1, had been as the נְקֻבֵי רֵאשִׁית הַגּוֹיִם; now they go off בְּרֹאשׁ גֹּלִים, at the head of the line of exiles.

Line Db: The colon-marker is *silluq* and the constraints are: 1 predicator, 2 constituents, and 3 units.

וְסָר. Qal *weqatal* 3 m s of סוּר. Normally meaning "turn aside" or "go away," it here means, "come to an end."

מִרְזַח סְרוּחִים. A construct chain with a qal passive participle m p of סרח (see 6:4) used substantively as the absolute noun. The מַרְזֵחַ is clearly a συμπόσιον ("symposium"; lit., "drinking together") such as is familiar from classical Greece. All of the major elements familiar from the classical world are present: revelers reclining on couches, music making, feasting, and drinking wine from bowls.

Line Dc: The colon-marker is *revia* and the constraints are: 1 predicator, 3 constituents, and 4 units.

נִשְׁבַּע. Niphal *qatal* 3 m s of שׁבע.

אֲדֹנָי יְהוִה. The subject.

בְּנַפְשׁוֹ. Prepositional phrase with בְּ for that by which one swears. נֶפֶשׁ here means "self." God is swearing by his own person.

6:8b-11: Judgment on the Houses of Samaria: This text is composed of two judgment oracles (6:8, 11), between which is a prose description of a grisly funerary scene (6:9-10), ironically making the point that, owing to the extent of the disaster, no lamentation is heard.

6:8b: Oracle against the Citadels of Samaria. This is a single strophe of four lines. It serves three functions. First, it uses a lengthy formula of divine speech (line a) to introduce a pronouncement of divine displeasure in lines c-d. Second, it links this displeasure to the oracles against the nations in Amos 1–2 and so treats Israel as one of the nations. God hates the "citadels" (אַרְמוֹן) of Samaria, and אַרְמוֹן is used in the judgments against all of the first seven nations. Also, Israel will be "handed over" (הסגיר) to its enemies (הסגיר is used in Amos 1:6,9 for carrying off captives into slavery). Third, it provides a lead-in to the following prose text, 6:9-10, in that line d speaks of the whole of the city being removed, and vv. 9-10 describe a large household that is entirely wiped out.

6:8b	a	נְאֻם־יְהוָה אֱלֹהֵי צְבָאוֹת
	b	מְתָאֵב אָנֹכִי אֶת־גְּאוֹן יַעֲקֹב
	c	וְאַרְמְנֹתָיו שָׂנֵאתִי
	d	וְהִסְגַּרְתִּי עִיר וּמְלֹאָהּ׃

Line a: The colon-marker is *zaqeph qaton* and the constraints are: 0 predicators, 1 constituent, and 4 units.

נְאֻם־יְהוָה אֱלֹהֵי צְבָאוֹת. This is another divine oracle formula, but it is made more solemn by the pleonastic divine title.

Line b: The colon-marker is *zaqeph qaton* and the constraints are: 1 predicator, 3 constituents, and 4 units.

מְתָאֵב. Piel participle m s of תאב II, used periphrastically. This root is *hapax legomenon* with the meaning "abhor" (it is clearly meant to be the parallel of שָׂנֵאתִי in line c). In Psalm 119:40, 174, a root תאב (qal) means to "long for." Notwithstanding the different stems, it is astonishing that two homonyms could have such diametrically opposite meanings. It is possible that a scribe has deliberately altered תעב to תאב for the sake of euphemism or that תאב, "abhor," is simply a by-form for תעב. Another possibility is that there is a deliberate wordplay here. God "abhors" the pride of Jacob (their wealth, citadels, etc.) but also "longs for" it in the sense that God himself ought to be their pride. The likelihood of such an interpretation is enhanced by the fact that God refers to himself as the "pride of Jacob" in 8:7. It is impossible to bring this out in translation, however.

אָנֹכִי. The first person subject has to be explicit because the verb is a participle.

אֶת־גְּאוֹן יַעֲקֹב. The direct object. The noun גָּאוֹן can refer to any kind of arrogance, but here it seems to refer specifically to their confidence in their military power and high walls, as the next line indicates.

Line c: The colon-marker is *athnach* and the constraints are: 1 predicator, 2 constituents, and 2 units.

וְאַרְמְנֹתָיו. The direct object. The chiastic structure of this and the previous line strongly suggests that the fortifications of Samaria are the basis for their pride (גְּאוֹן).

שָׂנֵאתִי. Qal *qatal* 1 c s of שׂנא. Note that here again a participle in one line is followed by a conjunction and finite verb in the next.

Line d: The colon-marker is *silluq* and the constraints are: 1 predicator, 3 constituents, and 3 units.

וְהִסְגַּרְתִּי. Hiphil *weqatal* 1 c s of סגר. This refers to sending the people into exile and slavery, as in Amos 1:6,9.

עִיר. The direct object. "City" is here synecdoche for the people of the city.

וּמְלֹאָהּ. A second direct object with a 3 f s suffix (the antecedent is עִיר). The "fullness" of the city is everything that enriches it, including its people, its treasures, and its prestige.

6:9-10: A Mass-Funeral without Lamentation: This text is not poetry. It is a kind of one-act play, a picture of the trauma that will overtake the arrogant nation, in which the only living and speaking characters are two gravediggers. The scene is grotesque, ironic, and not meant to be fully realistic. It portrays a land in which the normal conventions of mourning have been abandoned.

6:9 וְהָיָה אִם־יִוָּתְרוּ עֲשָׂרָה אֲנָשִׁים בְּבַיִת אֶחָד וָמֵתוּ׃

Prose Clause: וְהָיָה

The qal *weqatal* 3 m s of היה serves as a discourse marker to introduce an anticipatory (future oriented) narrative. On the pattern וְהָיָה אִם, see the discussion at 7:2.

Prose Clause: אִם־יִוָּתְרוּ עֲשָׂרָה אֲנָשִׁים בְּבַיִת אֶחָד

A protasis with יִוָּתְרוּ, a niphal *yiqtol* 3 m p of יתר, as predicate. The implied setting is some future calamity in which the population of the northern kingdom has been all but eradicated. An extended family may have once had fifty or even one hundred people in it (בַּיִת here is probably not a single structure but a בֵּית־אָב, a small interrelated community built around a local patriarch). After the devastation of the land, almost all will have been taken away or killed. But, the protasis asks, what if ten persons survive? (אֲנָשִׁים here is "persons" of either gender or any age.)

Prose Clause: וָמֵתוּ

The qal *weqatal* 3 c p of מוּת is the apodosis, and it responds to the indirect question with a startling, one-word answer: they will die. The point is that there will be no escape from the fury to come.

6:10 וּנְשָׂאוֹ דּוֹדוֹ וּמְסָרְפוֹ לְהוֹצִיא עֲצָמִים מִן־הַבַּיִת
וְאָמַר לַאֲשֶׁר בְּיַרְכְּתֵי הַבַּיִת הַעוֹד עִמָּךְ וְאָמַר אָפֶס
וְאָמַר הָס כִּי לֹא לְהַזְכִּיר בְּשֵׁם יְהוָה׃

Prose Clause: וּנְשָׂאוֹ דּוֹדוֹ וּמְסָרְפוֹ לְהוֹצִיא עֲצָמִים מִן־הַבַּיִת

וּנְשָׂאוֹ. a qal *weqatal* 3 m s of נשׂא with a 3 m s suffix, continues the apodosis with a second mainline clause. דּוֹדוֹ וּמְסָרְפוֹ is hendiadys for a person who is responsible for the disposal of a dead body. The basic meaning of דּוֹד is probably "uncle," but by extension it is a term of endearment and could probably be applied to a nonrelative performing the duties of a relative. Indeed, דּוֹד may be added to this man's title as a euphemism in light of how unpleasant his task is and because ideally it ought to be done by a family member. וּמְסָרְפוֹ appears to be a piel participle m s with a 3 m s suffix and conjunction. The root is either שׂרף I ("burn") or שׂרף II ("embalm"). In either case it refers to someone designated the task of taking care of a dead body, but it is probably from שׂרף II. Immolation not attested as a funerary rite in Iron Age Israel, and סרף is a known variant for שׂרף II but not for שׂרף I (Paul 1991, 215–16). Thus, in our terms and maintaining the euphemism, דּוֹדוֹ וּמְסָרְפוֹ is "his Uncle Undertaker." The 3 m s suffix on the verb (and the two nouns) refers to any deceased person that the "undertaker" must deal with; the suffix can be translated into English as "their." לְהוֹצִיא, a hiphil infinitive construct of יצא with לְ, expresses purpose. עֲצָמִים, "bones," is synecdoche for dead bodies (this verse does not refer to the ritual process of desiccating the bones, although that process may be behind referring to a dead body as "bones").

Prose Clause: וְאָמַר לַאֲשֶׁר בְּיַרְכְּתֵי הַבַּיִת

וְאָמַר. another qal *weqatal* 3 m s of אמר, continues the mainline predictive discourse. The subject is the undertaker, דּוֹדוֹ וּמְסָרְפוֹ, and he speaks to some slave or subordinate who is helping him find and remove bodies, here called אֲשֶׁר בְּיַרְכְּתֵי הַבַּיִת (this person, "who is in the back parts of the house," should not be regarded as one of the original inhabitants; he is in the house only because he is looking for dead bodies). In the Israelite "three-room" or "four-room" house of the Iron Age, יַרְכְּתֵי הַבַּיִת would probably be the storeroom that goes across the back part of the ground floor of the building (see King and Stager 2001, 28–30). Thus, the innermost recesses of the houses are being searched.

Prose Clause: הַעוֹד עִמָּךְ

Reported speech; a verbless clause with a prepositional phrase as the predicate and the subject unstated. The particle עוֹד has an interrogative ה; thus, "(Are) there still (any bodies) with you?" This is colloquial speech; it could be accurately rendered as, "Any more with you?" or "Still got any?"

Prose Clause: וְאָמַר

וְאָמַר. Another qal *weqatal* 3 m s of אמר, continues the mainline predictive discourse. The assistant "who is in the back of the house" responds.

Prose Clause: אָפֶס

Reported speech. Literally "end," אֶפֶס (in pausal form in this text) here means, "that's it" or "there are no more."

Prose Clause: וְאָמַר

וְאָמַר. Another qal *weqatal* 3 m s of אמר, continues the mainline predictive discourse. The undertaker speaks.

Prose Clause: הָס

Reported speech. Like the English "Hush!" this is an indeclinable imperative that calls for silence.

Prose Clause: כִּי לֹא לְהַזְכִּיר בְּשֵׁם יְהוָה

The reported speech of the undertaker continues. The pattern כִּי לֹא with לְ and an infinitive construct appears here and in Judges 1:19. In Judges, it means "although (they were) not (able) to." Here, however, it must mean, "for (it is) not (permissible) to." The hiphil of זכר, when used with בְּשֵׁם and the name of a deity, means to "make an invocation" in the deity's name (Josh 23:7; Ps 20:8 [E 7]; see also W. Smelik 1999). The "undertaker" is concerned that the "assistant" may casually, in his distress over the scene, invoke YHWH's name in some way (perhaps using something analogous to the English "Lord bless us!" as an apotropaic invocation). But why does the undertaker declare that it is not permissible to make an invocation in YHWH's name? The reason is that the land has become so defiled with death, bloodshed and gore that it would be blaspheming God's name to invoke it in such a place. In the context of the book, this has two functions. First, after the hollow exuberance of praise found at the shrines (5:21-23), the trauma and defilement will make it impossible to invoke YHWH's name in any manner, be it the formal liturgy of the shrines or a casual exclamation by an undertaker's assistant. Second, it ironically refers to the theme of lamentation that appears at 5:1-2; 5:16-17; and in the use of הוֹי at 5:18 and 6:1. That is, when lament is most called for, any lament that invokes the name of YHWH will be forbidden because of the excessive defilement present. The land of Israel will truly be God-forsaken, and one will not be allowed to call upon the name of God in any manner there.

6:11: Judgment Oracle: A second judgment oracle in one strophe concludes 6:8-11. This prophecy, introduced by כִּי הִנֵּה, is explanatory of the previous prose text. God will crush every household in the land.

כִּֽי־הִנֵּ֤ה יְהוָה֙ מְצַוֶּ֔ה 1a 6:11
וְהִכָּ֧ה הַבַּ֛יִת הַגָּד֖וֹל רְסִיסִ֑ים 1b
וְהַבַּ֥יִת הַקָּטֹ֖ן בְּקִעִֽים׃

Line 1a: The colon-marker is *zaqeph qaton* and the constraints are: 1 predicator, 3 constituents, and 3 units.

כִּֽי־הִנֵּ֤ה. With one exception, the expression כִּי הִנֵּה occurs only in the Latter Prophets (the one exception is Judges 13:5, in which an angelic visitor makes a prophecy). It almost always occurs in a prophecy which is explanatory of a prior text. For example, Jeremiah 30:10 reads, "But as for you, Jacob my servant, do not fear—the oracle of YHWH—nor be dismayed, O Israel; for behold (כִּי הִנֵּה), I will save you from far away. . . ." See also, e.g., Isa 26:20-21; 60:1-2; 65:16-17; Jer 1:14-15; 25:28-29; 50:8-9; Ezek 36:8-9; Mic 1:2-3. This not only explains the syntactical function of this line but also indicates that the oracle of 6:11 is attached to 6:9-10 in the structure of this section.

יְהוָה֙. The subject of the following participle.

מְצַוֶּ֔ה. Piel participle m s of צוה used periphrastically. Unusually, no reported speech follows this verb—we are not told what the command of YHWH is. The verb is used absolutely and means that YHWH is making a decree about how things should transpire.

Line 1b: The colon-marker is *athnach* and the constraints are: 1 predicator, 3 constituents, and 4 units.

וְהִכָּ֧ה. Hiphil *weqatal* 3 m s of נכה. The *weqatal* functions as an apodosis to the previous line to indicate what will happen as a result of YHWH's decree.

הַבַּ֛יִת הַגָּד֖וֹל. The direct object. "The large house" is either a household of an aristocrat or a household that has many people in it.

גָּדוֹל regularly refers to important and powerful people, but in light of the preceding prose text, we cannot exclude the possibility that a large family may equally be implied.

רְסִיסִים. These are the fragments or pieces that remain after something has been smashed. This word, רָסִיס II, is *hapax legomenon* unless רָסִיס I ("drop"; used only in Song 5:2) is actually the same word. But its meaning is not in doubt; cf. *HALOT.*

Line 1c: The colon-marker is *silluq* and the constraints are: 0 predicators, 2 constituents, and 3 units. There is gapping of the verb וְהִכָּה from the previous line.

וְהַבַּיִת הַקָּטֹן. This forms a merism with הַבַּיִת הַגָּדוֹל from the previous line. It is thus either the home of the commoner or a home with a small family in it.

בְּקִעִים. From the root בקע, to "split," this refers to fissures in walls and then also to the rubble that is left after a wall is breached.

6:12-14: Summary: The full series of accusations, exhortations and judgments in 5:1–6:11 is here summarized under the heading of a proverb.

6:12A: A Proverb: This is a single bicolon, and it speaks of absurd or irrational behavior (contrary to Cooper 1988). It is appropriate here since throughout 5:1–6:14 Amos has decried the Israelite behavior as fundamentally perverse. The holy shrines are places that the truly pious should avoid (5:5). The people worship God without paying attention to his demands (5:21-24), honor the sky gods instead of YHWH, ruler of the heavens (5:8, 26), and routinely turn right into wrong (5:7). They refuse to draw the right lessons from history (6:2) and place their faith in fortifications rather than God (6:3, 8).

6:12a a הַיְרֻצ֤וּן בַּסֶּ֙לַע֙ סוּסִ֔ים
b אִם־יַחֲר֖וֹשׁ בַּבְּקָרִ֑ים

Line a: The colon-marker is *zaqeph qaton* and the constraints are: 1 predicator, 3 constituents, and 3 units.

הֲיְרֻצ֤וּן. Qal *yiqtol* 3 m p of רוּץ, "run," with interrogative ה and paragogic ן. If the paragogic ן marks contrast (see *IBHS* §31.7.1b and comments at 6:3), the contrast here is not with the next line but with reality. In other words, the situation described in this line is inherently implausible.

בַּסֶּ֙לַע֙. Prepositional phrase with locative בְּ and definite article. סֶלַע normally refers to a cliff or rocky crag, and it can be a large stone. The rhetorical question, which expects an answer of "Obviously not," could be whether horses run up the face of a cliff. Probably, however, the word here refers to rocky ground that is badly broken with fissures, large stones, and sheer drops, such that a horse could not run on it without breaking his leg.

סוּסִ֔ים. The subject.

Line b: The colon-marker is *athnach* and the constraints are: 1 predicator, 2 constituents, and 2 units.

אִם־יַחֲר֖וֹשׁ. Qal *yiqtol* 3 m s of חרשׁ ("to plow") with אִם.

בַּבְּקָרִ֑ים. Prepositional phrase with instrumental בְּ. This line gave rise to a famous but misguided emendation. Thinking that "Or does one plow with oxen" in context makes no sense (because people obviously do plow with oxen, and context requires a negative answer), this has been emended to בבקר ים ("Does one plow with an ox [the] sea?"). This was followed by the RSV and NJB, for example. In reality, בַּסֶּלַע from line a is gapped here (i.e., does "double-duty"). The question is, "Does one plow stone with oxen?" Obviously, one does not.

6:12b-13: Proverb Exposition and Accusation: The exposition of the above proverb constitutes a summary accusation against Israel. It is a single strophe in five lines. The starting point for the accusation, lines a-b, is a metaphor of transforming as if by magic wholesome plants into noxious and poisonous plants. This summarizes the theme of moral perversity that dominates 5:1–6:14. After this, in lines c-e, the text returns to Israel's pride and joy over their military power (cf. 5:3; 6:2, 8.

6:12b	a	כִּֽי־הֲפַכְתֶּ֤ם לְרֹאשׁ֙ מִשְׁפָּ֔ט
	b	וּפְרִ֥י צְדָקָ֖ה לְלַעֲנָֽה׃
6:13	c	הַשְּׂמֵחִ֖ים לְלֹ֣א דָבָ֑ר
	d	הָאֹֽמְרִ֗ים
	e	הֲל֣וֹא בְחָזְקֵ֔נוּ לָקַ֥חְנוּ לָ֖נוּ קַרְנָֽיִם׃

Line a: The colon-marker is *zaqeph qaton* and the constraints are: 1 predicator, 3 constituents, and 3 units.

כִּֽי־הֲפַכְתֶּ֤ם. Qal *qatal* 2 m p of הפך (to "turn" or "change") with כִּי. The particle כִּי is at the same time explanatory (as in, "I say this because") and adversative (as in, "Horses and oxen are not so foolish, but you are").

לְרֹאשׁ֙. Prepositional phrase with לְ. The noun is ראשׁ II, a variety of poisonous plant, not ראשׁ I, "head." With הפך, the preposition לְ is that into which something is changed.

מִשְׁפָּ֔ט. The direct object.

Line b: The colon-marker is *silluq* and the constraints are: 0 predicators, 2 constituents, and 3 units. There is gapping of the verb הֲפַכְתֶּם.

וּפְרִ֥י צְדָקָ֖ה. A construct chain as the direct object. In construct with another noun, the noun פְּרִי ("fruit") is almost always bound to a genitive of source ("and the fruit of your ground" [וּפְרִי אַדְמָתְךָ], Deuteronomy 28:42; "like the fruit of his deeds" [כִּפְרִי מַעֲלָלָיו], Jeremiah 17:10; "from the fruit of your genitals" [מִפְּרִי בִטְנְךָ], Psalm 132:11, etc.). The relationship here, however, is probably not a genitive of source, as "the fruit that comes from righteousness." It is probably appositional or descriptive of the nature of the fruit, analogous to Song 4:13, פְּרִי מְגָדִים, "choice fruits." Thus, it is the "fruit (that is) righteousness."

לְלַעֲנָה. Prepositional phrase with לְ. The plant לַעֲנָה, "wormwood," is a stereotyped metaphor for bitterness in the OT and it often appears with רֹאשׁ (see Deut 29:18; Jer 23:15; Lam 3:19). In these two lines, the Israelites are something like demonic magicians or who take the good creation of God, justice and righteousness, here metaphorically portrayed as wholesome fruit, and transform it into bitter and poisonous plants. Specifically, they take Torah, the worship of God, and the justice system and turn them into means of exploitation.

Line c: The colon-marker is *athnach* and the constraints are: 1 predicator, 2 constituents, and 2 units, taking לֹא דָבָר as a proper name.

הַשְּׂמֵחִים. Qal active participle m p of שׂמח with definite article. This serves as a relative clause with "you" (the suffix of the verb הֲפַכְתֶּם) as its antecedent.

לְלֹא דָבָר. Prepositional phrase with causative לְ. Lo-debar was in the Transjordan near the Yarmuk River and in the area of Gilead. This was a hotly contested territory, with Damascus and Samaria both seeking to maintain control over it. Under Jeroboam II, Israel was ascendant over Syria and thus could claim this area for itself. The joy of the people over their victories against Syrian enemies is reflected also in 6:2. But there is an obvious wordplay here; לֹא דָבָר also means "nothing." Thus, they are rejoicing over nothing.

Line d: The colon-marker is *zaqeph qaton* and the constraints are: 1 predicator, 1 constituents, and 1 unit. This colometry violates the normal constraints, and its *zaqeph qaton*, being preceded by an *athnach* and having no subordinate disjunctive accent, does not normally constitute a colon-break. But lines d-e together are too long to be joined as one line, and this seems the best solution. See also 9:10.

הָאֹמְרִים. Qal active participle 3 m p of רוץ with definite article.

Line e: The colon-marker is *silluq* and the constraints are: 1 predicator, 4 constituents, and 4 units. This line is reported speech. The threefold repetition of the ending נוּ ("we, our, us") is ironic, mocking how pleased the people are with themselves.

הֲלוֹא בְחָזְקֵנוּ. Prepositional phrase with instrumental בְּ, a suffix 1 c p, and preceded by the rhetorical question marker הֲלוֹא. The noun חֹזֶק appears only here and in Exodus 13:3,14,16; Haggai 2:22, but it is from the well-attested root חזק and its meaning, "strength," is not in doubt.

לָקַחְנוּ. Qal *qatal* 3 c p of לקח.

לָנוּ. Prepositional phrase with לְ as a dative of advantage and 1 c p suffix.

קַרְנָיִם. Karnaim, like Lo-debar, was in the Transjordan and its capture reflects the triumph of Israel over their Syrian enemy. The dual form of the word קֶרֶן, it literally means "two horns." Since a horn could represent power, this could sound like a worthy boast. Taken literally, however ("We have captured two horns!"), it is absurd.

6:14: Oracle of Doom: A summary of the judgment against Israel concludes 5:1–6:14. It is marked by an expanded formula of divine speech, and (unusually for a judgment oracle) is in prose. The conclusion forms an inclusion with the introduction in 5:1-3. Like 5:3, this verse is a prophecy of doom introduced by כִּי. Also, 6:14 looks back ironically to 5:2, which lamented that there was no one to raise up (hiphil participle of קום) fallen Israel. In this verse, God will raise up (hiphil participle of קום) a nation against Israel. In addition, there is a conceptual inclusion. Amos 5:3 had spoken of calamitous military defeat, and here Israel suffers oppression at the hands of a Gentile nation. Finally, נְאֻם־יְהוָה אֱלֹהֵי הַצְּבָאוֹת here and in 6:8b forms an inclusion to demarcate this division's final sections, in which judgments are given in response to the accusations of 5:4–6:8a.

6:14 כִּ֡י הִנְנִי֩ מֵקִ֨ים עֲלֵיכֶ֜ם בֵּ֣ית יִשְׂרָאֵ֗ל נְאֻם־יְהוָ֛ה אֱלֹהֵ֥י
הַצְּבָא֖וֹת גּ֑וֹי וְלָחֲצ֥וּ אֶתְכֶ֛ם מִלְּב֥וֹא חֲמָ֖ת עַד־נַ֥חַל
הָעֲרָבָֽה׃

Prose Clause: כִּ֡י הִנְנִי֩ מֵקִ֨ים עֲלֵיכֶ֜ם . . . גּ֑וֹי

The 1 c s suffix on הִנְנִי functions as the subject of מֵקִים, a piel participle m p of קוּם. The direct object is גּוֹי, and the clause is interrupted by a divine speech formula. עֲלֵיכֶם has adversative force, and בֵּית יִשְׂרָאֵל is vocative.

Prose Clause: נְאֻם־יְהוָ֛ה אֱלֹהֵ֥י הַצְּבָא֖וֹת

A divine speech formula with a pleonastic divine title. It gives the prophecy suitable solemnity and indicates certainty of fulfillment.

Prose Clause: וְלָחֲצ֥וּ אֶתְכֶ֛ם מִלְּב֥וֹא חֲמָ֖ת עַד־נַ֥חַל הָעֲרָבָֽה

The *weqatal* 3 c p of לחץ continues the mainline of this predictive text and indeed makes the final and concluding prophecy of 5:1–6:14. The verb לחץ is used for the oppression done to the Hebrew slaves by the Egyptians (Exod 3:9; 22:20) and for the maltreatment of Israel by foreigners during the Judges period (Judg 2:18; 4:3; 6:9; 10:12). But the verb literally means to "push," and it here speaks of driving Israel into diaspora. Lebo-Hamath (לְבוֹא חֲמָת, "Entrance of Hamath") is a traditional northern border of Israel (Num 34:7-9; Josh 13:5; Ezek 47:16). Its mention here is appropriate because Hamath was one of the kingdoms Israel gloated over (6:2). The location of the נַחַל הָעֲרָבָה ("the Brook of the Arabah") is unknown, but it clearly was in the far south and is here in a merism with Lebo-Hamath. It thus represents the southern border of greater Israel. Normally, the OT uses the "Brook of Egypt" (נַחַל מִצְרַיִם) as a traditional designation for the southern border (Josh 15:4; Ezek 47:19). Amos' language, however, is deliberately shaped to reverse the prophecy spoken by Jonah the son of Amittai over Jeroboam II, that he would restore "the territory of Israel from (מִן) Lebo-hamath to (עַד) the Sea of the Arabah" (2 Kgs 14:25).

The glory of Jeroboam's reign would soon end and the people would be driven out of the land. In this text, מִלְּבוֹא חֲמָת עַד־נַחַל הָעֲרָבָה does not mean that they would be driven *from* Lebo-Hamath *to* the Brook of the Arabah; he uses מִן and עַד to parody Jonah. The point is that Israel would be expelled from all the land within those limits.

7:1–8:3: Amos the Seer

This is a collection of four visions (7:1-3, 4-6, 7-9; 8:1-3) interrupted by an account of Amos' encounter with Amaziah the priest of Bethel (7:10-17). Some scholars consider vv. 10-17 to be a later redactional insertion, although others argue for the original unity of the text (e.g., Noble 1998, although aspects of his presentation are not persuasive). The entire text is in prose except for four oracles of judgment appended to, respectively, Amaziah's complaint (7:11b), the Amos' response to Amaziah (7:17), and the third and fourth visions (7:8b-9; 8:2b-3). Because YHWH relents in visions one and two, these sections have no oracles of judgment.

7:1This is what Lord YHWH showed me: Behold, (he was) forming a locust swarm at the beginning of the sprouting of the latter crop—now it was the latter crop that is after the king's cut. 2And it would happen, whenever it finished eating the vegetation of the earth, that I said, "Lord YHWH, forgive! How will Jacob stand? After all, he is small." 3YHWH relented about this. "It will not happen," YHWH said.

4This is what Lord YHWH showed me: Behold, Lord YHWH was calling for a judgment with fire, and it consumed the great deep and was consuming the fields. 5And I said, "Lord YHWH, desist! How will Jacob stand? After all, he is small." 6YHWH relented about this. "It will not happen," Lord YHWH said.

7This is what he showed me: Behold, the Lord was standing at a wall of anak, and anak was in his hand. 8And YHWH said to me, "What do you see, Amos?" And I said, "Anak." And the Lord said,

Behold, I am setting anak
In the midst of my people, Israel.

I will no longer pass by him.
9And the high places of Isaac will be laid desolate,
And the sanctuaries of Israel will be laid waste.
And I will arise against the house of Jeroboam with a sword.

10And Amaziah, the priest of Bethel, sent (a message) to Jeroboam, the
king of Israel, as follows:

"Amos has conspired against you right in the middle of the house of Israel. The land is not able to contain all his words!
11For thus says Amos:

'Jeroboam will die by the sword
And Israel will wholly go from its land into exile!'"

12And Amaziah said to Amos, "Seer, go on and flee to the land of
Judah! So eat bread there and prophesy there!
13But never again prophesy
at Bethel! For it is a royal shrine, and it is a national structure."

14And Amos answered and said to Amaziah, "I am (was) not a prophet
and I am (was) not a son of a prophet. Rather, I am (was) a herdsman and
a cutter of sycamore figs.
15And YHWH took me from behind the flock.
And YHWH said to me, 'Go, prophesy to my people Israel!'
16Now listen to
the word of YHWH! You are saying, 'Do not prophesy against Israel and
do not preach against the house of Isaac!'
17Therefore, thus says YHWH:

Your wife will be used as a prostitute in the city
And your sons and your daughters will fall by the sword.
And your ground will be divided with a measuring line
And you will die on unclean ground.
And Israel will wholly go from its land into exile!'"

8:1This is what Lord YHWH showed me: Behold, a basket of summer
produce.
2And YHWH said to me, "What do you see, Amos?" And I said,
"A basket of summer produce." And the Lord said to me,

The end has come upon my people Israel.
I will no longer pass by him.
3And they shall wail temple songs on that day—
An oracle of the Lord YHWH:
"An abundance of corpses! They are thrown everywhere!
Hush!"

7:1-3: The Vision of Locusts

7:1 כֹּ֤ה הִרְאַ֙נִי֙ אֲדֹנָ֣י יְהוִ֔ה וְהִנֵּה֙ יוֹצֵ֣ר גֹּבַ֔י בִּתְחִלַּ֖ת עֲל֣וֹת
הַלָּ֑קֶשׁ וְהִנֵּה־לֶ֕קֶשׁ אַחַ֖ר גִּזֵּ֥י הַמֶּֽלֶךְ׃

Prose Clause: כֹּ֤ה הִרְאַ֙נִי֙ אֲדֹנָ֣י יְהוִ֔ה

Hiphil *qatal* 3 m s of ראה with 1 c s suffix. אֲדֹנָ֣י יְהוִ֔ה is the subject. This clause, headed by כֹּה, introduces a vision account in a manner analogous to how כה אמר יהוה introduces a prophetic speech.

Prose Clause: וְהִנֵּה֙ יוֹצֵ֣ר גֹּבַ֔י בִּתְחִלַּ֖ת עֲל֣וֹת הַלָּ֑קֶשׁ

The particle וְהִנֵּה gives the reader Amos' perspective on the vision. יוֹצֵר is a qal active participle m s of יצר. The verb יצר (to "form") may be a deliberate catchword with יצר in the doxology of 4:13; so also קרא occurs in the second vision at 7:4 and in the second doxology at 5:8 (see Paas 2002). After הִנֵּה, a participial phrase (rather than a finite verb) often serves as predicate, although a pronoun suffix is often added to הִנֵּה to indicate the subject. Here, a 3 m s pronoun (with YHWH as antecedent) is implied as the subject of the verb. The noun גֹּבַי refers to some variety of locust or grasshopper. It appears in only one other OT passage, Nahum 3:17, where it is parallel to אַרְבֶּה (which also means "locust"). The infinitive clause (עֲלוֹת, a qal infinitive construct of עלה) headed by בִּתְחִלַּת functions temporally, telling the reader when the vision took place. The verb עלה refers to the sprouting of young plants. The term לֶקֶשׁ ("latter crop") appears in the second line of the tenth century B.C. Gezer Calendar and only here in the OT.

Prose Clause: וְהִנֵּה־לֶ֕קֶשׁ אַחַ֖ר גִּזֵּ֥י הַמֶּֽלֶךְ׃

וְהִנֵּה. here introduces pertinent information, specifying for the reader when this vision occurred so that the reader may fully appreciate what a threat this was to the harvest. גִּזֵּי is the plural construct of the masculine noun גֵּז, which can mean either the fleece of sheep, as in Deuteronomy 18:4, or the cutting of grass or of a grain crop. It here refers to the "cut" of the harvest that the royal house takes for itself (the kind of grain tax that is condemned in Amos 5:11). On the surface, this clause is only a temporal marker. But it may also be a subtle attack on the royal taxation system. Note how similar this clause is to the previous, and especially how similar are the consonants of גבי, "locusts," and גזי "(the king's) cuttings," implying that the king was a locust to the yeoman farmers. Amos' choice of these words may not have been accidental.

7:2 וְהָיָ֗ה אִם־כִּלָּה֙ לֶֽאֱכוֹל֙ אֶת־עֵ֣שֶׂב הָאָ֔רֶץ וָאֹמַ֗ר אֲדֹנָ֤י
יְהוִה֙ סְלַח־נָ֔א מִ֥י יָק֖וּם יַעֲקֹ֑ב כִּ֥י קָטֹ֖ן הֽוּא׃

Prose Clause: וְהָיָ֗ה אִם־כִּלָּה֙ לֶֽאֱכוֹל֙ אֶת־עֵ֣שֶׂב הָאָ֔רֶץ

The qal *weqatal* 3 m s of היה is followed by אִם, which introduces a protasis. The pattern וְהָיָה אִם occurs five times in the Hebrew Bible (Jer 12:16; 17:24; Amos 6:9; 7:2; Zech 6:15). In every other case but this one, the pattern introduces a future contingency in a prophetic context (with the meaning, "and it shall happen, if . . ."). Here, this meaning is not possible, and scholars have suggested various emendations (see Paul 1991, 228 n. 20). But taking the text as it stands, one can treat the *weqatal* as a past imperfective, suggesting that the vision was repeated several times (such a scenario for visions is not unlikely; cf. Acts 10:9-16). We should note that Stuart creatively translates this as, "It seemed as if they would completely devour" (Stuart 1987, 370), but he gives no evidence to support this rendition. If that were the meaning, the Hebrew would probably have something like וַיְהִי כִּמְכַלֶּה לֶאֱכוֹל (see Gen 19:14; Num 13:33). The piel of כלה followed by לְ and an infinitive construct means to "complete" the verb of the infinitive, as in Genesis 24:45, אֲנִי טֶרֶם אֲכַלֶּה לְדַבֵּר ("before I finished speaking"). אֶת־עֵשֶׂב הָאָרֶץ refers to any kind of vegetation and is what the locust plague consumed during the exodus (Exod 10:12).

Prose Clause: וָאֹמַר

The *wayyiqtol* 1 c s of אמר introduces the apodosis (being past tense, the apodosis is a *wayyiqtol* and not a *weqatal*).

Prose Clause: אֲדֹנָ֤י יְהוִה֙ סְלַח־נָ֔א

After the vocative אֲדֹנָ֤י יְהוִה֙, the qal imperative m s of סלח with נָא gives the whole of Amos' request, what follows being merely argument that strengthens his appeal. The imperative of סלח also appears in the intercessions of Moses (Num 14:19) and Daniel (Dan 9:19). The parallel to Moses is particularly notable as Amos' imitation of Moses helps to authenticate his claim to being a true prophet.

Prose Clause: מִ֥י יָק֖וּם יַעֲקֹ֑ב

יָקוּם is a qal *yiqtol* 3 m s of קוּם with יַעֲקֹב as subject. The curious feature is מִי, which here seems to mean, "how." It also seems to mean "how" in Ruth 3:16. Here in Amos, the clause probably implies, "Who is Jacob that he should stand in the face of such a calamity?" But "How will Jacob stand?" is accurate. קוּם, literally to "arise," may connote recovery after a disaster.

Prose Clause: כִּ֥י קָטֹ֖ן הֽוּא

A nominal (verbless) clause introduced by explanatory כִּי. Israel is קָטֹן ("small") in the sense that it is too weak to withstand a divine assault. During the reign of Jeroboam II, of course, Israel's power was the greatest it had ever been, but before YHWH that is insignificant.

7:3 נִחַ֥ם יְהוָ֖ה עַל־זֹ֑את לֹ֥א תִהְיֶ֖ה אָמַ֥ר יְהוָֽה׃

Prose Clause: נִחַ֥ם יְהוָ֖ה עַל־זֹ֑את

נִחַם, morphologically either a niphal or piel *qatal* 3 m s of נחם, is here the niphal, to "regret" or "change one's mind." The verb also appears in Exodus 32:14, the most famous instance of God relenting over an intended judgment, setting up another parallel between Amos and Moses. The preposition עַל here means, "concerning." The choice of a *qatal* over a *wayyiqtol* here is noteworthy. It focuses more on the fact that YHWH relented than on the historical sequence.

Prose Clause: לֹא תִהְיֶה

Reported speech. The qal *yiqtol* 3 f s of היה. The verb is feminine, as is pronoun זֹאת in the previous clause, to indicate abstractly the hypothetical event of a locust plague.

Prose Clause: אָמַר יְהוָה

A divine speech formula with the qal *qatal* 3 m s of אמר.

7:4-6: The Vision of Drought

7:4 כֹּה הִרְאַנִי אֲדֹנָי יְהוִה וְהִנֵּה קֹרֵא לָרִב בָּאֵשׁ אֲדֹנָי
יְהוִה וַתֹּאכַל אֶת־תְּהוֹם רַבָּה וְאָכְלָה אֶת־הַחֵלֶק׃

Prose Clause: כֹּה הִרְאַנִי אֲדֹנָי יְהוִה

See 7:1.

Prose Clause: וְהִנֵּה קֹרֵא לָרִב בָּאֵשׁ אֲדֹנָי יְהוִה

The grammar of וְהִנֵּה קֹרֵא is like that of 7:1. לָרִב בָּאֵשׁ has the qal infinitive construct of רִיב (written defectively) headed by the preposition לְ followed by a prepositional phrase with בְּ. This could be taken to be something like a "trial by fire," but רִיב is not used for a judicial ordeal. A difficulty with this phrase is that in the formula ריב בְּ the preposition בְּ usually signifies the opposing party, as in Genesis 31:36; Judges 6:32, and with the noun רִיב, Jeremiah 25:31 (כִּי רִיב לַיהוָה בַּגּוֹיִם; "for YHWH has a contention with the nations"). Obviously the fire is not the opposing party. Thus, a number of scholars reconfigure the text as לִרְבִיב אֵשׁ, "for a rain of fire" (Wolff 1977, 292–93). Elsewhere in the Hebrew Bible, the word רביב appears only in the plural as רְבִיבִים, but a singular form is attested in Ugaritic. If this emendation is correct, it probably alludes to the fire that God rained down on Sodom according to Genesis 19:24. On the other hand, Limburg (1973) argues that ריב here means to "judge," since רִיב in Jeremiah 25:31 is paralleled by the niphal participle נִשְׁפָּט ("initiate a judgment"). Compare also Isaiah 66:16, כִּי בָאֵשׁ יְהוָה

נִשְׁפָּט ("for YHWH is bringing about a judgment with the fire"). In short, the point is that fire is punishment imposed after a judgment. Thus, it is best to leave the text unemended.

Prose Clause: וַתֹּ֙אכַל֙ אֶת־תְּה֣וֹם רַבָּ֔ה

אכל, here a qal *wayyiqtol* 3 f s, is often used for fire burning up its fuel. Here, however, it appears that the text does not mean a literal fire but a drought. The תְּהוֹם רַבָּה ("great deep") is not the Mediterranean Sea but the primeval ocean under the earth that feeds all the springs and other perennial water sources. In other words, all the springs and streams dried up.

Prose Clause: וְאָכְלָ֖ה אֶת־הַחֵֽלֶק

אכל appears again, but here it is a qal *weqatal* 3 f s. In the previous clause, the *wayyiqtol* is used perfectively and simply means that the springs dried up and had no water. Here, the *weqatal* is imperfective and means that the fields were getting progressively more parched, cracked and barren. חֵלֶק, "portion," here refers to the arable land apportioned out among the people.

7:5 וָאֹמַ֗ר אֲדֹנָ֤י יְהוִה֙ חֲדַל־נָ֔א מִ֥י יָק֖וּם יַעֲקֹ֑ב כִּ֥י קָטֹ֖ן
הֽוּא׃

Prose Clause: וָאֹמַ֗ר

The qal *wayyiqtol* 1 c s of אמר resumes the mainline of the narrative.

Prose Clause: אֲדֹנָ֤י יְהוִה֙ חֲדַל־נָ֔א

After the vocative אֲדֹנָי יְהוִה, the qal imperative m s of חדל calls on God to desist. This is not implying that the situation in 7:4-6 is somehow different from that in 7:1-3, where Amos called out, סְלַח־נָא ("forgive!"). In both cases, Amos wants God to forgive Jacob and stop ravaging the land.

Prose Clause: מִ֥י יָק֖וּם יַעֲקֹ֑ב

See 7:2.

Prose Clause: כִּ֥י קָטֹ֖ן הֽוּא

See 7:2.

7:6 נִחַ֥ם יְהוָ֖ה עַל־זֹ֑את גַּם־הִיא֙ לֹ֣א תִֽהְיֶ֔ה אָמַ֖ר אֲדֹנָ֥י
יְהוִֽה׃ ס

Prose Clause: נִחַ֥ם יְהוָ֖ה עַל־זֹ֑את

See 7:3.

Prose Clause: גַּם־הִיא֙ לֹ֣א תִֽהְיֶ֔ה

See 7:3.

Prose Clause: אָמַ֖ר אֲדֹנָ֥י יְהוִֽה

A divine speech formula.

7:7-9: The Vision of YHWH at the Wall

The prior vision narratives were in prose only. This one and the next (8:1-3) are each in two parts, with a prose vision narrative followed by a poetic oracle of doom.

7:7-8a: Prose Narrative: A change is signaled by a formal change in the narrative. Here, unlike the prior two vision narratives, YHWH questions Amos about the content of the vision before pronouncing doom. Amos, in turn, does not make intercession for Israel.

7:7 כֹּ֣ה הִרְאַ֔נִי וְהִנֵּ֧ה אֲדֹנָ֛י נִצָּ֖ב עַל־חוֹמַ֣ת אֲנָ֑ךְ וּבְיָד֖וֹ
אֲנָֽךְ׃

Prose Clause: כֹּ֣ה הִרְאַ֔נִי

See 7:1.

Prose Clause: וְהִנֵּ֧ה אֲדֹנָ֛י נִצָּ֖ב עַל־חוֹמַ֣ת אֲנָ֑ךְ

The grammar here is similar to that of 7:1, with נִצָּב, a niphal participle m s of נצב, "to stand." The preposition עַל may literally mean "upon" a wall or simply "at" or "beside" a wall. In the construct chain חוֹמַת אֲנָךְ, the wall is qualified as being "of אֲנָךְ," which may mean that אֲנָךְ was the material of which it was made, or that it was somehow characterized or made by אֲנָךְ.

Prose Clause: וּבְיָדוֹ אֲנָךְ

A verbless clause with אֲנָךְ as the subject and וּבְיָדוֹ as the predicate. YHWH held אֲנָךְ "in his hand," suggesting that אֲנָךְ was a substance or object that could be held. Whether a human could hold it, or only God could, is unclear.

7:8a וַיֹּאמֶר יְהוָה אֵלַי מָה־אַתָּה רֹאֶה עָמוֹס וָאֹמַר אֲנָךְ
וַיֹּאמֶר אֲדֹנָי

Prose Clause: וַיֹּאמֶר יְהוָה אֵלַי

The mainline of the narrative continues with the qal *wayyiqtol* 3 m s of אמר, which introduces reported speech. The express mention of the subject indicates that this is a new sentence.

Prose Clause: מָה־אַתָּה רֹאֶה עָמוֹס

Reported speech. The interrogative מָה is used here for the first time in the visions, since previously Amos had simply interpreted the visions for himself and on his own interceded with YHWH. The new pattern, a divine interrogation, suggests a new development, and it may imply that Amos, though he recognized the אֲנָךְ for what it was, did not understand its significance. The qal active participle m s of ראה suggests that God questioned Amos while the prophet was looking at the אֲנָךְ.

Prose Clause: וָאֹמַר

See 7:5.

Prose Clause: אֲנָךְ

Amos' answer is short and to the point. אֲנָךְ was obviously something that Amos could easily recognize; it is also noteworthy that he does not speak of the חוֹמַת אֲנָךְ but simply the אֲנָךְ itself; it is the אֲנָךְ in YHWH's hand, not the wall, that is the focus. The other clue about אֲנָךְ is that in 7:8b God places אֲנָךְ in the midst of Israel as a judgment. Thus, there was a wall of אֲנָךְ, but אֲנָךְ could be held in the hand (at least in God's hand), and Amos knew אֲנָךְ when he saw it, and it could be set in Israel as a mark of judgment. But what is אֲנָךְ? Options include: (1) אֲנָךְ is a plumbline. This is a medieval view and is based on the idea that אֲנָךְ is literally the metal lead but that by metonymy it is a plumbline, and this view until recently was widely followed (e.g., Maag 1951, 44–45, 66; Hammershaimb 1970, 111). This interpretation fits all the above conditions; a חוֹמַת אֲנָךְ would be a wall made with a plumbline (i.e., a wall that is plumb), it is something that can be held in the hand and that Amos would recognize, it signifies judgment, since setting it in the midst of Israel would imply a reckoning against a divine rule. Against this, recent analysis is fairly conclusive that אֲנָךְ does not mean "lead" and therefore that it does not signify a plumbline (Paul 1991, 233–34; see also *NIDOTTE* אֲנָךְ). In addition, no ancient version renders it as "plumbline," indicating that if it ever had that meaning, it was entirely lost on the earliest translators of the text. This is not a fatal objection to the translation "plumbline," but it does render it less likely. (2) אֲנָךְ means "tin." This is based on the Akkadian *annaku*, "tin." The problem is that this meaning fails every aspect of the context in Amos. First, "wall of tin" makes no sense. Some say that it might be metaphorical for weak defenses, just as "wall of iron" could be metaphorical for a strong army in heavy armor. One might well have such a verbal metaphor, but it is doubtful that one would *see* a wall of tin in a vision. What would such a wall look like? How could one make sense of it or even recognize it? Second, would it be meaningful for God to hold a lump of tin in his hand, and would Amos recognize it? In parallel visions, the thing observed is an everyday object and easily recognized (an almond branch in Jeremiah 1:11; a basket of summer fruit in Amos 8:1-2). A lump of tin is hardly the same. Third, it is difficult to see how setting tin in the midst of Israel signifies judgment. Some suggest that אֲנָךְ might mean "tin" but also be a wordplay on אֲנָקָה, "moaning," meaning that God intends to set "moaning" in Israel (e.g., Stuart 1987, 373). But in the parallel visions the wordplay is explicit (the significance of the summer fruit [קָיִץ] is explicitly that the end [קֵץ] has come in Amos 8:2; the significance of the almond [שָׁקֵד] is explicitly that God is watching [שֹׁקֵד] in Jer 1:11-12). This is not the case here. Fourth, the normal word for "tin" in biblical Hebrew is בְּדִיל, and thus it is likely that אֲנָךְ has some other meaning. (3) Ancient interpretations include that the אֲנָךְ is "adamant" (LXX: ἀδαμαντινος and ἀδάμας), or "plaster" and a "trowel" (Vulgate: *litum* and *trulla*), or "judgment" (Targum: דין). All of these appear to be guesswork and none suits the full context well. (4) Cripps (1929), working from the LXX, suggests that ἀδάμας may refer to "iron" and by metonymy mean a "sword" or "war-hammer." Rudolph (1971, 234–35) similarly, rendered it as *Brecheisen* ("crowbar"). This is rather far-fetched and lacks support in the Greek use of ἀδάμας, and few scholars follow it. (5) Andersen and Freedman (1989, 754) actually take אֲנָךְ to be first a wall of "plaster," then "tin" in YHWH's hand, and then "grief" that YHWH will set in the midst of Israel. This is altogether unsatisfactory. (5) On the other hand, Aquila here reads γανῶτα ("shining") and Theodotion has τηκόμενον ("molten"). Both suggest something like a glowing, molten metal, and this interpretation does make some sense in context: a melting, burning wall could suggest a collapse of Israel's defenses, God could hold a molten metal in his hand (cf. Isa 6:6) and Amos could recognize it, and setting such a substance in Israel could signify judgment and destruction. Unfortunately, we have no grounds on which to sustain this interpretation. (6) Another wordplay-based interpretation suggests that whatever אֲנָךְ originally meant, it is used as a wordplay for אָנֹכִי, "I," in v. 8, where God declares that he is setting אֲנָךְ in the midst of Israel (see Landy 2001, 165–66). The idea is that he is setting himself in the midst of Israel. This is grammatically peculiar and quite far-fetched. In short, the meaning of אֲנָךְ is lost.

Prose Clause: וַיֹּ֫אמֶר אֲדֹנָ֫י

A divine speech formula with a qal *wayyiqtol* 3 m s of אמר.

7:8b-9: Oracle of Doom: A poem of six lines. YHWH interprets the vision with an oracle predicting the destruction of Israel. In this case, he makes clear, there is no possibility that he will relent.

הִנְנִ֨י שָׂ֤ם אֲנָךְ֙	a	7:8b
בְּקֶ֨רֶב֙ עַמִּ֣י יִשְׂרָאֵ֔ל	b	
לֹֽא־אוֹסִ֥יף ע֖וֹד עֲב֥וֹר לֽוֹ׃	c	
וְנָשַׁ֙מּוּ֙ בָּמ֣וֹת יִשְׂחָ֔ק	d	7:9
וּמִקְדְּשֵׁ֥י יִשְׂרָאֵ֖ל יֶחֱרָ֑בוּ	e	
וְקַמְתִּ֛י עַל־בֵּ֥ית יָרָבְעָ֖ם בֶּחָֽרֶב׃ פ	f	

Line a: The colon-marker is *pashta* and the constraints are: 1 predicator, 3 constituents, and 3 units. It is rare but not unknown to have a line-break in Amos accented with *pashta*. If a break is not placed here, the resulting line would violate the constraints for both constituents and units. But ending the line here is probably correct because this ends the first line with a noun that is obviously very important here, אֲנָךְ֙.

הִנְנִ֨י. Particle הִנֵּה with 1 c s suffix as subject of participle. הִנֵּה can introduce a solemn divine disclosure.

שָׂ֤ם. Qal active participle m s of שִׂים.

אֲנָךְ֙. The direct object.

Line b: The colon-marker is *zaqeph qaton* and the constraints are: 0 predicators, 2 constituents, and 3 units.

בְּקֶ֨רֶב֙ עַמִּ֣י. Prepositional phrase with locative בְּ on a construct chain.

יִשְׂרָאֵ֔ל. This is in apposition to עַמִּ֣י.

Line c: The colon-marker is *silluq* and the constraints are: 1 predicator, 2 constituents, and 4 units.

לֹא־אוֹסִיף עוֹד עֲבוֹר. Negated hiphil *yiqtol* 1 c s of יסף. The expression לֹא עוֹד means, "no longer." עֲבוֹר, the qal infinitive construct of עבר, is used as an auxiliary to the finite verb.

לוֹ. The expression עבר לְ means to "pass by." It appears to mean to pass by without taking action (i.e., to overlook Israel's crimes). The expression עבר עַל־פֶּשַׁע, to "overlook an offense" (Mic 7:18; Prov 19:11) is illustrative.

Line d: The colon-marker is *zaqeph qaton* and the constraints are: 1 predicator, 2 constituents, and 3 units.

וְנָשַׁמּוּ. Niphal *weqatal* 3 c p of שׁמם. The niphal suggests that the shrines are the objects of violent action.

בָּמוֹת יִשְׂחָק. The subject (a construct chain). The unusual spelling for "Isaac" (יִשְׂחָק instead of יִצְחָק) occurs here and in v. 16, and also in Jeremiah 33:26. The use of "Isaac" to refer to the nation and in parallel with "Israel" is quite peculiar, but in Amos it occurs here and again in 7:16. The latter occurrence is most significant, because it appears there on the lips of Amaziah. This suggests that the use of יִשְׂחָק to designate the northern kingdom, and perhaps also the unusual spelling, is a local phenomenon at the Bethel shrine. See further discussion at v. 16.

Line e: The colon-marker is *athnach* and the constraints are: 1 predicator, 2 constituents, and 3 units. This line forms a chiasmus with the previous line.

וּמִקְדְּשֵׁי יִשְׂרָאֵל. The subject (a construct chain), set here as a parallel to בָּמוֹת יִשְׂחָק.

יֶחֱרָבוּ. Qal *yiqtol* 3 m p of חרב, "to be ruined, wasted." The *yiqtol* is offline, and is joined to the preceding *weqatal* in line d to speak of one single event and not two separate events. The third plural is impersonal and can be rendered as a passive. The choice of this verb may be driven by a desire to create a wordplay with חֶרֶב in line f.

Line f: The colon-marker is *silluq* and the constraints are: 1 predicator, 3 constituents, and 4 units.

וְקַמְתִּי. Qal *weqatal* 1 c s of קוּם. The *weqatal* is mainline and here introduces a prophecy that is separate from the one given in lines d-e.

עַל־בֵּית יָרָבְעָם. Prepositional phrase with עַל, here meaning "against." Several interpretations for "the house of Jeroboam" are possible. (1) His dynasty. But if that were the meaning, one would expect it to be the "house of Jehu" after the founder of the dynasty, as in Hos 1:4. On the other hand, Jeroboam II was so spectacularly successful the dynasty here could be named for him. (2) A royal palace located at Bethel. This interpretation is possible if at 7:13 וּבֵית מַמְלָכָה is taken to mean "and a royal palace," but that seems unlikely. (3) The Bethel shrine itself, which was sponsored by the king. Amos 7:13 does seem to describe Bethel as a "royal shrine," but on balance it is better to take "house of Jeroboam" to be a reference to the dynasty.

בֶּחָרֶב. Prepositional phrase with instrumental בְּ. The sword here represents coming to a violent end. On the end of the dynasty, see 2 Kings 15:8-10.

7:10-17: An Encounter with Amaziah: A biographical account of Amos' encounter with the chief priest of Bethel is abruptly inserted here. Calling this insertion "redactional" really does nothing to explain why it is here; it simply makes us ask questions about the redactor instead of the author. At minimum, this episode is inserted here to force us to reckon with this encounter in the context of Amos' four visions. Also, the arrogance of Amaziah enables the reader to see the justice in the verdicts that are given in the third and fourth visions. More significantly, this episode is highly ironic when set against the visions. Amaziah derisively calls Amos a "seer" (v. 12), and the reader knows from the vision accounts that this is precisely what Amos is. In addition, Amaziah sees Amos as an enemy of Israel, but the first two visions show him interceding with YHWH to pardon Israel. Finally, this section is probably put here because the prophecy of doom against the house of Jeroboam at the end of 7:9 is the basis for Amaziah's accusation in 7:11.

7:10-17a: Prose Narrative: The story of Amos' encounter with Amaziah is in prose, but it concludes with an oracle in poetic form.

7:10 וַיִּשְׁלַח אֲמַצְיָה כֹּהֵן בֵּית־אֵל אֶל־יָרָבְעָם מֶלֶךְ־
יִשְׂרָאֵל לֵאמֹר קָשַׁר עָלֶיךָ עָמוֹס בְּקֶרֶב בֵּית יִשְׂרָאֵל
לֹא־תוּכַל הָאָרֶץ לְהָכִיל אֶת־כָּל־דְּבָרָיו׃

Prose Clause: וַיִּשְׁלַח אֲמַצְיָה כֹּהֵן בֵּית־אֵל אֶל־יָרָבְעָם מֶלֶךְ־יִשְׂרָאֵל לֵאמֹר

The use of the qal *wayyiqtol* 3 m s of שׁלח sets the story of the encounter with Amaziah in the context of the visions, although it does not necessarily mean that the encounter actually occurred between the Amos' reception of the third and fourth visions. כֹּהֵן בֵּית־אֵל, in apposition to אֲמַצְיָה, suggests that he was a high-ranking priest at the shrine. לֵאמֹר, the qal infinitive construct of אמר with לְ, introduces the content of the implied letter to the king.

Prose Clause: קָשַׁר עָלֶיךָ עָמוֹס בְּקֶרֶב בֵּית יִשְׂרָאֵל

The qal *qatal* 3 m s of קשׁר introduces a factual summation (from Amaziah's perspective) of the situation. This is an abbreviated version of the letter; no doubt the full original would have contained a suitable salutation. The idiom קשׁר על can literally mean to tie something onto something (Jer 51:63), but often it means to "conspire against" (1 Sam 22:8; 1 Kgs 15:27; 2 Kgs 10:9). בְּקֶרֶב בֵּית יִשְׂרָאֵל probably connotes, "right in the middle of the house of Israel," suggesting that Amos was a danger to the royal house and was guilty of great effrontery. The "house of Israel" may refer to the nation or to the Bethel shrine.

Prose Clause: לֹא־תוּכַל הָאָרֶץ לְהָכִיל אֶת־כָּל־דְּבָרָיו׃

The negated qal *yiqtol* 3 f s of יכל with its auxiliary, a hiphil infinitive construct of כּוּל, literally says that the land cannot "contain" all his words (see 1 Kgs 7:26; 1 Kgs 8:64; Ezek 23:32). This could mean some or all of the following: (1) Amos' words are so many that they fill the land; that is, he won't stop preaching. (2) His message is spreading through all Israel and even spilling over into other nations, making them wonder what is happening here. (3) The land (referring to the people) cannot bear his preaching; in other words, he is discouraging and frightening them. (4) Amos' message is about to burst the land open like an overstuffed bag; that is, a violent reaction, possibly directed against the king, will soon erupt.

7:11a כִּי־כֹה אָמַר עָמוֹס

The above clause is prose, but Amaziah's citation of Amos below is poetry. Amaziah's introduction of Amos' words is strikingly similar to one of Amos' divine speech formulas, כֹּה אָמַר יְהוָה (1:3, 6, 8, etc.). In fact, this pattern is almost always used of God, and the exceptions cite the speech of a king or a king's representative (Isa 36:4; 14, 16; 37:3). This is ironic; whether he has intended to or not, Amaziah has cited Amos as a representative of God.

7:11b a בַּחֶרֶב יָמוּת יָרָבְעָם
b וְיִשְׂרָאֵל גָּלֹה יִגְלֶה מֵעַל אַדְמָתוֹ׃ ס

Line a: The colon-marker is *athnach* and the constraints are: 1 predicator, 3 constituents, and 3 units. The chiastic relationship of line a (prepositional phrase / verb / subject) to line b (subject / verb / prepositional phrase) indicates that Jeroboam's death and Israel's exile will be a single event taking place at about the same time. But we have no evidence that Amos actually said this; the words of line a subtly but critically distort line f in 7:9.

בַּחֶרֶב. Prepositional phrase with instrumental בְּ. The fronting of this phrase makes the violent nature of Jeroboam's death the focus.

יָמוּת. Qal *yiqtol* 3 m s of מות.

יָרָבְעָם. Proper name as subject.

Line b: The colon-marker is *silluq* and the constraints are: 1 predicator, 3 constituents, and 4 units. This line is cited verbatim in 7:17, and similar statements appear in 5:5 and 6:7.

וְיִשְׂרָאֵל. Proper name as subject with conjunction.

גָּלֹה יִגְלֶה. Qal infinitive absolute and qal *yiqtol* 3 m s of גלה. The infinitive absolute may imply certainty or totality.

מֵעַל אַדְמָתוֹ. Prepositional phrase with locative מִן and עַל.

7:12 וַיֹּאמֶר אֲמַצְיָה אֶל־עָמוֹס חֹזֶה לֵךְ בְּרַח־לְךָ אֶל־
אֶרֶץ יְהוּדָה וֶאֱכָל־שָׁם לֶחֶם וְשָׁם תִּנָּבֵא׃

Prose Clause: וַיֹּאמֶר אֲמַצְיָה אֶל־עָמוֹס

וַיֹּאמֶר, a qal *wayyiqtol* 3 m s of אמר, heads a mainline narrative clause and initiates the second episode of Amaziah's dealings with Amos; it also introduces Amaziah's reported speech.

Prose Clause: חֹזֶה לֵךְ בְּרַח־לְךָ אֶל־אֶרֶץ יְהוּדָה

This is reported speech. חֹזֶה, a qal active participle m s of חזה, is here a vocative substantive. The use of this title is unintended irony on Amaziah's part; he has derisively called Amos a "seer of visions," but the context indicates that this is precisely what Amos is. לֵךְ בְּרַח (qal imperatives m s of הלך and ברח), although two verbs, is really asyndetic hendiadys and not two separate clauses. Note the conjunctive *merka* with לֵךְ. The prepositional phrase לְךָ is an idiomatic verbal complement (the "ethical dative") and need not be translated. The prepositional phrase אֶל־אֶרֶץ יְהוּדָה is directive, giving the place to which Amos should flee.

Prose Clause: וֶאֱכָל־שָׁם לֶחֶם

וֶאֱכָל is a qal imperative m s with וְ, here subordinate to the previous clause and functioning as an implicit purpose clause, giving the reason Amos should flee there. The antecedent of שָׁם is יְהוּדָה in the previous clause. לֶחֶם is the direct object. Idiomatically, eating bread refers to earning a living.

Prose Clause: וְשָׁ֖ם תִּנָּבֵֽא

תִּנָּבֵא is a niphal *yiqtol* 2 m s functioning modally. The ו + [x] + *yiqtol* here is coordinated to the imperative וֶאֱכָל in the previous line, implying that the two actions are bound together as one. Note the chiastic structure of the two clauses:

וֶאֱכָל־שָׁ֣ם לֶ֔חֶם וְשָׁ֖ם תִּנָּבֵֽא

(verb + שָׁם + לֶחֶם + שָׁם + verb)

The lines mean that Amos should earn his living by performing his services as a professional prophet in Judah.

7:13 וּבֵֽית־אֵ֔ל לֹֽא־תוֹסִ֥יף ע֖וֹד לְהִנָּבֵ֑א כִּ֤י מִקְדַּשׁ־מֶ֙לֶךְ֙
ה֔וּא וּבֵ֥ית מַמְלָכָ֖ה הֽוּא׃ ס

Prose Clause: וּבֵֽית־אֵ֔ל לֹֽא־תוֹסִ֥יף ע֖וֹד לְהִנָּבֵ֑א

Heading the next clause with the locative וּבֵית־אֵל indicates that Amaziah does not care whether or where Amos prophesies, so long as he does not do it here. The hiphil modal *yiqtol* 2 m s of יסף with its auxiliary, the niphal infinitive construct of נבא, together with the strong negative לֹא and the temporal adverb עוֹד, imply that Amos must never prophesy there again.

Prose Clause: כִּ֤י מִקְדַּשׁ־מֶ֙לֶךְ֙ ה֔וּא

The explanation, introduced by כִּי, is that Bethel is a מִקְדַּשׁ־מֶלֶךְ. The construct chain probably designates a royally sponsored shrine. It is indefinite, suggesting that it is one of several (there was also one at Dan, and almost certainly one at Samaria as well).

Prose Clause: וּבֵ֥ית מַמְלָכָ֖ה הֽוּא

The phrase בֵּית מַמְלָכָה could be taken to mean that Bethel was also a royal residence, but this is unlikely. The phrase is probably simply a parallel to the preceding clause and may mean, “a national temple” (see Paul 1991, 243).

7:14 וַיַּ֤עַן עָמוֹס֙ וַיֹּ֣אמֶר אֶל־אֲמַצְיָ֔ה לֹא־נָבִ֣יא אָנֹ֔כִי וְלֹ֥א
בֶן־נָבִ֖יא אָנֹ֑כִי כִּֽי־בוֹקֵ֥ר אָנֹ֖כִי וּבוֹלֵ֥ס שִׁקְמִֽים׃

Prose Clause: וַיַּ֤עַן עָמוֹס֙

The *wayyiqtol* carries the mainline narrative forward. וַיַּ֤עַן is a qal *wayyiqtol* 3 m s of ענה.

Prose Clause: וַיֹּ֣אמֶר אֶל־אֲמַצְיָ֔ה

Epexegesis of וַיַּ֤עַן from the previous clause, introducing the content of Amos’ words. וַיֹּ֣אמֶר is a qal *wayyiqtol* 3 m s of אמר and אֶל־אֲמַצְיָ֔ה is a prepositional phrase with אֶל indicating the addressee.

Prose Clause: לֹא־נָבִ֣יא אָנֹ֔כִי

Negated verbless clause. As such, it is impossible to determine whether it is a present or past tense. Some prefer past tense on the grounds that Amos at this point obviously is a prophet and would not deny being such (see v. 15, which seems to establish the past tense meaning). But Amos may more precisely mean that he is not a *professional* prophet. In other words, he does not earn money by prophesying, in contrast to Amaziah’s sarcastic and implied accusation in v. 12. Probably Amos here and in the next clause is deliberately exploiting the temporal ambiguity of the verbless clauses: he *is not* a professional prophet but *continues* to earn his living as a herdsman; he *was not* a prophet but *was* a herdsman until God chose him to be a prophet. English cannot adequately convey this.

Prose Clause: וְלֹ֥א בֶן־נָבִ֖יא אָנֹ֑כִי

Another negated verbless clause. A בֶן־נָבִיא is a member of a prophetic guild, not a prophet’s biological son (2 Kgs 2:3,7; 6:1).

Prose Clause: כִּֽי־בוֹקֵ֥ר אָנֹ֖כִי וּבוֹלֵ֥ס שִׁקְמִֽים׃

A verbless clause with a compound predicate (בּוֹקֵר and בּוֹלֵס שִׁקְמִים). The particle כִּי is here adversative. Since בָּקָר often means "cattle," this would mean something like "cattleman," but it is anachronistic to suppose that this precludes his also being a shepherd, as he indicates he is in v. 15. Probably "herdsman" is a better rendition, indicating he managed sheep, goats and cattle. Another possibility is that בקר should be emended to דקר, giving the meaning "piercer." So emended, it would go with בּוֹלֵס שִׁקְמִים and refer to someone who pierces sycamore figs (as proposed by Zalcman 1980). A בּוֹלֵס שִׁקְמִים is apparently a person who cut the husk of the sycamore fig tree to enable the figs to ripen properly to an edible state. בּוֹלֵס, a qal active participle m s construct of בלס, is used substantively; בלס appears only here in the Hebrew Bible but there is fairly strong consensus about its meaning (for an alternative view, see Rosenbaum 1990, 47–50). The problem with the emendation of בקר to דקר is that, because of the word order, דקר cannot be in construct and conjoined to וּבוֹלֵס (to give the sense, "I am a piercer and cutter of sycamore figs"). For that to be the meaning, the word order would have to be אָנֹכִי דוֹקֵר וּבוֹלֵס שִׁקְמִים. Also, דקר is elsewhere used for the piercing of people, generally by the sword or in some act of violence. Thus, the text should not be emended. We cannot tell from these job descriptions how wealthy or poor Amos was, but clearly he identified himself with those who worked in the fields (see Giles 1992).

7:15 וַיִּקָּחֵנִי יְהוָה מֵאַחֲרֵי הַצֹּאן וַיֹּאמֶר אֵלַי יְהוָה לֵךְ הִנָּבֵא אֶל־עַמִּי יִשְׂרָאֵל׃

Prose Clause: וַיִּקָּחֵנִי יְהוָה מֵאַחֲרֵי הַצֹּאן

The preceding nominal clauses are background information and presented the setting for Amos' small narrative; this clause, headed by וַיִּקָּחֵנִי, a qal *wayyiqtol* 3 m s of לקח with a 1 c s suffix, is the first event of his narrative. The prepositional phrase מֵאַחֲרֵי הַצֹּאן combines מִן, indicating the situation from which God took him, and the construct plural of אַחַר, indicating his position relative to the flock that he watched over (he walked behind his herds and flocks).

Prose Clause: וַיֹּאמֶר אֵלַי יְהוָה

The *wayyiqtol* 3 m s of אמר continues the mainline sequence of Amos' narrative and introduces another reported speech. The subject of וַיֹּאמֶר is of course יְהוָה, but the position of the prepositional phrase אֵלַי between verb and subject is slightly unusual. It may be that the position of יהוה at the end of the clause is stronger than if in the middle (it cannot have the first position because of the *wayyiqtol*). Thus, what YHWH said to Amos here ("Prophesy!") is set in contrast to what Amaziah said ("Do not prophesy!"), as noted in the next verse. Be that as it may, the importance of this as a divine speech is not understated; the name YHWH is given twice in this verse as the subject of the two verbs וַיִּקָּחֵנִי and וַיֹּאמֶר; this is a divine commissioning.

Prose Clause: לֵךְ

A qal imperative m s of הלך; coming from Judah, Amos naturally had to "go" to Israel before he could prophesy there. Amaziah's command to Amos also began with לֵךְ.

Prose Clause: הִנָּבֵא אֶל־עַמִּי יִשְׂרָאֵל

This single clause is the whole of Amos' defense and explanation for his activity; he is prophesying in Israel because YHWH told him to do so. Contrast Amaziah's command in v. 12, which uses virtually identical language (לֵךְ . . . אֶל־אֶרֶץ יְהוּדָה . . . וְשָׁם תִּנָּבֵא). The word הִנָּבֵא, a niphal imperative m s of נבא, implies that Amos has the title of נָבִיא entirely by divine commission rather than by training or personal preference. The prepositional phrase אֶל־עַמִּי יִשְׂרָאֵל furthermore demonstrates that his area of prophetic activity, Israel rather than Judah, is by God's command in contrast to Amaziah's order.

7:16 וְעַתָּה שְׁמַע דְּבַר־יְהוָה אַתָּה אֹמֵר לֹא תִנָּבֵא עַל־
יִשְׂרָאֵל וְלֹא תַטִּיף עַל־בֵּית יִשְׂחָק׃

Prose Clause: וְעַתָּה שְׁמַע דְּבַר־יְהוָה

וְעַתָּה, literally "and now," is an inference marker that brings the previous historical discourse quickly to the present and describes the ramifications of prior events for the current situation. In another ironic touch, Amos, who had been forbidden to prophesy, responds to the command with another prophecy introduced by שְׁמַע, a qal imperative m s of שמע, and its object, דְּבַר־יְהוָה.

Prose Clause: אַתָּה אֹמֵר

Rather than using a finite verb (such as the *qatal* אָמַר), Amos employs a periphrastic qal active participle m s in אֹמֵר. This need not be taken to mean that Amaziah is repeating himself or speaking constantly; it only implies that this is the demand that Amaziah is currently putting forth.

Prose Clause: לֹא תִנָּבֵא עַל־יִשְׂרָאֵל

Amaziah's prohibition, לֹא תִנָּבֵא (with a niphal *yiqtol* 2 m s of נבא), here contrasts with YHWH's commission in the previous verse. The negative לֹא (in contrast to אַל) is legislative in nature (see *IBHS* 34.2.1b) and suggests a permanent injunction. The preposition עַל probably has the sense of "against."

Prose Clause: וְלֹא תַטִּיף עַל־בֵּית יִשְׂחָק

This clause is parallel to the previous, with another prohibitive לֹא with תַטִּיף, the hiphil *yiqtol* 2 m s of נטף, and another adversative use of עַל. The verb נטף (qal and hiphil stems) means to "secrete" or "drip," but it refers to prophetic preaching here and in Ezekel 21:2,7; Micah 2:6. The term is not of itself derisive, as God uses the word to direct Ezekiel to prophesy. Here again, "Isaac" is set as a parallel to "Israel," but it may be noteworthy that Amaziah also refers to the "house of Isaac." While this may be no more than an alternative name for the kingdom, the term may have special significance at the Bethel shrine. Of course, the Genesis stories primarily associate Bethel with Jacob, but this does not mean that the name Isaac was not used at the shrine.

7:17a לָכֵ֞ן כֹּֽה־אָמַ֣ר יְהוָ֗ה

The above is a divine speech formula in prose; it introduces the poetic oracle that follows.

7:17b: Oracle of Doom: Amos here gives a one-strophe, five-line oracle in which he predicts personal disaster for Amaziah on top of the general calamity coming to Israel. Every line begins with the subject, then has a prepositional phrase (with בְּ in lines a-c and עַל in lines d-e), and then has a *yiqtol* predicate at the end of the line (except for line e, which breaks the pattern by inverting the order of the verb and prepositional phrase). Also, each of the subjects in lines a-c has the 2 m s suffix (the other subjects obviously cannot have such a suffix), and lines c-e each have the noun אֲדָמָה. These lines have numerous interconnections and are in effect a list of coming disasters. These five lines are grouped into two couplets (lines a-b: wife and children; lines c-d: your ground and unclean ground) concluding with a final line that casts Amaziah's report to Jeroboam back into his face (compare line e to the second line of 7:11b).

7:17b a אִשְׁתְּךָ֞ בָּעִ֣יר תִּזְנֶ֗ה
b וּבָנֶ֤יךָ וּבְנֹתֶ֙יךָ֙ בַּחֶ֣רֶב יִפֹּ֔לוּ
c וְאַדְמָתְךָ֖ בַּחֶ֣בֶל תְּחֻלָּ֑ק
d וְאַתָּ֗ה עַל־אֲדָמָ֤ה טְמֵאָה֙ תָּמ֔וּת
e וְיִשְׂרָאֵ֕ל גָּלֹ֥ה יִגְלֶ֖ה מֵעַ֥ל אַדְמָתֽוֹ׃ ס

Line a: The colon-marker is *pashta* and the constraints are: 1 predicator, 3 constituents, and 3 units.

אִשְׁתְּךָ֞. The subject. Wolff notes that Akkadian treaties call for the sexual humiliation of the wives of covenant violators (Wolff 1977, 315 n. 59).

בָּעִ֣יר. Prepositional phrase with locative בְּ. Presumably the city meant here is the city of Amaziah's residence, Bethel. The phrase may imply that what she does, or what happens to her, will be a matter of public knowledge (cf. Deut 22:23–24).

תִּזְנֶה. Qal *yiqtol* 3 f s of זנה. The verb usually implies willful promiscuity. It seems very odd, however, that Amos should in this context predict that Amaziah's wife would become lustfully immoral. Every other line speaks of violence forcibly carried out against Israel, Amaziah and his children and possessions. זנה here probably connotes not willful promiscuity but sexual defilement either through rape or selling herself out of desperation to survive. As the wife of a priest, such defilement is particularly heinous. Her ruin may be symbolic of the desecration of the sanctity of the Bethel shrine.

Line b: The colon-marker is *zaqeph qaton* and the constraints are: 1 predicator, 3 constituents, and 4 units.

וּבָנֶ֤יךָ וּבְנֹתֶ֙יךָ֙. The subjects; it is not necessary to assume Amaziah's sons and daughters would be children at the time this prediction was fulfilled.

בַּחֶ֣רֶב. Prepositional phrase with instrumental בְּ. Falling "by the sword" represents a violent death. Amaziah's sons may have been combatants while his daughters may have been killed in the sack of the city.

יִפֹּ֔לוּ. Qal *yiqtol* 3 m p of נפל.

Line c: The colon-marker is *athnach* and the constraints are: 1 predicator, 3 constituents, and 3 units.

וְאַדְמָתְךָ֖. The subject; here it seems to be land that Amaziah privately owned.

בַּחֶ֣בֶל. Prepositional phrase with instrumental בְּ. The distribution of his land via a "measuring line" indicates that his land is broken up in an official process by a new administration that has no regard for his prior claim to the land. In other words, it is not simply occupied by squatters. This implies the fall of the government of Jeroboam II, Amaziah's patron. Also, it is fitting that members of the elite, who used judicial means to take the land of the poor, should have the same done to them.

תְּחֻלָּק. Pual *yiqtol* 3 f s of חלק, "be divided." Amaziah apparently owned an estate large enough for it to be divided and apportioned out by the conquerors. This suggests that Amaziah himself was one of the wealthy aristocrats that Amos inveighs against.

Line d: The colon-marker is *zaqeph qaton* and the constraints are: 1 predicator, 3 constituents, and 4 units.

וְאַתָּה. The subject.

עַל־אֲדָמָה טְמֵאָה. Prepositional phrase with locative עַל. The "unclean land" is a Gentile land where Israelite concerns for kosher foods, sabbath regulations, and so forth were not observed. We sometimes imagine that the prophets' opponents were so paganized that they had no regard for Torah requirements, and sometimes this is so (cf. 8:5). But Amaziah appears to have taken some aspects of his priesthood seriously.

תָּמוּת. Qal *yiqtol* 2 m s of מות.

Line e: The colon-marker is *silluq* and the constraints are: 1 predicator, 3 constituents, and 5 units. This line repeats Amaziah's charge about the content of Amos' prophecies (see 7:11), implying that Amos is asserting back to Amaziah that his prophecy will in fact come true.

וְיִשְׂרָאֵל. The subject; the final exile of Israel took place c. 722, and it appears that Amos' ministry was no later than c. 755 B.C. We need not assume, however, that all aspects of this oracle were fulfilled at the same time. His children's death and wife's humiliation, and his own death, could have occurred earlier and at different times.

גָּלֹה יִגְלֶה. Qal infinitive absolute and *yiqtol* 3 m s of גלה. The infinitive absolute here implies certainty and is in contrast to Amaziah's refusal to listen and implied denial.

מֵעַל אַדְמָתוֹ. Prepositional phrase with מִן and עַל, implying removal from their homeland.

8:1-3: A Basket of Summer Fruit

This vision is structurally parallel to the enigmatic third vision, but its meaning is much more clear.

8:1-2a: Prose Narrative: As before, Amos narrates the essential details of the vision in prose.

8:1 כֹּה הִרְאַנִי אֲדֹנָי יְהוִה וְהִנֵּה כְּלוּב קָיִץ׃

Prose Clause: כֹּה הִרְאַנִי אֲדֹנָי יְהוִה

See 7:1.

Prose Clause: וְהִנֵּה כְּלוּב קָיִץ

This is a clause with an implied הָיָה, "there was." וְהִנֵּה introduces Amos' perspective on the vision and provides the setting for the narrated conversation that follows. In the construct chain כְּלוּב קָיִץ, the term קַיִץ, literally "summer," connotes the produce of summer (cf. Jer 40:10). The late summer harvest would be figs and a late grape harvest (Mic 7:1). קַיִץ is also found in the seventh and last line of the Gezer Calendar (spelled as קץ; see also Rhatjen 1964).

8:2a וַיֹּאמֶר מָה־אַתָּה רֹאֶה עָמוֹס וָאֹמַר כְּלוּב קָיִץ
וַיֹּאמֶר יְהוָה אֵלַי

There are five prose clauses here; see 7:8a for a discussion of the grammar. Closely paralleling the third vision report, this introduces a new oracle.

8:2b-3: Oracle of Doom: Six lines in one strophe. The series of visions ends with an oracle that foretells the end of the kingdom. After a general statement to the effect that disaster is sure to come (lines a-b), there is a prophecy of wailing lamentation at the shrines (line c) and, after a parenthetical divine speech formula (line d), the lyrics of the lament songs are given (lines e-f).

בָּ֚א הַקֵּץ֙ אֶל־עַמִּ֣י יִשְׂרָאֵ֔ל	a	8:2b
לֹֽא־אוֹסִ֥יף ע֖וֹד עֲב֥וֹר לֽוֹ׃	b	
וְהֵילִ֜ילוּ שִׁיר֤וֹת הֵיכָל֙ בַּיּ֣וֹם הַה֔וּא	c	8:3
נְאֻ֖ם אֲדֹנָ֣י יְהוִ֑ה	d	
רַ֣ב הַפֶּ֔גֶר בְּכָל־מָק֖וֹם הִשְׁלִ֥יךְ	e	
הָֽס׃ פ	f	

Line a: The colon-marker is *zaqeph qaton* and the constraints are: 1 predicator, 3 constituents, and 4 units.

בָּ֚א. Qal *qatal* 3 m s of בּוֹא.

הַקֵּץ֙. The subject, "the end," is obviously a word-play on קַיִץ, "summer produce." The two words are from different roots (קַיִץ from קיץ, and קֵץ from קצץ; Paul 1991, 254) but they would have been pronounced the same in Samaria and, if the Gezer Calendar is any indication and unless *matres lectionis* were already employed in Amos' day, they were spelled the same (see also Wolters 1988). Also, the fact that the time of קַיִץ is at the end of the agricultural year is apropos to the wordplay.

אֶל־עַמִּ֣י יִשְׂרָאֵ֔ל. Prepositional phrase with אֶל.

Line b: See 7:8.

Line c: The colon-marker is *zaqeph qaton* and the constraints are: 1 predicator, 3 constituents, and 5 units.

וְהֵילִ֜ילוּ. Hiphil *weqatal* 3 m p of ילל, for future tense (mainline clause in an anticipatory text). The verb is generally intransitive, like the English "wail," but here it seems to be transitive, taking שִׁירוֹת ironically as its direct object. But just as the English counterpart, "they shall wail temple songs," is unusual but not unintelligible, the same is true of the Hebrew.

שִׁיר֤וֹת הֵיכָל֙. The direct object in a construct chain. שִׁירָה, "song," occurs twelve times in the MT but only here in the plural (the masculine plural שִׁירִים occurs seven times), but that is no reason to emend. Many interpreters (e.g., Noble 1998, 432–33) do emend שִׁירוֹת to שָׁרוֹת ("[female] singers"; thus, "the female singers of the temple shall wail"), but this is unpersuasive, and it is typical of how emendation often flattens the vivid language of the prophets. The phrase שִׁירוֹת הֵיכָל is, as described above, an ironic direct object to the verb. The meaning, of course, is that instead of harmonious singing there shall be wailing.

בַּיּ֣וֹם הַה֔וּא. Prepositional phrase with בְּ in a temporal phrase.

Line d: The colon-marker is *athnach* and the constraints are: 0 predicators, 3 constituents, and 3 units.

נְאֻ֖ם אֲדֹנָ֣י יְהֹוִ֑ה. A divine speech formula using a construct chain.

Line e: This line, as proposed here, does not follow the MT cantillation. The constraints are: 1 predicator, 4 constituents, and 4 units. There are two clauses, רַב הַפֶּגֶר and בְּכָל־מָקוֹם הִשְׁלִיךְ.

רַ֣ב. Adjective used as a predicate.

הַפֶּ֔גֶר. The subject; a collective noun, it represents a plurality.

בְּכָל־מָק֖וֹם. Prepositional phrase with locative בְּ on a construct chain.

הִשְׁלִ֥יךְ. Hiphil *yiqtol* 3 m s of שלך. The implied object is הַפֶּגֶר. The subject could be YHWH, but it is more likely that the verb is used impersonally and is a virtual passive.

Line f: The colon-marker is *silluq* and the constraints are: 1 predicator, 1 constituent, and 1 unit. This violates the constraints for having a one-unit line, but it is a dramatic end to the oracle. Most significantly, setting this word by itself dramatically recalls the grim scene in 6:10.

הָֽס. The imperative "Hush!" has here precisely the same conceptual context as in its use in 6:10: Samaria is filled with corpses and thus a city under taboo; it is so defiled that God's name must not even be mentioned there.

8:4–9:15: Final Condemnation and Redemption

The conclusion of Amos is a pair of lengthy poems (8:4-12; 9:1b-15). These poems are separated by a prose conclusion to the first poem (8:13-14) and a prose introduction to the second poem (9:1a). But the text divides into three major parts, as follows.

1. 8:4-6 is an introduction describing briefly the sins of the people. The offenses described here are the basis for the appropriate punishment God decrees in subsequent verses.
2. 8:7–9:6 gives YHWH's final judgment against Israel. This is in two parts, 8:7-14 and 9:1-6.
3. 9:7-15 predicts Israel's diaspora and recovery. It compares Israel to the nations, indicating that Israel is not really different from them in God's eyes (9:7-10). But then the text predicts the redemption of Israel and also draws the Gentiles into that redemption, asserting that God will bring the nations into Israel (9:11-12). The book ends with a promise of a great harvest and a robust population for the nation (9:13-15).

Several repeated themes bind this text together.

A. There is focus on what may be called *the fate of the Israelites.* First, the fate of impoverished Israelites is abuse and suffering. The more well-off members of society hunt them down and sell them into slavery (8:4,6). Second, and as a fitting judgment, God will hunt down the entire nation and slaughter Israelites wherever they hide (9:1b-4), and they will wander among the nations and face slaughter everywhere (9:9-10). Third, however, these judgments will be reversed and Israel will be secure in its land forever (9:14-15).
B. Another theme of the text may be broadly defined as *food.* First, the merchants cheat people when they sell grain (8:5). Second, the judgment on Israel is described as a "famine" for the word of God (8:11-13). In the restoration, however, Israel will experience a miraculously great harvest (9:13).

C. The matter of *oaths* appears three times. First, YHWH swears an oath by the pride of Jacob in 8:7. Second, the people swear by their shrines in 8:14. Third, YHWH makes a solemn decree against Israel while standing by an altar in 9:1, an act that is implicitly an oath.
D. The upheaval of the land *like the Nile* is two times a sign of the day of the YHWH (8:8; 9:5c).
E. The theme of *YHWH's cosmic power* appears three times: in his darkening of the daytime sky (8:9), in his causing the earth to melt (9:5a), and in the fact that his dominion extends from heaven to earth (9:6).
F. The *mourning* of the people is mentioned twice, in 8:10 and 9:5b.
G. Finally, the theme of *Israel and the Gentiles* is taken up in 9:7-8, 11-12. First, Israel is declared to be no better than the pagan nations (9:7-8). Second, however, the ancient promise that David's dynasty will have dominion over all the nations is reaffirmed, and even Gentiles are called the people of YHWH (9:11-12). This theme is also important for the structure of the whole book, as it creates an inclusion. The book begins with Israel no better than the Gentiles and like them facing YHWH's wrath (1:3–2:16). The book also ends with Israel no better than the Gentiles, but it includes the Gentiles in the blessings of YHWH's salvation of Israel (9:11-12).

The table below lays out the structure of this passage. On the left side, one can see how the two poems are divided into stanzas as well as where the prose boundary texts are placed. On the right side, the text is divided according to content, showing the major parts of this final division of the book. The thematic links described above are also presented here. These links are laid out to show where the various themes are located and to provide a map for following how Amos develops these themes, as described above. One can see, in fact, that the themes of Part I (the "fate of the Israelites" and "food") are taken up again in

Part III (with the addition of "Israel and the Gentiles"). Also, every theme Part IIa is taken up again in Part IIb, except that Part IIa deals with the theme of "food" but Part IIb does not, whereas Part IIb gives attention to the "fate of the Israelites" in 9:1b-4. Thus, one sees something of an inclusion pattern or chiasmus in this division, with Part I mirrored by Part III and Part IIa mirrored by Part IIb.

<table>
<tr><td rowspan="9">First Poem (8:4-14)</td><td rowspan="3">Stanza 1 (8:4-6)</td><td rowspan="3">I. Sin (8:4-6)</td><td>A. Fate of Israelites (8:4)</td></tr>
<tr><td>B. Food (8:5)</td></tr>
<tr><td>A. Fate of Israelites (8:6)</td></tr>
<tr><td>Stanza 2 (8:7)</td><td rowspan="6">IIa. Judgment (8:7-14)</td><td>C. Oath (8:7)</td></tr>
<tr><td>Stanza 3 (8:8)</td><td>D. Land like Nile (8:8)</td></tr>
<tr><td rowspan="2">Stanza 4 (8:9-10)</td><td>E. YHWH's Cosmic power (8:9)</td></tr>
<tr><td>F. Mourning (8:10)</td></tr>
<tr><td>Stanza 5 (8:11-12)</td><td>B. Food (8:11-13)</td></tr>
<tr><td>Prose (8:13-14)</td><td>C. Oath (8:14)</td></tr>
</table>

<table>
<tr><td rowspan="11">Second Poem (9:1-15)</td><td>Prose (9:1a)</td><td rowspan="6">IIb. Judgment 2 (9:1-6)</td><td>C. Oath (9:1a)</td></tr>
<tr><td>Stanza 1 (9:1b-4)</td><td>A. Fate of Israelites (9:1b-4)</td></tr>
<tr><td rowspan="4">Stanza 2 (9:5-6)</td><td>E. YHWH's Cosmic power (9:5a)</td></tr>
<tr><td>F. Mourning (9:5b)</td></tr>
<tr><td>D. Land like Nile (9:5c)</td></tr>
<tr><td>E. YHWH's Cosmic power (9:6)</td></tr>
<tr><td>Stanza 3 (9:7-8)</td><td rowspan="5">III. Recovery (9:7-15)</td><td>G. Israel and Gentiles (9:7-8)</td></tr>
<tr><td>Stanza 4 (9:9-10)</td><td>A. Fate of Israelites (9:9-10)</td></tr>
<tr><td>Stanza 5 (9:11-12)</td><td>G. Israel and Gentiles (9:11-12)</td></tr>
<tr><td rowspan="2">Stanza 6 (9:13-15)</td><td>B. Food (9:13)</td></tr>
<tr><td>A. Fate of Israelites (9:14-15)</td></tr>
</table>

8:4 Hear this, you who sniff after the poor
And who annihilate the impoverished in the land, 5 while saying:

"When will the new moon be over
So that we may sell grain,
And the Sabbath, so that we may open up the grain business—
By shrinking the ephah and enlarging the shekel,
By making twisted balance scales that deceive,
6 For obtaining poor people because of silver
And a poor man because of sandals—
And so that we may sell the bottom-of-the-barrel grain?"

7 YHWH has sworn by the pride of Jacob,
"I will never forget all their deeds!"
8 Isn't it for this reason that the earth will shake
And all who dwell on it will mourn,
And all of it will rise like the Nile,
And it will overflow and subside like the Egyptian Nile?

9 And it shall be on that day—
An oracle of Lord YHWH—
That I shall bring down the sun at noon
And I shall bring darkness to earth on a bright day.
10 And I will turn your festivals into mourning
And all your songs into lamentation.
And I shall bring sackcloth up around every waist
And baldness on every head.
And I shall make it as the mourning for an only son
And (I shall make) its outcome into a truly bitter day."

11 Behold, days are coming—
An oracle of Lord YHWH—
When I shall release a famine upon the earth.
(It will) not be a famine for bread and not be thirst for water.
Rather, (it will be a famine) for hearing the words of YHWH.

[12]And they will wander from sea to sea
And from the northlands to the rising of the sun.
They will rove about to seek the word of YHWH but not find (it).

[13]On that day they will collapse from thirst—the beautiful maidens
and the fine young men [14]who swear by the guilt of Samaria and say, "As
your gods live, Dan!" and "As the 'way' of Beersheba lives!"—and they
will fall never to rise again.

[9:1]I saw the Lord standing at the altar, and he said,

Strike the capital so that the door-frames shake!
And sever them at the top—all of them!
And I will slay the rest of them with the sword.

Not one of their fugitives will get away,
And not one of their refugees will escape.

[2]If they dig into Sheol,
From there my hand shall get them.
And if they ascend into heaven,
From there I shall bring them down.
[3]And if they hide on the top of Carmel,
From there I will hunt them down and get them.
And if they are concealed from before my eyes on the floor of the sea,
From there I will command the serpent to bite them.
[4]And if they go into captivity in the presence of their enemies,
From there I will command the sword to slay them.
And I shall set my eye upon them—
For evil and not for good.

[5]The Lord YHWH Sabaoth:
Who touches the earth and it melts,
So that all who inhabit it begin mourning,
And it—all of it—convulses like the Nile
And then sinks like the Nile of Egypt;
[6]Who builds in the heavens his (throne's) stairway
While laying his (throne's) foundation platform upon the earth;

Who calls to the waters of the sea
And then pours them out on the surface of the earth;
His name is YHWH!

[7]*Are you not like the sons of the Cushites as far as I am concerned,*
Sons of Israel? The oracle of YHWH.
Didn't I raise up Israel from the land of Egypt
And the Philistines from Caphtor and Aram from Kir?

[8]*Behold, the eyes of Lord YHWH are on the sinful kingdom*
And I shall annihilate it from the surface of the ground,
Except that I will not altogether annihilate the house of Jacob.
The oracle of YHWH.

[9]*For behold I am issuing a command,*
And I shall make the house of Israel wander among all the nations,
Just as when there is a jostling in a sieve
Without a pebble falling to earth.

[10]*They shall die by the sword—all the sinners of my people*
Who say,
"Trouble will not overtake or approach us."

[11]*In that day*
I will raise up the collapsing booth of David.
And I shall wall up its breaches
And raise up its ruins;
And I shall build it up as in the days of old,
[12]*So that they may possess the remnant of Edom and all the nations*
Who are called by my name.
The oracle of YHWH, who does this.

[13]*Behold the days are coming—the oracle of YHWH—*
When a plowman will be present with the harvester
And a grape treader will be present with the seed-spreader.
And the mountains will flow with grape juice
And all the hills will melt.

[14]And I shall bring about a restoration of my people, Israel.
And they will rebuild desolate cities and inhabit them.
And they will plant vineyards and drink their wine.
And they will make gardens and eat their fruit.

[15]And I shall plant them on their ground.
And they will never again be pulled up from their ground
That I gave to them,
Says YHWH your God.

8:4-14: First Poem and Prose Conclusion

8:4-6: First Stanza. This stanza is in two strophes. The first strophe, in two lines, calls on the merchant and aristocratic class to listen, and in summary fashion it makes an accusation (8:4). The second, in eight lines, makes a caricatured quotation of the merchants and in so doing sets forth a detailed accusation of their crimes (8:5-6). There is no reason to break the second strophe into two parts, as is done in the MT verse division.

8:4: First Strophe. Two lines, with the call to hear initiating 8:4–9:15.

8:4 שִׁמְעוּ־זֹ֔את הַשֹּׁאֲפִ֖ים אֶבְי֑וֹן
וְלַשְׁבִּ֖ית עֲנִיֵּי־אָֽרֶץ׃ לֵאמֹר

Line A1a: The colon-marker is *athnach* and the constraints are: 2 predicators, 4 constituents, and 4 units.

שִׁמְעוּ. Qal imperative m p of שמע.

זֹ֔את. The direct object of שִׁמְעוּ.

הַשֹּׁאֲפִ֖ים. Qal active participle m p absolute of שאף with definite article; it functions as a vocative relative clause and also as the subject of שִׁמְעוּ, and it takes a direct object. See the discussion at 2:7a, where emendation of this verb is rejected and it is suggested that it metaphorically represents the upper class of Samaria as dogs sniffing at the ground while they hunt their prey.

אֶבְיֽוֹן. The direct object of הַשֹּׁאֲפִים, the poor are the metaphorical prey of the powerful.

Line A1b: The colon-marker *silluq* at the end of 8:4 is disregarded here in favor of attaching לֵאמֹר to this line, and the constraints are: 2 predicators, 2 constituents, and 3 units.

וְלַשְׁבִּית. The hiphil infinitive construct of שׁבת. One would expect to see this as לְהַשְׁבִּית (Ps 8:2), but the preposition לְ has caused syncopation in a manner analogous to how the *yiqtol* form syncopates from hypothetical יְהַקְטִיל to יַקְטִיל (*GKC* §53a). The verb here means to "put an end to" and thus to "exterminate." Using שׁבת with this meaning is somewhat odd, but it is a wordplay on הַשַּׁבָּת ("the Sabbath"), which these persons are eager to see over according to line A2c. The infinitive construct could be taken as a clause expressing purpose or motive (a complement to הַשֹּׁאֲפִים). If so, the conjunction might be either emphatic ("even") or explanatory ("that is"), but GKC §114p observes that the infinitive construct with the conjunction ו and preposition לְ can express "the continuation of a previous finite verb." Psalm 104:21, הַכְּפִירִים שֹׁאֲגִים לַטָּרֶף וּלְבַקֵּשׁ מֵאֵל אָכְלָם ("the lions are roaring at the prey, and seek from God their food") is especially analogous here. See also *IBHS* §36.3.2, where this construction is described as the "equivalent of a finite verb." Here, the infinitive serves as a second relative clause after הַשֹּׁאֲפִים.

עֲנִיֵּי־אָֽרֶץ. A construct chain as the direct object.

לֵאמֹר. Qal infinitive construct of אמר introducing a quotation. Like וְלַשְׁבִּית, this counts as a predicator. Notwithstanding the MT verse division, this works better with this instead of the following strophe. What follows are the words of the oppressive mercantile class, but it seems odd that לֵאמֹר is not preceded by some word associated with speech (such as "boast" or "speak"). But לֵאמֹר can describe what one says while doing some other act, as in Isaiah 4:1 וְהֶחֱזִיקוּ שֶׁבַע נָשִׁים בְּאִישׁ אֶחָד בַּיּוֹם הַהוּא לֵאמֹר לַחְמֵנוּ נֹאכֵל ("And seven women will grab one man on that day while saying, 'We will eat our bread . . .'").

8:5-6: Second Strophe. Eight lines. This entire strophe (after לֵאמֹר) portrays itself as a quotation of the evil merchants. It seems unlikely that they were so brazen as to actually say these things; Amos is using this caricature or travesty as a literary device to portray their attitudes as betrayed by their actions.

8:5	A2a	מָתַי יַעֲבֹר הַחֹדֶשׁ
	A2b	וְנַשְׁבִּירָה שֶּׁבֶר
	A2c	וְהַשַּׁבָּת וְנִפְתְּחָה־בָּר
	A2d	לְהַקְטִין אֵיפָה וּלְהַגְדִּיל שֶׁקֶל
	A2e	וּלְעַוֵּת מֹאזְנֵי מִרְמָה׃
8:6	A2f	לִקְנוֹת בַּכֶּסֶף דַּלִּים
	A2g	וְאֶבְיוֹן בַּעֲבוּר נַעֲלָיִם
	A2h	וּמַפַּל בַּר נַשְׁבִּיר׃

Line A2a: The colon-marker is *pashta* and the constraints are: 1 predicator, 3 constituents, and 3 units.

מָתַי. Temporal interrogative pronoun.

יַעֲבֹר. Qal *yiqtol* 3 m s of עבר. The merchants long for the holy days to "pass by" so that they resume corrupt business practices, but ironically YHWH has just said that he will "pass by" Israel no longer (8:2).

הַחֹדֶשׁ. The subject. The Torah does not command Israelites to desist from labor on the day of the new moon, but apparently this was the standard practice (1 Sam 20:5; 2 Kgs 4:23).

Line A2b: The colon-marker is *zaqeph qaton* and the constraints are: 1 predicator, 2 constituents, and 2 units.

וְנַשְׁבִּירָה. Hiphil *weyiqtol* 1 c p of שׁבר with paragogic ה; it here expresses purpose or intent, "so that we may sell."

שֶּׁבֶר. The direct object, a cognate accusative with the verb. The daghesh in the שׁ is an example of a *daghesh forte conjunctivum* (*GKC* §20c).

Line A2c: The colon-marker is *athnach* and the constraints are: 1 predicator, 3 constituents, and 3 units. There is gapping of יַעֲבֹר from line A2a.

וְהַשַּׁבָּת. A second subject for יַעֲבֹר, the verb from A2a that is gapped.

וְנִפְתְּחָה. Qal *weyiqtol* 1 c p of פתח with paragogic ה; it here expresses purpose or intent, "so that we may open." The storage jars of grain would be opened up so that the contents could be measured out and sold. Cf. Genesis 41:56: וַיִּפְתַּח יוֹסֵף אֶת־כָּל־אֲשֶׁר בָּהֶם וַיִּשְׁבֹּר לְמִצְרַיִם ("and Joseph opened all [the storehouses] that were among them and he sold [it] to Egypt").

בָר. The direct object. בַּר III is threshed grain as opposed to cut stalks (עָמִיר) or unthreshed grain. It appears that שֶׁבֶר II and בַּר III are essentially synonymous, referring to grain that is threshed and suitable for purchase, but that דָּגָן is a more general term, as it can refer to grain either in the fields (Ezek 36:29; Ps 65:10 [E 9]) or threshed and ready for eat (Lam 2:12).

Line A2d: The colon-marker is *zaqeph qaton* and the constraints are: 2 predicators, 4 constituents, and 4 units.

לְהַקְטִין. Hiphil infinitive construct of קטן with לְ. This and the other infinitive construct forms in lines A2d-f function as gerundives explaining the nature of their grain selling (see *IBHS* 36.2.3e). As the gerundive functions within a clause governed by an actual or implied finite verb, it is debatable whether it can be considered a predicator. But as every gerundive here has a direct object, they are counted as predicators.

אֵיפָה. The direct object. "Shrinking the ephah," a dry measure of capacity, results in giving the customer less grain than he paid for. The precise size of an ephah is unknown, but it was certainly less than a bushel (for a full discussion, see *ABD*, "Weights and Measures").

וּלְהַגְדִּיל. Hiphil infinitive construct of גדל with לְ and the conjunction.

שֶׁקֶל. The direct object. "Enlarging the shekel," a weight against which silver was weighed, results in charging the customer more than the agreed price.

Line A2e: The colon-marker is *silluq* and the constraints are: 1 predicator, 2 constituents, and 3 units.

וּלְעַוֵּת. Piel infinitive construct of עות (to "bend") with לְ and conjunction. Apparently the scales were subtly distorted in a manner that caused unequal weights to appear to be in balance.

מֹאזְנֵי מִרְמָה. An adjectival construct chain, with "scales of deceit" meaning "deceitful scales."

Line A2f: The colon-marker is *zaqeph qaton* and the constraints are: 1 predicator, 3 constituents, and 3 units.

לִקְנוֹת. Qal infinitive construct of קנה with לְ. Here the gerundive describes not the means of cheating but the goal, "for getting for silver. . . ."

בַּכֶּסֶף. Prepositional phrase with בְּ, which could be considered a בְּ of price (*IBHS* §11.2.5d). But the point is not that they are buying slaves on the open market for silver, but that, by driving people into poverty and then lending them money, they can seize them as debt-slaves.

דַּלִּים. The direct object.

Line A2g: The colon-marker is *athnach* and the constraints are: 0 predicators, 2 constituents, and 3 units. There is gapping, with לִקְנוֹת in A2f governing the objects in both lines. This line repeats verbatim a line in 2:6, indicating that people are sold into slavery for as small a debt as the cost of a pair of sandals (see the discussion of A1d in 2:6b above).

וְאֶבְי֖וֹן. The direct object.

בַּעֲב֣וּר נַעֲלָ֑יִם. See 2:6b.

Line A2b: The colon-marker is *silluq* and the constraints are: 1 predicator, 2 constituents, and 3 units. This line has the pattern ו + [x] + *yiqtol*, and as such answers *weyiqtol* verb of the same root (שׁבר) in A2b. In addition, it also closes the above sequence of infinitive construct forms by breaking the chain of infinitive construct forms. It effectively means: "And on top of everything else, we will sell them grain that is almost worthless."

וּמַפַּ֥ל בַּ֖ר. A construct chain as the direct object. מַפַּל ("fallings") refers to grain from the bottom of the heap that is heavily contaminated with dirt and chaff.

נַשְׁבִּֽיר. Hiphil *yiqtol* 1 c p used to express intent.

8:7: Second Stanza. This stanza is in one strophe of two lines.

נִשְׁבַּ֥ע יְהוָ֖ה בִּגְא֣וֹן יַעֲקֹ֑ב	Ba	8:7
אִם־אֶשְׁכַּ֥ח לָנֶ֖צַח כָּל־מַעֲשֵׂיהֶֽם׃	Bb	

Line Ba: The colon-marker is *athnach* and the constraints are: 1 predicator, 3 constituents, and 4 units.

נִשְׁבַּ֥ע. Niphal *qatal* 3 m s of שׁבע.

יְהוָ֖ה. The subject.

בִּגְא֣וֹן יַעֲקֹ֑ב. Prepositional phrase with בְּ for that by which he swears. It is surprising that God would swear by the "pride of Jacob" since he said in 6:8 that he hates it. As suggested in our interpretation of that verse, however, there is probably ambiguity in the term גְּאוֹן יַעֲקֹב. The current and perverse pride of Jacob is their wealth and fortifications, but the right and proper pride of Jacob is their covenant

God. In swearing by the גְּאוֹן יַעֲקֹב, God is swearing by himself, as at 4:2 and 6:8.

Line Bb: The colon-marker is *silluq* and the constraints are: 1 predicator, 3 constituents, and 3 units.

אִם־אֶשְׁכַּח. The particle אִם in a truncated oath is a strong negative. The verb is qal *yiqtol* 1 c s of שׁכח, "forget."

לָנֶצַח. The prepositional phrase is adverbial ("forever").

כָּל־מַעֲשֵׂיהֶם. The direct object.

8:8: Third Stanza. This stanza is in one strophe of four lines. This is a comment on the previous stanza: since God has so sworn an oath against Israel, is it any surprise that the land reels and heaves?

8:8	Ca	הַעַל זֹאת לֹא־תִרְגַּז הָאָרֶץ
	Cb	וְאָבַל כָּל־יוֹשֵׁב בָּהּ
	Cc	וְעָלְתָה כָאֹר כֻּלָּהּ
	Cd	וְנִגְרְשָׁה וְנִשְׁקְעָה כִּיאוֹר מִצְרָיִם׃ ס

Line Ca: The colon-marker is *zaqeph qaton* and the constraints are: 1 predicator, 3 constituents, and 3 units.

הַעַל זֹאת. Prepositional phrase with the explanatory עַל ("on account of this") and the interrogative ה.

לֹא־תִרְגַּז. Negated qal *yiqtol* 3 f s of רגז, "shake." The *yiqtol* here signifies a future tense. The negative rhetorical question generally does not separate the interrogative ה from the negative לֹא, but writes it as הֲלֹא. But there are other examples like this one, such as 2 Samuel 19:22, הֲתַחַת זֹאת לֹא יוּמַת שִׁמְעִי ("Shouldn't Shimei be put to death on account of this?").

הָאָרֶץ. The subject.

Line Cb: The colon-marker is *athnach* and the constraints are: 1 predicator, 3 constituents, and 3 units.

וְאָבַל. Qal *weqatal* 3 m s of אבל in a mainline sequence with the initial verb תִּרְגַּז. There is a link here to the opening of the book at 1:2, where YHWH roars and the pastures wither (אבל II). Here, YHWH swears an oath, the earth shakes, and the inhabitants mourn (אבל I).

כָּל־יוֹשֵׁב. The subject, a qal active participle m s of ישׁב (used substantively) and כֹּל.

בָּהּ. Prepositional phrase with locative בְּ; the antecedent to the suffix is הָאָרֶץ.

Line Cc: The colon-marker is *zaqeph qaton* and the constraints are: 1 predicator, 3 constituents, and 3 units.

וְעָלְתָה. Qal *weqatal* 3 f s of עלה in a mainline sequence with the initial verb.

כָאֹר. Prepositional phrase with כְּ. There is a scribal error of כָאֹר ("like the light") for כַּיְאֹר ("like the Nile"). Cf. Vulgate *quasi fluvius* ("like a river").

כֻּלָּהּ. The subject. The antecedent to the suffix is הָאָרֶץ.

Line Cd: The colon-marker is *silluq* and the constraints are: 2 predicators, 3 constituents, and 4 units.

וְנִגְרְשָׁה. Niphal *weqatal* 3 f s of גרשׁ in a mainline sequence. As is done in *HALOT*, the root גרשׁ is often divided into two separate homonyms, גרשׁ I ("to drive out") and גרשׁ II ("to churn up [water]"), but this is needless and misleading. Used of a river, it does not mean to splash about or be unsettled, it means to overflow its banks and so toss up mud and silt (Isa 57:20). This is simply a function of the meaning "drive out."

וְנִשְׁקְעָה. Niphal *weqatal* 3 f s of שׁקע in a mainline sequence. The verb describes the subsidence of the river after the crest of the flood. This is the *qere* here; the *kethiv* וְנִשְׁקָה, an elsewhere unattested niphal of שׁקה ("to give water to drink") is plainly wrong.

כִּיאוֹר מִצְרָיִם. Prepositional phrase with כְּ on a construct chain identifying the יְאֹור specifically as the Nile. The term יְאֹור can be used of other rivers; in Daniel 12:5-7 it refers to the Tigris.

8:9-10: Fourth Stanza. This stanza is a single strophe of ten lines. It is of course possible to divide into smaller strophes, but that would seem arbitrary, as there is no clear strophic division. In fact, the whole stanza is a single protasis (line Da) and apodosis (lines Dc-j) construction. After the protasis and divine speech formula (Da-b), the apodosis is a judgment oracle of eight lines (note also that all of the verbs of the apodosis are first singular with YHWH as the subject). It is dominated by *weqatal* verbs, and in this is analogous to the full judgment oracles against the nations (1:4-5, 7-8, 14-15; 2:2-3) except that each of those has seven lines. It may be that the eight lines of Dc-j correspond to the fact that Israel is the eighth nation judged in 1:3–2:16. Also, the eight lines of judgment correspond to the eight lines of accusation in 8:5-6.

8:9	Da	וְהָיָ֣ה ׀ בַּיּ֣וֹם הַה֗וּא
	Db	נְאֻם֙ אֲדֹנָ֣י יְהוִ֔ה
	Dc	וְהֵבֵאתִ֥י הַשֶּׁ֖מֶשׁ בַּֽצָּהֳרָ֑יִם
	Dd	וְהַחֲשַׁכְתִּ֥י לָאָ֖רֶץ בְּי֥וֹם אֽוֹר׃
8:10	De	וְהָפַכְתִּ֨י חַגֵּיכֶ֜ם לְאֵ֗בֶל
	Df	וְכָל־שִׁירֵיכֶם֙ לְקִינָ֔ה
	Dg	וְהַעֲלֵיתִ֤י עַל־כָּל־מָתְנַ֙יִם֙ שָׂ֔ק
	Dh	וְעַל־כָּל־רֹ֖אשׁ קָרְחָ֑ה
	Di	וְשַׂמְתִּ֙יהָ֙ כְּאֵ֣בֶל יָחִ֔יד
	Dj	וְאַחֲרִיתָ֖הּ כְּי֥וֹם מָֽר׃

Line Da: The colon-marker is *revia* and the constraints are: 1 predicator, 2 constituents, and 3 units.

| וְהָיָה. Qal *weqatal* 3 m s of היה introducing an oracle and also serving as a protasis.

בַּיּוֹם הַהוּא. Noun with preposition בְּ and demonstrative. "That day" refers to the day of YHWH; it may include both the imminent destruction of Samaria and an eschatological final day. The language of this strophe, with the daylight turning to darkness, is standard prophetic language for the coming of the day of YHWH.

Line Db: The colon-marker is *zaqeph qaton* and the constraints are: 0 predicators, 1 constituent, and 3 units.

נְאֻם אֲדֹנָי יְהוִה. A divine speech formula.

Line Dc: The colon-marker is *athnach* and the constraints are: 1 predicator, 3 constituents, and 3 units.

וְהֵבֵאתִי. Hiphil *weqatal* 1 c s of בּוֹא introducing the apodosis and serving as the mainline verb in a predictive sequence. Used with שֶׁמֶשׁ, the root בּוֹא means to "go down" (Gen 15:12; Exod 17:12). Thus, the hiphil here means to "bring down."

הַשֶּׁמֶשׁ. The subject.

בַּצָּהֳרָיִם. Prepositional phrase with temporal בְּ, "at noon."

Line Dd: The colon-marker is *silluq* and the constraints are: 1 predicator, 3 constituents, and 4 units.

וְהַחֲשַׁכְתִּי. Hiphil *weqatal* 1 c s of חשׁך continuing the predictive mainline sequence.

לָאָרֶץ. Prepositional phrase with לְ serving either to mark אֶרֶץ as the object or used in a directional sense, as in "bring darkness *to* the earth."

בְּיוֹם אוֹר. Prepositional phrase with temporal בְּ. The genitive is adjectival, meaning "a bright day."

Line De: The colon-marker is *revia* and the constraints are: 1 predicator, 3 constituents, and 3 units.

וְהָפַכְתִּי. Qal *weqatal* 1 c s of הפך continuing the predictive mainline sequence.

חַגֵּיכֶם. The direct object, "your festivals." In light of 5:26, these feasts may related to astral deities. At the least, they probably were tied to astronomical events in the calendar. Thus, the cosmic darkening of the sky is directly relevant.

לְאֵבֶל. Prepositional phrase with לְ indicating the outcome of the transformation described by וְהָפַכְתִּי, as in the English "to turn X into Y."

Line Df: The colon-marker is *zaqeph qaton* and the constraints are: 0 predicators, 2 constituents, and 2 units. There is gapping, with וְהָפַכְתִּי from line De also governing this line.

וְכָל־שִׁירֵיכֶם. The direct object.

לְקִינָה. Another prepositional phrase with לְ indicating the result of the transformation. A קִינָה is a song of lament.

Line Dg: The colon-marker is *zaqeph qaton* and the constraints are: 1 predicator, 3 constituents, and 3 units.

וְהַעֲלֵיתִי. Hiphil *weqatal* 1 c s of עלה continuing the predictive mainline sequence.

עַל־כָּל־מָתְנַיִם. Prepositional phrase with locative עַל. The word מָתְנַיִם refers to the hips, lower abdomen and crotch, and thus the sackcloth referred to here was apparently worn as a loin cloth.

שָׂק. The direct object. Jeremiah 48:37 also attests to the wearing of sackcloth about the waist and the shaving of the head (see line Dh) as a sign of lamentation. See also Isaiah 3:24.

Line Dh: The colon-marker is *athnach* and the constraints are: 0 predicators, 2 constituents, and 2 units. There is gapping of וְהַעֲלֵיתִי.

וְעַל־כָּל־רֹאשׁ. Prepositional phrase with locative עַל.

קָרְחָה. The direct object, "baldness." Women pulling out their hair as a sign of lament is mentioned as early as the Sumerian lament over the fall of Ur (*ANET* 461:299).

Line Di: The colon-marker is *zaqeph qaton* and the constraints are: 1 predicator, 2 constituents, and 3 units.

וְשַׂמְתִּיהָ. Qal *weqatal* 1 c s of שִׂים and a 3 f s suffix continuing the predictive mainline sequence. But what is the antecedent of the feminine suffix? One could take it to be either the city of Samaria or the land of Israel, but it probably is a neutrum referring to an unspecific antecedent or to the whole situation, like the English "it."

כְּאֵבֶל יָחִיד. Prepositional phrase with כְּ, for an analogy, on a construct chain in an objective genitive relationship; that is, the יָחִיד ("only son") is what is "mourned." But this is not merely a simile; in 2:14-16 we see that many sons will in fact need to be mourned because they will have fallen in battle.

Line Dj: The colon-marker is *silluq* and the constraints are: 0 predicators, 2 constituents, and 3 units.

וְאַחֲרִיתָהּ. Again, the 3 f s suffix probably refers to the entire situation. Literally "Its outcome" or "The end of it," this could be the subject of a nominal clause, but probably it is the object of וְשַׂמְתִּיהָ due to gapping.

כְּיוֹם מָר. Prepositional phrase with כְּ. This is the *kaph veritatis*, a כְּ preposition with an event that literally comes to pass. In other words, it is not simply "like" a bitter day, it is a bitter day in the fullest sense. *GKC* §118x is somewhat skeptical about the *kaph veritatis*, but it is clear that this is not simply an analogy. *IBHS* 11.2.9b describes *kaph veritatis* as follows: "The agreement of the things compared is complete, insofar as the discourse is concerned." It aptly illustrates this with Nehemiah 7:2: כִּי־הוּא כְּאִישׁ אֱמֶת ("For he is in every way an honest guy").

8:11-12: Fifth Stanza. Like the previous stanza this begins with a reference to the coming days serving as an initial protasis (compare line Da to E1a), and it repeats the same divine speech formula (compare line Db to E1b). Unlike the previous stanza, however, this is in two strophes. The first strophe begins the apodosis with a first person *weqatal* verb, just as was done before. But the second strophe (8:12) is marked by a change to third plural verbs.

8:11: First Strophe. Five lines. Lines E1a and E1c, serving respectively as the protasis and apodosis, are the structural heart of this strophe.

הִנֵּ֣ה ׀ יָמִ֣ים בָּאִ֗ים E1a 8:11
נְאֻם֙ אֲדֹנָ֣י יְהוִ֔ה E1b
וְהִשְׁלַחְתִּ֥י רָעָ֖ב בָּאָ֑רֶץ E1c
לֹֽא־רָעָ֤ב לַלֶּ֙חֶם֙ וְלֹֽא־צָמָ֣א לַמַּ֔יִם E1d
כִּ֣י אִם־לִשְׁמֹ֔עַ אֵ֖ת דִּבְרֵ֥י יְהוָֽה׃ E1e

Line E1a: The colon-marker is *revia* and the constraints are: 1 predicator, 3 constituents, and 3 units.

הִנֵּ֣ה ׀. The expression הִנֵּה יָמִים בָּאִים occurs three times in Amos, always at the head of a divine judgment regarding the future of Israel. In 4:2 it announces the judgment that will befall the women of Samaria when the city falls, and in 9:13 it announces eschatological salvation for Israel. Here, it announces a prolonged period of diaspora during which time Israel with be without the word of God.

יָמִ֣ים. The subject of the periphrastic sentence with בָּאִים.

בָּאִ֗ים. Qal active participle m p of בּוֹא; it is here used periphrastically as a predicator.

Line E1b: The colon-marker is *zaqeph qaton* and the constraints are: 0 predicators, 1 constituent, and 3 units.

נְאֻם֙ אֲדֹנָ֣י יְהוִ֔ה. A divine speech formula.

Line E1c: The colon-marker is *athnach* and the constraints are: 1 predicator, 3 constituents, and 3 units.

וְהִשְׁלַחְתִּ֥י. Hiphil *weqatal* 1 c s of שׁלח. It here introduces the apodosis. The hiphil of שׁלח is used five times in the Hebrew Bible (Exod 8:17; Lev 26:22; 2 Kgs 15:37; Ezek 14:13; here). God is always the subject, and it always involves the dispatch of a plague or calamity upon God's enemy. This is in contrast to the other stems of שׁלח, which often do not imply hostile action (where the verb might be used for sending a messenger, the release of a person, etc.) Especially illustrative is Exodus 8:17, where YHWH says to the pharaoh, "Or else, if you will not dismiss (שׁלח piel) my people, behold, I will dispatch (שׁלח hiphil) swarms of flies on you."

רָעָב. The direct object.

בָּאָרֶץ. Prepositional phrase with locative בְּ.

Line E1d: The colon-marker is *zaqeph qaton* and the constraints are: 0 predicators, 4 constituents, and 4 units. This line is parenthetical, explaining the nature of the famine predicted in E1c.

לֹא־רָעָב. The subject רָעָב from the previous line is repeated in order to clarify what kind of famine is meant.

לַלֶּחֶם. Prepositional phrase with לְ marking the object of hunger.

וְלֹא־צָמָא. "Thirst" is here used in parallel with "famine," as the two often go together. See also the description of thirst in 4:7-8.

לַמַּיִם. Same pattern as לַלֶּחֶם.

Line E1e: The colon-marker is *silluq* and the constraints are: 0 predicators, 2 constituents, and 3 units. The entire line after כִּי אִם qualifies the implied topic word רָעָב: "Rather, (it is a famine) for hearing the words of YHWH."

כִּי אִם־לִשְׁמֹעַ. The particles כִּי אִם, as is common, here together mean "but" or "rather." The qal infinitive construct of שׁמע with preposition לְ here parallels the usage of לְ in the previous line (לַלֶּחֶם and לַמַּיִם); the infinitive has a gerund function as the object of לְ ("for hearing").

אֵת דִּבְרֵי יְהוָה. The direct object of לִשְׁמֹעַ.

8:12: Second Strophe. Three lines. This strophe explains how the people will respond to the famine for the word of God with which YHWH will afflict them.

8:12 E2a וְנָ֨עוּ מִיָּ֣ם עַד־יָ֔ם

E2b וּמִצָּפ֖וֹן וְעַד־מִזְרָ֑ח

E2c יְשֽׁוֹטְט֛וּ לְבַקֵּ֥שׁ אֶת־דְּבַר־יְהוָ֖ה וְלֹ֥א יִמְצָֽאוּ׃

Line E2a: The colon-marker is *zaqeph qaton* and the constraints are: 1 predicator, 3 constituents, and 3 units.

וְנָ֨עוּ. Qal *weqatal* 3 c p of נוע, "wander." It is a mainline predictive text. The action of this verb is subsequent to and follows upon the condition described in the previous strophe, that there would be a famine for the word of God.

מִיָּ֣ם. Prepositional phrase with locative מִן. The preposition refers to the beginning point of their wandering.

עַד־יָ֔ם. Prepositional phrase with עַד, indicating the endpoint of their wandering. But the identities of the two seas is left unstated, and the verb "wander" by definition implies a lack of specificity regarding one's origin and destination. Thus, it is unlikely that one should identify the seas mentioned here as some specific seas. Some interpreters believe that, on the analogy of Joel 2:20, the two seas are the Mediterranean and the Dead Sea. The idea is that the people will wander about the territory of Judah (Paul 1991, 266). Another view is that Amos has the four cardinal directions in mind, and that since line E2b clearly refers to north and east, this line must refer to west and south (Andersen and Freedman 1989, 825–26). On this reckoning, one of the seas must be the Mediterranean (west) and the other must be either the Dead Sea or perhaps the Gulf of Aqaba (south). Neither interpretation is convincing. Against the first interpretation, it is really rather absurd to picture the fugitives "wandering" the small space between the Dead Sea and Mediterranean. Also, unlike this text, Joel 2:20 specifically identifies its two seas as the "eastern" and "western" seas. Amos' refusal to specify a particular "sea" cannot be disregarded. Against the second interpretation, it is not at all clear that Amos has the points of the compass in mind (see the comments on the next line). Rather, as in Zecheriah 9:10 and Psalm 72:8, מִיָּם עַד־יָם in effect means "to the most distant regions of the earth" and is not confined to the southern Levant. Why does Amos speak of wandering "from sea to sea" instead of saying "from land to land"? Probably because he is implying that they will cross many seas and go far away into unknown territory.

Line E2b: The colon-marker is *athnach* and the constraints are: 0 predicators, 2 constituents, and 2 units.

וּמִצָּפ֖וֹן. Prepositional phrase with מִן. Although צָפוֹן means "north," it connotes more than a compass point. צָפוֹן is the place of the divine mountain (Isa 14:13; Ps 48:3 [E 2]). It stretches out into a great void (Job 26:7). To wander צָפוֹן implies not just being somewhere in the north but being unimaginably far away. It is the sense of great distance, not the geographical direction, that is the real point.

וְעַד־מִזְרָ֑ח. Prepositional phrase with עַד and the conjunction. מִזְרָח is the sunrise and therefore by extension the east, but it is by implication a limitless distance, as no human can ever get to the place from which the sun rises. Thus, this line also speaks of wandering far and wide and not strictly of compass points.

Line E2c: The colon-marker is *silluq* and the constraints are: 2 predicators, 4 constituents, and 5 units.

יְשׁוֹטְט֛וּ. Polel *yiqtol* 3 m p of שׁוט. Being a *yiqtol*, rather than another *weqatal*, this verb introduces not another mainline predictive clause but an offline clause, a prediction that summarizes and concludes the message of the whole stanza. The polel of שׁוט connotes going back and forth, moving all about a territory, as if in search of something. Cf. 2 Chr 16:9: כִּי יְהוָה עֵינָיו מְשֹׁטְטוֹת בְּכָל־הָאָרֶץ ("For YHWH's eyes rove about in all the earth").

לְבַקֵּ֥שׁ. Piel infinitive construct of בקשׁ ("seek") used as a complement with the main verb.

אֶת־דְּבַר־יְהוָ֖ה. The direct object of לְבַקֵּשׁ.

וְלֹ֥א יִמְצָֽאוּ. Negated qal *yiqtol* 3 m p of מצא with conjunction. This offline clause is contrastive to the previous clause headed by יְשׁוֹטְטוּ.

8:13-14: Prose Conclusion: The structure of this passage indicates that it is prose. If it were treated as poetry, the colon break would have to be after הַיָּפוֹת. This fits the formal requirements of the constraints, but it is unusually long for a line in Amos, and the essential prepositional phrase בַּצָּמָא does not appear until the next line. The second colon would have to be וְהַבַּחוּרִים בַּצָּמָא, which would be absurdly truncated after the previous line. In addition, the cantillation suggests that the Masoretes did not regard this as poetry (note the lack of any major disjunctive in v. 13 before the *silluq*). In order to see the clause structure, the two verses must be considered together.

8:13-14 בַּיּוֹם הַהוּא תִּתְעַלַּפְנָה הַבְּתוּלֹת הַיָּפוֹת
וְהַבַּחוּרִים בַּצָּמָא׃ הַנִּשְׁבָּעִים בְּאַשְׁמַת שֹׁמְרוֹן
וְאָמְרוּ חֵי אֱלֹהֶיךָ דָּן וְחֵי דֶּרֶךְ בְּאֵר־שָׁבַע
וְנָפְלוּ וְלֹא־יָקוּמוּ עוֹד׃ ס

Prose Clause: בַּיּוֹם הַהוּא תִּתְעַלַּפְנָה הַבְּתוּלֹת הַיָּפוֹת וְהַבַּחוּרִים בַּצָּמָא׃

All of v. 13 is a single clause. The main verb תִּתְעַלַּפְנָה (hithpael *yiqtol* 3 f p of עלף, to "faint") has both הַבְּתוּלֹת and וְהַבַּחוּרִים as subject. The word בַּצָּמָא ("by thirst") is adverbial and it applies to both subject nouns. It has the preposition בְּ (used instrumentally) to describe what causes the healthy young people to collapse. The definite articles on הַבְּתוּלֹת and וְהַבַּחוּרִים as well as on בַּצָּמָא refer to a class or type and not to some specific persons or thing. בָּחוּר ("young man") is derived from בחר ("choose") and refers to young men of quality (see *NIDOTTE*, בָּחוּר).

Prose Clause: הַנִּשְׁבָּעִים בְּאַשְׁמַת שֹׁמְרוֹן

The beginning of v. 14, הַנִּשְׁבָּעִים בְּאַשְׁמַת שֹׁמְרוֹן, is headed by a niphal participle m p of שׁבע serving as a relative clause whose antecedent is both וְהַבַּחוּרִים and הַבְּתוּלֹת (the participle is masculine by virtue of the gender of the nearer antecedent, just as תִּתְעַלַּפְנָה, the main verb, is feminine by virtue of the nearer subject noun). Thus, although הַנִּשְׁבָּעִים בְּאַשְׁמַת שֹׁמְרוֹן is a relative clause, it is closely bound to the preceding clause as it functions as an adjectival phrase with the subjects, and a translation needs to reflect that. The phrase בְּאַשְׁמַת שֹׁמְרוֹן is emended by some to בַּאֲשִׁימַת שֹׁמְרוֹן ("by [the deity] Ashima of Samaria"). But Ashima was not introduced into the land until after the destruction of Samaria in 722 (see *ABD*, "Ashima"), and there is no reason to suppose that Ashima was ever known as "Ashima of Samaria." בְּאַשְׁמַת שֹׁמְרוֹן should be left as is, "by the guilt of Samaria." It refers to rival shrines such as that set up at Dan, elsewhere referred to in similar terms, such as the "the sins of Jeroboam the son of Nebat" (2 Kgs 15:9, etc.). That is, the "god of Dan" and the "way of Beersheba" that are mentioned below together constitute examples of the "guilt of Samaria" by which they swear.

Prose Clause: וְאָמְרוּ

A qal *weqatal* 3 c p of אמר, this verb is linked to the participle הַנִּשְׁבָּעִים and gives the content of the oaths spoken by the men and women of Samaria. The text could have used the familiar לֵאמֹר for this purpose, but the *weqatal* more strongly suggests that they use the oath formulas repeatedly or routinely.

Prose Clause: חֵי אֱלֹהֶיךָ דָּן

A verbless oath clause. The form חַי is normally used for swearing by YHWH while the form חֵי is used for swearing by men (e.g., 2 Kgs 2:6, חַי־יְהוָה וְחֵי־נַפְשְׁךָ, "as YHWH lives and as your soul lives"). But we do have the example of the angel's oath in Daniel 12:7, וַיִּשָּׁבַע בְּחֵי הָעוֹלָם, "and he swore by the life of the eternal," so perhaps we should not make too much of this. אֱלֹהֶיךָ could be taken to mean "your gods" and to refer to shrines for pagan deities at Dan. On the other hand, it could mean "your God" and refer to YHWH. If the latter, it implies that the Israelites regarded YHWH as a localized shrine deity.

Prose Clause: וְחֵי דֶּרֶךְ בְּאֵר־שָׁבַע

Another verbless oath clause. Swearing by the "way of Beersheba" seems odd, and interpreters have proposed various emendations, none of which is convincing (see Wolff 1977, 323–24, and Paul 1991, 271–72). דֶּרֶךְ here apparently refers to the pilgrimage to Beersheba and by extension to the God there (Paul [1991, 272] compares it to a Muslim custom of swearing by the pilgrimage to Mecca). As Beersheba was relatively far from Samaria, it makes sense that they might swear by the pilgrimage as a euphemism for the deity.

Prose Clause: וְנָפְלוּ וְלֹא־יָקוּמוּ עוֹד

Formally this is two clauses, but the negated qal *yiqtol* 3 m p of קום in וְלֹא־יָקוּמוּ עוֹד serves to modify adverbially וְנָפְלוּ and could be translated, "never to rise again." וְנָפְלוּ, a qal *weqatal* 3 c p of נפל, resumes the mainline of the prophecy after תִּתְעַלַּפְנָה, a verb with which it shares some semantic overlap.

9:1-15: Second Poem with Prose Introduction

9:1a: Prose Introduction: This text describes a vision of YHWH and as such gives context to the final oracles of the book.

9:1a רָאִיתִי אֶת־אֲדֹנָי נִצָּב עַל־הַמִּזְבֵּחַ וַיֹּאמֶר

Prose Clause: רָאִיתִי אֶת־אֲדֹנָי נִצָּב עַל־הַמִּזְבֵּחַ

The initial verb, a qal *qatal* 1 c s of ראה, indicates that this is a vision report, although this report is formally different from the other four (7:1-9; 8:1-3). YHWH does not address Amos directly, and there is no wordplay based on some object in the vision. YHWH is standing (niphal participle m s of נצב; an adjectival participle) עַל the altar. Does עַל here mean "upon"? This is possible but not necessary; the meaning "beside" is well attested (e.g., Jer 17:2). The pattern נצב עַל as "stand beside" appears in Genesis 24:13; Numbers 23:6 and elsewhere. The altar in question is probably at one of the major shrines, such as Bethel or Dan.

Prose Clause: וַיֹּ֗אמֶר

The qal *wayyiqtol* 3 m s of אמר continues the mainline of the narrative of the vision. Although context indicates that YHWH is the speaker, this is not a divine speech formula.

9:1b-4: First Stanza. This stanza is in three strophes. It describes YHWH's purpose to hunt down and exterminate the Israelites (particularly the leaders) in response to 8:5-6. The first strophe speaks of the destruction of the people under the metaphor of striking a pillared structure, the second declares that none will escape, and the third elaborates on how it is that none will get away.

9:1b: First Strophe. Three lines. It is a command to cut down the pillars of some edifice, such as a shrine or palace, and to so bring down the whole structure. It is metaphorical for bringing down all of society, starting with its most high-ranking members (the capitals of the pillars).

9:1b	A1a	הַ֨ךְ הַכַּפְתּ֜וֹר וְיִרְעֲשׁ֣וּ הַסִּפִּ֗ים
	A1b	וּבְצַ֙עַם֙ בְּרֹ֣אשׁ כֻּלָּ֔ם
	A1c	וְאַחֲרִיתָ֖ם בַּחֶ֣רֶב אֶהֱרֹ֑ג

Line A1a: The colon-marker is *revia* and the constraints are: 2 predicators, 4 constituents, and 4 units.

הַ֨ךְ. Hiphil imperative m s of נכה.

הַכַּפְתּ֜וֹר. "The capital," the direct object of הַ֨ךְ. It has the definite article.

וְיִרְעֲשׁ֣וּ. Qal *weyiqtol* 3 m p of רעשׁ. The *weyiqtol* is here a purpose clause, "so that they shake."

הַסִּפִּים. The subject of וְיִרְעֲשׁוּ, it means, "the door-frames."

Line A1b: The colon-marker is *zaqeph qaton* and the constraints are: 1 predicator, 3 constituents, and 3 units.

וּבְצַעַם. Qal imperative m s of בצע with 3 m p suffix and conjunction. The verb means to "sever"; it does not mean to "shatter" (ESV) or "bring down" (NIV). See *HALOT* בצע.

בְּרֹאשׁ. Prepositional phrase with locative בְּ. The columns are to be severed at the "top" (the meaning of ראשׁ in this context; this is ראשׁ I and not ראשׁ II, "poison," contrary to Cathcart 1994 [one cannot "sever" with poison]). Many interpreters take ראשׁ to be a construct before כֻּלָּם and read the line to mean, "and sever them on the head(s) of all of them" (i.e., "on all their heads"). Cf. ESV, NIV, RSV, NRSV. The pattern "construct noun + כֹּל + suffix does appear; cf. Judges 7:16, "and he placed shofars in the hands of each one of them (בְּיַד־כֻּלָּם)," where the pattern has a distributive function. But "and sever them on(to) the head(s) of all of them" is very awkward, and one would expect, if the meaning were that the pillars were to be severed and fall down onto all of their heads, that the text would instead use the pattern בְּכָל־רָאשֵׁיהֶם (see Ezek 7:18 [וּבְכָל־רָאשֵׁיהֶם]; also compare Nehemiah 9:32 [וּלְכָל־עַמֶּךָ]; Psalm 143:5 [בְּכָל־פָּעֳלֶךָ]; Jeremiah 16:17 [עַל־כָּל־דַּרְכֵיהֶם]). It is better (notwithstanding the accent *munah*) to read ראשׁ as an absolute noun and take כֻּלָּם to be in apposition to the pronoun suffix on the verb וּבְצַעַם: "and sever them at the head—all of them!" An analogous case is in Micah 3:7, וְעָטוּ עַל־שָׂפָם כֻּלָּם, "and they shall cover the upper lip—all of them" (שָׂפָם clearly is not in construct). We have another similar example in this very context, in Amos 9:5, וְעָלְתָה כַיְאֹר כֻּלָּהּ, "and (the land) shall rise like the Nile—all of it," where יְאֹר obviously is not in construct.

כֻּלָּם. As stated above, this is in apposition to the suffix on וּבְצַעַם.

Line A1c: The colon-marker is *athnach* and the constraints are: 1 predicator, 3 constituents, and 3 units.

וְאַחֲרִיתָם. This does not form a merism with בְּרֹאשׁ from line A1b. רֹאשׁ, "head" or "top," is not the antonym to אַחֲרִית, "ending" or "remainder." The two terms appear together in Isaiah 2:2; Amos 8:10; 9:1; Micah 4:1 and in the Aramaic of Daniel 2:28, but they never form a merism. There is a kind of merism in this text, but not specifically with רֹאשׁ. Rather, the pillars, that according to lines A1a-b, are to be struck down are metaphorically the leading members of society (cf. Gal 2:9), and וְאַחֲרִיתָם refers to the rest of the populace, the common people.

בַּחֶרֶב. Prepositional phrase with instrumental בְּ.

אֶהֱרֹג. Qal *yiqtol* 1 c s of הרג. The pattern וְ + [X] + *yiqtol* used here probably marks this line as an offline future following the imperative הַךְ in line A1a. It is an additional comment making the point that God will deal with the rest of the people after his command concerning the leaders is carried out.

9:1c: Second Strophe. Two lines. This bicolon with syntactic and semantic parallelism makes the point that no one will escape. The third strophe elaborates on this theme in much more detail. The impossibility of flight from death and disaster looks back to 2:14-16 (where the verbs נוס and מלט are prominent) and forms something of an inclusion for the book.

לֹא־יָנוּס לָהֶם נָס A2a 9:1c
וְלֹא־יִמָּלֵט לָהֶם פָּלִיט׃ A2b

Line A2a: The colon-marker is *zaqeph qaton* and the constraints are: 1 predicator, 3 constituents, and 3 units.

לֹא־יָנוּס. Negated qal *yiqtol* 3 m s of נוס.

לָהֶם. Prepositional phrase with לְ and a 3 m p suffix. This could be an "ethical dative" (*GKC* §119s), but one would expect the suffix to be singular, like the verb, if that were the case. It is probably functioning as a partitive genitive, as in "no one of them."

נָס. Qal active participle of נוּס used substantively as a cognate nominative with the main verb.

Line A2b: The colon-marker is *silluq* and the constraints are: 1 predicator, 3 constituents, and 3 units.

וְלֹא־יִמָּלֵט. Negated niphal *yiqtol* 3 m s of מלט.

לָהֶם. Same as A2a.

פָּלִיט. The subject; it is not cognate with its verb (יִמָּלֵט), but it has assonance with it, creating another layer of parallelism with the previous line.

9:2-4: Third Strophe. Twelve lines in six sub-strophe couplets. This has a series of five protasis-apodosis bicola, with A3a, c, e, g, i being the protasis lines and A3b, d, f, h, j being the apodosis lines. The last two lines of the strophe, A3k-l, do not follow this pattern and could be regarded as a separate strophe, but in Hebrew poetry, a lengthy parallel series is often terminated by a final element that breaks the formal pattern. Throughout the strophe, until the end at line A3k, the verbs are primarily *yiqtol*, marking the potential future conditions of the protases and apodoses.

9:2 A3a אִם־יַחְתְּרוּ בִשְׁאוֹל
A3b מִשָּׁם יָדִי תִקָּחֵם
A3c וְאִם־יַעֲלוּ הַשָּׁמַיִם
A3d מִשָּׁם אוֹרִידֵם׃
9:3 A3e וְאִם־יֵחָבְאוּ בְּרֹאשׁ הַכַּרְמֶל
A3f מִשָּׁם אֲחַפֵּשׂ וּלְקַחְתִּים
A3g וְאִם־יִסָּתְרוּ מִנֶּגֶד עֵינַי בְּקַרְקַע הַיָּם
A3h מִשָּׁם אֲצַוֶּה אֶת־הַנָּחָשׁ וּנְשָׁכָם׃
9:4 A3i וְאִם־יֵלְכוּ בַשְּׁבִי לִפְנֵי אֹיְבֵיהֶם
A3j מִשָּׁם אֲצַוֶּה אֶת־הַחֶרֶב וַהֲרָגָתַם

A3k וְשַׂמְתִּ֨י עֵינִ֧י עֲלֵיהֶ֛ם
A3l לְרָעָ֖ה וְלֹ֥א לְטוֹבָֽה׃

Line A3a: The colon-marker is *zaqeph qaton* and the constraints are: 1 predicator, 2 constituents, and 2 units.

אִם־יַחְתְּר֣וּ. Qal *yiqtol* 3 m p of חתר ("dig") with אִם marking the protasis.

בִשְׁא֔וֹל. Prepositional phrase with locative or directive בְּ. Sheol, like the Greek Hades, is here conceived of as being underground. In lines A3a-j, the first four hiding places are vertical in nature: Sheol (down), heaven (up), Mt. Carmel (up), and the bottom of the sea (down). Sheol is often thought of as the place where one is ultimately and finally removed from God (Ps 6:6 [E 5]; 9:18 [E 17], but see also Ps 139:8).

Line A3b: The colon-marker is *athnach* and the constraints are: 1 predicator, 3 constituents, and 3 units.

מִשָּׁ֖ם. Prepositional phrase with מִן, "from there."

יָדִ֣י. The subject.

תִקָּחֵ֑ם. Qal *yiqtol* 3 f s of לקח with 3 m p suffix.

Line A3c: The colon-marker is *zaqeph qaton* and the constraints are: 1 predicator, 2 constituents, and 2 units.

וְאִם־יַעֲלוּ֙. Qal *yiqtol* 3 m p of עלה with אִם marking the protasis.

הַשָּׁמַ֔יִם. Heaven is here in a merism with Sheol representing the hypothetical highest and lowest places in the cosmos, and so indicating that there is no place where they can go to hide. This is an ironic treatment of what we see in Psalm 139:8, which takes comfort in the fact that even in heaven and in Sheol no one is beyond God's reach. Here, that fact is a threat.

Line A3d: The colon-marker is *silluq* and the constraints are: 1 predicator, 2 constituents, and 2 units.

מִשָּׁם. Prepositional phrase with מִן.

אוֹרִידֵם. Hiphil *yiqtol* 1 c s of ירד ("bring down") with 3 m p suffix. This verb may be used of God bringing down the proud (e.g., Jer 49:16: כִּי־תַגְבִּיהַ כַּנֶּשֶׁר קִנֶּךָ מִשָּׁם אוֹרִידְךָ ["although you, like the eagle, make your nest high, from there I will bring you down"]). Here, however, the people are up high not out of pride but out of a desire to escape God.

Line A3e: The colon-marker is *zaqeph qaton* and the constraints are: 1 predicator, 2 constituents, and 3 units.

וְאִם־יֵחָבְאוּ. Niphal *yiqtol* 3 m p of חבא ("hide") with אִם marking the protasis.

בְּרֹאשׁ הַכַּרְמֶל. Prepositional phrase with בְּ on a construct chain. But why is Mt. Carmel mentioned as a place of hiding? Crenshaw suggests that it was because of its height (second only to Mt. Tabor in Israel), its dense forests and its many caves. He notes that the classical geographer Strabo says that robbers hid there. Also, since Carmel juts out into the Mediterranean, it sets the stage for the next hiding place, the bottom of the sea (Crenshaw 1975, 133). It is remarkable, however, that a local and certainly accessible mountain is mentioned as a hiding place among three other places that involve mythological voyages (into Sheol, heaven, and the bottom of the sea). It may be that Carmel was considered a sacred place at this time (note especially the association of Mt. Carmel with Elijah [1 Kgs 18], who died some 40 years before Amos' ministry).

Line A3f: The colon-marker is *athnach* and the constraints are: 2 predicators, 3 constituents, and 3 units.

מִשָּׁם. Prepositional phrase with מִן.

אֲחַפֵּשׂ. Piel *yiqtol* 1 c s of חפשׂ. The piel of חפשׂ often means to seek out in a hostile sense (Gen 44:12; 1 Sam 23:23; 1 Kgs 20:6; 2 Kgs 10:23). This forcefully develops the metaphor of God hunting down the fleeing Israelites.

וּלְקַחְתִּים. Qal *weqatal* 1 c s of לקח with 3 m p suffix. The *weqatal* adds a second prediction to the apodosis verb אֲחַפֵּשׂ. This should not be rendered as a purpose clause; if that were the meaning, a *weyiqtol* verb probably would have been used.

Line A3g: The colon-marker is *zaqeph qaton* and the constraints are: 1 predicator, 3 constituents, and 5 units.

וְאִם־יִסָּתְרוּ. Niphal *yiqtol* 3 m p of סתר ("hide") with אִם marking the protasis.

מִנֶּגֶד עֵינַי. The idiom מִנֶּגֶד עַיִן occurs five times in the Old Testament. In these examples, it always connotes being out of God's sight and thus presumably out of his thoughts as well. Isa 1:16 exhorts the people to remove their evil deeds from before God's eyes, and Jeremiah 16:17 says that their iniquity is not hidden from God's eyes. In Jonah 2:5 and Psalm 31:23, the psalmist is alarmed at the thought of being removed from God's sight (i.e., abandoned by him). Here in Amos, however, the people try to remove themselves from God's sight, as though they want him to forget about them.

בְּקַרְקַע הַיָּם. "On the floor of the sea." In Gilgamesh, the hero dives to the bottom of the sea to recover the plant of eternal life (*ANET* 96). Here, instead of being on a hero's quest, Israelite refugees plunge into the deep to escape God. The bottom of the sea could also represent the realm of the dead in parallel with Sheol in line A3a (cf. Rev 20:13). Of course, it does not seem to make sense that someone who is already in the realm of the dead would be punished by being put to death. But rational coherence of that sort is not the point here; rather, the message is that there is no place to hide.

Line A3h: The colon-marker is *silluq* and the constraints are: 2 predicators, 4 constituents, and 4 units.

מִשָּׁם. Prepositional phrase with מִן.

אֲצַוֶּה. Piel *yiqtol* 1 c s of צוה.

אֶת־הַנָּחָשׁ. The direct object of אֲצַוֶּה. Again there is a parallel to Gilgamesh's quest, in that it was a serpent that thwarted his quest by carrying away the plant of eternal life (*ANET* 96). Here, the serpent is an agent of God and it attacks the Israelites directly. In addition, this parallels Amos 5:19, where the serpent's bite frustrates the flight of the man seeking refuge from a lion or bear.

וּנְשָׁכָם. Qal *weqatal* 3 m s of נשׁך with 3 m p suffix. The *weqatal* again indicates a second prediction, which here is the outcome of God's command.

Line A3i: The colon-marker is *zaqeph qaton* and the constraints are: 1 predicator, 3 constituents, and 4 units.

וְאִם־יֵלְכוּ. Qal *yiqtol* 3 m p of הלך.

בַשְּׁבִי. The last hiding place, the captivity, is remarkable in two ways. First, it is not a hypothetical voyage escape God but corresponds to the reality of Israel's exile and diaspora. Second, Israelites are here portrayed as thinking of exile and diaspora, the ultimate punishment from God, as a way to hide from God. It is as thought they wanted to meld into the crowd of Gentiles and disappear, hoping that God and they themselves would forget that they are the covenant people.

לִפְנֵי אֹיְבֵיהֶם. The preposition לִפְנֵי, "in the presence of," instead of בְּ, "in," or בְּתוֹךְ, "in the midst of," suggests that they will still stand out as Jews. The choice of אֹיְבֵיהֶם, "their enemies," instead of a more neutral term such as הַגּוֹיִם, "the nations," reminds them that their hosts retain a level of hostility toward them.

Line A3j: The colon-marker is *athnach* and the constraints are: 2 predicators, 4 constituents, and 4 units.

מִשָּׁם. Prepositional phrase with מִן.

אֲצַוֶּה. Piel *yiqtol* 1 c s of צוה.

אֶת־הַחֶרֶב. The direct object of אֲצַוֶּה, the sword is here personified as the agent of God's wrath, and it is concretely realized in the literal swords of the enemies of the diaspora Jews.

וַהֲרָגָתַם. Qal *weqatal* 3 f s of הרג with 3 m p suffix. חֶרֶב is a feminine noun, in agreement with this verb. The *weqatal* again indicates the outcome of the action of the apodosis verb.

Line A3k: The colon-marker is *tevir* and the constraints are: 1 predicator, 3 constituents, and 3 units. *Tevir* does not normally signal a line break, but it would violate the constraints (too many constituents) to have no break between A3k and A3l. The break is preferable, moreover, because A3k creates a suspension ("To what end will God keep his eye upon them?") that A3l brings to a tragic resolution.

וְשַׂמְתִּי. Qal *weqatal* 1 c s of שׂים. This acts as a mainline verb continuing the sequence of predictions in all the apodosis lines above. Breaking the pattern of protasis and apodosis line-pairs and being the last verb of this lengthy strophe, moreover, it describes the abiding condition in which the Israelites will find themselves *vis-à-vis* God.

עֵינִי. Reference to YHWH's eye recalls line A3g.

עֲלֵיהֶם. Prepositional phrase with עַל. "My eye upon you" has a benevolent sense in Psalm 32:8, and the reader might anticipate the same meaning here, but the next line shows that it has a hostile sense here.

Line A3l: The colon-marker is *silluq* and the constraints are: 0 predicators, 2 constituents, and 2 units. This line is dependent on the previous line.

לְרָעָה. Prepositional phrase with לְ here denoting goal or purpose. This is in effect an abbreviated way of saying, "for the purpose of harming them."

וְלֹא לְטוֹבָה. Amos' dire prediction is reversed in the eschatological redemption predicted in Jeremiah 24:6: "I will set my eyes on them for good" (וְשַׂמְתִּי עֵינִי עֲלֵיהֶם לְטוֹבָה).

9:5-6: Second Stanza. This doxological stanza is in one strophe. The stanza is opened in Ba with וַאדֹנָי יְהוִה הַצְּבָאוֹת, and is closed in Bj with יְהוָה שְׁמוֹ, forming an inclusion. Setting aside these two lines, there are three sub-strophes each headed by a definite qal active participle (הַנּוֹגֵעַ in Bb, הַבּוֹנֶה in Bf, and הַקֹּרֵא in Bh). It is tempting to break this into three strophes at each participle line, but this stanza is in fact a single sentence ("The Lord YHWH Sabaoth . . ., his name is YHWH") within which there are three complex relative clauses, each formed by a participle and one or more finite verbs. Amos' tendency to have one or more participles lines followed by lines headed by the conjunction and predicated with a finite verb has already been noted; see 6:3-6. He does the same thing here in Bb-e (one participle line and three finite verb lines), Bf-g (one participle line and one finite verb line) and Bh-i (one participle line and one finite verb line). In each of these we have a participial relative clause extended by the addition of one or more finite verb lines. The divine title (וַאדֹנָ֨י יְהוִ֜ה הַצְּבָא֗וֹת) serves as the antecedent for all three complex relative clauses. This stanza asserts God's authority over all things by virtue of his intrinsic power (first relative clause [Bb-e]) and his royal authority (second relative clause [Bf-g]). These two concepts are combined in the third relative clause (Bh-i), where God calls (קרא) the waters up from the sea and pours them on earth. The stress on divine authority arises from the prophet's assertion that God would deal with Israel by issuing judgmental commands (note the use of צוה in 9:3, 4, 9).

וַאדֹנָ֨י יְהוִ֜ה הַצְּבָא֗וֹת Ba 9:5
הַנּוֹגֵ֤עַ בָּאָ֙רֶץ֙ וַתָּמ֔וֹג Bb
וְאָבְל֖וּ כָּל־י֣וֹשְׁבֵי בָ֑הּ Bc
וְעָלְתָ֤ה כַיְאֹר֙ כֻּלָּ֔הּ Bd
וְשָׁקְעָ֖ה כִּיאֹ֥ר מִצְרָֽיִם׃ Be
הַבּוֹנֶ֤ה בַשָּׁמַ֙יִם֙ מַעֲלוֹתָ֔יו Bf 9:6
וַאֲגֻדָּת֖וֹ עַל־אֶ֣רֶץ יְסָדָ֑הּ Bg
הַקֹּרֵ֣א לְמֵי־הַיָּ֗ם Bh
וַֽיִּשְׁפְּכֵ֛ם עַל־פְּנֵ֥י הָאָ֖רֶץ Bi
יְהוָ֥ה שְׁמֽוֹ׃ Bj

Line Ba: The colon-marker is *revia* and the constraints are: 0 predicators, 1 constituent, and 3 units.

וַאדֹנָ֨י יְהוִ֜ה הַצְּבָא֗וֹת. YHWH's name is proclaimed in a pleonastic manner to prepare the reader for the attributes and powers that will be predicated to him in the following lines. This is a title ("Lord YHWH of the Sabaoth"), not a clause ("YHWH of the Sabaoth is Lord"). Since אדני יהוה appears as a title almost 300 times in the Hebrew Bible (twenty times in Amos), it is impossible that אדני is here a predicate.

Line Bb: The colon-marker is *zaqeph qaton* and the constraints are: 2 predicators, 3 constituents, and 3 units.

הַנּוֹגֵ֤עַ. Qal active participle m s of נגע ("touch") with the article. It is a predicator, as indicated by the *wayyiqtol* verb coordinated with it in this line. As indicated above, it serves as a relative clause.

בָּאָ֙רֶץ֙. Prepositional phrase with locative בְּ. The earth is here the domain of human habitation, unlike sea and sky.

וַתָּמ֔וֹג. Qal *wayyiqtol* 3 f s of מוג ("melt"). The subject is הָאָרֶץ. The perfective *wayyiqtol* is here gnomic and not in reference to past action, although the choice of a *wayyiqtol* (instead of a pattern ו + [X] + *qatal*) makes the point that the action of this verb is sequential to the action of the preceding participle. The "melting" of the earth probably refers to an earthquake.

Line Bc: The colon-marker is *athnach* and the constraints are: 1 predicator, 2 constituents, and 3 units.

וְאָבְל֖וּ. Qal *weqatal* 3 m p of אבל. The use of a *weqatal* after a *wayyiqtol* is noteworthy. The action is both resultative and ingressive ("so that they begin to mourn").

כָּל־י֣וֹשְׁבֵי בָ֑הּ. After כֹּל, the qal active participle m p construct of ישׁב is joined to a prepositional phrase with בְּ. The use of a construct before the preposition בְּ is unusual but not without analogy. Cf. Isaiah 5:11, הוֹי מַשְׁכִּימֵי בַבֹּקֶר ("Woe to those who rise early in the morning . . ."), and 9:1, יֹשְׁבֵי בְּאֶרֶץ צַלְמָוֶת ("inhabitants in a land of deep darkness"). In each of these cases, the construct is a participle.

Line Bd: The colon-marker is *zaqeph qaton* and the constraints are: 1 predicator, 3 constituents, and 3 units.

וְעָלְתָה. Qal *weqatal* 3 f s of עלה. The imperfective *weqatal* here describes repeated action; the land does not simply heave up once but rises and falls many times.

כַיְאֹר. Prepositional phrase with כְּ.

כֻלָּהּ. This is in apposition to אֶרֶץ in line B1b, the implied subject of the verb וְעָלְתָה.

Line Be: The colon-marker is *silluq* and the constraints are: 1 predicator, 2 constituents, and 3 units.

וְשָׁקְעָה. Qal *weqatal* 3 f s of שׁקע. Again, the *weqatal* expresses repeated action.

כִּיאֹר מִצְרָיִם. See 8:8.

Line Bf: The colon-marker is *zaqeph qaton* and the constraints are: 1 predicator, 3 constituents, and 3 units.

הַבּוֹנֶה. The relative clause, like the first, begins with a qal active participle m s (here of בנה) with the article.

בַשָּׁמַיִם. Prepositional phrase with locative בְּ.

מַעֲלוֹתָיו. The direct object. The word מַעֲלָה consistently refers to the steps of a stairway (Exod 20:26; 1 Kgs 10:19; etc.), although it can refer metaphorically to the direction of one's thoughts (Ezek 11:5). This may explain the mysterious psalm designation שִׁיר לַמַּעֲלוֹת ("song of ascents"). But it seems odd that God would build his "steps" in heaven. Some therefore emend to עֲלִיָּתוֹ, "his upper chamber" (עֲלִיָּה); thus *HALOT* מַעֲלָה. But Mur XII (88) 8:16 (from the Wadi Murabbaat texts from the Judean Desert) attests to the reading מעלותו, and this renders emendation doubtful. One should not simply translate the word as "upper chamber" as though מַעֲלָה and עֲלִיָּה meant the same thing. But if מַעֲלוֹתָיו means "his stair steps," it obviously cannot refer to a stairway to some higher place (What could be above heaven?). However, in 1 Kings 10:19 and 2 Kings 9:13 the term refers to steps up to a throne or place of royal authority. Thus, it may be that the "steps" are part of YHWH's throne or judgment seat and that by synecdoche the steps refer to the throne itself.

Line Bg: The colon-marker is *athnach* and the constraints are: 1 predicator, 3 constituents, and 3 units.

וַאֲגֻדָּתוֹ. The direct object with a 3 m s suffix and a conjunction. The noun אֲגֻדָּה refers to something that is closely bound together (it is apparently from the root גדד II, "to join together"). It can refer to a bunch of hyssop (Exod 12:22) or to a disciplined body of troops (2 Sam 2:25). English translations persistently render this as "vault," but it is not clear what they mean by that. A vault is often an arched or domed structure of the Romanesque type, but such architecture did not exist in Iron Age Israel. A vault may be an underground church crypt, but this, too, does not exist in Israelite architecture. Stuart (1987, 393) takes it to mean "storeroom" but he does not indicate what is his evidence for this rendering (nor does he say what is supposed to be kept in this storeroom). Mays translates it without explanation as "reservoir" (Mays 1969, 151), possibly justifying this translation from the next line. But this is wrong; the participle הַקֹּרֵא in line Bh below indicates that this is a separate, third relative clause and is unrelated to the אֲגֻדָּה. The אֲגֻדָּה is here apparently some architectural feature which, in keeping with the root meaning of the word ("bound together"), is made very secure and uniform. Since it is "founded" (יסד) we might speculate that the אֲגֻדָּה is the foundation itself, a platform that is precisely joined together so that it is very secure, like a well-made footing of cut stone or wood. Furthermore, if מַעֲלוֹתָיו in 2Ba refers to God's throne, the אֲגֻדָּה may be the platform for the throne. This concept, that the upper part of God's throne is in heaven and the lower part on earth, may be based upon a concept such as in Deuteronomy 4:39, יְהוָה הוּא הָאֱלֹהִים בַּשָּׁמַיִם מִמַּעַל וְעַל־הָאָרֶץ מִתָּחַת ("YHWH is God in heaven above and on earth below"). Thus, lines Bf-g assert that God's throne occupies heaven and earth, as in Isaiah 66:1, "Heaven is my throne and the earth is my footstool."

עַל־אֶ֫רֶץ. Prepositional phrase with locative עַל.

יְסָדָ֑הּ. Qal *qatal* 3 m s of יסד ("fix, establish") with 3 f s suffix (antecedent is אֶרֶץ).

Line Bh: The colon-marker is *revia* and the constraints are: 1 predicator, 2 constituents, and 3 units. Lines Bh-j repeat verbatim three lines from 5:8.

הַקֹּרֵ֣א. Qal active participle of קרא with definite article; it is coordinated with the following *wayyiqtol* וַֽיִּשְׁפְּכֵם in line Bi and is therefore a predicator. The use of קרא here is analogous, on the one hand, to a king who issues commands to his subjects, and on the other hand, to a conjuror who summons up the power of the deep. See Amos 7:4.

לְמֵֽי־הַיָּם. Prepositional phrase with לְ and a construct chain; indicates the addressee.

Line Bi: The colon-marker is *tifha* and the constraints are: 1 predicator, 2 constituents, and 3 units.

וַֽיִּשְׁפְּכֵ֖ם. Qal *wayyiqtol* 3 m s of שפך ("pour out") with 3 m p suffix. The *wayyiqtol* is here sequential but gnomic (not past tense).

עַל־פְּנֵ֣י הָאָ֑רֶץ. Prepositional phrase with directional עַל. The construct פְּנֵי is not prepositional but is literally the "face of" (i.e., the surface of) the ground.

Line Bj: The colon-marker is *silluq* and the constraints are: 0 predicators, 2 constituents, and 2 units.

See the discussion of line 1f in 5:8.

9:7-8: Third Stanza. This stanza is in two strophes. There is an inclusion structure here; נְאֻם־יְהוָה appears at the beginning of the stanza in C1b and at its end in C2e. This stanza concerns Israel's place as one of the nations, stating in the first strophe that Israel cannot cite the exodus as proof that God especially favors Israel, since God also led other nations in something of an exodus. Significantly, the last two nations named in strophe one (the Philistines and Aram in C1d) are the first two nations judged in Amos 1:3-8, creating another inclusion for the beginning and ending of the book. The second strophe indicates that like those Gentile nations, Israel, too, will be judged, but it also asserts that Israel will not be eradicated.

9:7: First Strophe. Four lines. Astoundingly, the exodus, elsewhere described as the singular event that marked Israel as the elect people, is here demoted to the level of being analogous to the early migrations of other peoples. Why does Amos do this? Against Hoffman (1989), it is not because Amos, as a representative of the southern kingdom, rejected the belief (supposedly particularly predominant in the northern kingdom) that the exodus was a constitutive theological event. If one takes 9:7 to mean that Amos did not regard the exodus as a crucial event in redemption history, then one would also have to conclude that Amos rejected also the very idea of Israel's election (see lines C1a-b below). This he manifestly does not do (3:1-2). Rather, Amos is continuing to attack the exaggerated and perverse significance Israel attached to its election and exodus. Negatively, he had argued that just as God judges the Gentiles, so he will also judge Israel (Amos 1–2). Here, he argues more positively that just as God had created and redeemed Israel, so also he supervised the births of the other nations. In short, the distance between elect Israel and the Gentile outsiders was not nearly so great as Amos' audience had imagined.

9:7 C1a הֲל֣וֹא כִבְנֵי֩ כֻשִׁיִּ֨ים אַתֶּ֥ם לִ֛י
C1b בְּנֵ֥י יִשְׂרָאֵ֖ל נְאֻם־יְהוָ֑ה
C1c הֲל֣וֹא אֶת־יִשְׂרָאֵ֗ל הֶֽעֱלֵ֙יתִי֙ מֵאֶ֣רֶץ מִצְרַ֔יִם
C1d וּפְלִשְׁתִּיִּ֥ים מִכַּפְתּ֖וֹר וַאֲרָ֥ם מִקִּֽיר׃

Line C1a: The colon-marker is *tevir* and the constraints are: 0 predicators, 3 constituents, and 3 units (taking בְּנֵי כֻשִׁיִּים as a proper name). This is a verbless clause.

הֲלוֹא כִבְנֵי כֻשִׁיִּים. After the rhetorical interrogative marker הֲלוֹא and the preposition כְּ, the construct chain "sons of the Cushites" heads this strophe, giving rhetorical prominence to the Cushites. In other words, by naming the Cushites first, they are made more prominent and Israel is, by comparison, diminished.

אַתֶּם. The subject.

לִי. "To me" here means, "as far as it concerns me." Cf. the idiom מַה־לִּי וָלָךְ (or, מַה־לִּי וְלָכֶם), "What dealings are there between me and you?" as in Judges 11:12; 2 Samuel 16:10; 2 Kings 3:13. The point here is not simply that the Israelites are like the Cushites in God's opinion, but that the Israelites have no greater claim on God than do the Cushites.

Line C1b: The colon-marker is *athnach* and the constraints are: 1 predicator, 2 constituents, and 3 units.

בְּנֵי יִשְׂרָאֵל. A vocative (a predicator according to the constraints). By using the same formula for both peoples (בְּנֵי כֻשִׁיִּים and בְּנֵי יִשְׂרָאֵל), the prophet rhetorically removes any distinction between them.

נְאֻם־יְהוָה. A divine speech formula.

Line C1c: The colon-marker is *zaqeph qaton* and the constraints are: 1 predicator, 3 constituents, and 4 units.

הֲלוֹא אֶת־יִשְׂרָאֵל. The second rhetorical question (also headed by הֲלוֹא) here places Israel first, making it the focus. Rhetorically, this deliberately misdirects the reader. By making Israel the focus and referring to the exodus, it appears to be ready to affirm that Israel does indeed have a unique relationship to God. The following line, however, undercuts this completely by assigning the same status to Philistia and Syria.

הֶעֱלֵיתִי. Hiphil *qatal* 1 c s of עלה. Amos uses the hiphil of עלה to refer to God taking Israel from Egypt in the exodus also in 2:10 and 3:1.

מֵאֶ֣רֶץ מִצְרַ֔יִם. Prepositional phrase with מִן on a construct chain. This obviously refers to the exodus.

Line C1d: The colon-marker is *silluq* and the constraints are: 0 predicators, 4 constituents, and 4 units. There is gapping of the verb הֶֽעֱלֵ֗יתִי. This gapping is rhetorically effective; the one verb refers to the movements of Israel, Philistia, and Syria, and thus the possibility of there being a qualitative difference among them is eliminated.

וּפְלִשְׁתִּיִּ֥ים. The subject of the (gapped) second clause.

מִכַּפְתּ֖וֹר. Prepositional phrase with מִן for place of origin. Crete, Cyprus, and Cilicia have all been suggested as the location of Caphtor, but Crete is probably correct (Rainey and Notley 2006, 108).

וַאֲרָ֥ם. The subject of the (gapped) third clause.

מִקִּֽיר. Prepositional phrase with מִן for place of origin. On Kir, see comments on 1:5.

9:8: Second Strophe. Four lines. The text speaks of God's determination to destroy "the sinful kingdom" (which can be any sinful kingdom) but asserts that Israel will not be totally destroyed. Israel is therefore both like and unlike the other nations of earth.

9:8 C2a הִנֵּ֞ה עֵינֵ֣י ׀ אֲדֹנָ֣י יְהוִ֗ה בַּמַּמְלָכָה֮ הַֽחַטָּאָה֒

C2b וְהִשְׁמַדְתִּ֣י אֹתָ֔הּ מֵעַ֖ל פְּנֵ֣י הָֽאֲדָמָ֑ה

C2c אֶ֗פֶס כִּ֠י לֹ֣א הַשְׁמֵ֥יד אַשְׁמִ֛יד אֶת־בֵּ֥ית יַֽעֲקֹ֖ב

C2d נְאֻם־יְהוָֽה׃

Line C2a: The colon-marker is *zaqeph qaton* and the constraints are: 0 predicators, 3 constituents, and 6 units. This violates the normal constraints (too many units), but all the lines of this strophe (except the divine speech formula in C2d) are unusually long for Amos.

הִנֵּ֞ה. As always, הִנֵּה draws attention to what follows. In this case, however, it probably also looks back to the preceding context, in which Israel enjoys no favoritism from God over against Cush, Philistia and Syria. Thus, הִנֵּה functions here almost as if it were וְעַתָּה הִנֵּה (cf. Gen 12:19; Num 24:14; Josh 9:12; Jer 40:4, etc., where וְעַתָּה הִנֵּה occupies a kind of Janus position, looking back to the former reality and ahead to what follows).

עֵינֵ֣י ׀ אֲדֹנָ֣י יְהוִ֗ה. A construct chain serving as the subject of a verbless clause. After 9:4, it is clear that the "eyes of YHWH" are on people "for evil and not for good."

בַּמַּמְלָכָה֮ הַֽחַטָּאָה֒. Prepositional phrase with locative or objective בְּ on a noun with adjective. The "sinful kingdom" is not identified here. After the preceding indictments of Israel, there can be no doubt that Israel is included in this concept. But Israel is not the only "sinful kingdom," as the opening oracles of the book indicate. Thus, Israel is once again grouped together with sinful Gentile states that God is ready to destroy.

Line C2b: The colon-marker is *athnach* and the constraints are: 1 predicator, 3 constituents, and 4 units.

וְהִשְׁמַדְתִּ֣י. Hiphil *weqatal* 1 c s of שׁמד ("destroy").

אֹתָ֔הּ. The direct object.

מֵעַ֖ל פְּנֵ֣י הָאֲדָמָ֑ה. Prepositional phrase with מִן and עַל. This expression is often used to describe the divine annihilation of a person or people (Gen 6:7; 7:4; Exod 32:12; Deut 6:15; 1 Kgs 9:7; Jer 28:16; Zeph 1:2).

Line C2c: The colon-marker is *tifha* and the constraints are: 1 predicator, 3 constituents, and 4 units (taking בֵּית יַעֲקֹב as a proper name).

אֶ֗פֶס כִּ֠י. This idiom appears here and in Numbers 13:28; Deuteronomy 15:4; Judges 4:9; and 2 Samuel 12:14. It means "nevertheless."

לֹ֣א הַשְׁמֵ֥יד אַשְׁמִ֛יד. Negated hiphil infinitive absolute of שׁמד with Hiphil *yiqtol* 1 c s of שׁמד. The infinitive is used adverbially to indicate totality; here, of course, it is negated. It seems a self-contradiction to say in one line that God will wipe them off the face of the earth and in the next line say that he will not utterly destroy them. Note, however, that YHWH did not specify in lines C2a-b that he would utterly destroy Israel; rather, he would utterly destroy "the sinful kingdom." Israel, Aram and Philistia all fall into this category, but YHWH makes a partial exception Israel's case.

אֶת־בֵּ֥ית יַעֲקֹ֖ב. The direct object.

Line C2d: The colon-marker is *silluq* and the constraints are: 0 predicators, 1 constituent, and 2 units.

נְאֻם־יְהוָֽה. A divine speech formula.

9:9-10: Fourth Stanza. This stanza is in two strophes. The stanza is introduced by כִּֽי־הִנֵּ֤ה אָנֹכִי֙ מְצַוֶּ֔ה in D1a, a line that acts as a protasis for the whole stanza. The apodosis, the content of what YHWH commands, is in two parts, the first apodosis being at D1b and the second at D2a. Setting aside the protasis at D1a, each strophe has a three-line apodosis. The content of the stanza concerns Israel in diaspora among the nations.

9:9: First Strophe. Four lines, making the point that exiled Israel will not stop wandering from place to place.

9:9 D1a כִּֽי־הִנֵּ֤ה אָנֹכִי֙ מְצַוֶּ֔ה
D1b וַהֲנִע֥וֹתִי בְכָֽל־הַגּוֹיִ֖ם אֶת־בֵּ֣ית יִשְׂרָאֵ֑ל
D1c כַּאֲשֶׁ֤ר יִנּ֙וֹעַ֙ בַּכְּבָרָ֔ה
D1d וְלֹֽא־יִפּ֥וֹל צְר֖וֹר אָֽרֶץ׃

Line D1a: The colon-marker is *zaqeph qaton* and the constraints are: 1 predicator, 3 constituents, and 3 units. This line is identical to the first line of 6:11 except that the subject is first person.

כִּֽי־הִנֵּ֤ה. The expression כִּֽי־הִנֵּה is almost always explanatory (as opposed to כִּי by itself, which has a wide range of meanings). It is often used in the prophets to introduce some predicted act of God that is the basis for a warning, exhortation, or appeal (e.g., Isa 26:20; 60:2; 65:17; Jer 1:15; 25:29; 49:15; Amos 6:11).

אָנֹכִי. Note that צוה appears with a first person subject in 9:3-4 also.

מְצַוֶּה. Piel participle m s of צוה. This parallels the use of צוה in 6:11 and 9:3-4, where God decrees judgment on Israel. Here, as in 6:11, צוה has no addressee.

Line D1b: The colon-marker is *athnach* and the constraints are: 1 predicator, 3 constituents, and 3 units (taking בֵּית יִשְׂרָאֵל as a proper name).

וַהֲנִעוֹתִי. Hiphil *weqatal* 1 c s of נוע. The hiphil of נוע is used with ראשׁ to mean, "to shake the head" (as a sign of derision), as in Lam 2:15. The verb also means to make something totter (before brining it down) in Psalm 59:12 (E 11). In 2 Kings 23:18 it is used for disturbing the bones of a deceased person. In Numbers 32:13 and 2 Samuel 15:20 (qere) it is used for making people wander about. In general, the root נוע means either to "wander" (of people; Gen 4:12,14; Ps 109:10; Lam 4:14) or to "sway," "tremble" or "quiver" (of trees [Judg 9:9], or of a person's hand [Zeph 2:15] or lips [1 Sam 1:13], or of a person or his heart, signifying fear [Exod 20:18; Isa 7:2]). In its other uses in Amos (4:8; 8:12) it refers to the wandering of people. That is the meaning here as well.

בְּכָל־הַגּוֹיִם. Prepositional phrase with locative בְּ.

אֶת־בֵּית יִשְׂרָאֵל. The direct object.

Line D1c: The colon-marker is *zaqeph qaton* and the constraints are: 1 predicator, 3 constituents, and 3 units.

כַּאֲשֶׁר. As is normal, this means "just as." It here sets up an analogy.

יִנּוֹעַ. Niphal *yiqtol* 3 m s of נוע. Used only here and in Nahum 3:12, the niphal means to be "shaken about" or "jostled." The subject is not indicated; it could be צְרוֹר ("pebble") from the next line. The subject cannot be בֵּית יִשְׂרָאֵל from the preceding line since this line describes the analogy and not the thing itself. Probably, however, an impersonal translation is best: "Just as when there is a shaking. . . ."

בַּכְּבָרָה. Prepositional phrase with locative בְּ. The word כְּבָרָה is *hapax legomenon* in the Hebrew Bible. כברה occurs on a jar stamp from Tell el-Judeideh, but this is probably a homonym with no relevance to Amos 9:9 (see Bliss 1900, 221–22). The standard translation for כְּבָרָה here, "sieve," is based on later Hebrew. Several scholars believe that Sirach 27:4 may refer to the כְּבָרָה. The LXX of that text reads ἐν σείσματι κοσκίνου διαμένει κοπρία ("When a sieve is shaken, dung remains"). Wolff (1977, 349) indicates that the Hebrew for the Sirach text is בְּהָנִיעַ כְּבָרָה יַעֲמֹד עָפָר, but he provides no source for this. In fact, no extant Hebrew manuscript of Sirach contains 27:4 (see Skehan and Di Lella 1987, 52–53; see also Levi 1951; Yadin 1965), and no extant Hebrew text of Sirach contains the word כְּבָרָה (according to Ben-Hayyim 1973). It appears that Wolff's Hebrew text is his own retroversion and thus is of no value for lexical analysis. A Ugaritic parallel, *kbrt*, appears in the Baal myth (*CTA* 6:v:16), where the line is translated by Dennis Pardee as "on account of [you] I experienced [being strained] with a sieve." However, only a single letter the verb is extant ([...*y*]; see *COS* 1, 272 [especially n. 270]), making this interpretation less certain and perhaps dependent on later Hebrew texts. Thus, the Ugaritic text adds little clarity. כְּבָרָה has several possible cognates in biblical Hebrew, including כָּבִיר, a goat-hair quilt or pillow (1 Sam 19:13, 16), מַכְבֵּר, another kind of quilt (2 Kgs 8:15), and מִכְבָּר, the bronze grating found in the bronze altar (Exod 27:4; 35:16; 38:4,5,30; 39:39). The common element in all of these may have been an interlaced construction. On the other hand, the construction and purposes of these various cognate nouns vary significantly and their relationship to one another is uncertain. The nature and purpose of the כְּבָרָה is particularly opaque. If it was a sieve, it is not certain whether it was something like a basket with a lattice bottom, or a bag made with crisscrossed cords, or something entirely different. Shalom Paul argues that it was used for cleansing grain, and says that the grain would fall through the lattice work while the impurities would remain in the כְּבָרָה (Paul 1991, 286 n. 39; see also Stuart 1987, 393). This is implausible; it is unlikely that kernels of grain would fall through a sieve but that pebbles, which would often be smaller, smoother, and heavier, would not (see line D1d). On the other hand, others claim that the grain would remain in the sieve while the impurities fell through. If so, why does Amos point out that no pebbles fall through? In fact, there is no indication here that the כְּבָרָה was used for sifting grain.

Line D1d: The colon-marker is *silluq* and the constraints are: 1 predicator, 3 constituents, and 3 units.

וְלֹא־יִפּוֹל. Negated qal *yiqtol* 3 m s of נפל with conjunction. The negated *yiqtol* here adverbially modifies the preceding verb יִנּוֹעַ and could be translated, "without a pebble falling to earth" (lit., "and a pebble doesn't fall to earth").

צְרוֹר. From 2 Samuel 17:13, where the word describes what remains after a wall is brought down, this word probably means "small stone" or "pebble." It does not mean "kernel (of wheat)," against Andersen and Freedman (1989, 870–71) (who appear to want to emend on the basis of the LXX to שֶׁבֶר II, but this emendation is far-fetched) and Smith (1998, 367).

אָרֶץ. A locative sense, "to the earth," is implied despite the lack of a preposition or directive ה. The standard interpretation of these lines is that there will be a sifting out the good or elect from the evil or rejected. But problems here are numerous. Is the "pebble" the good or the bad? What is the substance (apart from the pebbles) that is being sifted? What falls through the sieve? Is it something good (wheat) or something bad (dirt)? Is the fact that not a pebble falls out a judgment or salvation? Issues in the interpretation of the analogy are equally obscure. If there is a sifting, are Israelites being separated from Gentiles? Are sinful Israelites being separated from repentant ones? In short, every aspect of the "sifting" interpretation is unclear both in terms of the details of the cultural analogy and in terms of the theological meaning of its symbols. Wolff (1977, 349) argues on the basis of Sirach 27:4 that the pebbles are sinners and that the ones that fall out are the remnant (also Paul 1991, 286). But this text says nothing about a remnant; it only describes the jostling of the pebbles. Elsewhere in the Bible, when there is an analogy involving sifting or separating, it is generally separating grain from chaff, and it is at a threshing floor or using the wind, a sledge or a threshing fork, and not a sieve. In such texts, the analogy is transparent in both cultural context and interpretation (e.g., Job 21:18; Ps 1:4; Isa 29:5; 41:15; Mal 4:1; Luke 3:17). The present text is nothing like that. We therefore conclude that this text does not mention either sifting or a remnant. Rather, the pebbles shaking about within the כְּבָרָה is itself the point. The meaning, following the usage of נוע in Amos 8:12, is that the Israelites will wander to and fro among the nations. The reason that a "sieve" (if that is the meaning of כְּבָרָה) is mentioned is simply that this is something which is likely to be shaken. The statement that no pebble falls to earth only means that no Jew will escape the buffeting of being bounced about from place to place. That is, they will not be released from their wandering. This is a prediction of diaspora, not of separating out a remnant.

9:10: Second Strophe. Three lines. The stanza describes how the Israelites/Jews will find themselves violently attacked in places where they thought that they had obtained refuge. The slaughter of Jews in diaspora, and not just the destruction of Samaria, is in view here.

9:10 D2a בַּחֶ֣רֶב יָמ֔וּתוּ כֹּ֖ל חַטָּאֵ֣י עַמִּ֑י
D2b הָאֹמְרִ֗ים
D2c לֹֽא־תַגִּ֧ישׁ וְתַקְדִּ֛ים בַּעֲדֵ֖ינוּ הָרָעָֽה׃

Line D2a: The colon-marker is *athnach* and the constraints are: 1 predicator, 3 constituents, and 4 units.

בַּחֶ֣רֶב. Prepositional phrase with instrumental use of בְּ. The "sword" is here metonymy for the violence of an enemy.

יָמ֔וּתוּ. Qal *yiqtol* 3 m p of מוּת.

כֹּל חַטָּאֵי עַמִּי. This is a construct chain and the subject of יָמוּתוּ. The word כֹּל appears to be absolute but it is construct; cf. Amos 3:2 and 4:6. An important question is whether the construct chain חַטָּאֵי עַמִּי creates a partitive genitive, indicating that God will select out the sinners of the nation and set them aside for punishment but spare the rest, who might be defined as a remnant. Analogous construct chains appear at Exodus 23:11 (אֶבְיֹנֵי עַמֶּךָ) 1 Samuel 15:30 (זִקְנֵי־עַמִּי); Isaiah 3:14 (זִקְנֵי עַמּוֹ); 10:2 (עֲנִיֵּי עַמִּי); 14:32 (עֲנִיֵּי עַמּוֹ); Psalm 113:8 (נְדִיבֵי עַמּוֹ); and Ruth 4:4 (זִקְנֵי עַמִּי). In each of these the genitive relationship would be better defined as "focal" than as "partitive." In other words, those who are defined as the "poor" or "elders" or "nobles" of the people are the *focus* of their respective sentences, but they are not conceived of as being somehow separated from the rest of the population. For example, in 1 Samuel 15:30, when Saul asks Samuel to honor him "before the elders of my people," he does not mean that the elders are to be set apart from the rest of Israel, much less that he will not be honored by the rest of the nation; he merely gives focus to the men of high standing (Saul's full request is כַּבְּדֵנִי נָא נֶגֶד זִקְנֵי־עַמִּי וְנֶגֶד יִשְׂרָאֵל ["Honor me before the elders of my people and before Israel"]). Similarly, when Isaiah 10:2 criticizes those who "rob the poor of my people," it does not mean that the robbers single out the poor for robbery or that it is of no consequence if they rob people who are not poor; the text merely focuses on the heinous nature of the crime as committed against the poor. Amos does not mean that only a part of Israel will be singled out for punishment. The phrase חַטָּאֵי עַמִּי focuses on those who have committed the crimes this chapter has described. Amos only leaves the door open for the survival of some, but he has here nothing here like a full-fledged remnant theology. See also Noble (1997).

Line D2b: The colon-marker is *revia* and the constraints are: 1 predicator, 1 constituent, and 1 unit. This violates the constraints but seems the best solution for the colometry of this strophe.

הָאֹמְרִים. Qal active participle m p of אמר with article; it serves as a relative clause with כֹּל חַטָּאֵי עַמִּי as its antecedent.

Line D2c: The colon-marker is *silluq* and the constraints are: 2 predicators, 4 constituents, and 4 units. This is reported speech.

לֹא־תַגִּישׁ. Hiphil *yiqtol* 3 f s of נגשׁ. But the hiphil ("offer, bring near") makes little sense here, and it may be better to emend it to the qal תִּגַּשׁ ("approach, come near"). The hiphil of the MT may be accounted for by attraction to וְתַקְדִּים. The subject is left undefined until the last word of the line.

וְתַקְדִּים. Hiphil *weyiqtol* 3 f s of קדם ("meet"). This does not function as a *weyiqtol* normally does (e.g., to introduce a final clause). Instead, לֹא־תַגִּישׁ וְתַקְדִּים is a compounded verb clause, with the negative לֹא governing both verbs. Note the conjunctive accent *darga* in תַגִּישׁ.

בַּעֲדֵינוּ. Prepositional phrase with בַּעַד. The word generally connotes being behind or around something either to entrap it (Jonah 2:7) or protect it (Zech 12:8). It can also mean "for the sake of" or "beyond." In this context, it seems to imply entrapping or catching up with the people.

הָרָעָה. The subject. "The trouble" here connotes the problems and violence that aristocracy of Israel supposes it can escape.

9:11-12: Fifth Stanza. This stanza is a single strophe headed by בַּיּוֹם הַהוּא in line Ea and concluded with נְאֻם־יְהוָה עֹשֶׂה זֹּאת in line Eh. A predictive text, this stanza has a series of *weqatal* verbs at Ec-e, analogous to how *weqatal* verbs dominate the predictions of doom in Amos 1–2. Also, this stanza has eight lines, analogous to the seven-line doom predictions in 1:4–5, 7-8, 14-15; 2:2-3. The eight-line stanza here may reflect the fact that in Amos 1–2 Israel is the eighth nation named. In content, however, this text reverses the others in that it is a prediction of restoration. Many scholars, of course, believe that 9:11-15 is a secondary addition to the book (cf. Hasel 1991, 105–20), but that conclusion is unnecessary. Structurally, this material is integrated into the whole of 8:4–9:15, as illustrated by the focus on matters involving food and agriculture in 8:5, 11-13 and 9:13. Also, 8:4–9:10 is essential to understanding 9:11-15. After God's promise to hunt down and slaughter Israelites wherever they go, the survival and renewal of Israel is a surprising work of God and so dramatic a reversal of the foregoing pronouncements of doom that the latter text can only be explained as a resurrection. This is more fully developed in later prophets, especially Ezekiel 37. But 9:11-15 depends upon the earlier sentence of death. The astonishing, counter-intuitive nature of the text is intentional.

בַּיּ֣וֹם הַה֔וּא	Ea	9:11
אָקִ֛ים אֶת־סֻכַּ֥ת דָּוִ֖יד הַנֹּפֶ֑לֶת	Eb	
וְגָדַרְתִּ֣י אֶת־פִּרְצֵיהֶ֗ן	Ec	
וַהֲרִֽסֹתָיו֙ אָקִ֔ים	Ed	
וּבְנִיתִ֖יהָ כִּימֵ֥י עוֹלָֽם׃	Ee	
לְמַ֨עַן יִֽירְשׁ֜וּ אֶת־שְׁאֵרִ֤ית אֱדוֹם֙ וְכָל־הַגּוֹיִ֔ם	Ef	9:12
אֲשֶׁר־נִקְרָ֥א שְׁמִ֖י עֲלֵיהֶ֑ם	Eg	
נְאֻם־יְהוָ֖ה עֹ֥שֶׂה זֹּֽאת׃ פ	Eh	

Line Ea: The colon-marker is *zaqeph qaton* and the constraints are: 0 predicators, 1 constituent, and 2 units.

בַּיּ֣וֹם הַה֔וּא. The familiar prophetic temporal marker here refers to some time at the end of Israel's diaspora.

Line Eb: The colon-marker is *athnach* and the constraints are: 1 predicator, 2 constituents, and 4 units.

אָקִ֛ים. Hiphil *yiqtol* 1 c s of קוּם.

אֶת־סֻכַּ֥ת דָּוִ֖יד הַנֹּפֶ֑לֶת. A construct chain with a participle (הַנֹּפֶ֑לֶת: qal active participle f s of נפל with definite article) serving as an attributive adjective to סֻכַּת. A סֻכָּה is either a lean-to made of branches or a tent; it is some kind of temporary shelter. (Richardson 1973 argues that the word here refers to the town Succoth, but this is not persuasive. Similarly, interpreting the סֻכַּת דָּוִיד as a shrine by tying it to the discredited idea that דוד in the Tel Dan inscription is a god [Davies 1994] should be rejected.) David's "house" (בַּיִת, a "dynasty" in 2 Sam 7:11) is here called a סֻכָּה to indicate the wretched state into which the Davidic dynasty and empire had fallen.

Line Ec: The colon-marker is *revia* and the constraints are: 1 predicator, 2 constituents, and 2 units.

וְגָדַרְתִּ֣י. Qal *weqatal* 1 c s of גדר (to "wall up"). It is a mainline verb in a predictive text.

אֶת־פִּרְצֵיהֶ֗ן. The direct object. The "breaches" function on two levels here. They are the breaches in the walls of the conquered city and so reflect the destruction of Israel's great cities, but they are also breaches in the walls of a decrepit house, a metaphor for the Davidic dynasty.

Line Ed: The colon-marker is *zaqeph qaton* and the constraints are: 1 predicator, 2 constituents, and 2 units.

וַהֲרִסֹתָיו֙. The direct object. הֲרִיסָה is *hapax legomenon* in the Hebrew Bible, but it is derivative of הרס, to "ruin" or "tear down," so its meaning, "ruins," is not in doubt.

אָקִ֔ים. Hiphil *yiqtol* 1 c s of קום. This line and clause has a ו + [X] + *yiqtol* pattern and is not mainline (which would require a *weqatal*). Instead, line Ed is bound to line Ec as a parallel clause.

Line Ee: The colon-marker is *silluq* and the constraints are: 1 predicator, 2 constituents, and 3 units.

וּבְנִיתִ֖יהָ. Qal *weqatal* 1 c s of בנה with 3 f s suffix. The antecedent to the feminine suffix is סֻכַּת דָּוִיד (line Eb). This resumes the mainline prediction. Lines Ec-d describe the making of essential repairs; this line describes the enlargement and aggrandizement of the house of David.

כִּימֵ֥י עוֹלָֽם. Prepositional phrase with כְּ. The construct chain creates an adjectival genitive, in which "as in days of age" means "as in ancient times."

Line Ef: The colon-marker is *zaqeph qaton* and the constraints are: 1 predicator, 3 constituents, and 5 units. כֹּל should be counted as a unit only if it is in the absolute or is suffixed; thus this line conforms to the constraints and has only five units. The LXX here reads ὅπως ἐκζητήσωσιν οἱ κατάλοιποι των ἀνθρώπων καὶ πάντα τὰ ἔθνη, "so that the remaining ones of the peoples and all the nations may seek." This is an unintelligible translation because ἐκζητήσωσιν has no direct object unless καὶ πάντα τὰ ἔθνη be treated as the object, but this is unlikely because of the καὶ (and also because the resultant sentence, "the remaining ones of the peoples may seek also all the nations," makes no sense). The citation of this line in Acts 15:17 emends the difficulty by inserting τὸν κύριον as a direct object. The Greek appears to have as its *Vorlage* ידרשׁו for יירשׁו and אדם ("humanity") for אדום. The LXX of Amos, however, is of poor quality, and one should not emend the text on the basis of the Greek.

לְמַ֨עַן יִֽירְשׁ֜וּ. Qal *yiqtol* 3 m p of ירשׁ ("possess") with לְמַעַן, indicating purpose.

אֶת־שְׁאֵרִ֤ית אֱדוֹם. The direct object. The noun שְׁאֵרִית suggests that Edom will decline to the point that it has only a fraction of its former glory. On the other hand, שְׁאֵרִית is used for an elect remnant saved from destruction (e.g., Mic 2:12). There is a tension here, as throughout the Old Testament, between an eschatology in which Israel rules the Gentiles and one in which Gentiles are brought into the blessings of the covenant (e.g., Ps 87). In New Testament theology, this tension is resolved by the coming of Gentiles into the church (thereby submitting themselves to the Davidic Messiah) and by the eschatological dominion of Christ in the new earth (thereby placing a Davidic king over all the nations of earth). But why is Edom singled out at all, since the next words tell us that Israel will possess "all the nations"? Probably Edom is here representative of all Gentile hostility to Israel.

וְכָל־הַגּוֹיִם. A second direct object. Having wandered among all the nations, Israel will possess all the nations. This sounds imperialistic in nature, but the following line gives new meaning to the Israelite "possession" of the Gentiles.

Line Eg: The colon-marker is *athnach* and the constraints are: 1 predicator, 3 constituents, and 4 units. This line speaks of the Gentiles not as conquered peoples but as the elect of God.

אֲשֶׁר . . . עֲלֵיהֶם. Relative with a resumptive pronoun on the preposition עַל, "upon whom."

נִקְרָא. Niphal *qatal* 3 m s (or participle m s) of קרא.

שְׁמִי. The subject of נִקְרָא. The expression, "upon whom my name is called," means that the Gentiles are treated as God's own possession (2 Chr 7:14, עַמִּי אֲשֶׁר נִקְרָא־שְׁמִי עֲלֵיהֶם ["my people upon whom is my name called"]).

Line Eh: The colon-marker is *silluq* and the constraints are: 1 predicator, 3 constituents, and 4 units.

נְאֻם־יְהוָה. A divine speech formula.

עֹשֶׂה. The qal active participle m s of עשׂה. It is probably best to take this as a relative clause with an implied אֲשֶׁר.

זֹאת. The direct object. The feminine singular pronoun is here a neutrum, representing all that is predicted in this stanza.

9:13-15: Sixth Stanza. This stanza has three strophes. One should note that in this stanza, as in the previous, the lines are dominated by the *weqatal* that describe the glories of the restored kingdom. This recalls the long judgment strophes in chapters 1–2, in which lines were dominated by the *weqatal* (1:4-5, 7-8, 14-15; 2:2-3). Thus, the sufferings of Israel's judgment are repaid in the restoration. In response to the earlier famine motif (8:11), the image of agricultural abundance dominates this stanza.

9:13: First Strophe. Five lines depicting agricultural bounty.

9:13 F1a הִנֵּ֨ה יָמִ֤ים בָּאִים֙ נְאֻם־יְהוָ֔ה
F1b וְנִגַּ֤שׁ חוֹרֵשׁ֙ בַּקֹּצֵ֔ר
F1c וְדֹרֵ֥ךְ עֲנָבִ֖ים בְּמֹשֵׁ֣ךְ הַזָּ֑רַע
F1d וְהִטִּ֤יפוּ הֶֽהָרִים֙ עָסִ֔יס
F1e וְכָל־הַגְּבָע֖וֹת תִּתְמוֹגַֽגְנָה׃

Line F1a: The colon-marker is *zaqeph qaton* and the constraints are: 1 predicator, 4 constituents, and 5 units.

הִנֵּ֨ה. In Amos, הנה often introduces a statement of judgment (4:2; 6:11,14; 7:1,4,7,8; 8:1,11; 9:8,9). Here, it introduces a message is of salvation.

יָמִ֤ים. This masculine plural of יוֹם is the subject of the periphrastic participle that follows.

בָּאִים֙. Qal active participle m p of בּוֹא. The temporal clause יָמִים בָּאִים is here a protasis.

נְאֻם־יְהוָ֔ה. A divine speech formula.

Line F1b: The colon-marker is *zaqeph qaton* and the constraints are: 1 predicator, 3 constituents, and 3 units.

וְנִגַּ֤שׁ. Niphal *weqatal* 3 m s of נגשׁ. The *weqatal* is the apodosis to line F1a. As in Isaiah 29:13 and Jeremiah 30:21, the verb means to "approach" or "come close to."

חוֹרֵשׁ֙. Qal active participle m s of חרשׁ (to "plow") used substantively.

בַּקֹּצֵ֔ר. Qal active participle m s of קצר (to "harvest," used substantively) with preposition בְּ and definite article. In this text alone the niphal of נגשׁ seems to have בְּ with its object; it is usually used absolutely or has אֶל with its object. Isaiah 65:5 and Job 41:8 have בְּ with the qal of נגשׁ and so are not fully parallel. For further discussion, see comments on the next line. In the Israelite agricultural year, plowing took place in October-November and the grain harvest occurred in April-May, which meant that there was a dormant period, so far as the grain crops were concerned, from June until early October. In the new ecosystem, plowing for the grain crop will begin again immediately after the harvest.

Line F1c: The colon-marker is *athnach* and the constraints are: 0 predicators, 2 constituents, and 4 units. There is gapping of the verb וְנִגַּשׁ from the previous line.

וְדֹרֵךְ עֲנָבִים. Qal active participle m s construct of דרךְ (to "tread," used substantively) with conjunction.

בְּמֹשֵׁךְ הַזָּרַע. Qal active participle m s construct of משׁךְ (used substantively) with preposition בְּ. The word משׁךְ (which normally means to "pull" or "drag") here describes the sower leaving a trail of seed behind himself. The participle is definite by virtue of the absolute noun הַזָּרַע. Thus, in both F1b and F1c, the first participle is indefinite and the second participle has בְּ and is definite. But why is וְדֹרֵךְ עֲנָבִים (and חוֹרֵשׁ in the previous line) indefinite? The point may be that there are some starting to do the first activity while the second activity is still in full swing. This may also help us to understand the peculiar niphal of נגשׁ with בְּ. The בְּ here does not really mark a direct object; the verb is used absolutely. The proximity is temporal, not spatial. בְּ here means "with" and the meaning is that a man might begin to plow or spread seed while the harvesters or grape-treaders still have plenty of work ahead of them. The grape harvest and subsequent treading of the grapes took place in at the end of the agricultural year in August-September, with the sowing of new crops taking place in November-December. In the new ecosystem, the gap between the end of one agricultural year and the beginning of the next will be eliminated, with the result that crops will be enormous.

Line F1d: The colon-marker is *zaqeph qaton* and the constraints are: 1 predicator, 3 constituents, and 3 units.

וְהִטִּיפוּ. Hiphil *weqatal* 3 c p of נטף. Literally to "cause to flow," the point here is that the hills will be so fertile that the grapes upon them will be numerous and will swell to the point of bursting. There appears to be little difference between the qal and hiphil for this root; see Joel 4:18.

הֶהָרִים. The subject, here referring to the hill country of Israel.

עָסִיס. The direct object. The word refers to unfermented or fresh grape juice.

Line F1e: The colon-marker is *silluq* and the constraints are: 1 predicator, 2 constituents, and 2 units. This forms a chiastic couplet with the previous line.

וְכָל־הַגְּבָעוֹת. The subject; in parallel with הֶהָרִים.

תִּתְמוֹגַגְנָה. Hithpolel *yiqtol* 3 f p of מוג. The ו + [X] + yiqtol pattern is offline, implying here that this line does not move the prediction forward to a subsequent event but is parallel to the previous line. In Amos 9:5, the verb מוג described chaotic upheavals of the land as a divine judgment. Here, the hills "melt" in that a harvest of plenty flows down from them.

9:14: Second Strophe. Four lines depicting the rebuilding of cities and farms.

9:14 F2a וְשַׁבְתִּי אֶת־שְׁבוּת עַמִּי יִשְׂרָאֵל
F2b וּבָנוּ עָרִים נְשַׁמּוֹת וְיָשָׁבוּ
F2c וְנָטְעוּ כְרָמִים וְשָׁתוּ אֶת־יֵינָם
F2d וְעָשׂוּ גַנּוֹת וְאָכְלוּ אֶת־פְּרִיהֶם׃

Line F2a: The colon-marker is *segholta* and the constraints are: 1 predicator, 3 constituents, and 4 units.

וְשַׁבְתִּי. Qal *weqatal* 1 c s of שוב. The *weqatal* resumes a mainline sequence of predictions.

אֶת־שְׁבוּת עַמִּי. A construct chain direct object. The word שְׁבוּת functions as a cognate accusative to the verb; it should be rendered, "I will bring about a restoration of . . ." and not, "I will bring back the captivity of . . ." (see Paul 1991, 294).

יִשְׂרָאֵ֑ל. A proper name in apposition to עַמִּי.

Line F2b: The colon-marker is *zaqeph qaton* and the constraints are: 2 predicators, 3 constituents, and 4 units.

וּבָ֨נוּ. Qal *weqatal* 3 c p of בנה. This is a mainline clause and is sequential to the previous clause.

עָרִ֤ים נְשַׁמּוֹת֙. Plural noun עָרִים (from עִיר) with adjectival niphal participle f p of שׁמם, "desolate." It here serves as the direct object.

וְיָשָׁ֔בוּ. Qal *weqatal* 3 c p of ישׁב. As another *weqatal*, this is another mainline prediction. It could be a final clause, "so that they may inhabit (them)." The *weyiqtol* would more clearly mark a final clause.

Line F2c: The colon-marker is *athnach* and the constraints are: 2 predicators, 4 constituents, and 4 units.

וְנָטְע֣וּ. Qal *weqatal* 3 c p of נטע. This is another mainline prediction.

כְרָמִ֔ים. The direct object.

וְשָׁת֖וּ. Qal *weqatal* 3 c p of שׁתה. As with וְיָשָׁבוּ in F2b, this could be a final clause.

אֶת־יֵינָ֑ם. The direct object.

Line F2d: The colon-marker is *silluq* and the constraints are: 2 predicators, 4 constituents, and 4 units.

וְעָשׂ֣וּ. Qal *weqatal* 3 c p of עשׂה.

גַנּ֔וֹת. The direct object.

וְאָכְל֖וּ. Qal *weqatal* 3 c p of אכל. This is another possible final clause.

אֶת־פְּרִיהֶֽם. The direct object.

9:15: Third Strophe. Four lines, using an agricultural metaphor depicting Israel as a plant that YHWH places in the ground never to be uprooted again.

9:15 F3a וּנְטַעְתִּ֖ים עַל־אַדְמָתָ֑ם
F3b וְלֹ֨א יִנָּתְשׁ֜וּ ע֗וֹד מֵעַ֤ל אַדְמָתָם֙
F3c אֲשֶׁ֣ר נָתַ֣תִּי לָהֶ֔ם
F3d אָמַ֖ר יְהוָ֥ה אֱלֹהֶֽיךָ׃

Line F3a: The colon-marker is *athnach* and the constraints are: 1 predicator, 2 constituents, and 2 units.

וּנְטַעְתִּים. Qal *weqatal* 1 c s of נטע with 3 m p suffix. Agricultural language dominates this text; Israel "plants" vineyards and YHWH "plants" Israel.

עַל־אַדְמָתָם. Prepositional phrase with עַל. The use of אֲדָמָה ("arable ground") instead of אֶרֶץ ("land") is probably a function of the agricultural image.

Line F3b: The colon-marker is *pashta* and the constraints are: 1 predicator, 2 constituents, and 3 units.

וְלֹא יִנָּתְשׁוּ עוֹד. Negated niphal *yiqtol* 3 m p of נתשׁ with conjunction and adverb עוֹד. Although the verb is often used to describe the uprooting of peoples from their homelands (e.g., Jer 12:14-17), it is fundamentally an agricultural term that describes pulling a plant up from the soil. Cf. Ezekiel 19:12, "but (the vine) was uprooted (וַתֻּתַּשׁ) in anger."

מֵעַל אַדְמָתָם. Prepositional phrase with מִן and עַל. Again, the picture is of a plant pulled out of the soil.

Line F3c: The colon-marker is *zaqeph qaton* and the constraints are: 1 predicator, 3 constituents, and 3 units.

אֲשֶׁר. Relative pronoun serving as the direct object of נָתַתִּי. The antecedent is אַדְמָתָם.

נָתַתִּי. Qal *qatal* 1 c s of נתן. This is probably not a "prophetic perfect" but a true past tense. It looks back to the original giving of the land to Israel.

לָהֶם. Indirect object; preposition לְ with 3 m p suffix.

Line F3d: The colon-marker is *silluq* and the constraints are: 1 predicator, 2 constituents, and 3 units.

אָמַר. Qal *qatal* 3 m s of אמר in the last divine speech formula of the book.

יְהוָה אֱלֹהֶיךָ. The subject. Here alone in the divine speech formulas YHWH is called "your God." This indicates that in the restoration, Israel's prior relationship to God is resumed.

Glossary

Adjectival genitive: A construction in which the genitive (absolute) substantive is in some manner adjectivally modifying the governing (construct) substantive, as in Amos 6:4, מִטּוֹת שֵׁן, "beds of ivory," where שֵׁן describes the material that decorates מִטּוֹת.

Appositional genitive: A construction in which the genitive (absolute) substantive is in apposition to the governing (construct) substantive, as in Amos 6:1, נְקֻבֵי רֵאשִׁית, "designated as finest," where רֵאשִׁית is in apposition to נְקֻבֵי.

Constituent: One of the **poetic constraints**. It is a word or phrase that fills one grammatical slot. Examples would be a subject, a predicate, or a prepositional phrase. A construct chain functioning as a subject or direct object, for example, is a single constituent.

Dependence: A **trope** in which a line is grammatically incomplete and depends upon either the previous or following line. For example, in 1:3, lines Aa and Ac both depend on line Ab.

Gapping: A **trope** in which a word in one line also governs or modifies an adjacent line. For example, the verb וְהִכְרַתִּי in line Bd of 1:5 also governs line Be. This is traditionally described as a word doing "double-duty."

Hapax legomenon: A word that occurs only one time in the Hebrew Bible and thus is difficult to define.

Hendiadys: Expressing a single idea by means of two words. תֹהוּ וָבֹהוּ, "empty and void," in Gen 1:2 is an example.

Mainline: In Hebrew discourse, mainline clauses make up the basic structure of the text. In historical narrative, for example, clauses predicated by the ***wayyiqtol*** generally form the mainline sequence, giving the essential chain of events in a storyline. In a predictive text, the ***weqatal*** generally gives the mainline sequence. Mainline clauses generally form a chain that is either logically or chronologically sequential. For example, in Amos 1:4-5, a series of *weqatal* verbs sets up a sequence of predictions, that God will send fire on Damascus, that it will consume the city, that the fortifications will be destroyed, and the that the people will go into exile. Mainline clauses generally do not have **prominence**.

Neutrum: A pronoun such as "this" or "it" used to refer to an assertion or a situation rather than to a concrete item or a specific noun. For example, in Amos 2:11 זֹאת ("this") refers to the prior assertion that God had sent prophets and Nazirites to Israel.

Objective genitive: A construction in which the genitive (absolute) substantive is the direct object of the governing (construct) substantive, as in Amos 1:8, וְתוֹמֵךְ שֵׁבֶט, "and (the) holder of (the) scepter."

Offline: In Hebrew discourse, offline clauses in some way add detail to or qualify the **mainline** clauses. An offline clause may give background information, or it may describe an act that is conceptually or chronologically concurrent with the previous mainline clause, or it may in some way have **prominence**. In historical narrative, וְ + [X] + ***qatal*** clauses are often offline, and in predictive texts, וְ + [X] + ***yiqtol*** clauses are often offline. Negated clauses and copular clauses are almost always offline. For example, in Amos 7:9, the clause יִשְׂחָק בָּמוֹת וְנָשַׁמּוּ: ("And the high places of Isaac will be laid desolate") is mainline and the clause יֶחֱרָבוּ יִשְׂרָאֵל וּמִקְדְּשֵׁי ("And the sanctuaries of Israel will be laid waste") is offline. In this case, the two clauses are conceptually simultaneous.

Partitive: A grammatical function in which a subset is separated from a larger group. A construct chain may have a partitive function, as in רֵאשִׁית הַגּוֹיִם, "finest of the nations," in Amos 6:1. The preposition מִן sometimes is partitive, as in וּמִבַּחוּרֵיכֶם, "some of your young men," in Amos 2:11.

Poetic constraint: Following the research of Michael O'Connor, this model asserts that a line of Hebrew poetry generally will have from 0 to 3 **predicators**, from 1 to 4 **constituents**, and from 2 to 5 **units**. That is, for example, a line of Hebrew poetry will not contain only 1 unit, or have 5 constituents.

Predicator: One of the **poetic constraints**. A predicator may be a finite verb, an infinitive absolute that functions as a finite verb, an infinitive construct phrase functioning as a finite verb, a participle functioning as a periphrastic finite verb, and the particles אֵין and יֵשׁ, or a vocative.

Prominence: A clause, phrase or word that is prominent in some way stands out from the text around it. The prominence may be a contrast to the context, or the sentence structure may draw attention to something unexpected or dramatic, or some individual item or person may be given greater attention.

Qatal: The conjugation traditionally called "perfect."

Semantic matching: A **trope** in which a word or phrase in one line is synonymous or nearly synonymous with a word in an adjacent line. See line b of 1:2.

Semantic parallelism: A **trope** in which one line more-or-less has the same meaning as an adjacent line. See lines a and b in 1:2. usually the second line in some way advances or in some way modifies the thought of the first.

Substantival: When a participle functions as a noun rather than as verb, it is substantival. For example, שֹׁפֵט, "judge," is a substantival use of the verb שׁפט.

Syntactic parallelism: A **trope** in which two adjacent lines have the same grammatical structure, as in lines c and d in 1:2.

Trope: In this commentary, this refers to devices used in constructing a line of Hebrew poetry. Common tropes include **gapping**, **dependence**, **semantic matching**, and **syntactic parallelism**.

Unit: One of the **poetic constraints**. A unit is basically a word, but small particles such as כִּי or אִם or prepositions such as אֶל do not count as units. In this commentary, לֹא is regarded as a non-unit, and כֹּל is counted as a unit only if it is absolute.

Volitive: A verb form used to express the desire of the speaker. Volitives include cohortatives, jussives, and imperatives.

Wayyiqtol: The conjugation traditionally called "vav conversive" or "vav consecutive."

Weqatal: The conjugation traditionally called "imperfect" with a simple conjunction, as in וְיִקְטֹל.

Weyiqtol: The conjugation traditionally called "perfect" with a simple conjunction, as in וְקָטַל.

Yiqtol: The conjugation traditionally called "imperfect."

Bibliography

Andersen, Francis I., and David Noel Freedman. *Amos* (*AB*). New York: Doubleday, 1989.

Barton, John. *Amos's Oracles Against the Nations: A Study of Amos 1.3–2.5*. Cambridge: Cambridge University Press, 1980.

Barré, Michael. "Amos 1:11 Reconsidered." *CBQ* 47 (1985): 420–27.

Ben-Hayyim, Z., ed. ספר בן סירא: המקור, קונקורדנציה וניתוח אוצר המלים [*The Book of Ben Sira: Text, Concordance and Analysis of the Vocabulary*]. Jerusalem: The Academy of Hebrew Language and the Shrine of the Book, 1973.

Bliss, F. J. "Second Report on the Excavations at Tell el-Judeideh." *Palestine Exploration Fund* 32 (1900): 199–222.

Boyle, Marjorie O'Rourke. "The Covenant Lawsuit of the Prophet: Amos III 1–IV 13." *VT* 21 (1971) 338–62.

Bronznick, Norman. "More on *HLK 'L*." *VT* 35 (1985): 98–99.

Cathcart, Kevin J. "RŌ'Š, 'Poison,' in Amos IX 1." *VT* 44 (1994): 393–95.

Cathcart, Kevin J., and Robert P. Gordon. *The Targum of the Minor Prophets: Translated, with a Critical Introduction, Apparatus, and Notes*. Wilmington, Del.: M. Glazier, 1989.

Cooper, Alan. "The Absurdity of Amos 6:12a." *JBL* 107 (1988): 725–27.

Coote, Robert. "Amos 1:11: *RHMYW*." *JBL* 90 (1971): 206–8.

Crenshaw, James L. *Hymnic Affirmation of Divine Justice: The Doxologies of Amos and Related Texts in the Old Testament*. Missoula, Mont.: Scholars Press, 1975.

———. "*Wedōrēk 'al-bāmŏtê 'āres*." *CBQ* 34 (1972): 39–53.

Cripps, Richard S. *A Critical and Exegetical Commentary on the Book of Amos*. London: SPCK, 1929.

Davies, Philip R. "*Bytdwd* and *Swkt Dwyd*: A Comparison." *JSOT* 64 (1994): 23–24.

Dell, Katharine J. "The Misuse of Forms in Amos." *VT* 45 (1995): 45–61.

Fishbane, Michael. "Additional Notes on *RHMYW*: Amos 1:11." *JBL* 91 (1972): 391–92.

———. "The Treaty Background of Amos 1:11 and Related Matters." *JBL* 89 (1970): 313–18.

Garrett, Duane A. *Rethinking Genesis*. Grand Rapids: Baker, 1991.

Gelston, A. "Some Hebrew Misreadings in the Septuagint of Amos." *VT* 52 (2002): 493–500.

Giles, Terry. "A Note on the Vocation of Amos in 7:14." *JBL* 111 (1992): 690–92.

Gitay, Yehoshua. "A Study of Amos's Art of Speech: A Rhetorical Analysis of 3:1-15." *CBQ* 42 (1980): 293–309.

Hammershaimb, Erling. *The Book of Amos: A Commentary*. Translated by John Sturdy. New York: Schocken Books, 1970.

Hasel, Gerhard. *Understanding the Book of Amos: Basic Issues in Current Interpretations*. Grand Rapids: Baker, 1991.

Hayes, John H. *Amos: The Eighth-Century Prophet: His Times and His Preaching*. Nashville: Abingdon, 1988.

Hoffman, Yair. "A North Israelite Typological Myth and a Judean Historical Tradition: The Exodus in Amos and Hosea." *VT* 39 (1989): 169–82.

Holladay, William. "Amos VI 1Bβ: A Suggested Solution." *VT* 22 (1972): 107–10.

———. "*Hebrew Verse Structure* Revisited (I): Which Words Count?" *JBL* 118 (1999): 19–32.

———. "*Hebrew Verse Structure* Revisited (II): Conjoint Cola, and Further Suggestions." *JBL* 118 (1999): 401–16.

Hoop, Raymond de. "The Colometry of Hebrew Verse and the Masoretic Accents: Evaluation of a Recent Approach, Part 1." *Journal of Northwest Semitic Languages* 26 (2000): 47–73.

———. "The Colometry of Hebrew Verse and the Masoretic Accents: Evaluation of a Recent Approach, Part 2." *Journal of Northwest Semitic Languages* 26 (2000): 65–100.

Isbell, Charles. "Another Look at Amos 5:26." *JBL* 97 (1978): 97–99.

King, Philip J., and Lawrence E. Stager. *Life in Biblical Israel.* Louisville: Westminster John Knox, 2001.

Kleven, Terence. "The Cows of Bashan: A Single Metaphor at Amos 4:1–3." *CBQ* 58 (1996): 215–27.

Koch, Klaus. "Die Rolle der hymnischen Abschnitte in der Komposition des Amos-Buches." *ZAW* 86 (1974): 504–37.

Kugel, James L. *The Idea of Biblical Poetry: Parallelism and its History.* New Haven: Yale University Press, 1981.

Landy, Francis. *Beauty and the Enigma: And Other Essays on the Hebrew Bible.* Sheffield: Sheffield Academic, 2001.

Lévi, Israel. *The Hebrew Text of the Book of Ecclesiasticus.* Leiden: Brill, 1904.

Limburg, James. "Amos 7:4: A Judgment with Fire?" *CBQ* 35 (1973): 346–49.

Limburg, James. "Sevenfold Structures in the Book of Amos." *JBL* 106 (1987): 217–22.

Maag, Victor. *Text, Wortschatz und Begriffswelt des Buches Amos.* Leiden: Brill, 1951.

Maeir, Aren M. "The Historical Background and Dating of Amos vi 2: An Archaeological Perspective from Tell es-Sâfi/Gath." *VT* 54 (2004): 319–34.

Markert, Ludwig. *Struktur und Bezeichnung des Scheltworts: eine gattungskritische Studie anhand des Amosbuches.* Berlin: de Gruyter, 1977.

Mauchline, John. "Implicit Signs of a Persistent Belief in the Davidic Empire." *VT* 20 (1970): 287–303.

Mays, James Luther. *Amos* (*OTL*). Philadelphia: Westminster, 1969.

Miller, Cynthia L. "Discourse Functions in Quotative Frames in Biblical Hebrew Narrative." Pages 155–82 in *Discourse Analysis of*

Biblical Literature: What It Is and What It Offers. Edited by Walter R. Bodine. Atlanta: Scholars, 1995.

Möller, Karl. *A Prophet In Debate: The Rhetoric of Persuasion in the Book of Amos*. Sheffield: Sheffield Academic, 2003.

Möller, Karl. "'Hear This Word against You': A Fresh Look at the Arrangement and the Rhetorical Strategy of the Book of Amos." *VT* 50 (2000): 499–518.

———. "Reconstructing and Interpreting Amos's Literary Prehistory." Pages 397–441 in *"Behind" the Text: History and Biblical Interpretation*. Edited by Craig Bartholomew, C. Stephan Evans, Mary Healy, and Murray Rae. Grand Rapids: Zondervan, 2003.

Noble, Paul R. "Amos' Absolute 'No.'" *VT* 47 (1997): 329–40.

———. "Amos and Amaziah in Context: Synchronic and Diachronic Approaches to Amos 7–8." *CBQ* 60 (1998): 423–39.

———. "The Literary Structure of Amos." *JBL* 114 (1995): 209–26.

O'Connell, Robert H. "Telescoping N + 1 Patterns in the Book of Amos." *VT* 46 (1996): 56–73.

O'Connor, Michael P. *Hebrew Verse Structure*. Winona Lake, Ind.: Eisenbrauns, 1980.

Paas, Stefan. "Seeing and Singing: Visions and Hymns in the Book of Amos." *VT* 52 (2002): 253–74.

Park, Aaron. *The Book of Amos as Composed and Read in Antiquity*. New York: Peter Lang, 2001.

Paul, Shalom. *Amos*. Hermeneia. Minneapolis: Fortress, 1991.

———. "Amos 1:3–2:3: A Concatenous Literary Pattern." *JBL* 90 (1971): 397–403.

———. "Fishing Imagery in Amos 4:2." *JBL* 97 (1978): 183–90.

———. "Two Cognate Semitic Terms for Mating and Copulation." *VT* 32 (1982): 492–93.

Priest, John. "The Covenant of Brothers." *JBL* 84 (1965): 400–6.

Rosenbaum, Stanley N. *Amos of Israel: A New Interpretation*. Macon, Ga.: Mercer University Press, 1990.

Rudolph, Wilhelm. *Joel, Amos, Obadja, Jona*. Gütersloh: G. Mohn, 1971.

Sherwood, Yvonne. "Of Fruits and Corpses and Wordplay Visions: Picturing Amos 8:1-3." *JSOT* 92 (2001): 5–27.

Sivan, Daniel. "The Gezer Calendar and Northwest Semitic Linguistics." *Israel Exploration Journal* 48 (1998): 101–5.

Skehan, Patrick W., and Alexander A. Di Lella. *The Wisdom of Ben Sira*. AB. New York: Doubleday, 1987.

Smelik, K. A. D. "The Meaning of Amos V 18-20." *VT* 36 (1986): 246–47.

Smelik, Willem. "The Use of הזכיר בשׁם in Classical Hebrew: Josh 23:7; Amos 6:10; Ps 20:8; 4Q504 III 4; 1QS 6:27." *JBL* 118 (1999): 321–32.

Smith, Gary V. *Amos*. Ross-shire, U.K.: Christian Focus, 1998.

———. "Amos 5:13: The Deadly Silence of the Prosperous." *JBL* 107 (1988): 289–94.

Snyman, S. D. "A Note on Ashdod and Egypt in Amos III 9." *VT* 44 (1994): 559–62.

Steinmann, Andrew E. "The Order of Amos's Oracles Against the Nations: 1:3–2:16." *JBL* 111 (1992): 683–89.

Rabinowitz, Isaac. "The Crux at Amos III 12." *VT* 11 (1961): 228–31.

Rainey, Anson F., and R. Steven Notley. *The Sacred Bridge*. Jerusalem: Carta, 2006.

Rhatjen, Bruce. "A Critical Note on Amos 8:1-2." *JBL* 83 (1964): 416–17.

Richardson, H. Neil. "*SKT* (Amos 9:11: 'Booth' or 'Succoth')." *JBL* 92 (1973): 375–81.

Rottzoll, D. U. *Studien zur Redaktion und Komposition des Amosbuchs*. BZAW 24. Berlin: de Gruyter, 1996.

Stuart, Douglas K. *Hosea-Jonah*. WBC. Waco: Word Books, 1987.

Tsumura. D. T. "'Inserted Bicolon,' the AXYB Pattern, in Amos I 5 and Psalm IX 7." *VT* 38 (1988): 234–36.

Waard, Jan de. "The Chiastic Structure of Amos V 1-17." *VT* 27 (1977): 170–77.

Waard, Jan de, and William A. Smalley. *A Translator's Handbook on the Book of Amos*. New York: United Bible Societies, 1979.

Williams, A. J. "A Further Suggestion about Amos IV 1–3." *VT* 29 (1979) 206–11.

Wolff, Hans Walter. *Joel and Amos.* Hermeneia. Philadelphia: Fortress, 1977.

Wood, Joyce Rilett. *Amos in Song and Book Culture.* JSOTSS 337. London: Sheffield Academic, 2002.

Wolters, Al. "Wordplay and Dialect in Amos 8:1-2." *JETS* 31 (1988): 407–10.

Yadin, Yigael. *The Ben Sira Scroll from Masada*. Jerusalem: The Israel Exploration Society and the Shrine of the Book, 1965.

Youngblood, Ronald. "לקראת in Amos 4:12." *JBL* 90 (1971): 98.

Zalcman, Lawrence. "Astronomical Allusions in Amos." *JBL* 100 (1981): 53–81.

———. "Laying DMŠQ 'RŚ to Rest (Amos III 12)." *VT* 52 (2002): 557–59.

———. "Piercing the Darkness at (Amos VII 14)." *VT* 30 (1980): 252–55.

INDEX OF MODERN AUTHORS

SUBJECT INDEX